THE ESSEX SYMPOSIA
literature / politics / theory

Colonial discourse / postcolonial theory

Since the early 1980s the issues of colonialism and imperialism have, for the first time, come to the forefront of thinking in the humanities. Disciplines such as history, literature and anthropology are taking stock of their extensive and usually unacknowledged legacy of Empire. At the same time, contemporary cultural theory has had to respond to *post*colonial pressure, with its different registers and agendas.

This truly global volume ranges geographically from Brazil to India and South Africa, from the Andes to the Caribbean and the USA. This range is matched by a breadth of historical perspectives. The contributors focus on theoretical matters, though their references cover diverse topics. Central to the whole volume is a critique of the very idea of the 'postcolonial' itself.

Contributors include Annie E. Coombes, Simon During, Peter Hulme, Neil Lazarus, David Lloyd, Anne McClintock, Zita Nunes, Benita Parry, Graham Pechey, Mary Louise Pratt, Renato Rosaldo and Gayatri Chakravorty Spivak.

Francis Barker is a Reader and Peter Hulme is a Professor in the Department of Literature, and Margaret Iversen is a Lecturer in the Department of Art History, all at the University of Essex.

already published in the series
Francis Barker, Peter Hulme and Margaret Iversen, eds.

Uses of history: Marxism, postmodernism and the Renaissance

Postmodernism and the re-reading of modernity

Colonial discourse /
postcolonial theory

EDITED BY
FRANCIS BARKER, PETER HULME
AND MARGARET IVERSEN

MANCHESTER UNIVERSITY PRESS
MANCHESTER AND NEW YORK

Distributed exclusively in the USA and Canada by
ST. MARTIN'S PRESS

Published by Manchester University Press
Oxford Road, Manchester M13 9PL, UK
and Room 400, 175 Fifth Avenue,
New York, NY 10010, USA

Distributed exclusively in the USA and Canada
by St. Martin's Press, Inc.,
175 Fifth Avenue, New York, NY 10010, USA

British Library Cataloguing-in-Publication Data
A catalogue record for this book is available from the British Library

Library of Congress Cataloging-in-Publication Data

Colonial discourse, postcolonial theory / edited by Francis Barker, Peter Hulme and Margaret Iversen.
    p.   cm. — (The Essex symposia, literature, politics, theory)
    Includes index.
    ISBN 0–7190–3979–7
    1. Literature, Modern—History and criticism. 2. Colonies in literature. 3. Developing countries in literature. 4. Imperialism in literature. 5. Literature and history. I. Barker, Francis, 1952–.
II. Hulme, Peter. III. Iversen, Margaret. IV. Series.
PN56.C63C65   1993
809′.93358—dc20
                                                                                    93–28950

ISBN 0 7190 3979 7 *hardback*

Printed in Great Britain
by Biddles Limited, Guildford and King's Lynn

Contents

THE ESSEX SYMPOSIA
literature / politics / theory

Preface to the series

In the 1990s the new critical theory of the 1970s and 1980s is firmly established in university departments and publishing houses alike, but with the constant risk that its original cutting edge will be blunted by its currency. Hence our insistence on the three terms of the title of this series: the engagement of theory with literature needs to grasp the political questions at its centre.

Between 1976 and 1984 the annual Sociology of Literature conference at Essex provided an important forum for those interested in left literary and cultural theory in England. Ten volumes of proceedings were published, and some of the papers were collected under the title we now use for this series. The sequence of volumes to which this book belongs has a different configuration from that first series, but builds upon its work. The principles behind the intervention remain the same: the process is different. These books present advanced research by people working in this new critical field. Contributors have been invited with a view to achieving a mix of established and younger writers from Britain and abroad, representing a variety of relevant theoretical approaches. In each case participants have been asked to prepare a draft paper in advance of a symposium held at Essex. At the symposium the pre-circulated papers have been discussed, and the direction of the volume assumed a clearer shape. Papers have then been rewritten in the light of the discussions, the underlying commitment being to collective and dialogic methods of work and publication. The resulting volume has a much greater coherence (though not necessarily internal agreement) than the normal collection of essays, to register the terms of current debates, and to offer perspectives for future work.

The Editors

Introduction

There is little doubt that matters of colony and empire have moved centre stage in Anglo-American literary and cultural theory over the last fifteen years or so. And not before time. One factor involved in this move is the increasing globalisation of culture, especially the publishing phenomenon – first seen with the Latin American 'boom' of the 1970s – whereby so-called 'Third World' or 'post-colonial' writers, either writing directly in English or quickly translated, have been so successfully marketed. Another factor is the insistent pressure from 'the periphery' (India, Africa, Australia, Canada), with the development there of various critical and theoretical schools that have been 'writing back' to the metropolitan centres with a confidence and sophistication that have demanded attention. Indeed not just *writing* back: the movement of communities has become a complicating feature to which much attention has been paid, with terms like 'migration', 'diaspora' and 'nomadism' taking on new burdens of significance.

In addition – over a longer term – one could also chart a growing awareness within US and British political and intellectual culture that imperialism and colonialism, either directly or in their aftermaths, are still constitutive elements of the modern world and its conflicts. The evidence of Algeria, Cuba, Vietnam, Central America and South Africa eventually had its impact on at least sections of the left, and on the theory that had for the most part developed in isolation and ignorance of such matters.

If, as David Lloyd puts it in his paper, 'western theory' has been transformed and reconfigured as a result of its encounter with 'non-western cultures', then there is little dispute that the catalyst for much of the new work that has resulted, and still an indispensable reference point, was Edward Said's *Orientalism*, published in 1978. In July 1982, at the Essex conference on 'The Politics of Theory', Homi Bhabha gave a paper in which the notion of 'colonial discourse' received one of its earliest elaborations through a generalising and sympathetic critique of the argument made by *Orientalism*. Said, along with Bhabha and Gayatri Chakravorty Spivak, were at Essex in 1984 when colonial issues were the central topic on the agenda for the conference 'Europe and its Others' although, interestingly, the term 'postcolonial' nowhere features in those discussions. At the end of the decade, when we were discussing topics for the new symposium series, there was no doubt that enough innovative and important work had been done in the relatively few years since 'Europe and its Others' to justify another sustained investigation of current issues in the field of colonial and postcolonial studies. (For the relevant volumes of conference proceedings, see Barker *et al.*, eds 1983 and 1985.)

The Symposium was held in Wivenhoe House at the University of Essex on 7–10 July 1991. Following the model established by the two previous symposia, the draft papers, circulated in advance, were briefly introduced by their authors and then either discussed directly or allowed to trigger wider consideration of problems in the field. We have not thought it appropriate to give a detailed account of the discussions which took place at the Symposium: the papers, which have been revised – in some cases lightly, in other cases very fully – subsequent to the Symposium and in the light of those discussions, will speak for themselves, as must the implicit and explicit relations among them. However, we have drawn upon our notes of the discussions – particularly the final open session – in the following sketch of some of the issues that seemed of general concern to the people around that table.

The title of the Symposium, 'Colonial discourse / postcolonial theory', which, after some discussion, we have kept for this volume, incorporates two notions separated by that discrete slash which leaves their relationship undetermined. 'Colonial discourse' attracted little debate: over the last ten years it has become a widely used phrase, and there has been little dissent to the idea that there is an area of general and quite novel interest designated by the term. Two of the undoubted benefits of 'colonial discourse' as a phrase are that, firstly, it directs attention towards the interrelatedness of a whole variety of texts and practices more conventionally seen as belonging to their 'own' disciplinary realms, and then, secondly, it politicises that network by implicating it with the power relations of colonial hegemony. Said's deployment of Michel Foucault's terminology in *Orientalism* has been the subject of considerable debate, but the enabling consequences of that usage are evident in several of the symposium papers, perhaps especially in the five that open this volume, those by Mary Louise Pratt, Simon During, Peter Hulme, Annie E. Coombes and Zita Nunes.

The situation is, however, more complicated than a simple colonial/postcolonial divide might suggest, in at least two ways. For one thing, the phrase 'colonial discourse' itself belongs to the critical vocabulary of postcoloniality: indeed it has recently been endowed with the dubious privilege of the upper case in Aijaz Ahmad's distancing formulation 'Colonial Discourse Analysis'. 'Discourse' is a word inextricably associated with the post-structuralism of the 1980s (though its actual range of users is much broader), and in particular with Michel Foucault's project of the genealogical analysis of modernity. The second complication is that, although 'postcolonialism' is often used in easy tandem with its apparent cousin 'postmodernism', one of the phenomena to which it presumably relates – viz. societies that have been colonies and are now not – would include (thinking just of the modern period) the USA, Haiti and most of the Latin American countries, all of which became in this particular sense 'post-colonial' during the eighteenth and nineteenth centuries. The advantages and drawbacks of this historical time-depth to the notion of the 'post-colonial' have yet to be determined, although it is certainly true that the term's unnuanced use in the US case – as more recently, say, with Indonesia – would foreclose the vicissitudes of the actual processes of decolonisation and their various aftermaths.

Similarly, the (largely) Australian attempt to generalise the term to include just about all English literary works produced by societies affected by colonialism has been widely criticised as tending to ditch any specificity at all (Ashcroft *et al.* 1989; McClintock below, Shohat 1992, p. 102). Yet it could be argued that there is a wider sense in which, for example, Britain in the 1990s is a post-colonial country – a usage which asserts that the having of colonies cannot just be sloughed off by the gesture of sending a minor member of the Royal Family to preside over the raising of a new flag. The effects of having been a colonising power are still visible in political life, and still permeate that society's cultural production.

'Postmodernism' and its cognates have been at the centre of cultural debate in the west – and especially in Britain and the USA – at least since Fredric Jameson's 1984 article 'Postmodernism, or the cultural logic of late capitalism' – although the term itself was regularly used by critics such as Ihab Hassan in the 1970s and was generalised into a cultural concept of some scope in 1979 by Jean-François Lyotard's *La Condition postmoderne*, the immediate stimulus for Jameson's attempts to think through the phenomenon of the postmodern as the cultural correlate of late capitalism. Whatever one's views of what is now commonly referred to as 'postmodern theory' – and the contributors to the three Essex symposia have been mostly although not unanimously hostile to its concerns and tendencies – the volume of analysis and discussion has at least allowed certain discriminations to emerge, between 'the postmodern', 'postmodernity' and 'postmodernism' for example, or even between 'post-modern' and 'postmodern', discriminations that have perhaps been most useful when returned to questions of 'modernity' and 'modernism' (cf. Barker *et al.*, eds 1992). Although it shows distinct signs of generating the same heat, and although the equivalent cognates are presumably available, the field of the 'post-colonial' has not yet been developed in the same (arguably scholastic) manner in the relatively few years since its entry into theory (though see Shohat 1992, p. 101 and Mishra and Hodge 1991). The editors have not, therefore, tried to impose any uniformity on the various formulations in the papers that follow – nor should variations of usage

be taken as the tokens of significant theoretical claims; though in this Introduction we have distinguished between 'post-colonial' used as a temporal
marker and 'postcolonial' etc. to indicate the analytical concept of greater
range and ambition, as in 'postcolonial theory' or the 'postcolonial condition'
persuasively defined by Graham Pechey (below p. 153).

Nobody at the Essex symposium wanted simply to defend the term 'post-
colonialism' *tout court*, though opinions varied as to its usefulness as an
initial marker. The indiscriminate and often unhelpful proliferation of the
term 'postmodernism' has prompted a healthy scepticism towards the rapid
and often merely fashionable adoption of easy labels – a scepticism no doubt
strengthened by the attacks on Fredric Jameson's attempt to make use of the
idea of a literature of the 'Third World', a term of similar scope (Jameson
1988 and Ahmad 1989; and see the recent contextualisation of Ahmad's
argument provided by his *In theory* (1992)).

We have maintained 'postcolonial theory' in our title, in part because –
although initially intended only as a phrase within the working title – it was
the rubric under which the papers at the Symposium were given; and in part
because an interrogation of the implications of the term can to our minds be
the stimulus to necessary reflections on the current state of literary and
cultural studies within a global context. Herein lies the hub of an arguably
crucial distinction between the areas designated by the signifers that cluster
around the poles of 'the postmodern' and 'the postcolonial' respectively.
Whatever its descriptive currency, 'postmodern' remains a problematic analytic concept because there is little agreement as to whether the term that
forms its second part belongs to the register of the historical, the cultural, the
socio-economic or the literary, all of which use 'modern' in different and in
some cases quite incompatible ways (*pace* Marshall Berman's attempt to hold
them all together). 'Colonial' is less of a problem: there may be legitimate
discussion as to when European colonialism began (1095, 1292, and 1492
could all make claims), as to the very different forms colonialism has taken
(Spain in America, England in India, etc.), and as to the immensely complex
business by which the ends of colonialism are often now achieved by other
means. Certain places in the world are also likely to remain challenges to
such a formulation (though this is hardly uniquely true of 'postcolonial'):
Ireland, Puerto Rico, South Africa. It would, however, be naive to imagine
that such discussions and further discriminations are in any way *prevented* by
the currency of the term 'postcolonial'. Just the opposite would appear to be
the case to date, as Anne McClintock's chapter here on the 'pitfalls' of the
term both exemplifies and acknowledges.

European colonialism was a real historical phenomenon that has had
massive consequences for the world order. The currency of postcolonial
theory has tended to bring into focus (or at least has been part of a larger
process which has brought into focus) the centrality of imperial and colonial

issues to areas of study, such as the early modern period or the nineteenth-century novel, from where they traditionally have been given scant attention; and has encouraged the development of a critical and theoretical vocabulary which can deal with such phenomena – a trend to which this present volume bears witness.

Until the currency of 'post-structuralism' as a term coincided with the widespread adoption of Derridean-inspired reading practices (which inter-rogated prefixes with inquisitorial enthusiasm) – culminating in the familiar brouhaha surrounding 'postmodernism' and creating the vortex into which 'postcolonialism' as a term was sucked – 'post-colonial' seems to have proceeded along its own trajectory relatively unnoticed, being employed largely as a catch-all term to refer to countries that had once been colonies and are now independent: *Europe and Africa: issues in post-colonial relations* (Cornell, ed. 1981) is a representative title of this kind, although the formu-lation goes back at least as far as the well-known UNESCO collection from 1970, *Race and class in post-colonial society*. Other, more recent examples of the kind suggest that this generally unreflective but not especially problematic descriptive use continues to gain ground (see, for example, Olinder 1984, Neuberger 1986, Bayliss-Smith *et al.* 1989, Mitra 1990, Mayall and Payne, eds 1991).

In their Introduction to the collection of essays *Past the last post: theorizing post-colonialism and post-modernism*, Ian Adam and Helen Tiffin (1991) suggest that postcolonialism can be characterised as having two archives, related but not co-extensive, one which constructs it as 'writing . . . grounded in those societies whose subjectivity has been constituted in part by the subordinating power of European colonialism', and a second in which the postcolonial is conceived of as a set of discursive practices involving '*resistance* to colonialism, colonialist ideologies, and their contemporary forms and subjectificatory legacies' (1991, p. vii). This is a useful formulation. The different emphases of the two 'archives' are certainly to be seen throughout the range of chapters in the present volume, and there is clearly an internal debate over the relationship between the two, especially on the question of identifying and recovering the voices of resistance (see the chapters by Benita Parry and Neil Lazarus).

It might also be argued, though, *contra* the emphasis of Adam and Tiffin's volume, that postcolonialism, as scholarship and theory, relates more closely in its development (in the work of Said, Spivak and Bhabha, say) to the insights of that broad body of theory referred to as post-structuralism than to the postmodern phenomenon with which it is now contemporary. Simply put, postcolonial theory began from the recognition that the complex processes of colonialism and its aftermath needed for their proper analysis – especially at the discursive and psychological levels – a conceptual vocabulary made possible by post-structuralist theory (although in no sense simply *provided* by it). (Cf. Shohat's suggestion that it is most usefully thought of as 'post-anti-colonial-critique' (1992, p. 108.) 'Aftermath' is Gayatri Chakravorty Spivak's term, a useful metaphor inasmuch as it both hints at the destructive effect of the colonial mower (read Gatling gun) and suggests in the rich mixture of the 'math' something of that transculturated residue that will form, for better or worse, the loam of future cultural production. 'Hybridity' and – to name the process – 'hybridisation' are the terms now most commonly associated with the attempt to theorise the ambivalence of this colonial aftermath. Annie Coombes's chapter contains an extended discussion of the terms, but they also provided a recurrent motif throughout the Symposium (for further discussion, see Bhabha 1993).

Mary Louise Pratt's chapter, 'Transculturation and autoethnography: Peru 1615/1980', gives several salutary reminders about the complexity of the issues at hand. To begin with she takes us back to Peru in the sixteenth century, the high period of Spanish imperialism in the Americas, paradigmatic of one kind of relationship between metropolis and colony, and of a sort very different from the deeply intimate relationship between Europe and the Orient, as studied by Edward Said, or from the genocidal clearing of the land that would mark the territorial establishment of later American nation states such as the USA and Argentina.

Three useful terms form the foundations of Pratt's chapter, the two in the title plus 'contact zone', a phrase she uses, as she explains in her recent book *Imperial eyes*: 'to refer to the space of colonial encounters, the space in which peoples geographically and historically separated come into contact with each other and establish ongoing relations, usually involving conditions of coercion, radical inequality, and intractable conflict . . .'. 'Contact zone' might sometimes look synonymous with 'colonial frontier', but while that latter term is grounded within a European expansionist perspective, 'contact zone' attempts to 'invoke the spatial and temporal copresence of subjects previously separated by geographic and historical disjunctures, and whose trajectories now intersect' (Pratt 1992, pp. 6–7).

In fact, 'contact zone' correlates closely with the introduction of the term 'tribal zone' into recent anthropological work on colonial warfare: 'that area continuously affected by the proximity of a state, but not under state administration' (Ferguson and Whitehead, eds 1992, p. 3). In both cases the use of the word 'zone' indicates the importance of seeing the colonial encounter as productive of novelty – new spaces, new languages, new tribes – rather than simply a matter of subjugation or imposition. 'Contact' is a term that Pratt takes from linguistics, where contact languages refer to improvised languages that develop among speakers of different native languages who need to communicate with each other, usually in the context of trade. Such 'pidgins', as they are also called, become 'creoles' when they have native speakers of their own (Pratt 1992, p. 6).

This 'zone' is, amongst other things, a space in which the colonised respond and resist, collaborate and adapt, communicate and imitate. 'Transculturation' is a term that suits both characterisations of the zone: coined by a Cuban sociologist in the 1940s to replace the reductive concepts of acculturation and deculturation, it has been adapted into anthropological discussions of the colonial process and is here used by Pratt as a key term to help understand the ways in which 'members of subordinated or marginal groups select and invent from materials transmitted by a dominant or metropolitan culture'.

Pratt offers two particular examples from the contact zone, Guaman Poma's extraordinary *New chronicle and good government* (1615) and the *tablas de Sarhua* (1980), contemporary painted panels, in both of which cases text and image stand in complex relationship to each other. Both are termed by Pratt 'autoethnographies', one of the characteristic indigenous responses from within the contact zone, and defined as texts 'in which people undertake to describe themselves in ways that engage with representations others have made of them', constructed in response to and in dialogue with those representations and involving a selective collaboration with and appropriation of the idioms of the metropolis or conqueror.

There is here some recasting of literary history with a newly defined Latin American literature seen not as an offshoot of Spanish, or even as an adaptation of it, but as a fulled creolised development in which indigenous forms had a part to play: *testimonio* is one contemporary genre whose understanding can be enriched by this historical sense. In the particular case of Guaman Poma, his book was originally not recognised as text at all (because partly in Quechua), then not recognised as having anything to do with the colonial encounter, then not read with any understanding of its discursive complexity. It is still in no sense a canonical text, but Pratt – along with the critics she cites – has moved it on to the stage.

In not dissimilar vein to Pratt's analysis of the 'contact zone', Simon During discusses the border that was supposed to exist between the self-designated 'civilised' and their 'primitive' others and which runs like a stripe through the colonial period, constantly changing locations, thicker in some places than others, but never shrinking to the bare line which metropolitan thought imagined. At its widest that 'border' becomes a fully-fledged contact zone of the kind that Guaman Poma inhabited; at its narrowest it is merely the beach that European sailors walked across in the Caribbean or Pacific islands (cf. Dening 1980). During's chapter focuses, though, not on the experiences of those who actually crossed and re-crossed that border, such as Jean-Baptiste Du Tertre or Louis-Antoine de Bougainville, but on the Enlightenment writers who straddled or traversed it in fiction or in theory.

During's chapter is cast as an enquiry into the problem of identity-formation in the Enlightenment period, when traditional, filiative forms of identity were being challenged. It asks what new signs of individuality were invented in a society which had repudiated inherited rank and family position. The title of the paper, 'Rousseau's patrimony', is half ironic – for Rousseau notoriously abandoned his children – and half serious since he was a key figure in the theorisation of legitimate power based on something other than family lineages. A host of intellectuals, including those that During calls 'modernist primitives', can be said to share in Rousseau's patrimony. Yet the notion of 'inheritance' is in this context, he shows, deeply problematic. Accordingly, During re-conceptualises 'inheritance' in terms of a repeated negotiation of a metaphorical border formed by the opposition between the present and the past, superstition and reason, despotism and liberty. More often than not this border passes between one generation and the next, especially between father and children. Or again, the border might be construed geographically as the division between the 'civilised' and 'savage' worlds. What makes this enquiry so complex and interesting is that the figures at its centre, Rousseau and Diderot, do not unequivocally occupy one side of the border or the other.

The patriarchal form of society, which Rousseau projected into the immaturity of the species, could easily be displacced on to the geographical plane. It is only a short step, then, to twist an enlightened opposition to patriarchal forms of power into a legitimation of colonial expansionism. More often, though, 'unpoliced' societies were themselves seen to be crossed by a conceptual border: as During remarks, 'they were patriarchal *and* they marked the threshold of that state of nature on which society ought to be grounded'. The contradictions this double valence caused in Rousseau's thought are clear: society marks a loss because children accept patriarchal authority and so lose their natural autonomy; yet at the same time it is the gain of knowledge passing from generation to generation.

From generational struggles, During moves to the way in which the relationship between husbands and wives was theorised. Again, the setting for this enquiry is displaced on to the 'unpoliced'. In Diderot's 'Supplement to Bougainville's Voyage', for example, an anti-patriarchal conception of familial freedom sits uncomfortably with a notion of male sexuality as naturally more aggressive and urgent. In this text and others, sexual violence is seen as one of the components of a destructive but necessary energy which propels men over the 'border' into the future, annihilating identity on the way.

A final identity dissolving/forming technique discussed by During is what he calls 'self-othering', which involves the appropriation of elements of another's identity. This could take the form of transvestism, adopting Oriental or other exotic attire, 'going native' or, somewhat later, becoming a 'Bohemian' artist. More important though, and certainly more available to women, is the fictional realm of romance in which self-othering is propelled by sexual desire. Here the unique self is precipitated through fusion with a particular object-choice. The individuating effect is all the more pronounced when the choice is exotic: During offers a reading of Rousseau's *La Nouvelle Héloïse* as just such a self-othering romance, which rounds off a paper which is a contribution to the postcolonial re-reading of the relationship between the dominant European intellectual tradition and the literature produced during the colonial era, but which also contributes to a process of re-thinking the Enlightenment that works counter to the simplicities propounded by Lyotard (cf. Hulme and Jordanova, eds 1990).

One of the threads running through the Symposium discussions and inflecting the fairly constant interrogation of the notion of the postcolonial was the pedagogic context. In the final session there was a discussion of 'transnational literacy' as an increasingly common and desirable skill which enables teachers to construct ambitious courses which challenge canonical orthodoxies without those teachers necessarily claiming 'expert' knowledge – in the traditional sense – of what they teach: even having, it was claimed, a responsibility to 'refuse to refuse', that is not to use 'lack of expertise' as a reason not to accept the pedagogic challenges. A certain degree of 'constitutive ignorance' could be, it was argued, a positive factor – especially given the obfuscatory role that claims to 'expertise' have often played within the academy.

This pedagogical situation was invoked by Peter Hulme, as he explains at the beginning of his chapter, 'The locked heart: the creole family romance of *Wide sargasso sea*', as a possible justification for the terminology of postcolonialism: it operates with some effectivity precisely at the level of such transnational literacy, a function which should not be scorned. Even here, though, the argument can work both ways. In a recent essay Ella Shohat writes about the *negative* implications of the very acceptability of 'postcolonial' as a term in the academy when sharper formulations such as 'imperialism' and 'geopolitics' frighten the horses at curriculum committees (Shohat 1992, p. 99). For Hulme – and this may be one example among many we came across of different nuances on different sides of the Atlantic – there are genuine gains made by the introduction of such terms as 'postcolonial' into the atrophied course-lists of British universities; with the corollary that real gains do not become disastrous losses just because cases are successfully made and demands acceded to.

Hulme's case with respect to *Wide sargasso sea* and postcoloniality is, however, a modulated one since he is responding to the danger of using the term as a loose catch-all which fails to acknowledge, or to see the need even to account for, the specificities of particular texts produced in particular historical circumstances, dangers that Anne McClintock (this volume) is as aware of as Ella Shohat. The proper response to this danger, Hulme argues, is to treat texts like *Wide sargasso sea* with the same amount of historically-informed attention as has conventionally been lavished on the canonical texts of the western tradition – if employing it to more point. In other words, the specificity of *Wide sargasso sea*'s rootedness in the West Indian, and even more particularly the Dominican, situation needs recognition and study – however many more difficulties that study might entail (cf. Hulme, note 4). The substance of Hulme's chapter offers a preliminary account of what such 'local knowledge' (as he calls it) might suggest for a reading of the novel, reconstructing the work of literary production as a familial 'compensation' which re-inscribes – in compelling fashion – the colonial violence of the 1840s through a rewriting of one of the most resonant English fictions of that decade, Charlotte Brontë's *Jane Eyre*. Hulme traces in some detail the changes that *Wide sargasso sea* makes in the course of that 're-writing': chronological adaptation brings it into line with Rhys's own family history; topographical transpositions represent not simply a substitution of Dominica for Jamaica but the 'intertwining of "Jamaica" and "Dominica"'; and changes in the family relationships also inflect the materials closer to Rhys's (Lockhart) family history. But even behind the family romance, there is, arguably, another history: Hulme's reconstruction of the Dominican record from archival material of one sort or another, while not wishing to short-circuit the 'fraught relationship between literature and history', none the less suggests the occlusion involved in the process of compensation.

But if part of Hulme's project is, as he says, 'to validate the local and the particular, even the familial', and thus to affirm the cultural differences that colonial discourse characteristically homogenises, this is not to say that it is impossible to move out from the particular to a wider historical context, in contrast to the postmodernism which begins and ends with the anecdote or the *petit récit*. Invoking Paul Gilroy's revisionist notion of the Atlantic world, Hulme is able to emphasise what Brontë and Rhys ultimately share in 'a larger world of which the locality forms only a part'. But this, in turn, is not again to 'collapse differences, but to argue for the need to understand the complex trafficking that exists between texts (and their authors)'.

This distinction is worth pausing over. In the postcolonial context the arguments for giving due consideration to the local are firstly that the discourse of colonialism has always operated by making the local (colonised) place secondary to the metropolitan centre, its history calibrated according to an external norm; and secondly that the stereotyping simplification of colonial discourse works by a similarly reductive dismissal of 'local' distinctions: its theatre is populated by figures like 'the Oriental', 'the savage', and 'the Indian', who have been divorced from particular times and places. Postcolonial work is, then, to a degree re-constitutive: to begin to understand local geographies and histories and to allow them to count in a way previously denied, are crucial counter-hegemonic moves.

There are, however, dangers to be avoided, notably that of falling back into an obsession with specificities, which can become another version of the empiricist fallacy in which all attempts to theorise are answered by the supposedly irrefutable case of a counter-example – a fallacy of which the anti-theoretical theoreticism of some postmodern thinking is merely a special, and specially pernicious, case. As Bruce Robbins puts it, in an excellent discussion of these issues: while we must always avoid the 'easy generalisation', we need to retain the right to formulate difficult generalisations (1992, pp. 174–5). In other words, a commitment to 'particularity' is not *ipso facto* a rejection of the very possibility of any totalising knowledge and of the grounding of a politics in that knowledge; nor is it an end in itself – the local must be valued for something other than its 'localness'. Indeed, at the end of the day, like most terms that form binary oppositions (usually in this case with 'cosmopolitan'), a way will have to be found of overcoming the dualism (cf. Robbins 1992; Pechey below, pp. 154–7).

As we have already mentioned, one of the most prominent concepts – if it is a concept – of the postcolonial theoretical debate is represented by the term 'hybridity'. Certainly it was much invoked, and criticised, at the Symposium. In her chapter, 'The recalcitrant object: culture contact and the question of hybridity', Annie E. Coombes interrogates this term from the perspective of a critical discussion of an important recent series of exhibitions which, in a strategy that seemingly departs from the binary culturalist model of 'the west' and 'its other', foregrounded instead transculturated objects, and declared themselves harbingers of a new postcolonial consciousness. While accepting the potential strategic value of hybridity 'as an important cultural strategy for the political project of decolonisation', Coombes none the less questions critically the ways in which hybridity 'is transformed . . . in the narratives of the western art and ethnographic museum and [asks] what relations of power and transgression it can still articulate there'. In doing so, she argues with some trenchancy the need to avoid what she sees as the uncritical celebration in museum culture of a hybridity which collapses the heterogeneous experience of racism into some kind of scopic feast where the goods are displayed in enticing configurations which do nothing to challenge or expose the ways in which such difference is constituted in the first place and operates as a mechanism for oppression.

In tracing some of the terms which the notion of hybridity has given rise to historically – it is part of her case that this notion has a sedimented history, 'a particular pedigree in the discourse of both art history and anthropology' – Coombes turns back to a moment in the disciplinary history of British ethnography when debates over the assignation of aesthetic value to material culture devolved around precisely one such term: the issue of 'racial purity'. The example chosen is that of the Benin bronzes which, along with the Elgin marbles, have been at the centre of the museological and political debate about the restitution of cultural property. In 1897 the British Museum put on public exhibition three hundred cast brass plaques from Benin, causing considerable popular and scientific speculation about how works showing such extraordinary technical skill and naturalism had been found in such quantities in Africa, including suggestions that their origin was the product of trans-culturation with Portuguese or Egyptian influences.

In charting the multiple discourses in which the significance of the Benin bronzes and ivories was imbricated, Coombes discusses the two key instances of representation of Beni women and that of Benin City from different discursive sites, in particular drawings and photographs in the contemporary illustrated press, and the supposedly more academic representations produced by the anthropological community. Then, focusing closely on the complex ethnographic and art-historical debate about the presumed 'degeneracy' of colonised, and particularly African, races and their material cultures, she demonstrates that there is a complicated, and often contradictory, ensemble of interests at work in this discursive formation, not least those of anthro-pology itself as it increasingly sought a public audience, professional re-cognition, disciplinary status as a science and state funding. Even when a 'purely' African origin was attributed to the bronzes – at some risk to the prevailing stereotypes of European racial superiority – it was arguably part of a strategy to enhance the status of the Ethnographic Department of the British Museum (at the expense of Egyptology) as the keeper of such anomalous works of African art; and more generally that of ethnography as such, as the scientific and ideological 'keeper' of the power to determine such questions.

Coombes brings the theme of the professionalisation of anthropology up to date by tracing the way in which it has sought to legitimate itself by proclaiming the need to conserve and preserve the artefacts in the custody of art and ethnographic museums, a rhetoric she dubs 'the disappearing world' phenomenon. But this in turn raises issues of the extent to which the museo-logical discourse is in fact complicit with the colonial subjugation, the silencing and extinction, of the cultural producers themselves. The picketing by Survival International of the 'Hidden Peoples of the Amazon' exhibition at the London Museum of Mankind in 1985, and the boycott by the Lubicon Lake Cree of the exhibition 'The Spirit Sings: Artistic Traditions of Canada's First Peoples' which was mounted in Calgary in 1988 to coincide with the Winter Olympics and sponsored by Shell Oil, both exposed the way in which these recent exhibitions, while devoted to the 'hybridity' of cultural contact, none the less suppressed the indigenous peoples' accounts of such contact, and in particular neglected their continuing struggles for land rights which the museum's discourse of cultural conservation occludes.

Finally Coombes discusses the 1989 exhibition 'Les Magiciens de la Terre' at the Centre Beaubourg, 'one of the more notorious exhibitions to foreground hybridity as a condition of post-coloniality'. Coombes questions whether the exhibition's postmodern technique of bricolage, assembling artefacts indif-ferently from a wide variety of different cultures, does not in fact 'simply revert to the pitfalls of the older cultural relativist model, concealing the distances between cultures while insisting that all are equal'. Coombes concludes her critique of the museological discourse of hybridity by suggesting that, in contrast to the 'philosophical relativism' of postmodernism's 'celebration of flux and indeterminacy as the product of the mobility of global capital', we need 'an account of "difference" which acknowledges the inequality of access to economic and political power... and would articulate the ways in which such differences are constituted, not only in relation to the western metropolitan centres', allowing us to explore the 'specific conditions' of hybridity, 'the how and the who of it'.

Ethnographic writing also features in Zita Nunes's chapter, 'Anthropology and race in Brazilian modernism', although in Brazil – in another salutary reminder of the complexity of these matters – the ethnography concerned was not charting a 'primitive' or 'savage' otherness across the civilisational divide, as in the cases studied by During and Coombes, but was in the process of forging a *national* identity which would – so the story went – break free of available European models. The problem which such writing had to confront was that the national search conducted by the political elites for a moment of authentic origin on which to construct a fixed identity for present and future always foundered on the irredeemably miscegenated reality of the Brazilian population. This conflict was addressed, Nunes writes, 'through the elaboration of a myth of racial democracy', a myth her chapter is concerned to unpick. In the course of her argument, Nunes takes issue with the well-intentioned efforts to define race as a construct independent of biology and with the optimistic view that Brazil has succeeded in 'deconstructing' race by means of miscegenation. Both views, she claims, can be used as a smokescreen behind which profoundly racist hierarchies continue to operate.

Her chapter focuses on the *modernista* movement of the 1920s, still an indispensable reference point for all discusions of Brazilian life and culture, and increasingly turned to as a forerunner of 'hybrid' cultural movements on account of its innovative and imaginative mixture of indigenous and avant-gardist motifs, symbolised by the famous *Manifesto antropófago* (*Cannibalist manifesto*). However, in an unusual move, Nunes sets her study of *modernismo* – and in particular of its classic text, Mario de Andrade's *Macunaíma* – against the anthropological and ethnographic writing of the 1920s and 1930s which had been investigating and theorising the racial complexity of modern Brazil. The key figures here are Gilberto Freyre, author of *The masters and the slaves*, and Paulo Prado, to whom Andrade dedicated *Macunaíma*. This contextualisation enables Nunes to pose some difficult questions to *Macunaíma*'s classic status within and outside Brazil, unravelling and exposing its occluded relationship to a 'local history' – looking at the materials from which Andrade drew and the alternatives he ignored –

in a way which has parallels with Hulme's reading of *Wide sargasso sea*.

The 'cannibalistic' thought of the Brazilian *modernistas* is tied in quite overt fashion to the metaphorics of the body – eating, incorporation, sickness. In these texts, however, Nunes finds expressed the fear that Brazilian modernisation – which would link Brazil to Europe and the USA – is threatened by a weakness and illness perpetuated by miscegenation, the black body figured as an alien being that may weaken the healthy (white) body. The implicit strategy for overcoming the threat was to eliminate the black race by assimilation into the white, even though the demographics of Brazil make that an absurd proposition.

The technique advocated in the 'Cannibalist manifesto' is to digest what European sources are useful to the creation of a national culture and to excrete the rest. *Macunaíma*, selectively borrowing from indigenous myth, re-inscribes the connection between race, contagion and illness and re-enforces a tripartite hierarchy of the races. Nunes demonstrates that the metaphor of ingestion turns out to apply to a white digestive system into which African and Indians are fed, assimilating what it can use, excreting the rest: 'For all the celebration of racial mixing that the cannibalistic approach to writing implies, and contrary to the usual readings of *Macunaíma*, there is no racial mixture in this book.' Instead we have the narration of racial democracy *and its residue*.

On one level Gayatri Chakravorty Spivak's chapter, 'How to read a "culturally different" book', is, as she says, about the representation of a temple dancer. Amongst other things. Interwoven with reflections on teaching practice (what it means to work in Cultural Studies), on situatedness (what 'a feminist reader or teacher in the USA might wish to know'), and on the relationship between English and the vernacular languages (a topic also discussed by Graham Pechey for South Africa), is Spivak's analysis of R. K. Narayan's 1958 novel, *The guide*, contrasting the book with the later film version. The dancer, Miss Nalini, the temple dancer or *devadāsi*, is the character in the novel to whom Spivak gives most attention, looking at the available sources for grasping the kind of representation that Narayan makes, notably at Frédérique Marglin's uncritical *Wives of the god-king* (1985), and at the evidence available from the 'ancient texts'.

Spivak's careful reading of *The guide* is a gesture in itself, affirming the need to take seriously – from a postcolonial perspective – the realist fictions associated with an emerging sense of nationhood, recovering, in other words, what might otherwise be sloughed off as uninterestingly pre-post-colonial, in the most dangerous and shallow use of the term 'postcolonial' as roughly equivalent to 'magical realist' in its promise of a hyper-reality of international or at least mythical proportions cut adrift from any of those moorings in the muddy estuaries of local realities that might baffle – or so the argument goes – that 'casual unmoored international audience'.

Spivak wants, through her reading and the reflections that accompany it, to convey some sense of the complexity of what she calls the 'neocolonial traffic in cultural identity': the 'differences and deferments within "national identity" and "ethnic minority"'. In these circumstances the worst move is to slap down the label 'postcolonial' and move on; so, to describe the novel, she insists on the term 'Indo-Anglian' which, through its very unfamiliarity, provides what she elsewhere calls 'a clue to the road-blocks to a too-quick enthusiasm for the other', a further correlate to the 'sargasso' that Hulme discusses at the end of his chapter.

By contrast, the film version of *The guide* belongs to an era of post-Independence India when multi-lingualism and secularist multi-communalism were still the official ideology. With an eye on current tendencies in India, Spivak reads this as particularly instructive as a symptom of the erosion of decolonisation.

At a moment when questions of canonicity and pedagogy are so central to discussions in the humanities, Spivak offers an object-lesson in how the texts of 'global English' need to be read historically and/or politically in order to make the multicultural canon really count.

Graham Pechey's chapter, 'Post-apartheid narratives', brings the 'post' of a particular social regime in South Africa into connection with the 'posts' of postcolonialism and postmodernism, and opens with some valuable reflections on these terms in the context of recent South African history. In that country, Pechey suggests, the project of rapid modernisation by force and the stable if violent oppositions it engendered have come to an end. It is a moment when the long-standing discourses of anti-apartheid must undergo some reconsideration. These had typically aligned themselves unproblematically with modernity against what was construed as the anti-modern system of apartheid. The limited conception of the political conceived by these discourses is also now in question: for Pechey, the time has come to 'listen to the unconscious of political reason' and to engage with its cultural and spiritual repressed.

Pechey argues that the thesis which has long informed ANC policy, that apartheid constitutes a form of 'internal colonialism', needs to be re-read in this new context. That thesis maintains that in South Africa the metropolis and colony co-exist geographically in a tiered class-formation; it is a version of the Leninist narrative of history tailored to the special circumstances of South Africa. Against this vision, Pechey insists on the importance of the micropolitical and on the validity of the co-existence of heterogeneous histories which can be brought to light by putting *discourse* at the centre of analysis and looking at the multifarious ways in which collectivities and subjectivities actually constitute and reconstitute themselves. Yet, at the same time, he is prepared to concede that in actual fact the Enlightenment discourse of universal humanism as embodied in the Freedom Charter of 1955 was 'the most powerfully mobilising document of the country's leading democratic movement'. Still, in its widely divergent receptions among a diversity of groups it might equally be considered a postmodern document.

The second section of Pechey's chapter looks closely at the polyglossic linguistic situation in South Africa. The Charter's authorised version is in English and, given the political prominence of Afrikaans, it is perhaps obvious that English should be touted as the language of neutrality, of the public sphere, and even of resistance. Pechey's post-apartheid perspective would seek to complicate this obviousness first by pointing out that the initial chapter of South Africa's forced modernisation was 'written in English' and then by observing that Afrikaans is far from being a 'white' language since it originates as a Dutch creole, which in turn developed from a pidgin spoken to and by slaves. As a product of 'the contact zone' it has, perhaps, richer resources for 'carnivalisation': Pechey certainly regards writing in the new hybrid forms of Afrikaans and English as a powerful decolonising gesture.

There is, however, a darker side to the post-apartheid situation. After the breakdown of the simple confrontation of state violence met by revolutionary counter-violence, there appears a proliferation of forms of violence. In the shadow of assimilationist ideologies we find movements of both the black and white right seeking to revive the old narratives of resistance to modernis-ation. Yet the binary logic of confrontation was also significantly altered, he shows, by the rise of Black Consciousness, a movement which shifted emphasis away from exclusively political aims and means and towards psycho-cultural and spiritual issues.

Writing in the 1980s demonstrates, on the one hand, blacks finally be-coming the authors of their own narratives and, on the other, whites re-sponding to the shock of the demise of liberalism. Pechey writes out of a conviction that postcolonial writing in South Africa (always clearly post-modern too, as an institution) challenges some of the assumptions associated with the Marxist/post-structuralist conception of literature as the imaginary solution of ideological contradictions. Ending on an optimistic note, Pechey sees both sorts of writing in South Africa as now working to reduce polar conflicts and engage in 'a dialogue of creoles of all "colours" overheard by the world'; though this optimism is immediately tempered by a postscript. The last word on apartheid is clearly yet to be written.

For obvious reasons, an examination of nationalism has once again become unavoidable for social and cultural theorists – as was reflected in the dis-cussions at Essex, where nationalism was the only topic that threatened to polarise opinion. Both Benita Parry and Neil Lazarus start from the overlap between dominant (western-centred) disparagements of nationalism and deconstructive readings of the phenomenon in current theories of colonial discourse. Both look again at anticolonial nationalism and its contemporary theorisation by way of suggesting the continuing indispensability of national consciousness to the decolonising project, a perspective that can usefully be contrasted with Pechey's.

The eventual topic of Benita Parry's chapter ('Resistance theory / theorising resistance, or two cheers for nativism') is Négritude, the forerunner of various kinds of 'nativism' that have tended to receive short shrift from the more theoretically sophisticated forms of postcolonial theory. She encourages a fresh consideration of Négritude as part of a larger project to theorise the variety of *resistances* to colonial power. Like Neil Lazarus, whose chapter Glissant follows hers, Parry is drawn back to the seminal work of Frantz Fanon, on which much postcolonial theory has been a commentary; to which she adds a consideration of his Martinican mentor, the poet and teacher Aimé Césaire, one of the founders of the Négritude movement in the 1930s.

Parry begins by identifying a fault-line within contemporary counter-hegemonic work around the question of whether or not the objective of restoring the colonised as the subject of its own history simply inverts but perpetuates the terms established by colonial discourse, while remaining complicit with its assumptions. Crucial issues of ethnic, national and cultural identity are raised by such a question, which is also addressed in many of the other chapters in this volume – especially those by Lazarus, Lloyd and Rosaldo. Parry's own position clearly asserts the value of attention to those moments of clandestine or overt countervailance, arguing that no system of coercion or hegemony can ever wholly determine the range of possible subject-positions. Her prolegomenon to the case of Négritude considers the arguments against this view, accepting the force of some but arguing the case for the 'unsententious interrogation' of even the most infrequently defended – of which Négritude is now the paradigm case. Her conclusion is that 'two cheers' can still be raised for this nativist project.

The usual criticism of the recuperation of figures of colonial resistance is that some mythical aboriginal essence is being sought, a quest both theoretically absurd – since we no longer accept even the idea of authentic *origins* – and historically blind – since the effects of colonial oppression cannot simply be wished away. Parry shows that the modes of resistance are themselves more subtle than this criticism would suggest, citing Wilson Harris's example of limbo-dancing and Edouard Glissant's theory of *métissage*, and drawing support from Stuart Hall's 'carefully modulated case' for a form of ethnic identitarianism.

Parry's reassessment of Négritude involves re-reading its dialogue with its critics, notably the Haitian René Depestre, who attacked its lack of political edge, and the 1960s generation of African philosophers and scholars, who were keen to distance themselves from what they saw as the spurious 'African-ism' of their predecessors. These sections of Parry's chapter also provide a useful background for Lazarus's discussion of Christopher Miller's *Theories of Africans* (1990), a book which takes such criticisms of supposedly

European-derived 'nativisms' much further. One of Miller's main targets is
the work of Frantz Fanon: Parry, as one might expect, offers a usefully
modulated account of Fanon as an ironic figure, recognising the literary
subtlety and ideological complexity of his work, especially the early *Black
skin, white masks* – her account of which complements Neil Lazarus's equally
sympathetic but not uncritical reading of Fanon's second masterpiece, *The
wretched of the earth*.

In his 'National consciousness and the specificity of (post)colonial intellectualism' Lazarus addresses the significance of forms of nationalism in the
struggle against colonial domination, and considers the role of this term
in some postcolonial theory. He begins by embracing Fanon's critique of
bourgeois nationalism in the essay 'The pitfalls of national consciousness'
written at the height of the Algerian war of independence, while wanting,
with Fanon, to keep a space open for what, following Anwar Abdel-Malek,
he terms a 'nationalitarian' consciousness as indispensable for the anti-
imperialist aspiration of oppressed peoples. Lazarus examines the problematic
character of Fanon's nationalitarianism in relation to the specific history of
the Algerian revolution, and also discusses the complexity of such a notion in
relation to the Marxist tradition of thought on the national question – Fanon
having been criticised both for abandoning Marxism by having dissolved the
perspectives of class struggle and socialist revolution into national aspirations;
and for not abandoning a Marxism inextricably wedded to European paradigms such as that of the nation, which are seen by many as wholly inap-
propriate to African societies, as no more than colonial impositions.

As the title of his chapter implies, a central issue for Lazarus in the debate
about national consciousness involves the role of the intellectual, a question
which has been aggravated by recent debates in postcolonial theory where it
has been in many ways a key concern – as indeed it was at the Symposium.
He cites Benita Parry's criticism of the disparaging of nationalist discourse
in recent, especially post-structuralist, scholarship on (post)colonialism, and
notes how this is linked, in Parry's view of Gayatri Chakravorty Spivak's
work specifically, to an ' "exorbitation" or exaltation of intellectualism'. A
corollary of the apotheosis of the postcolonial intellectual is the subordination
or erasure of the evidence of what Parry calls 'native agency'. Lazarus doubts
whether this charge can be consistently brought against Spivak, seeing the
latter's theory of subalternity as more a theory of colonial representation
than an account of native agency, even at the risk of privileging a 'deconstructive interrogation' over a 'radical historiography'.

Lazarus gives an extended and illuminating account of what he constitutes
as a debate between Parry and Spivak, endorsing and criticising aspects of
both their positions. He is particularly struck by Spivak's warning that we
should be as watchful for the continuing construction of the subalternity in
nationalist discourse as in that of imperialism, but none the less, where

Spivak 'balks' at the claim of a Ranajit Guha or an Edward Said that 'it is indeed possible for a movement or an alliance or a party to "speak for the nation"', it is on the possibility of this possibility – the nationalitarian rather than nationalist perspective – that Lazarus ultimately insists.

Crucial to this insistence is the relationship between the intellectuals and 'the masses'. Lazarus acknowledges the dangers of speaking *to* (rather than *for* or *with*) the people. But if there has been an 'exultation of the intellectual', there has also been an equally irresponsible '*intellectualist anti-intellectualism*, a post-Foucauldian disavowal of the problematic of representation, such that the very idea of speaking for others comes to be viewed as a discredited aspiration, and secretly authoritarian'. But Lazarus is convinced, with Adorno, that the socially instituted division between the intellectuals and the masses can be dissolved only by the transformation of society, and that until then theoretical dissolutions of the problem are merely ideological. Indeed, opposition to the notion of a national consciousness, and to a role for intellectuals in its formation, can itself become a radical elitism when in disparaging nationalism as a European derivative it ignores the 'huge investment of "the masses" in various kinds of nationalist struggle'. Citing the work of an intellectual and activist like Amilcar Cabral as an instance, Lazarus speaks of a dialectical process, a passage, in which intellectuals must play a key role, from 'local knowledge' – the terms are Cabral's – to 'the principles of national and social revolution', an 'articulation' which can be 'forged' between 'cosmopolitan intellectualism and popular consciousness'.

Lazarus invokes Partha Chatterjee's view of anticolonial nationalist discourse having a relation of difference from the bourgeois nationalism from which it none the less derives. He is, however, keen to separate this sense of the 'difference' of nationalitarian consciousness from Homi Bhabha's sense of the 'ambivalence' of colonised subjectivity, finding the latter's account of colonial mimicry, for example, too much the generalisation of a specific form, and thus too inattentive to the 'vastly differential thrusts, effects and modes of domination/subjection of colonialism as practised at different times by different powers in different parts of the world, or even within single but "unevenly developed" colonies'.

Lazarus concludes with a firm defence of the role of the intellectual in the formation of an appropriate nationalitarian consciousness. He cites Said on the contribution of intellectuals *as intellectuals* to the cause of anti-imperialism in the post-1945 era, and, evoking Lenin on the necessity of revolutionary theory, stresses the pressing need to construct – in Gates's phrase – a 'counternarrative of liberation'. Returning finally to the Fanon of the conclusion of *The wretched of the earth*, Lazarus invokes the idea of the possibility of a new humanism 'predicated upon a formal repudiation of the degraded European form'. Rather than abandoning 'the terrain of universality' to the projection of European forms (and still less buying into the postmodernist response to the indefensibility of bourgeois humanism by 'abandoning the very idea of totality'), Lazarus affirms instead 'the specific role of postcolonial intellectualism: to construct a standpoint – nationalitarian, liberationist, internationalist – from which it is possible to assume the burden of speaking for all humanity'.

'Ethnic cultures, minority discourse and the state' by David Lloyd begins by defining the difference between the first two phrases of his title. While ethnic culture concerns the traditions, histories and internal differences of a community, minority discourse is formed in the teeth of the dominant state formation which threatens to destroy it. These terms are deployed to contest the major conceptions of culture circulating in the relatively new academic field of Cultural Studies. According to Lloyd there are three fundamental definitions in circulation: the notion of the autonomy of the aesthetic sphere prefiguring a moment of freedom and reconciliation; the Marxist critique of autonomy which makes culture determined by socio-economic factors; and finally, the anthropological definition of culture as the life-world generally. None of these accounts is ultimately acceptable. The first option is particularly suspect since for an ethnic culture reconciliation with the dominant culture would mean its own demise. Yet the other options also have weaknesses, not least that they do not treat their objects as specifically *cultural* products.

The particular problems thrown up by ethnic cultural formations are used by Lloyd to unsettle and re-conceptualise the whole field of Cultural Studies. In their light we are better able, for example, to reflect on the function of the aesthetic within the state. The aesthetic sphere has a synchronic position in its distinction from political and economic spheres and a diachronic moment as the imagined apex of the human narrative. From this vantage, ethnic cultures are often seen as not yet having developed autonomous art because of historical damage. The same is often said of working-class culture by those who seek in it a simulacrum of high cultural forms. This, Lloyd implies, is another function of the aesthetic.

Lloyd also shows how the particular circumstances of ethnic/minority culture cast doubt on the defining terms of aesthetic high cultural theory – totalisation and typicality. This is because of their deep heteronomy, formed as they are not only by the shift between the ethnic culture and its relation to the state but also by divisions within such communities which are crossed by differences of gender, class and even ethnicity. The typical Mexican or black is a concept imposed from outside. Or, as Lloyd observes, ethnicity is a 'retrospective hypothesis'. This leads on to another observation concerning the double and contradictory formation of the ethnic minority by the dominant culture: it wants to assimilate individuals so that they become subjects of the state, yet at the same time it wants generic representatives of their culture of origin. The exigencies of minorities throw the whole discourse of 'equal rights' into question. That discourse, Lloyd claims, 'is inseparable from the racist structure of its political formation' as it demands an abstract public sphere in which people constitute themselves as individuals and as such it is in direct contradiction with the constitution of minorities, that is, as generic not as individual subjects.

Like Neil Lazarus, Renato Rosaldo focuses in his chapter, 'Social justice and the crisis of national communities', on the emancipatory possibilities still extant in the idea of 'nation', though he wants to imagine national communities whose solidarity emerges more from diversity than it does from the usual calls for homogeneity. This desire, Rosaldo begins by admitting, is partly conditioned by what he calls the 'dreamtime' of the Gulf War, a frequent refererence point in Symposium discussions and a conflict Rosaldo likens to the battle of Wounded Knee when US cavalry massacred the Sioux at Pine Ridge.

Rosaldo adds two other initial vantage points for his discussion. The first pits two Mexican positions on national culture: that the very idea is the invention of a few urban intellectuals who ignore the pervasive presence of the indigenous cultures throughout the country; and that there is a real Mexican national culture which is precisely a culture of resistance to attempts at US domination. The second, Chicano perspective sees national culture from the point of view of a marginalised and excluded group whose history does not appear in the school textbooks – any more than does that of the Native Americans, African Americans or Asian Americans. The materials of Rosaldo's essay primarily concern the Philippines, but the underlying questions relate equally closely to the pressing matter of national community in the USA and are hardly without relevance to other 'western' societies.

Rosaldo charts some of the changes over the last twenty-five years in the Ilongot relationship to the nation state of the Philippines. The Ilongot simply do not regard themselves as Filipino, and yet have to respond as 'the nation' imposes itself in their land in. a variety of ways – through landgrabbing, mining, resettlement projects, etc. As a result, over a very short span of years, Ilongot children have come to belong to a world very different from that of their parents – to the extent that the older generation now speaks of the younger as no longer Ilongot.

The Ilongot case allows Rosaldo to float the idea of 'cultural citizenship', which he takes to encompass both legal definitions and more local and informal notions of membership and entitlement: a hybrid term appropriate for an era in which ethnic minority groups constantly have to negotiate the vertiginous straits between strictly local identities and participation in the state. Rosaldo is interested in the consequent testing of the often tacit and fluctuating boundaries of imagined local and national communities.

The argument proceeds by way of an extended discussion of Benedict Anderson's influential book, *Imagined communities: reflections on the origins and spread of nationalism* (1983), noting in particular his use as an example of the Philippine novel *Noli me tangere* by José Rizal, a text to which Rosaldo returns later in his chapter to demonstrate now the 'horizontal egalitarian relations among men' in the novel are hydraulically related, as he puts it, to the exclusion of women, a dimension of the imagined community's fraternal bonds somewhat lacking in Anderson's analysis.

Anne McClintock's chapter, 'The angel of progress: pitfalls of the term "postcolonialism"', has frequently been referred to in this Introduction for its cautionary scrutinising of the term 'postcolonialism'. Her essay interrogates the theoretical and critical assumptions built into the very idea of post-colonialism, and represents a sustained address to the analytic and descriptive usefulness of the term when applied to the variety of contemporary national and regional situations. Many of the contributors to this book find the term useful, even indispensable, in some contexts (as McClintock herself does): none would deny the dangers of its slack deployment or want to suggest that it does not contain the kinds of pitfalls she outlines.

McClintock begins by examining the contradictory ideas of history that lay behind the presentation of the 1991 New York 'Hybrid State Exhibit'. While it was committed to a 'postcolonial' understanding of hybrid or multiple historical time, the physical organisation of the exhibition none the less articulated a linear, progressivist model of historical development, or, in McClintock's words, 'one of the most tenacious tropes of colonialism'. If postcolonial *theory* has 'sought to challenge the grandmarch of western historicism', as a *term*, ' "postcolonialism" none the less re-orients the globe around a single, binary opposition'. McClintock remarks that this results in 'an entranced suspension of history', and the term 'reduces the cultures of the peoples beyond colonialism to *prepositional* time. The term confers on colonialism the prestige of history proper.' In other words, the world's multitudinous cultures are marked, 'not positively by what distinguishes them, but by a subordinate, retrospective relation to linear, European time'.

If the term is theoretically reductive, equally it radically oversimplifies descriptively the variety of 'crucial geopolitical distinctions'. It flattens the uneven development of post-colonialism; in its Eurocentrism it obscures who the colonisers and who the colonised may be or have been; it may be 'prematurely celebratory'; it is unable to distinguish the different forms of global domination that are extant (for example, 'colonisation', 'internal colonisation', and 'imperial colonisation'); it obscures the difference among the forms of decolonisation which have taken place; and so on. Citing a host of examples from throughout the world, McClintock's emphasis is on the variety and difference among types of colonial, neocolonial and post-colonial situations.

The reductionism of the term – from which McClintock wants to rescue the orientation of the newly emerging discipline of postcolonial studies – is part of a broader problem of historical theory. In a concluding section of her essay McClintock seeks to account for the ubiquity of ' "post"-words' in contemporary intellectual life. She attributes this phenomenom to a 'global crisis in ideologies of the future, particularly the ideology of "progress" '. According to her argument, the combined collapse of the US myth of progress (attendant on a shift of foreign policy after the global economic crisis of the late 1970s), and the later breakdown of 'communist progress' with the demise of the Soviet Union, has produced a 'doubled and overdetermined crisis in images of future time'.

'For this reason', McClintock contends, 'there is some urgency in the need for innovative theories of history and popular memory, . . . a *proliferation* of historically nuanced theories and strategies . . . which may enable us to engage more effectively in the politics of affiliation, and the currently catastrophic dispensations of power'. The alternative will be to 'face being becalmed in an historically empty space in which our sole direction is found by gazing back, spellbound, at the epoch behind us, in a perpetual present marked only as "post" '.

The Symposium itself was a valuable, entertaining and comradely event, and we would like to thank all the participants for making it so, and for their contributions to the volume that has resulted. In addition we would like to acknowledge the help of the following: The University of Essex, and the Departments of Art History and Theory and of Literature at Essex for contributions to the funding of the project; Lesley Theophilus for hospitality; Wendy Harfield for secretarial assistance; and Ian Pindar for making the index.

Francis Barker
Peter Hulme
Margaret Iversen
University of Essex

Transculturation and autoethnography: Peru, 1615/1980

MARY LOUISE PRATT

Que se nos guarden nuestras buenas costumbres y leyes que entre nosotros a abido y ay, justas para nuestro gouierno e justicia, y otras cosas que soliamos tener en tiempo de nuestra ynfidelidad.

May our good customs and laws be retained that among us have existed and exist, suitable for our government and justice, and other things that we were accustomed to having in the time of our infidelity. (Quoted in Murra 1980, I, p. xix)

So stated a group of several hundred Andean indigenous leaders in a petition addressed to the Spanish crown in 1562, some thirty years after Pizarro's landing at Cajamarca, and ten years before the fall of the last Inca, Tupac Amaru, in 1572. This one-sentence item (like any other in this remarkable document) exemplifies the intricate transcultural pragmatics of communication under conquest. I begin, then, with a brief reflection on it. The language is Spanish, of course, native to none of the addressors of the document. It was produced here almost certainly by a bilingual scribe from conversation conducted in more than one Andean language. The mode of communication, alphabetic writing, is also European, there being no systems of writing indigenous to the Andes. The speech act, a royal petition, is also Spanish but probably intersected with the indigenous speech repertoire.

'Que se nos guarden' the statement begins, in a Spanish construction that is grammatically neither active nor passive voice, and translates as something like 'May it be brought about that [our laws and customs] are maintained for us' or 'May we be enabled to maintain [them]'. The subjunctive mode refers, as subjunctives do, to an uncertain future from a present marked in this case by cataclysmic upheaval. It calls forth a possibility, as subjunctives also do, from the position not simply of the conquered subject, but of the leadership of the conquered – authorised to address the conqueror, but in his language and discourse, and in tones of supplication. Who will determine this future? Who could and might ensure the retention of customs and laws, and how? The Spanish construction states no agent. In the aftermath of the clash between empires, lines of power and legitimacy are unclear, and the mutual responsibilities of conquerors and conquered to each other are under negotiation.

'The good laws and customs that exist and have existed among us', says the second clause. The sequence of perfect and present verb tenses ('exist and have existed') marks the historical watershed of the European invasion in the invader's language, but from the point of view of the invaded. And of course, on this side of that before-and-after is the pronoun 'we', the collective Amerindian subject brought into being by the rapacious descent of the Spanish you/they. In the Andean petition that 'we' asserts itself (in the conqueror's language) as a subject specifically of culture (our laws, customs, other things it was our custom to have) and of history (that which existed, exists, should be maintained). Paradoxically (for such is the post-conquest state), the indigenous demand for continuity is predicated of a moral universe already assumed to be radically altered. The alteration is expressed by two terms: *buenas*, 'good', and *ynfidelidad*, 'infidelity' – may we keep the *good* laws and customs from the time of our *infidelity*. The bifurcated bases of Christianity – good/evil; Christian/infidel – are presupposed by the Andean speakers, or perhaps invoked as the shared basis for communication between themselves and Spanish authorities. The Andean leaders, so it seems, agree to insert themselves into these moral paradigms. Thus while calling for continuity with the pre-conquest world, they constitute themselves as other to their pre-conquest selves. Addressing the invader the leaders situate themselves within the Christian moral universe, and outside the Spanish legal, political and social universe. A highly strategic manipulation of the invader's linguistic and ideological apparatuses, surely. And a potentially challenging one, too, given its premise that goodness and infidelity can and did co-exist.

The invader's language appropriated by the invadee to address the invader; the invadee's interests expressed in discursive apparatuses adapted from the invader and redirected back at him. Not an unusual situation historically, not at all. But perhaps one that could bear more reflection, both by students of colonialism and imperialism and by students of language. One of the significant projects of what is called postcolonial scholarship has been to work out ways of studying colonialism and imperialism from the perspective of its non-European subjects. Perhaps it is this project that most clearly links postcolonial scholarship on the one hand and anti-imperial and decolonisation movements on the other. What, it has been asked, are the forms of socio-historical agency of the subordinated subjects of colonialism and imperialism? How can the negotiated, radically conflicted character of colonial relations be more fully represented? Work on such questions has made possible readings such as the one just done of the Andean petition, and indeed has brought texts like that one into the sphere of scholarly and political understanding. New questions have been raised by such inquiry.

What is to be the field of reference of the categories of resistance and sub-version? Co-optation and assimilation? Syncretism and hybridity? Cultural heterogeneity at the level of social structure and of consciousness? Can one move from identifying these dimensions of imperial interaction to assessing their effects and their effectiveness? How?

In the segment quoted from the Andean petition, the subject of negotiation is culture itself. Cultures, as students of colonialism must often be reminded, are not 'overthrown' like empires, or 'taken over' like capital cities, or 'razed' like temples and palaces. They don't simply 'fall'. Under conquest, culture in both broad and narrow senses enters the realm of that which 'has existed and exists', that which continues to be but not at all as it was before. It is an elementary point, but easy to lose track of as one studies the violent dramas of invasion, overthrow, occupation and enslavement. Except in the face of outright genocide, conquest does not simply 'bring down' cultures, societies, languages as it brings down political hegemonies. Consciousness and memory cannot simply be put an end to by an act of either force or volition. (A person cannot choose, or be compelled, to sit down and forget their language or religion from one moment to the next, for instance.) Under conquest social and cultural formations enter long-term, often permanent states of crisis that cannot be resolved by either conquerer or conquered. Rather, the relations of conquered/conqueror, invader/invadee, past hegemony/present hegemony become the medium in which and out of which culture, language, society and consciousness get constructed. The constructing itself, as the Andean leaders of 1562 knew, involves continuous negotiation, among radically hetero-geneous groups making up the imperial power structure, among radically heterogeneous systems of meaning put into contact by the colonial encounter, and within the relations of radical inequality enforced by imperial violence.

Within what has come to be known as the colonial discourse movement, terms such as hybridity (Bhabha, García Canclini), syncretism (JanMohamed) and mimicry (Bhabha, Spivak) have been brilliantly used to examine cultural and linguistic interfaces between coloniser and colonised, the dynamics of what I have elsewhere called 'contact zones' (Pratt 1991, 1992). In what follows I propose to consider further questions of how culture is negotiated in situations of conquest and occupation, and to enrich the terminology by a couple of terms. Like the Andean text with which I began, the materials I will consider are indigenous responses to the Spanish invasion of the Americas. They might serve, it is hoped, to counterbalance the understandable but disproportionate focus in colonial studies on British imperialism of the last two centuries.

In 1908 a Peruvianist named Richard Pietschmann was exploring in the Danish Royal Archive in Copenhagen and came across a manuscript.[1] It was dated in the city of Cuzco in Peru, in the year 1613 and signed with an unmistakably Andean indigenous name: Felipe Guaman Poma de Ayala. Written in a mixture of Quechua and ungrammatical, expressive Spanish, the manuscript was a letter addressed by an unknown but apparently literate Andean to King Philip III of Spain. What stunned Pietschmann was that the letter was twelve hundred pages long. There were almost eight hundred pages of written text and four hundred captioned line drawings. The letter bore the title *La primera nueva coronica y buen gouierno* (*The first new chronicle and good government*). No one knew (or knows) how the manuscript got to the library in Copenhagen or how long it had been there. No one, it appeared, had ever bothered to read it or figured out how. Quechua was not thought of as a written language in 1908, nor Andean culture as a literate culture. Pietschmann prepared a paper on his find, which he presented in London in 1912, a year after Hiram Bingham 'discovered' Machu Picchu. Reception, by an international congress of Americanists, was apparently confused. It took twenty-five years for a facsimile edition of the work to appear, in Paris. It was not till the late 1970s, as positivist reading habits gave way to interpretive studies and colonial ethnocentrisms to postcolonial pluralisms, that western scholars found ways of reading Guaman Poma's *New chronicle and good government* as the extraordinary intercultural tour de force that it was.[2] The letter got there, only 350 years late, a miracle and a terrible tragedy.

In so far as anything is known about him at all, Guaman Poma exemplified the socio-cultural complexities produced by conquest and empire. He was an indigenous Andean who claimed noble descent and who had adopted (at least in some sense) Christianity. He may have worked in the Spanish colonial administration as an interpreter, scribe or assistant to a Spanish tax collector – as a mediator, in short. He says he learned to write from his half-brother, a *mestizo* whose Spanish father had given him access to religious education.

Guaman Poma's letter to the king is written in two languages and two parts.[3] The first is called the *Nueva coronica* (*New chronicle*). The title is important. The chronicle of course was the main writing apparatus through which the Spanish represented their American conquests to themselves. It constituted one of the main official discourses. In writing a 'new chronicle', Guaman Poma took over the official Spanish genre for his own ends. Those ends were, roughly, to construct a new picture of the world, a picture of a Christian world with Andean rather than European peoples at the centre of it – Cuzco, not Jerusalem. In the *New chronicle* Guaman Poma begins by rewriting the Christian history of the world from Adam and Eve (fig. 1), incorporating the Amerindians into it as offspring of one of the sons of Noah. He identifies five ages of Christian history that he links in parallel with the five ages of canonical Andean history – separate but equal trajectories that diverge with Noah and reintersect not with Columbus but with St Bartholomew, claimed to have preceded Columbus in the Americas. In a couple of hundred pages, Guaman Poma constructs a veritable encyclopedia of Inca and pre-Incaic history, customs, laws, social forms, public offices and dynastic leaders. The depictions resemble European 'manners and customs' descriptions, but also reproduce the meticulous detail with which knowledge in Inca society was stored on *quipus* and in the oral memory of elders.

Guaman Poma's *New chronicle* is an instance of what I have proposed to call an *autoethnographic* text (Pratt 1991, 1992), by which I mean a text in which people undertake to describe themselves in ways that engage with representations others have made of them. Thus if ethnographic texts are those in which European metropolitan subjects represent to themselves their others (usually their subjugated others), autoethnographic texts are representations that the so-defined others construct *in response to* or in dialogue with those texts. Autoethnographic texts are not, then, what are usually thought of as autochthonous or 'authentic' forms of self-representation (as the Andean *quipus* were, for instance). Rather they involve a selective collaboration with and appropriation of idioms of the metropolis or conqueror. These are merged or infiltrated to varying degrees with indigenous idioms to create self-representations intended to *intervene* in metropolitan modes of understanding. A remarkable range of European descriptive modes are appropriated by Guaman Poma to depict Andean society and history. He includes a creation story, a genealogy of rulers, a cycle of the seasons, a cycle of feast days,

Figs 1, 2 Guaman Poma, 22, 369

generalised manners-and-customs description and, at the end of the work, a tour of the cities of the New World *à la* John Mandeville.

Autoethnographic works are often addressed to both metropolitan audiences and the speaker's own community. Their reception is thus highly indeterminate. Such texts often seem to be a marginalised group's point of entry into the dominant circuits of print culture. It is interesting to think, for example, of American slave autobiography in its autoethnographic dimensions, which in some respects distinguish it from Euro-American autobiographical tradition. Autoethnographic representation often involves concrete collaborations between people, as between literate ex-slaves and abolitionist intellectuals, or between Guaman Poma, the Inca elders who were his informants and perhaps the bilingual scribe who took his dictation. Often, as in Guaman Poma, it involves more than one language. In recent decades autoethnography, critique and resistance have reconnected with writing in a contemporary creation of the contact zone, the *testimonio*.

Guaman Poma's *New chronicle* ends with a revisionist account of the Spanish conquest. This, he argues, should have been a peaceful encounter of equals with the potential for benefiting both. Only the mindless greed of the Spanish turned it into the campaign of destruction that ensued. He parodies Spanish history. Following contact with the Incas, he writes, 'In all Castille, there was a great commotion. All day and at night in their dreams, the Spaniards were saying "Yndias, yndias, oro, plata, oro, plata del Piru"' ('Indies, Indies, gold, silver, gold, silver from Peru', Guaman Poma 1980 [1613], I, p. 372). See fig. 2. The Spanish, he writes, brought nothing of value to share with the Andeans, nothing but armour and guns 'con la codicia de oro, plata, oro y plata, yndias, a las Yndias, Piru' ('with the lust for gold, silver, gold and silver, Indies, the Indies, Peru', *ibid.*). I quote these words as an example of a conquered subject using the conqueror's language to construct a parodic, oppositional representation of the conqueror's own speech. Guaman Poma mirrors back to the Spanish – in their language, which is alien to him – an image of themselves that they often suppress and will therefore surely recognise. Such are the dynamics of language, writing and representation in the contact zones of European expansion.

The second half of Guaman Poma's epistle continues the critique. It is titled *Buen gobierno y justicia* (*Good government and justice*), and combines a description of colonial society in the Andean region with a passionate denunciation of Spanish exploitation and abuse. (These, at the time he was writing, were destroying the indigenous population at a genocidal rate. In fact, the potential loss of the labour force became a main catalyst for reform of the system.) Guaman Poma's most implacable hostility is aimed at the clergy, followed by the dreaded *corregidores*, or colonial overseers (see fig. 3). He also praises good works, Christian habits and just men where he finds them, and offers at length his views as to what constitutes 'good government and justice'. The Indies, he argues, should be administered through a collaboration of Inca and Spanish elites. The epistle ends with a remarkable imaginary interview between Guaman Poma and the King of Spain. It takes the form of a question-and-answer session in which, in a reversal of hierarchy, the King is depicted asking Guaman Poma for advice about how to reform the empire. Here is a dialogue imagined across the many lines of hierarchy, difference and distance that divide Andean scribe from imperial monarch, in which the subordinated subject single-handedly gives himself authority in the coloniser's language and verbal repertoire. In a way, it worked – the extraordinary text did get written – but in a way it did not, for the letter never reached its chief addressee. The absence of structures of reception made Guaman Poma's project an impossible speech act.

To grasp the import of Guaman Poma's project in the *New chronicle and good government* one needs to keep in mind that the Incas had no system of writing. Their huge empire is said to be the only known instance of a full-blown bureaucratic state society built and administered without writing (Collier *et al.* 1982). Guaman Poma constructs his text by appropriating and adapting pieces of the representational repertoire of the invaders. He does not simply imitate or reproduce it; he selects and adapts it along Andean lines to express (bilingually, mind you) Andean interests and aspirations. Cultural

Figs 3, 4 Guaman Poma, 525, 366

theorists (Ortiz, Rama) have used the term *transculturation* to describe processes whereby members of subordinated or marginal groups select and invent from materials transmitted by a dominant or metropolitan culture. The term, originally coined in the 1940s by Cuban sociologist Fernando Ortiz (Ortiz 1978 [1947]), aimed to replace overly reductive concepts of acculturation and cultural loss used to characterise culture under colonialism. While subordinate peoples do not usually control what emanates from the dominant culture, they do determine to varying extents what gets absorbed into their own, and what it gets used for. Transculturation, like autoethnography, is a phenomenon of the contact zone.

The transcultural character of Guaman Poma's text is intricately apparent in its visual component as well. Recent studies of the *Nueva coronica y buen gobierno* have paid particular attention to the four hundred line drawings it includes, a corpus absolutely unique in the voluminous body of chronicles on colonial Peru. (Some scholars argue that the drawings in fact make up the basic scaffolding of the book, and that the written text is appended to them rather than the reverse.) The genre of the four hundred captioned line drawings is European. There seems to have been no practice of representational drawing among the Incas. But in their execution, Guaman Poma's drawings deploy specifically Andean systems of spatial symbolism that express Andean values and aspirations.

Most of the drawings are representational, accompanied by a title and a telegraphic explanatory text in Spanish, Quechua or a mixture of the two. Fig. 1 for example, from the beginning of the *New chronicle*, depicts Adam and Eve and their two sons at the beginning of the world. The caption reads 'El primer mundo / Adan, Eva' ('the first world / Adam, Eve'). The phrase 'en el mundo' ('in the world') is written across the bottom. The commentary accompanying the drawing sums up the genealogy of people from Adam via Methuselah to Noah, all of whom 'lived many years. Adam and Eve alone are said to have lived two or three thousand years' (I, p. 21 [23]). Fig. 4 depicts Guaman Poma himself (centre) in Europeanised dress consulting with elders on the history of the ancients. In a typical mix of Spanish and Quechua, the caption reads 'Pregunta el autor / Ma uillauay achamitama' ('The author asks, "Tell me, old ones"'). In the bottom right-hand corner the phrase 'y muestra' ('and he shows') is explained by the textual commentary that accompanies the picture:

> He tells the author and shows him the *quipus* and tells him, and the Incas and the Chinchaysusyos, Andesuyos, Collasuyos, Condesuyos [lords of the four quadrants of the Inca empire – MLP] relate stories to the author . . . telling him from the first Indian that God brought to this kingdom, of the offspring of Adam and Eve, of Noah and the flood, the first Indian named Uari Uiracocha and Uari Indians, Purun Indians, Auca Indians, Incapacha Indians, told and explained everything so he will write it down in this book so the society will go forward. (I, p. 264 [367])

In a carefully planned juxtaposition, this picture of Guaman Poma as chronicler—author—ethnographer appears immediately following another one of almost, but not quite, identical composition (fig. 5), depicting the Royal Council of the Incas who governed the four sectors of the city of Cuzco and the four sectors of the Inca empire. (I will be discussing these drawings further below.)

Figs 6 and 7 are taken from sections of the *New chronicle* describing Inca society and customs. Fig. 6 shows an agricultural scene, fig. 7 depicts the traditional ceremonial fiesta of one quadrant of the Inca empire. The *Good government and justice* is introduced by the drawing in fig. 8. This drawing depicts one of the Spanish viceroys, Don Andres Marquis de Canete, meeting with Sairi Topa Inga, labelled 'King of Peru'. Its spatial symmetry suggests what for Guaman Poma was an ideal of 'good government' based on co-operation and mutual respect between Spanish and Inca hierarchies. Such a view of the Euro-American contact contrasts dramatically with Spanish versions of fierce battles against bloodthirsty antagonists. In the *Good government* the pictorial agenda often foregrounds the violence, brutality and dehumanisation of Spanish imperialism. Many drawings depict forms of mistreatment suffered by indigenous Andeans at the hands of Spanish authorities, emphasising its systematic character. Fig. 3 above summarises several kinds of punishment inflicted on Indians by the notorious Spanish *corregidores*. Sitting in the upper right-hand corner the colonial official presides

Figs 5, 6 Guaman Poma, 364, 1103

while one man is beaten sitting on a llama (perhaps suggesting high rank); others are beaten tied to posts, and another (lower right) is put in the stocks. 'Corregidor de minas,' ('overseer of mines') reads the text, 'how he cruelly punishes chieftains; *corregidores* and judges with no fear of reprisals, with different punishments, with no godly pity for the poor in the mines.' Fig. 9 shows parents defending their daughter from the advances of a lascivious Spaniard. 'Indians', reads the caption, 'the mother and father defend their daughter from the Spaniard / The poor Indians / pride and licentiousness [bottom line].' Church officials likewise come under attack. A section of fully 90 pages called 'Padres' describes in highly critical fashion the activities of Spanish priests among the indigenous population. Their physical brutality and habitual sexual hypocrisy are recurring themes. Fig. 10 titled 'Mala confesion' ('bad confession') depicts a weeping, pregnant woman convert on her knees before a rather fierce-looking padre who, as he admonishes her to virtue, kicks her with his foot. The caption reads:

> Mala conficion que haze los padres y curas de las dotrinas. Aporrea a las yndias prenadas y a las biejas y a yndios. Y a las dichas solteras no las quiere confezar de edad de beynte anos, no se confiesa ni ay rremedio de ellas.

> Bad confession made by the fathers and priests of the doctrines. He beats the pregnant Indians and the old women and men. And the young single women he

Figs 7, 8 Guaman Poma, 324, 440

does not wish to confess at the age of twenty years they do not confess and there is no hope for them.

The refusal to confess the young women follows from the priests' own sexual intentions toward them. The text on the adjacent page elaborates the critique: 'So the padres confess the Indian women in houses of the church and the baptismal font and the sacristy in the dark and suspicious hidden places the single women they commit fornication and sin with them, worthy of punishment and good example in this kingdom that there may be Christianity' (II, p. 23 [577]).

In other sections of the *Buen gobierno*, vices within the indigenous masses also come under attack. Fig. 11 for example gives Guaman Poma's description of drunkenness with a colourful text in Quechua: 'auaya ayauaya machac, machaclla tucuy cay – upyac, upycalla tucuy cay – quimnac, quipnaclla tucuy cay camca serui suyulla mina suyulla' ('Awayay, ayawaya the drunk is only a drunk, the drinker only a drinker, he who vomits only vomits, what he deserves is to serve you, devil, what he deserves is the mines').

Recent scholarship (Adorno, López-Baralt) has shown that Guaman Poma's drawings are often composed according to an Andean system of spatial symbolism developed before contact with Europe, and still operative in the region today. The traditional Andean cosmological order was a quadripartite

Figs 9, 10 Guaman Poma, 868, 576

one organised by sets of binary complementarities governed by the verbal terms *hanan* 'above' and *hurin* 'below'. Horizontally, *hanan* is associated with right and *hurin* with left. Spatially, these relations are marked out by two diagonals which define four symbolic sectors (up, down, right, left), and whose point of intersection marks a privileged fifth position. The paradigm is associated, among other things, with the Southern Cross (interpreted as an X). The diagonal running from upper right (*hanan*) to lower left (*hurin*) is the primary symbolic axis. This symbolic order determined the administrative organisation of the Inca Empire, which was divided into the four quadrants Guaman Poma mentions in his depiction of the Royal Council (fig. 5 above). The city of Cuzco was likewise divided into upper and lower zones, and each of these into two others. (Andean villages today are commonly divided into moieties that are crossed by other binary forms of organisation such as gender.) It is important to note that in the Andean schema these positions are understood not as embodying *intrinsic* values but as expressing *relations*, notably relations of complementarity. Fig. 12 is one of Guaman Poma's *tours de force*, a 'World map of the Indies' ('Mapa mundi de las indias') deploying this symbolic system. The two diagonals, linked to the sun and the moon, intersect at Cuzco and mark out the four quadrants. The heraldic shield of the Pope stands to the left of Cuzco, and that of Castile and Leon to the right.

Fig. 11 Guaman Poma, 862

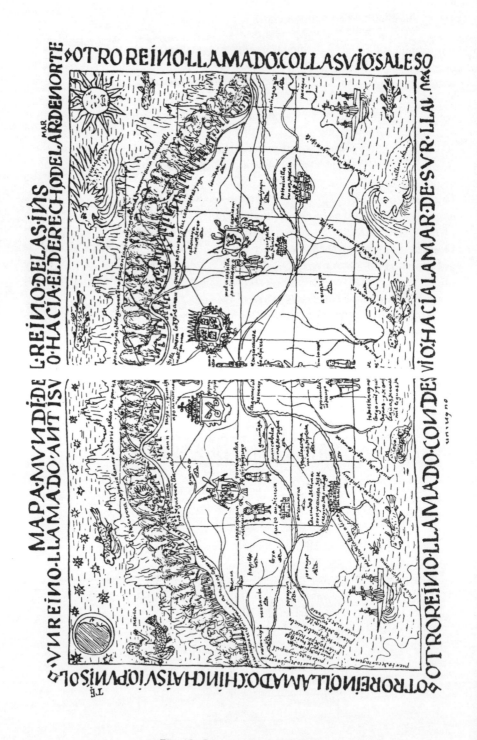

Fig. 12 Guaman Poma, 983–4

Roughly speaking, this diagonal paradigm produces two kinds of symbolic organisation. Read vertically it expresses hierarchical relations in which higher (*hanan*) positions are distinguished from lower (*hurin*) ones. Read horizontally it expresses relations of complementarity, in which left is associated with female and right with male. Contemporary Andean ethnographers have documented the ways these associations continue to structure many aspects of life in Andean communities, such as the allocation of lands, social groupings, marital patterns, assignment of ceremonial duties, religious cycles and so forth (see, for example, Isbell, Palomino Flores).

Adorno (1982, 1986) and López-Baralt (1979) demonstrate that many of Guaman Poma's drawings make systematic use of diagonal organisation and vertical and horizontal symbolism to express relations or judgements of value. Consider the arrangement of elements in fig. 1, for instance. 'Read' according to the Andean spatial order, Adam's digging stick (an Andean, not a biblical, allusion) divides the drawing along a rough diagonal one side of which is masculine, containing Adam, the rooster, the sun, and the other feminine, containing Eve and her babies, the hen and the moon. On the vertical axis, Adam stands above Eve (as in the Bible), the Sun-deity above Adam, and the moon above Eve. While the subject matter of the picture is biblical and Christian, its iconography and spatial organisation are Andean. So Guaman Poma appropriates Christianity into a world defined in non-European terms.

A word of explanation is required here. I noted above that the Andean gender paradigm assigns females to the left position and males to the right. In the pictorial representations, however, the paradigm is deployed from the viewpoint of a person standing behind the picture. The viewer must interpret the schema as mirror-imaged: in fig. 1 the symbolic (male) right is on the visual left and vice versa. Similarly in fig. 7 the woman drummer and child are on the visual right, or symbolic left, opposite from the male flautists. The basic diagonal dividing *hanan* and *hurin* is likewise mirror-imaged, running, like Adam's digging stick in fig. 1, from visual lower right to upper left. So it is plotted again in fig. 5, where the Royal Inca stands in the middle as the central power, while his diagonally held staff defines the *hanan/hurin* line and the positions of the lords who govern the various regions of the Empire. In the otherwise similar fig. 4, the absence of this very diagonal denotes, as I shall discuss below, the disruption of the imperial order.

Only a handful of Guaman Poma's drawings deploy the Andean symbolic spatial order as fully and literally as figs 1, 5 or 12. But, in fact, that is just the point. Adorno and others argue that in many of Guaman Poma's drawings the spatial order is violated in systematic ways that express the disorder and disruption brought about by the conquest, or the evil and illegitimacy of Spanish domination. As mentioned above, fig. 4 depicting Guaman Poma himself lacks the clear diagonal marker found in the pre-

conquest version in fig. 5, and is 'off centre' in a number of other ways as
well, such as the position of Guaman Poma's body. The highly symmetrical
fig. 8 reads rather differently when the spatial symbolism is brought into
play. Again the Inca king's staff of office marks out the basic diagonal. With
reference to that diagonal, it becomes significant that the Inca king is sitting
ever so slightly lower than the Spanish viceroy, and on the visual right
(female) side. The symbolism, in short, contradicts the message of equality
and symmetry, conveying, perhaps, a scepticism or cynicism only Guaman
Poma's Andean readers would detect.

Adorno notes that, in many drawings, Andean victims of the Spanish are
found in the upper left corner which in the normative schema marks the seat
of legitimate authority (where the sun is in fig. 1, for example). Spanish
oppressors are often located on the upper right. Fig. 3 exemplifies this
strategy. Here the basic diagonal organisation runs in the 'wrong' direction,
from lower left to upper right, marked clearly by the parallel staffs of the
corregidor and his assistant. In this mundo al rreves ('world in reverse') as
Guaman Poma called it, the Spanish corregidor occupies a position of power
diametrically opposed to the seat of legitimate authority in the upper left
corner. That position is occupied, as in many other drawings, by an Indian
victim. In fig. 10, 'Mala confesion', both the diagonal and the gender signs
are reversed. The evil priest occupies the upper position on the 'wrong' side
both in terms of authority and in terms of gender. Not surprisingly, Guaman
Poma's depiction of confession as it should be conducted (fig. 13) puts the
priest in the position of legitimate male authority (visual left), and adds
balance with a second window.

The point here is not of course to argue that Guaman Poma's book is
'really' Andean beneath an appearance of assimilation. Such an argument
would be trapped in an ideology of authenticity whose limitations are brought
to the fore by transculturated texts like this one. Guaman Poma's book is a
polemic; it is not a naive expression of what he thinks his world is and ought
to be, but an engagement with what he thinks the Spanish think his world
is and ought to be. This engagement is central to what I am calling its
autoethnographic dimensions. If one thinks of cultures as discrete, coherently
structured, monolingual edifices, Guaman Poma's text, and indeed any
autoethnographic work, appears anomalous or chaotic – it apparently did to
the European scholars Pietschmann addressed in 1912. If one does not think
of cultures this way, then Guaman Poma's text is not chaotic, but heterogeneous (cf. Cornejo Polar), as the Andean region was itself and remains
today. Such a text is heterogeneous on the reception end as well as the production end. That is, it will read differently to people in different positions in
the contact situation. Because it deploys European and Andean systems of
signification, the letter necessarily means differently to bilingual Spanish–
Quechua speakers and to monolingual speakers in either language. The

Fig. 13 Guaman Poma, 615

drawings likewise mean differently to monocultural readers, Spanish or Andean, and to bicultural readers responding to the Andean symbolic structures embodied in European genres. Guaman Poma himself acknowledged the heterogeneity of his potential audience when he declared that his book 'es para todo el mundo y cristiandad hasta los infieles se debe verlo para la dicha buena justicia y policia y ley del mundo' ('is for all the world and Christendom and even infidels should look at it for the above mentioned good justice and policy and law of the world', II, p. 447 [1168]).

In the Andes in the early 1600s there existed a literate public with considerable intercultural competence and degrees of bilingualism. Unfortunately, such a community did not exist in the Spanish court with which Guaman Poma was trying to make contact. It is interesting to note that in roughly the same year Guaman Poma sent off his letter, a text by another Peruvian was adopted in official circles in Spain as the canonical Christian mediation between the Spanish conquest and Inca history. It was another huge encyclopedic work, titled the *Royal commentaries of the Incas* (*Comentarios reales de los Incas*) written, tellingly, by a *mestizo*, known as Inca Garcilaso de la Vega. Like the *mestizo* half-brother who taught Guaman Poma to read and write, Inca Garcilaso was the son of an Inca noblewoman and a Spanish official, and had lived in Spain since he was seventeen. Though he too spoke Quechua, his book is written in eloquent, standard Spanish, without illustrations. It too is highly critical of Spanish abuses and disrespect for Inca traditions. While Guaman Poma's life's work sat somewhere unread, the *Royal commentaries* were edited and re-edited in Spain and the New World, a mediation that coded the Andean past and present in ways more recognisable and congenial to the colonial hierarchy. The situation persists. The *Royal commentaries* have long been a staple item on Ph.D. reading lists in Spanish, while the *New chronicle and good government*, despite the availability of several fine editions, is still seldom found.

While Guaman Poma's letter sat unread, in Peru Andeans continued to elaborate transcultural currents of expression, less in writing than in storytelling, ritual, song, dance-drama, painting and sculpture, dress, textile art, religious belief, forms of governance, and these forms have continued to enact what has been called their resistant adaptation to the European invasion (Stern 1987). Since the 1960s, Andean ways of life have faced interventions and transformations as radical as those lived out by Guaman Poma, and these too have been registered in new forms of transcultural and intercultural expression. Beginning in the 1960s, modernity and modernisation hit the Andean region full force in all its guises: anthropology, education, western medicine, mass communications, machine transportation, prefabricated commodities, tourism, agronomy and the capitalist labour machine which produced, among other things, large-scale migrations to coastal urban centres, especially Lima. I propose to end this essay with a brief, speculative consideration of a contemporary form of autoethnographic expression arising from this accelerated contact between Andean society and the metropolis. It is an art form to which I was introduced by the Peruvian Andeanist Luis Millones, and which (except for the brief treatment in Millones and Pratt 1989/1990) has not been the subject of published scholarship. In the absence of art-historical studies, my aim here is simply to suggest some of the ways those contemporary productions are illuminated by a juxtaposition with the work of Guaman Poma.

The contemporary Peruvian paintings of a genre known as the *tablas de Sarhua* (*tabla* = 'board') are an art form created by painters from the Andean town of Sarhua in the province of Ayacucho, a region know among ethnographers for its adherence to Andean traditions (Isbell 1978, Palomino Flores 1984). The *tablas* are panels painted in vivid colours on wood. The paintings depict traditional Andean lifeways, each *tabla* usually exemplifying a particular event, practice or tradition. A written label in the upper corner names the custom or event portrayed, usually in Quechua but sometimes in Spanish. In one, for instance, the label 'Tarpuy' means 'Sowing' (cf. Guaman Poma's drawing in fig. 6 above). Often in the *tablas de Sarhua* a few lines of text follow explaining what is depicted in telegraphic, unpunctuated Spanish. Another depicts a betrothal scene in which two families formally agree on the marriage of their children.[4] The Quechua title 'Ari Nichey' translates roughly as 'saying yes', and the text that follows in Spanish says literally: 'The young man and his family after convincing the girl's parents of the marriage will again convince the girl promising fidelity of eternal pure love' ('El mozo y sus familiares despues de convencer a los padres de la novia para el casamiento reconvencera a la novia prometiendo fidelidad de amor eterno puro').

While many *tablas* depict the observance of community customs and rituals, others dramatise what happens when norms of conduct are breached. Another, for example, pictures the meeting of an adulterous couple, surrounded by the devils who have tempted them, one carrying a snake (cf. Guaman Poma's devils in fig. 11 above). A woman looks on from behind a rock while the text, held up by a devil, states 'Act against morality insult to the community a man a woman commit adultery in hidden places tempted by the devils those who come bring harm to the families of the adulterers' ('Acto contrario a la moral insulto a la comunidad un varon una mujer cometen adulterio en sitios ocultos tentados por los demonios quienes acuden llevan el mal a sus familias de los adulteros'). A further *tabla* depicts the public punishment suffered by adulterous couples who are discovered. 'It is absolutely forbidden', the text reads, 'to commit adultery if the offender is discovered the authorities punish drastically make run through streets with horns put in stocks cut hair ear whipping spitting' ('Es sumamente prohibido adulterar al infractor si le descubren autoridades castigan drasticamente hacen recorrer por calles con cuernos ponen al sepo cortan pelo oreja azotando escupen').

Guaman Poma, we saw earlier, appropriated and adapted European apparatuses (alphabetic writing, representational drawing) in order to enter into communication with the European metropolis. The painters of Sarhua, on the other hand, appropriated and adapted an art form indigenous to village culture to develop a commodifiable expression to sell to outsiders. The *tablas* described here derive from a pre-existing artistic tradition unique to the town of Sarhua. When new households formed in the village, it was customary to adorn the new house with a painted panel on which multiple scenes depicted the household's genealogy. The panel was mounted on the roof beam of the couple's new house. Another more recent, highly stylised *tabla* appearing in a calendar in 1990,[5] depicts this traditional practice. Needless to say, this local art form, like the whole rich tradition of Andean painting, has its origins in the transculturated world of colonial contact that gave rise to the drawings of Guaman Poma. Thus though it would be difficult to characterise the traditional Sarhuino paintings as anything but an 'authentic' indigenous art form, their transcultural origins in contact with the metropolis are part of what makes them (unlike the *quipu*, for instance) a springboard for an attempt to place messages into circulation in the metropolis. Such is what Michael Taussig has called the 'mirror dance' of colonial meaning-making (Taussig 1988).

The development of the commercialised 'folk art' form of the Sarhua panels was a direct result of Sarhua's increased contact with the metropolis in the 1960s, and of the expanding national and international market for Andean cultural productions. As with a great many Andean villages, migrants from Sarhua formed a satellite community in Lima in the 1970s. A group of painters from the village set up shop there, developing and marketing the outer-directed genre of the *tablas*. This outer-directed genre bears the clear markings of the metropolitan category of 'folk' or 'vernacular' art (Spanish *arte típica*): the paintings are sold for money and seek a collectors' market; works are identified only by the label 'Artes de Sarhua' ('Arts of Sarhua'), not individual artists' names; the style fits into the metropolitan category of 'naive realism', depicting rural life and an autonomous social world in a normalised, and sometimes miniaturised and idealised way that does not correspond to a lived experience thrown into upheaval by the penetration of capitalism and modernity. Indeed, modernisation is conspicuous in the *tablas* by its complete absence as a referent. Like Guaman Poma's autoethnographic depictions of Inca life, the *tablas* depict life-ways understood to have been lost or threatened by radical change.

Just as the capitalist 'modernisation' and 'development' of the 1960s are historically linked to the Spanish imperialism of the sixteenth century, so the autoethnographic work of the Sarhua painters (or so I would suggest) is linked to Guaman Poma's effort in the *New chronicle* to document histories and life-ways subject to transformation, devaluation and misinterpretation by the metropolitan invaders. Unlike Guaman Poma, the *tabla* painters undertake no critical or polemical project comparable to the eloquent denunciations of the *New government and justice*.[6] Conflict among whites, mestizos and Indians, though a crucial determinant of contemporary Peruvian reality, is nowhere to be found in the *tablas*. The present-day reality of the Sendero Luminoso ('Shining Path') insurgency is not alluded to. In the era of commodification, politics and critique are left outside the doorway of the art market.

Three centuries after Guaman Poma, the *tablas de Sarhua* portray an Andean culture that has internalised many institutions originating in Europe. For example, the *tabla* painters depict at least three distinct versions of the marriage ceremony: Andean village marriage, Christian church marriage and secular state marriage.[7] In the *tablas* these differing traditions are each represented separately, and with different iconography. They are portrayed neither as clashing nor as blending into each other but as coexisting in difference. Tension among them, which certainly exists in real life, is not part of the representation. Icons that Guaman Poma used to depict Spanish colonial violence turn up in the *tablas* depicting conflict and violence *within* indigenous society. So for example the stocks and the whip which appear in fig. 3 as weapons of Spanish violence against Andeans appear in the *tablas* as the local punishment for adultery. The term *maltrato*, 'mistreatment', in Guaman Poma refers to Spanish abuse of Indians, while in the *tablas de Sarhua* it labels paintings of parents punishing recalcitrant daughters who try to elope. The horses on which Spaniards carried off indigenous women turn up in the *tablas* as the horses on which a suitor tries to steal his lover from her family. The pointed rock wall that in Guaman Poma's *mapa mundi* (fig. 12 above) defines the borders of the Indies appears in the *tablas* as the wall separating the domain of community morality from the wild spaces of desire and wrongdoing. In short, the historic, and unresolved, struggle between Spaniards and Indians is not a referent in the *tablas*, yet the co-ordinates of that conflict continue, it seems, to shape the portrayal of society in ways illuminated by Guaman Poma's work. Commodification manifestly does not separate the *tablas de Sarhua* from the long history of Andean cultural expression. Rather little about them can be explained solely in terms of the marketplace, and in many ways they are not organised by the perceptual habits and expectations of the metropolis.

The *tablas de Sarhua* exhibit some rather specific conventions of their own to encode postcolonial coexistence-in-difference. Consider for instance the two depictions of marital infidelity described above. One, a Quechua-titled panel 'Huanchillo', deploys motifs of both pre- and post-contact origin. Its devils and serpent are originally Christian; its tall green cactus plant is an Andean motif marking 'wild' spaces outside village boundaries (Isbell 1978). Thematically the *tabla* depicts the sexual violation itself, the acting out of desire and the voyeuristic dynamic of discovery. The roots of adultery in desire are foregrounded through the tempter-devils. Community morality is embodied in a person *observing* the seduction, but the question of sanctions is not raised. The Spanish-titled *tabla* 'Adulterio' approaches the subject differently. Here the theme is the shame and violence of punishment, not the desire and wrongdoing themselves. Official morality appears in the guise not of a witness figure but of authorities carrying out a standardised punishment. The site is not the wild spaces but the village centre where the violators are displayed in stocks. Similar contrasts recur in other *tablas*. Panels with the Spanish titles 'Maltrato' ('mistreatment') and 'Madre soltera' ('single mother') depict public punishment for violations of community morality. *Tablas* bearing the Quechua title 'Ronday' ('party') display not the ill effects of sexual licence but the licence itself in its sensual dimensions. The historically disjunct forms of social organisation and discipline which determine contemporary Andean life seem to be distinguished in the *tablas* through language and composition, but not depicted in conflict or contradictoin.

I have defined autoethnography as expression aimed specifically at *intervening* in the discursive economy of a dominant group; a subordinate group asserts an alternative to the dominant group's representations of them, in part by transculturating the latter's own discourses. Do the *tablas de Sarhua* in any way constitute such an intervention? If so, how? The questions can be posed of many commodified 'folk' and 'ethnic' art forms. Like European-based genres of ethnography and manners and customs description, the *tablas de Sarhua* represent culture through practices of codifying, objectifying, normalising, collectivising. In purely formal terms, the elliptical captions on the paintings might well remind anthropologists of their own field notes. At the same time, the *tablas de Sarhua* seem to approach the workings of society rather differently from conventional ethnography. Though they strongly valorise rituals, they do not privilege them over everyday life practices and events. Relatedly, the *tablas* do not privilege what in western terms would be seen as society's patterns of order over dysfunction and disorder. Many *tablas* display moments of crisis or breakdown. Taboos, conventionally treated in ethnography as rules which must not be broken, are treated in the *tablas* as the rules that inevitably *are* broken, and whose breaking constitutes much of the drama of social life. Desire is routinely pitted against authority and morality, and scenes of passion are privileged points of reference.

It is perfectly coherent to regard such contrasts between the *tablas* and ethnographic convention as the result of absolute cultural difference: ethnography is western, the *tablas* are Andean. However I believe it is worth asking whether such differences are also the result of their *contact*, the result of an active engagement by the Sarhuino painters with the institution of ethnography that arrived in their midst in the 1960s. Are the written descriptive labels an appropriation (not a reproduction) of the ethnographer's objectivist rhetoric? The Quechua terms, for example, are not translated. Do the *tablas*, as their bilingualism suggests, anticipate a heterogeneous audience? Certainly they will not 'read' the same to Andeans and non-Andeans, bilinguals and monolinguals, Sarhuinos and outsiders. Yet they seem to interpellate all these audiences. To Andean viewers, whether or not they are potential owners of the paintings, the *tablas* recall village life prior to the disruptions of modernisation and urban migration. Nostalgia and a profound sense of loss are important dimensions of experience for urban migrants, and urban autoethnographic art expresses these dimensions often through idealised portrayals received by outsiders as exotic and folkloric.[8]

What I have been calling autoethnographic expression suggests a particular kind of cultural self-consciousness, an awareness of one's life-ways or customs *as they have been singled out by the metropolis*, be it for objectification in knowledge, for suppression or for extermination. Autoethnography selectively appropriates some tools of objectification both to counter eradication ('We are still here despite your/their efforts') and to counter objectification ('We are not as you/they see us'). So the Sarhua paintings are shaped, as I have been suggesting, not only by the way the Sarhuino painters imagine or wish or remember their community to be but also by ways the Sarhuino painters imagine that metropolitan outsiders imagine or wish or remember them to be. Autoethnographic art involves an assertion not of self-as-other, but of self-as-another's-other, and of self as more-than-the-other's-other. Reception of such art either in terms of assimilation and co-optation, or in terms of purity, authenticity or naivety, suppresses its dialogic, transcultural dimensions.

Do autoethnographic interventions 'work'? Probably not in any direct or systematic sense. Guaman Poma's letter reached Europe all right, but apparently sat unread for three hundred years. In the era of commodity culture, autoethnographic art like that of the Sarhuino painters may do little more than silently *occupy* the metropolis, on walls, shelves, behind frames, in the pages of books. Perhaps its most profound effects are on the consciousness of the community that produced it. Meanwhile in Peru as elsewhere, the problem of 'good government and justice' is pretty much where Guaman Poma left it three hundred years ago. Indeed, in 1991, in anticipation of the Columbus quincentennial, a group of American indigenous leaders met in Quito and produced a declaration remarkably similar to the petition of 1562 with which this essay began (Declaration of Quito 1991). The victory concinues to be in survival, a fact with which metropolitan social theory has yet to come to grips.

Notes

1 Part of what follows is revised from Pratt 1991.

2 Raul Porras Barrenechea pioneered Guaman Poma studies in the 1940s. John Murra's work of the early 1960s was followed in the early 1970s by the writings of Juan M. Ossio. Since 1980 principal contributors to Guaman Poma studies have included Mercedes López-Baralt, Raquel Chang-Rodríguez, Lorenzo López y Sebastián, Abraham Padilla Bendezú and Rolena Adorno.

3 References in this paper are to the Biblioteca Ayacucho edition of Guaman Poma's text, edited in two volumes by Franklin Pease (1980). I refer to Guaman Poma's text by the volume and page number in this edition, followed in square brackets by the (slightly irregular) pagination of the manuscript. Guaman Poma's drawings carry their page number in the upper right-hand corner.

4 The *tablas* described here are from a corpus of twenty-eight paintings photographed in the early 1980s by Josephine Nolte in the painters' studio in Lima. They represent the work of three artists, Victor Sebastián Yucra, Primitivo Evanan Poma and Juan Gualberto Quispe Michue. I am grateful to Luis Millones for making available to me slides of these paintings.

5 I am indebted to the generosity of Rolena Adorno and David Adorno for providing me with this calendar.

6 The exception, in the corpus with which I worked, is a painting which, like Guaman Poma's 'Mala conficion', criticises the abuses by priests of the power of confession.

7 In the corpus of *tablas* to which I have had access, traditional village marriage is depicted as a procession with musicians, Roman Catholic marriage by a scene in church during the wedding mass, and secular state marriage by a gathering around a table at which the newly-weds are signing a register.

8 Needless to say, Andeans do not have a monopoly on nostalgia for village life in the context of modernisation. Ilona Szombati-Fabian and Johannes Fabian (1976) study a Zairian vernacular art form called Shaba paintings that displays intriguing parallels with the Sarhua *tablas*. Here too the idealisation of traditional village life is a major theme. Szombati-Fabian and Fabian make the crucial observation that the chief market for the Shaba paintings is urban migrants and ex-villagers who have come to acquire both cash to buy the paintings and houses with walls to hang them on.

Rousseau's patrimony: primitivism, romance and becoming other

SIMON DURING

In this chapter I want to elaborate and problematise the familiar claim that, as Chris Bongie has recently stated it: 'Montesquieu, Rousseau, and Diderot provide nineteenth-century exoticism [for which we can read "primitivism"] with much of its conceptual apparatus' (Bongie 1991, p. 14). The work published here deals only with eighteenth-century theorists, not with modern primitivists like Pierre Loti and Paul Gauguin, but the central contention of my argument remains – that modern primitivism needs to be understood in the light of the Enlightenment attempt to establish a non-filiative basis for personal identity. I want to argue, conventionally enough, that anti-filiative theory and practice were embedded within large transformations of European discourses and life-ways in which relations between family-members, men and women, the public and the private, the art work and its audience and, finally, the western and non-western world shifted. I also want to argue, more specifically, that this transformation pivoted around new values and functions given to what I will call 'self-othering', that is, means for constructing or finding a self as another or by identification with others. My ultimate aim is to trace a number of trajectories from the enlightened critique of filiation through modes of self-othering to the larger processes of European expansion and back. This will allow me, in work which will follow, to examine certain exchanges between European and non-European modes of resisting and reincorporating filiation and patriarchy.

Forefathers

The genealogy of modern primitivism would be easier to explore if the always uncertain relations between past and present were not there particularly tangled. Even if we accept that some eighteenth-century concepts (the 'noble savage', the celebration of nature as a realm of self-recovery and freedom, for instance) lie behind the later aestheticisation of the primitive, it is not as if the methods of current academic intellectual history can be taken for granted when it comes to describing relations between eighteenth-century theorists and their successors. This is apparent as soon as we pose the relation in terms of a particular, if loaded, question – when we ask, in what sense are men like Gauguin and Loti heirs of Jean-Jacques Rousseau? Taken literally, it is an unanswerable question. After all, Rousseau abandoned his children, all five of them, so that his offspring down the generations do not know that they have a famous forebear. To take the question literally like this, even for a moment, may seem odd – ultimately because we work in institutions designed to weaken the degree to which our ancestors' position determines our own. But filiation and kinship's function in social and cultural reproduction was far from a dead issue for Rousseau and his 'heirs'. It posed a problem. And it did so finally because, for them (as for later academic knowledge) the division between Enlightened and non-Enlightened societies was defined in terms of a distinction between societies organised around kin-relations and lineages and those not – or less – so organised. This, of course, was an ethical and political as much as an analytic distinction. For Enlightened thought, a society was considered just when it minimised the degree to which one's parents' wealth and status determined one's own – when, at this familial level, the past was least determinative of the present. The distinction was not simply theoretical however. 'What kind of kin one should be?' was an urgent, practical question for those attempting to ground life-practices on general principles. An Enlightened father – to take the crucial instance – had to ask himself (if reasonably well-off like the middle-aged Denis Diderot): should I arrange my children's marriages? or (if poor like Rousseau): should I abandon them to the Foundling Hospital? – a fate then shared by about a quarter of all urban children. (See Boswell 1988, pp. 16ff.) Indeed, as we shall see, modern primitivism develops out of the difficulty of taking the position of the 'legitimate' father, as felt by, and forced upon, men who worked against, as Diderot put it, 'the abuse of authority, religion, government; vice, errors, prejudices' (Diderot 1971, p. 190).

To consider the relation between modern primitivists and eighteenth-century theorists in filiative terms, even for a moment, is to begin to recognise that the formulation of Enlightened theory (and hopes for its future) were not independent of intellectuals' management of family life. This was especially so because 'legitimate' family life was difficult for progressive intellectuals – particularly those with little inherited money or status. We should remember that their work paid badly: much of their writing, the object of censorship, could not be distributed through the market, being publishable only abroad or after their death. Leaving censorship aside, print was not an efficiently protected commodity, even if, tantalisingly and tellingly, the 1777 reform of the book trade in France gave publishing *privilèges* to the author and the author's heirs in perpetuity (Chartier 1991, p. 60). Enlightened intellectuals had few career opportunities other than writing; higher educational institutions were all but totally closed to them. Because it was difficult for these men to provide financially for a family, it was also hard for them to live satisfactory domestic lives, 'satisfactory' according to ethical criteria that they were formulating, based on the value of individual autonomy, the free, public exchange of ideas and the importance of domestic space for a child's development – all of which were designed to detach future generations from received ideas and institutions. Leaving aside larger questions of gender justice, Diderot and Rousseau both felt their wives not to be their social peers – their wives, in fact, functioned more or less as their servants. Both men were, on occasion, infatuated with rich and educated women for whom they had considerable intellectual respect. But their lives would have been easier had they not conceived of the future quite concretely as populated by their offspring and desired so to populate it. Despite their poverty and the impediments to their taking up the sanctioned paternal position, they were driven towards becoming prolific fathers in a nation, indeed, a world that was almost universally considered to be threatened by depopulation (the old belief that the classical world was more heavily populated than the modern was only beginning to wane) and where biological generation was thought to be inseparable from the economic productivity of the population as a whole, a belief that only the publication of Thomas Malthus's 1798 *Essay on the principle of population* would undo.[1] Strangely, for them the broadest and 'highest' concepts that could be used to conceive of peoples across time and space – concepts like 'humanity' and 'man' – tacitly denoted that mass of individuals who will spring from their (and their readership's) loins. When, for instance, Diderot dreams of the 'most glorious' moment that might befall his *Encyclopaedia* – the book which, as he says, places 'man' at the centre of the world – he thinks of a future 'generation' who might read it 'in the wake of some catastrophe to suspend the progress of science . . . and plunge a portion of our hemisphere into darkness' (Diderot 1964, p. 290). The connection between the *Encyclopaedia*'s authors and these imaginary readers, separated from one another by the apocalyptic descent of ignorance and superstition, is that of generation. The *Encyclopaedia*'s authors are not just these readers' cultural and intellectual guides but – in a broad sense – their forefathers, though relations between the transmission of knowledge and genealogical continuity was for them an unstable one.

This is to begin to see that inheritors of European Enlightened ideals and problems (not least, modern academics like 'us') live and work in a framework that makes our uncertainty as to whether a figure like Rousseau *literally* is our forebear or not an exemplification of that patrimony. In broad terms, this is because that 'patrimony' was elaborated and gifted to the future around three poles: (1) a theoretical critique of filiation and patriarchy as the dominant forms of arbitrary authority, (2) a model of propriety and progress which affirmed both biological generation and accumulation, and (3) a system of cultural and discursive production which could rely neither on market relations nor on patronage for its transmission and preservation, partly because its content was finally aimed against those state and religious institutions which had secured the longevity of western culture hitherto. In this situation, it is better not to say that certain nineteenth-century intellectuals (in particular its 'modernist primitivists') inherit the Enlightenment (with all the problems surrounding the notion 'inherit'), but that they return to a shared border, if we conceive of a border undergoing constant fraying, displacement and re-forming. This border lies between parents and children, husband and wives, the present (and future) and past, as each generation inherits these oppositions in a new form. Around this border, generative, familial and intellectual bonds continually unthread one other, never more so than when the demand for a future freed from the tyranny of the past stands against the order by which the future is to be generated from the present within legitimate families. More specifically, this border comes into existence when, at the level of grand theory, the past is considered to be threatened with extinction by the forward movement of time, either under affirmative glosses such as 'perfectibility' and 'progress' (in eighteenth-century France associated with the struggle against 'despotism' and underproductivity), or under negative ones like 'loss' and 'degeneration' (associated with Rousseau in his resistance to the denaturalising effects of urbanisation and artificiality), or neutral ones like 'inevitability' (as we shall see, associated with the blind flow of energy that Diderot posits as the ground of Being). In each case the ever-shifting border between the past and the present is marked by the shadow of death. The past dies as the present (and future) come into existence. If, in the public arena, this dark border marks the difference between superstition and reason, between despotism and liberty, even between protectionism and free trade, in the private sphere it may separate one generation from the next, especially a father from his children.

Driven by familial tropes, this border passes from the public to the private sphere remarkably easily – nowhere more famously than in Kant's essay 'What is Enlightenment?' where the past is figured as the species's *Unmundigkeit*, its nonage or (legal) 'immaturity', given a concept of 'maturity' as that which transcends the dominance/subservience relation (Kant 1867, 4, p. 159). Crucially, though, the border between past and present could also take a spatial – a geographical – form: it divided the 'civilised', or, as was said in eighteenth-century France, the 'policed' world from those lands and peoples available for European colonisation or annexation. Let me put this another way: the oppositions around which Enlightened critique turned were continually orientated towards, and grounded on, the differences and conflicts between the 'civilised' and the 'savage', that is to say, white travellers and (especially in the nineteenth century) settlers and those they encountered. The group of men that I am mainly concerned with here are distinguished because they haunt this border rather than remain inside either of the zones that it separates. In both cases, they either cross and recross from one side to other, unable to move steadfastly in one direction; or they attempt to straddle it; or they re-encounter it where they had long since thought to have left it behind. All have a sense that at least some of the messages they send, especially messages with energy enough to speak to the distant future, pass across it but cannot leave it behind.

These are rather abstract and difficult propositions. Can we conceive of this 'border', so available for displacement, more concretely? We can begin by concentrating on it not as a geographical actuality at the edges of European expansion but as a set of discursive practices which separated the present from the past and inserted that division inside western families, marking off both authoritarian fathers from their children and men from women. Let us begin by thinking, specifically, about the figure of the father. There were wide-ranging religious, institutional and legal reasons why eighteenth-century anti-patriarchal writers emphasised authority as held by the male head of the household, particularly in his role as father. The Christian God was a father. The notion of the 'patriarch' overlapped with that of the 'despot', ever since Nicolas-Antoine Boulanger in his *Recherches sur l'origine du despotisme oriental* (1761) connected despotism to lordship of the harem. Absolute monarchs, as 'divine kings', were conceived of as 'father of the nation' (as the French 1789 *cahiers de doléances* show), a trope that could underpin absolutist political theory as in Sir Robert Filmer's tract, *Patriarchia*.[2] Of course, male heads of households had real power over the property and bodies or other family members.[3] In pre-revolutionary France, for instance, they could arrange to have *lettres de cachet* sent to control their children's choice of a marriage partner, it being illegal, since a Council of Trent Edict of 1556 (directed against 'clandestine marriages') for a man to marry without parental consent until he was thirty years old and a woman until she was twenty-five, though with parental consent a man could marry at fourteen, a woman at twelve (Ourliac and De Malafosse 1968, pp. 205–15). Diderot himself was imprisoned on a letter organised by his father and married a month after his thirtieth birthday; in turn, he tried to arrange his daughter's marriage when she was fourteen.[4] After 1639, sex in a marriage that had no parental consent was regarded as rape (*rapt de séduction*), and was punishable by death (Traer 1980, p. 35). In England, to take one of many instances, until the early nineteenth century the murder of a husband was a form of petty treason – a crime against the state. There it seems that most fathers expected to control the career choices of their sons (as well as the marriage choices of their daughter) until the late eighteenth century (Stone 1977, p. 447). In both countries marriage was almost indissoluble. Outside the family social legitimacy ended: a non-marital child was a *filius nullius*, without legal recognition – or as English Common Law put it 'once a bastard, always a bastard' (a principle that was revoked only in 1926).

As many family historians have argued, the legal authority invested in the father as head of the household increased throughout Europe from at least the sixteenth century on, though at different rates in different regions.

Ecclesiastical law which had insisted on the publicity of marriage vows since the fourteenth century (as well as a canon of proscribed 'affinities' and indissolubility) was increasingly backed up by Roman and written law which emphasised paternal and husbandly power. Apart from the profitable trade in dispensations, such legislation seems to have had two main purposes. Firstly, to anchor individuals geographically, genealogically and socially, especially to prevent the birth of nomadic individuals – those who lacked strong connections to particular localities and existing social institutions, in particular the victims of the slow process of rural enclosure.[5] Secondly, to push individuals, for whom property was increasingly easy to acquire and bequeath, towards a structure of patrilinear inheritance. In England, that was the effect of Lord Hardwicke's 1753 Marriage Act, designed to control clandestine marriages two centuries after the Council of Trent.[6] In France, where regional differences remained strong and where the Church had a much tighter control over marriage rites than in England, a sacramental view of marriage became fused into state administrative apparatuses which appealed to marriage as contract, involving dowries. This strengthened the power of coverture and tightened the link between a household-head's private power and his economic assets, primarily inherited through the male blood-line.[7]

All this is worth noting at some length because the *philosophes* who articulated Enlightened ideals projected a version of these relatively recent historical formations on to the species's so-called immaturity. For them, most societies that lacked Enlightenment, whether 'savage' or 'despotic', were controlled by primordial patriarchs – whose marriages, however, were (like the ancient Romans') dissoluble or (like those of the Northern European 'barbarians' who brought Rome down) polygamous. Thus Rousseau who, in his *Second discourse*, his 'hypothetical history of governments', historicised the development of social institutions, regarded the first socialised individuals (though not the earth's autochthonous inhabitants) as living in patriarchal clans linked by broad kinship ties (Rousseau 1984, p. 72). The belief in primordial patriarchy helped order Buffon's, Rousseau's and Diderot's emergent, monogenetic and anthropological understanding of the human species as a unity dispersed across the globe differentiated by variations of climate and custom (cf. Duchet 1971, p. 21).

It was an understanding which, though formulated in familial terms, appeared around the time that western nations began to conceive of themselves as genuine world powers with a global reach; when, to take a couple of British instances, politicians began to consider the implications of their policy for the 'whole Globe' (cited in Brewer 1990, p. 175), and when Captain Cook, with support of the Royal Society and enabled by new navigational technology and medical knowledge, began his explorations in the Pacific so that twenty years after his first voyage, and, against fears of underpopulation, the United Kingdom (in 1788) established a colony at the very end of the earth in New South Wales.[8] Around 1760 too, western productive capacities, transportation systems and technology began decisively to overtake those of other societies. To take perhaps the most dramatic and culturally significant instance of all: it was only then that the Europeans developed a textile industry competitive with that of India, especially Bengal (Wolf 1982, p. 270). As the west's productive capacity and military reach increased, civilisations which had previously been regarded respectfully, like that of the Chinese, began to be increasingly defined as petrified, rigidly hierarchical – as, influentially, by Adam Smith (Smith 1937, p. 73). Tropes like the 'wheel of Empire' or the 'revolutions of nations' slowly began to lose their persuasiveness too. In the play between the anthropological sense of a unified if fragmented species, and the progressive requirement to denote non-European societies as 'backward', differences between nations and family-structures, as well as what we would call 'cultures', were frozen into an us/them opposition: the broad distinction between Europe and the rest of the world became spatial *and* conceptual. The west was autonomous and active, the non-west patriarchal or despotic; the west was open to the future and on the historical path to perfectibility; the non-west was stuck in the past, degenerative (unreproductive) and without history.[9] To use a more contemporary phrasing, the west was modern, the non-west non-modern. At any rate the west was where the future happened first. But the point I want to insist on is that this shift from difference into opposition (in what we might call the 'paradigm of modernity') was an element of a larger set of articulations of the border between authority and freedom, past and present, the civil and the 'savage', which included the contestation of inherited privilege and authority, most concretely imaged and practised as a resistance to patriarchal power.

This involved more than one paradox. The conceptual structure within which the future began to be imagined and worked towards also required a past to which to return. For to escape the stasis of non-western societies, especially of peoples without nation states, to move out of *that* past, was also to distance oneself from that natural law which was considered to be a measure of freedom and social justice. For the *philosophes*, unpoliced societies lay at a crossroads: they were patriarchal *and* they marked the threshold of that state of nature on which society ought to be grounded. As the latter, such societies provided an image for how life should be lived by men when they achieved their maturity and autonomy – especially because 'primitive' societies were thought to permit the dissolution of marriage. Indeed, one strand in the history of modern ethnography is to be found in older 'natural law' theorists like Jean Bodin and Hugo Grotius who used (vague and inaccurate) accounts of non-western societies as a form of legal critique, in particular to argue against ecclesiastical resistance to divorce. The contradictions embedded in this dual impulse to imagine primordial society as simultaneously a ground for natural law and as patriarchal are most clearly apparent in Rousseau, for whom the relations between nature and the family remained fluid. For him, depending on the polemical context, the family could belong *either* neither wholly to nature nor wholly to society *or* to both nature and society. In the *Second Discourse*, for instance, he insisted against John Locke that the family is no more a part of nature than property, and that neither a child's dependency on its parents nor a woman's on a man, belongs to natural law (Rousseau 1984, pp. 161–6). Against this, in *The Social Contract*, he claimed that 'The oldest of all societies, and the only natural one, is the family' (Rousseau 1968, p. 50). The family is only natural, though, where the bond between 'fathers' and children lasts no longer than a child's biological dependence. For Rousseau, society (as against nature) begins when children do not take advantage of their capacity for autonomy, when they do not reject paternal authority. It is within this frame that Rousseau judges – as against analyses – the history of socialization. In the first instance, the emergence of society is a loss because, in it, children are 'born in chains' – placed in an inherited submission that they are doomed to contest. It is a gain for the opposite reason, to the degree that once parents recognise their children, then knowlege can be transmitted and history-as-progress can begin, so that 'man' will no longer 'remain eternally a child' – a phrase that anticipates Kant's familial figure for Enlightenment (Rousseau 1968, p. 105). And here we see that the border which fenced primitivism out of history, only to reengage it, was also developed within a logic by which the species's maturity required 'men' to transmit their knowledge to future generations as if these future generations both were, and were not, their offspring committed to filial respect and a certain cultural repetition.

Property, power and moral struggles between a father and his heirs, between the present-as-rejection-of-the-past and the past-as-future were inseparable from struggles over another relation of authority – that between husband and wife. Husbandly power was questioned, narrativised and re-narrativised in contemporary, progressive fiction and theory where, as in Rousseau's novel *La Nouvelle Héloïse* and Diderot's play *Le Père de famille*, it took the form of promoting the *pater familias* against the patriarch. Yet such preferences led back to a problem at once theoretical and historical: why did a *man* head the family that joined nature to society – the family of natural law? Rousseau was committed to the genderlessness of the earth's autochthonous inhabitants, so it was Diderot who engaged the question, especially in his posthumously published 'Supplement to Bougainville's Voyage' (written 1772, published 1796). This text used the recently expanded possibilities of prose fiction to rework the tradition of ethnographic natural-law theorising, and here again divisions between individuals in families mobilises divisions between the 'policed' and the 'primitive'. Cast as a dialogue between two men who have just finished reading Bougainville's account of his recent voyage to the Pacific, Diderot's text invents words,

thoughts and feelings for the Polynesians – including an impassioned critique
of European impact on Tahiti. For Diderot, Tahiti is a real place, an island
recently visited by a French naval expedition, but it is also a concept: the
embodiment of nature. The state of nature here is not, as in Rousseau's
Second Discourse, merely hypothetical, it has been travelled to. As both
nature-in-general and a particular place, Diderot's Tahiti's primary use is to
deliver truths about the social organisation of sexuality within an argument
for the value of biological generation. It is within this frame that Diderot
addresses the crucial issue of 'natural subjection' – the natural basis for social
hierarchies.

Diderot's Tahiti is so close to nature that no disguise is possible; there no
distinction between the public and the private is permitted. Diderot tells a
story about a white woman who dressed as a man in order to sail with
Bougainville. (The story – not to be found in Bougainville's account – is
based on the adventures of Jeanne Baré who did in fact sail in the expedition:
see Withey (1987), p. 102). When Baré arrived at Tahiti, so Diderot writes,
the Maohi (to give the locals their non-colonising name) immediately
recognised her as a woman, though the Europeans had not. The locals see
through all 'civilised' masquerade. It is because nature knows no family/
population or public/private division (in Tahiti, sex can take place for
everyone to see and women remain at home with their sexual wants) that
biological generation is inseparable from economic productivity. Private
benefit coincides with the general good because patrilinear and legitimate
inheritance does not exist there. Here we see the beginnings of a legitimation
of settler-colonies as regenerating old stock which will become widespread
(particularly in Britain) only after 1840. But in Tahiti all exogamy whatso-
ever has been banished – even incest between siblings and parents and
children is possible. To make the point, Diderot puts in the mouth of an
imaginary Tahitian an old defence of incestuous acts previously given to the
famous criminal Marguerite de Ravalet (executed with her brother for the
crime in 1603) by another pioneer of modern fiction, François de Rosset, in
his *Les Amours incestueuses d'un frère et d'une sœur* (1614) (see Pillorget
1979, p. 224).

For Diderot, Tahiti shows that the most natural and productive form of
sexual relationship is serial monogamy. This allows him to argue that both
economic and political inequity in general is based on a 'male tyranny' that
transforms 'possession of women into property' (Diderot 1875, 2, p. 245).
How then to assert women's natural subjection? Strangely, the message of the
'Supplement' is (in part) carried by a dialogue between a cleric and Orou, a
Tahitian, in which Orou invites the European to sleep with his wife and
daughters as a gesture of hospitality. Sexual equality here effectively relies
upon a man's ability to dispose of 'his' women. Not that Diderot quite
disavows the contradiction between his work's anti-male-tyranny thrust and

its dramatic framing, for Tahiti-as-nature teaches us that social relations are, in the last instance, based on men's power over women. Men are more sexually aggressive, naturally more proprietorial, not because (unlike women) their physiology sometimes prevents them from performing sexually, not because one can never be certain who a child's father is (though these are possibilities that Diderot floats), but because a woman's sexual response is slower than a man's. Women need to be pressured into sexual activity: every sexual act is a rape *in petto* – where I am using 'rape' in its modern sense as an act of sexual violence rather than in its eighteenth-century legal sense as a sexual act between individuals who belong to groups which may not legally have intercourse. Diderot argues (implicitly solving Rousseau's problem of accounting for the gap between nature and society) that it is from this primordial difference that socio-political hierarchies develop – in a form which ensures that they can break male power only at the risk of offending their own basis in nature. Diderot's Tahiti, then, offers both a glimpse of familial freedom (a society in which monogamous domesticity does not exist) and a confrontation with equality's limits (just because men always come first). Which means that Diderot's Tahiti also shows that to cross the border from the civil to the natural, to move out from the modern family towards freedom and full generative productivity, entails, paradoxically, a partial return to patriarchy's base. And we should recognise that Diderot's theoretical work also expresses his private life, that is, his own inability to remove himself from husbandly and fatherly authority – in part, at least, because of the economic conditions under which he, as an enlightened writer, lived. The difficulties of banishing patriarchy at the level of theory are not disconnected to the difficulties of the theoretician's living a just and happy familial life.

The anti-patriarchal impulse (which ultimately returned to patriarchy) also shifted the frame in which art's function was thought about. The problem was posed like this: if future society was radically to separate itself from its past, how to produce art now that would last? How to communicate in perpetuity? This aesthetic question concerning 'longevity and perfection' (to use Diderot's phrase) was addressed in relation to the financial, ethical and generative problems that I have been considering (Diderot 1990, p. 62). Diderot's evaluation of the 1767 Salon shows this best. Diderot introduced his account of the exhibition by appealing for reforms to artists' working conditions. For him, patronage was, at least in principle, unacceptable because it was an instance of arbitrary and filiative authority. But, still more to the point, aesthetic appreciation was not to be dissociated from the economic appreciation of art works; after all, he notes, artists needed to be able to provide for a family and a lineage (we should note that this was the moment when, in Britain, the Society of Artists Associated for the Relief of Their Distressed Brethren was about to compete with the Royal Academy and other associations for public support via public exhibitions). Unlike a system of public exhibition, patronage was unable to guarantee the artist's ability to take on the role of good father, a patron's tastes, whims and means being too private and unpredictable. The Salon, in exposing paintings to public view and providing the framework for a cultural market, could offer spectators and purchasers a full range of knowledge and choice as well the opportunity for 'public censure' (p. 59). Thus it began to make possible a means for aligning artistic to economic value. Further, given a monetary index of value, paintings would become investments able to support families after an artist's death (pp. 61–2). To ensure that, Diderot wanted the king – the state – to force painters to expose their works to public view.

At this point Diderot's argument for the commodification and public exhibition of art, based on the priority of family life is – once again – seduced by the appeal of savage, patriarchal, freedom. For art that will retain its value in the future cannot be contaminated by the here-and-now, by what will become obsolete, dead. At a very general level this means that it cannot be merely mimetic, reflective of the passing moment. Instead it needs to be based on a formal 'line of beauty' (p. 71). At a more concrete level, it must avoid the merely fashionable – that is, forms of life which are neither close to nature nor made obsolete by the sweep of 'progress' or shifts in consumer desire. In the decades in which the European textile and clothing industry was beginning to dominate international commerce, and fashion magazines were increasingly widespread (with Paris at the centre of the fashion world), this meant, most of all for Diderot, that artists must avoid painting modern clothes (Diderot 1955, pp. 88–9).[10] To bolster his case, Diderot appealed to going native and cross-cultural (un)dressing as a natural means of avoiding fashion: 'one sees many men strip themselves and make themselves savages' ('se dépouiller et se faire sauvages') he writes approvingly (Diderot 1955, p. 89). Approvingly, because this turn to savagery underpins the commodification of the art-object in assuring that the work will never become undesirable.

For Diderot, conventionally enough, artists who produce work that will survive their death are 'geniuses', defined, like the images they create, by their lack of localness, their ability to aim at the ideal. His example of a great artist is not a painter but an actor – David Garrick who, more than anyone, 'is never himself' (Diderot 1990, p. 75). The tension between being other to oneself and as a savage, close to nature, is at least papered over by the role that travelling plays in Diderot's criticism. This is particularly clear in his encomium to the young artist–traveller, Hubert Robert, painter of Roman ruins. What the artist and the traveller share is a superabundance of energy, a blind and 'cruel energy' that disrupts identities fixed by genealogical and social networks and family relations (Diderot 1990, p. 327). But – and this reads rather strangely today I think – if this energy drives the policed away from fashion into savagery, it also drives 'savages' into civil life. Diderot borrows an anecdote from the traveller Lepage du Pratz to make the point:

'The savage Moncacht-Apé will reply to the chief of a foreign nation who asks him, "Who are you?" "Where are you going?" "What are you searching for with your short hair?" "I'm in search of reason, and I'm visiting you so you can provide it to me."' To which Diderot as narrator–critic replies: 'My dear Apé, everything you've said is very fine. But understand that you travel because you cannot stay still [rester]. You're over-charged with energy and are embellishing that secret force that is killing you' (Diderot 1990, p. 326). The border between policed and unpoliced societies, whose unsurpassability provides grounds by which aesthetic (and economic) value may be secured in the future, can be crossed from both sides. What each generation shares, what 'savages' and the policed also share, is an energy which crosses this border and which, in its deadliness, also maintains it.

We have come a long way from the argument's point of departure. The destructive energy that drives 'savages' into rationality and Europeans out of family-relations, as well as charging communication with a power to remain relevant in the future, has a source and direction very different from that reservoir of capital and taste upon which art appreciated and was, in turn, appreciated so as to ground happy and 'legitimate' families. Yet the distance between the market economy of the family and the aesthetic on the one side, and the 'cruel energy' of transgressive and self-othering genius and savage on the other, is at least somewhat reduced when we re-read certain of Diderot's almost throw-away remarks threaded through his commentaries on the Salon – which, also, return us to the 'Supplement'. Among the little that he has learnt from reading Abbé Richard's *Description historique et critique de l'Italie*, Diderot declares, was the fact that a Genovese senator could legitimate his ex-nuptial son and that, in Bologna, men could choose an heir among the children of the Foundling Hospitals. Why are these seemingly trivial comments central to Diderot's criticism? Because they presuppose that the future generations who will inherit the value embodied in art might be produced outside the family – by (so to say) geniuses on the move, on the road. At this point the logic of Diderot's argument becomes somewhat opaque, but its thrust is that the capital stored in these art works, which is not being put to productive use, can help undo the connection between filiative and legal inheritance just because it is portable and idle. Capitalised paintings, whose aesthetic value is best secured by their connection to the fatal border between the modern and non-modern, can be easily bequeathed to those who do not inherit a name, land, means of production, fixity. (Thus, for instance, it was as governors of the Foundling Hospital in London that British artists organised themselves into an Academy.) Timeless art works may emerge out of conditions in which genealogical chains are broken, but because they have economic value and do not require active management, they can help incorporate those born 'illegitimately' (including children of artists and intellectuals who haunt the border) into the economy.

These ideas were posed within a larger framework still. Both the philosophical attack on current conditions and the need for art and individuals to
transcend unforeseeable cultural change relied on a vision of history which
accepted that the cultures which embodied the species's immaturity would die
– Diderot's paean to the generative powers of Tahitians notwithstanding.
This line of thought reflected and ultimately legitimated the ethnocides of the
period. In the third edition of Abbé Raynal's popular *Histoire des deux
Indes*, for instance, Diderot wrote (anonymously) that in three centuries the
Indians 'will have disappeared from the earth'. He continued: 'What will our
descendants think about this species of men who will then exist only in
travellers' stories [*l'histoire des voyageurs*]? Won't the era of savage man be
for posterity what the fabled era of antiquity is for us? Won't it speak of him
in the way that we speak of centaurs and Lapiths . . . they will prove that
Man was never naked, nomadic [*errant*], without police, without laws, in fact
reduced to the animal condition' (Diderot 1875, 4, p. 45). In his articulation
of the fatal impact theme, Diderot, characteristically, imagines the distant
future in loose genealogical terms: posterity is inhabited by 'our' rather than
'their' 'descendants' – including, presumably, settlers. Here he faces a new
difficulty: what if death erases that savagery which is the most transparent
sign of the energy that draws human beings to their death? For him, history
can become myth in the future both because we – and not others – are the
ancestors of those who will populate the earth, but also because we do not
control our heirs' minds and memories. Diderot's prophecy, however, is
subtly ironic – as befits one who could also colonise the consciousness
of Europe's victims and put vehement and impassioned speeches into the
mouths of natives in protest against their colonisers. What is required for
'our' wholly civilised and policed descendants not to receive truth as myth,
for our messages to cross the border into the future, given the threatened end
of savagery? What would be required for them to remember that people
could live naked, lawlessly? The usual answer – by the production of art
which remains timeless because it simultaneously expresses the energy and
the loss of identity and destruction through which the future continuously
detaches itself from the past – was no longer sufficient. So another solution
appeared: by representing oneself (a cultural forefather) as nakedly as possible
so as to reassert that state of nature which remains a horizon of the species. It
was partly in these terms, it would seem, that Diderot posed naked to Anna
Therbouche for a portrait to be displayed in the 1767 Salon – by his own
account pondering an erection that might swell and unswell throughout the
sitting. It was almost as if the exhibited vicissitudes of his phallus, though
unrepresentable in the Salon, could communicate to his heirs the savagery
that they were in danger of forgetting but none the less should not leave
behind, the uncontrollable energy to which male primacy was tied. And if we
may surmise that the painter's response to Diderot's penis was tepid then that

too was foreseen and an exemplification of patriarchy's unsurpassability. Here the grounds of primitivism stand exposed.

Others

The rejection of patriarchy as a mode of familial and political existence returned Enlightened thinkers to patriarchy as a state of nature only by passing through a problem concerning the nature of identity. The problem can be stated quite simply in theoretical terms: if identities are neither to be inherited nor 'naturally' given but to be open to choice and change – whence their grounds and stability? Not surprisingly, the writings which most clearly articulated the possibility of constructed identity in theoretical terms were those that compared one society to another. In his *Histoire de deux Indes*, for instance, Raynal wrote (believing that the 'Hottentots' habitually cut off one of their testicles): 'Through the amputation of the prepuce, one Jew says to another, "I am a Jew too." Through the amputation of a testicle, one Hottentot says to another, "I am a Hottentot too"'(Raynal 1783, 1, p. 203). For Raynal, such techniques of identity construction are both conventional and universal, being found not just in 'savage' lands but in 'policed societies' especially in times of revolution. And Raynal offers a standard progressive account of how the arbitrariness of identity-construction has been forgotten: priests have frozen signifiers of identity into cosmologies, passed them off as God's bequest to man so as to protect territorial claims. However easy it may be to reject a conspiracy theory of this kind, here it becomes possible to conceive of (male) individuals inventing their own identities by constructing markers of individuality – not least by exposing their penises.

For Raynal's Enlightened anthropology, identity-construction had been frozen into filiative and cosmological chains. How to dissolve them in the interests of Enlightenment? By what means could new identities be constructed? One solution was to proliferate what I will call 'self-othering' – occasions and techniques for constructing an identity by appropriating elements of another's identity, a deeply problematic example of which is Diderot's gestures towards being-savage. In general terms these techniques can be divided into those which remained outside organised and very widespread social institutions and technologies (in particular, the family and print) and those which were incorporated into such institutions. The first were available for purposes of radical self-individuation; the second – and here, as we shall see, I am thinking about forms of self-othering made available through the fictional romance – quickly became conventionalised. In both cases, self-othering could shade into something else, 'becoming another' – a transformation, rather than a more or less reversable reconstruction or invention, of identity. Each of these kinds of self-othering, however, continued to operate in relation to that border between modernity and non-modernity,

Enlightenment and patriarchy, which I have been describing and whose geographical correlate and reference point was the violent frontier of empire. This relation was not, of course, directly referred to in all cultural aids to self-othering; none the less it helped to order the large discursive and material structures within which those aids were produced.

The difficulty with analysing the emergence of modern self-othering and becoming another are twofold. Firstly, non-filiative identity – being oneself on one's own terms, outside of caste, family and so on – was developed by individuals both within old religious practices (confession, testaments of faith and backsliding etc.) and within the newer apparatus of government in the Foucauldian sense, especially education. So non-filiative identities were not produced primarily through techniques of self-othering. Indeed, as formal education in particular was directed towards more and more of the population and regarded as more and more capable of forming personalities, the re-sonance of self-othering and becoming another shifted. As we shall see, Rousseau was already driven to imagine his 'self' as, on the one hand, just his own (neither inherited nor produced by techniques of self-othering or modes of governmentality), while, on the other, he was forcefully driven to become another against the conventional selves being produced by religious and state institutions. Secondly, the distinction between self-othering and becoming another, though analytically quite easy to grasp, was in fact very fluid because both appeared within social and cultural fields in which their charac-teristic practices were widespread and used quite casually. We can note a few of these tactical uses of self-othering. As commodity-markets expanded, taking the place of another had economic functions. In the 1740s, for in-stance, *The London tradesman* enthused, 'a Tradesman must be a perfect Proteus, Change Shapes as often as the Moon, and still find something new' (cited in McKendrick *et al.* 1982, p. 50). Various kinds of self-othering were also presupposed by progressive pedagogy – Diderot himself, famously, took on a disguise to learn the skills of tradesmen and communicate them to readers of the *Encyclopaedia* (Wilson 1972, p. 199). Markers of gender and caste identity were constantly appropriated by those to whom they did not 'belong': we know that women dressing as men, in particular, have been common as far back as records go, the most pressing motive for cross-dressing being women's need to gain access to work. But there were more particular reasons; for instance, in those clandestine 'Fleet marriages' that Lord Hardwicke closed down upon, it was not unusual for women dressed as men to marry other women not necessarily for reasons of sexual preference but to avoid the financial implications of coverture. Even less meaningfully, the poor could dress as an 'other' simply by acquiring clothes as cast-offs or through theft. In a world where fashion had not yet been rationalised, exotic dressing was common among the rich too – a practice which, as we shall see, had some important cultural consequences.

It is impossible firmly to fix a threshold at which such tactical forms of disguise or appropriation of signifiers of otherness were transmuted into forms of self-othering or becoming another. But two cultural sites seem to be particularly important to the emergence of self-othering. The first involved specific kinds of transaction between individuals for ethical and political purposes, in particular in order to construct an ordered public sphere and to minimise the opacity of one individual for another. Importantly, these transactions required individuals to cultivate feelings saturated with moral and political values. One thinks, for instance, of the way in which in Enlightened theory, a large and disparate public may become an audience – a single group attending to the same message or representation – by virtue of communicators' ability to transform themselves into the sensibilities of those they address – a capacity connected to that conventionally theorised as 'sympathy' or as 'pity' (by Rousseau). Sympathy and pity involved entering empathetically into the subjectivity of another – a moral practice grounded on the possibility of becoming another for a particular occasion. Thus, again, Diderot on the popular painter Greuze: 'He is a ceaseless observer in the streets, in the churches, in the markets, in the theaters, in the promenades, in public assemblies ... Even his personality is affected: he is brusque, gentle, insinuating, caustic, gallant, sad, gay, cold, serious, or mad, according to the object he is rendering' (cited in Crow 1985, p. 142). Through the second form of self-othering, individuals could become objects of widespread public attention outside of religious, state or legal ceremonies. However this mode remained entangled with practices of ceremonial self-spectacularisation common to aristocrats, and which became increasingly privatised through the seventeenth and eighteenth centuries. It was not at all uncommon for rich men to have their portraits painted in exotic dress (members of the Society of Dilettanti club were so painted), and Oriental costume was particularly popular in eighteenth-century masquerades (Ribeiro 1979). But self-spectacularisation could also help poorer people make a living: early in the eighteenth century, George Pzsalmanzar became famous by passing himself off as a 'Formosan' in London (dressing suitably, inventing an alphabet and language etc.) in order to gain access to the London literary world, for instance.

Rousseau is important to the history of self-othering and becoming another both because he combines each of these separate modes and because he is so sensitive to the contradictions involved in becoming another to become oneself. He too becomes other as the exotic object of public attention. When Boswell, a long-time admirer at a distance, first met Rousseau, he found his host to be a 'genteel black man in the dress of an Armenian' – an especially strange get-up in a thinker so committed to being what he was and not another (Boswell 1953, p. 216). At one level Rousseau has given up on western dress because of an embarrassing, perhaps psychosomatic, problem that required him to urinate frequently. More to the point, in allowing more access to the naked body than contemporary European male dress, his Armenian outfit permitted a minimum of conventionality and a self-spectacularisation. (We should note that as a young man he had been an assisitant to an itinerant, exotically dressed false priest *à la* Pzsalmanzar.) But Rousseau's clothing also hinted at a Diderot-like exhibitionism, a form of sexual expression to which he had been addicted, as we know from *The confessions*. To choose a signifier of identity by thinly veiling the phallus is to hint at the limits of self-othering within self-othering, given that, for Enlightened thought, the phallus was the horizon of nature and a marker of stable meaning. At moments, though, Rousseau tried to cross even that horizon, in a drive motivated by a paranoia which seems inseparable from the very success of his tactics of self-othering: 'I have thought like a man, I have written like a man and people have disapproved of me, so now I will become a woman' (cited in Guéhenno 1966, 2, p. 120). Rousseau attempted to become a woman by turning to sewing – embroidering and de-commodifying garments that he presented to women who promised to breast-feed their children, as if by making such a gift he could transform embroidery into nakedness and naturalness and end the reproduction of merely cul-tural and, thus, arbitrary, identities. In fact the conditions of possibility of Rousseau's modes of self-othering were exactly those he would deny. Sewing, appearing publicly in his Armenian costume, Rousseau attracted staring crowds. He was individuating himself, differentiating himself from others in an effort of self-individuation that could be based neither on a 'natural' difference (a given body) nor on a 'conventional' one (the determinations of an inherited class or culture) but on a willed difference only to be expressed by taking the place of another, wearing another's costume or, even (as a 'black'), acquiring the body of another. It was as if Rousseau could simul-taneously acquire universality in becoming other to himself and be a unique individual through the acquisition of another identity. This public use of self-othering for purposes of self-individuation was, of course, a tactic often to be repeated by the modern, 'Bohemian' artist. And, as we shall see in more detail, in Rousseau's case the presentation of oneself as other, as exotic is in-timately intertwined with the possibility of 'deeper' identity transformations.

Becoming another itself could become routinised. In particular, it could be-come necessary to those who traded between Europeans and non-Europeans, especially when that trade involved, sporadically, violence. In the late seven-teenth and early eighteenth century, the *coureurs de bois*, fur-traders in what is today Canada, were famous for their 'savagery', their being like Indians.[11] Even in Britain, where images of this kind were less common, 'West Indians' were characteristically represented as rough and brutal, touched not just by the harsh authority they wielded, the stringency and remoteness of their life, but, at least implicitly, by the 'savagery' of those with whom they had contact.[12] (By the late nineteenth century, a wing of social science had formulated the supposed tendency of colonial settlers to 'degenerate' into the 'savages' whom they had displaced, as a law.) The anti-colonialist movement recoiled from the 'metamorphosis of the expatriate European' with ambivalent horror: Diderot, as one might expect, described settlers who went native in terms analogous to those in which he conceived of transgressive geniuses (Raynal 1783, 3, p. 1). Yet settler becoming-another could revert to self-spectacularisation, the most famous British case being the Scot Peter Williamson, who was captured by a group of indigenous people in Canada in the 1780s and who exhibited himself as an exotic spectacle; his memoirs and portrait dressed in the style of his captors becoming very popular around 1800, by which time he had turned into a successful businessman. No identity-exchange was in question in Williamson's case. Although settler becoming-another through going native never gained widespread metropolitan or colonial approval at the level of public culture, it did remain attractive to certain advanced intellectuals and, later, avant-garde artists – like Loti and Gauguin – who moved from 'self-othering' through self-spectacularisation (like Williamson) to becoming another by making 'savages' of themselves, 'going native' to enter the timeless order of victorious western culture at a later stage of colonialism.

Yet in the eighteenth century, the strongest forms of self-othering were less spectacular than cross-dressing; less commercial than, for instance, a tradesman's empathy with the myriad forms of commodity-desire; less specialised than the 'going native' which was almost essential in early colonial settlement. They were to be found in reading and writing which, unlike the forms of self-othering and becoming another with which I have been concerned, were easily available to women. Why women in distinction to men? The reason why self-spectacularisation was fundamentally a male practice was not just that it was connected, at its determining margins, to going native and the phallus, but because it was public. So-called 'public' spaces were accessible to unaccompanied women only with great stress and difficulty, both because women were ideologically bound to domesticity (a woman unaccompanied in public was regarded, almost automatically, as selling sex) and because such spaces were in fact dangerous for women. To choose one of hundreds of instances because, though important, it has been somewhat neglected: through the second half of the eighteenth century, a number of public debates and discussions, attended by both men and women, were held in London halls under titles like the 'Disputing Society', the 'University for Rational Amusements' and the 'School of Eloquence'. These halls were not public in the way the streets and fairs were – they had an admission fee of 1s – but they were public enough to cause difficulties for women. They were also especially important for women; topics like the rights of women, the value of love and virtue, were prominent. But women were at risk even in public spaces like these halls: not only was their reputation jeopardised, they were sexually assailed by men. So advertisements reassured women that veils were permissable, masks and dominoes were often handed out and some of the halls were made off-limits to men. Not especially successfully – at least one women-only group was chaired by a man dressed as a woman, and attended by several such, presumably to prey on women sexually.[13] If a woman's (especially a single woman's) presence in this kind of space required so much care, other forms of self-othering were no less difficult. Gender cross-dressing seems to have become increasingly difficult as public spaces were placed under more vigilant surveillance; as reading secured domestic ideology, as education and religion disseminated 'respectability' more efficiently, and as cloth and clothing became cheaper and more uniform. There were also sanctions against women self-othering themselves by emigrating and establishing themselves as (uncivil) settlers – it was only in the 1840s that it became possible to represent women colonial settlers affirmatively at least in the mainstream press, and then only because the women encouraged to emigrate came from the poorest section of the working class, especially the so-called 'slop-workers' or 'needlewomen' – in the famous campaign supported by the Queen and the *Morning chronicle*. The strongest forms of self-othering, then, were provided in reading and writing – which, just because they could be enjoyed in private, were accessible to women, including single women.

But we must be careful in drawing too firm a distinction between print- and non-print-based forms of self-othering. Ever since the sixteenth century, prose fiction and dramas had represented dressing as another so as to demonstrate the unsurpassability of filiative, caste and guild inheritance. In such fictions, taking on the appearance of another merely led to a dénouement which revealed that caste and gender differences were so deeply embedded as to be untransformable. But through the eighteenth century, the threat to filiation and patriarchy which such narratives presupposed became increasingly less easily deflected. To take one of the most intriguing English examples, Tobias Smollett's *Ferdinand Count Fathom* tells the story of a no-status, extra-marital child – Ferdinand Fathom – who attempts to use both caste cross-dressing and class-exogamy to 'rise' in the world. He fails; natural filiative order reasserts itself, yet what is at stake is different here from what it would have been even in a Shakespearean comedy. The text gains its particular narrative energy, its hook, because it cannot hold off the possibility that Ferdinand might indeed transform his identity (as, to some degree, Defoe's Moll Flanders had) – that the camp-follower might become a gentleman. The possibility of identity-transformation is powerful because the reader is given so much of Ferdinand's self to take pleasure in and identify with.

In Smollett, self-othering, becoming another and self-invention threaten, but do not replace, patriarchal filiation. From around 1740, however, writing in the interests of self-othering and becoming another became commonplace.

Before considering the dominant means for encouraging textual identity transformation, it is important to note that, once Enlightened values dominated public discourse, becoming a patriarch was itself transformed into a form of self-othering, more than it had been for the Diderot who exposed himself to Anna Therbouche. On 'our' side of modernity and Enlightenment, becoming a patriarch acquired a new social and cultural use-value, because it was associated with aggressive, militarised masculinity. In particular, it was required to preserve the nation state. The greatest theorist of this post-Enlightened self-othering, of the masculinist recrossing of the border which separated Enlightenment from darkness, was the Marquis de Sade. The Marquis believed it was crucial that Enlightenment should not eliminate patriarchy entirely. Firstly, he equated freedom with nature so literally that, for him, all desires and power relations were 'natural'. Most of all, a man's patriarchal need 'to command, to be obeyed, to surround himself with slaves' (de Sade 1966, p. 317) was natural and should not be repressed. Next, the need to do and be everything and anything – including an old patriarch – overcomes that 'fear in dark places' characteristic of both 'despotism' and religion (p. 305). 'Being a patriarch' has been transformed into a mode of becoming 'other' with full theoretical sanction. But how to re-enact patriarchy, now a sign of liberty, in modern society – in a republic? The answer is – orgies, which (in opposition to Tahiti) privatise the play of dominance and submission and render it harmless. Or better than harmless, because a republic will continue to depend on patriarchal power relations in its military struggle for self-determination. In short, de Sade – especially in his instructive *Philosophy in the bedroom* – attempts to establish a political and ethical order for self-othering, prescribing times and places at which it remains proper to take non-Enlightened positions for Enlightenment's sake. What de Sade recognises is that modernity cannot erase inherited identity: individuals are still born into membership of a particular nation. A (male) disposition to violence must be preserved to secure that identity, which, for Enlightened governmentality, grounds other freedoms – just as violence was required of the savage settler.

Smollett's fragile affirmation of filiation and de Sade's arguments for patriarchy's use-value both stand against, and presuppose, the dominance of another, far more powerful and seductive genre – romance as developed by Richardson and (once again) Rousseau. In modern romance reading, writing and living become entwined – I am tempted to say 'fused'. In romance, becoming another reaches into zones of subjectivity that had previously lain inert; in romance, the self becomes another propelled by (fictionalised) sexual desire and the promise of a unique self, in order to establish modern love and families. At the heart of romance lies what Freud was to call 'object-choice'. For Freud, especially in *Group psychology and the analysis of the ego*, 'object-choice' names the attempt to 'have' the Other in love (Freud 1985, p.

99). Object-choice (unlike cross-dressing for instance) is felt and acted out with another; it falls outside of detached and distancing inspection. It is directed not at signifiers of identity but at the other as a whole person, and, indeed, what is 'deepest' in them. Grounded on sexual desire, it seems to belong more to nature conceived of as a domain of freedom and choice than to society conceived of as a structuring framework. The romance is the narrative expression of reciprocal and free object-choice: when romances are circulated in the public sphere, they allow readers to identify with fictional characters (also, sometimes, the implied author) by having those characters make and be free object-choices. (And, let us remind ourselves, fiction becomes powerful in the eighteenth century partly because it imagines actions for, and puts words in the mouths of, those who, like Diderot's Tahitians or maid-servants like Richardson's Pamela, have limited access to educated discourses and very partial access to metropolitan 'public' spaces.) The identificatory flow which moves from the reader's private space to a public world which is fictional and 'other' but not completely different from the real (as the old 'chivalric romances' were, say) grounds the amazing capacity of romances to pluck a love-object from the far side of exclusionary social divisions, most profoundly that between the legitimate and the illegitimate, the policed and the unpoliced. In romantic love object-choosing and being chosen is represented as happening simultaneously in a magical moment of 'crystalisation' (to borrow Stendhal's term) at which identities fuse, change and, for a moment, settle. The paradigmatic statement of fictional, romantic self-othering is, no doubt, Cathy Earnshaw's 'I am Heathcliffe' – Heathcliffe being exactly a non-nuptial, sea-port baby; Catherine the daughter of a respectable, non-nomadic family. The more exotic the object-choice, the more different and, thus, unique both lovers become as they fuse together.

So modern romance was a literary technique for drawing the border between the past and the present, law and desire, parent and lover, familiar and exotic, into the largely imagined geography shared by a reading public dispersed into private houses (or rooms or beds). By drawing this border into the civil order, romances also, if weakly, disrupt civility. The logic is simple enough: the border appears, however diagrammatically, whenever a father is rejected – and one cannot love to a father's order. Yet confrontation with the father turned into negotiation just because, in the 'policed' world, romance also provided legitimation and guidance for the reproduction of affectionate nuclear families made up of aggregates of autonomous individuals – families placed on the map of the civil. Romances turned into marriages that generated that kind of family – as in Samuel Richardson's *Pamela* where a patriarch/rake becomes a *paterfamilias* and the young woman a domesticated mother. However the passage from lover to parent, from patriarchy to paternalism, from child to adult, from dependency to autonomy, and, indeed, from transgression to legitimacy, can be neither smooth nor complete any more than they were in Enlightened social theory or in Diderot and Rousseau's lives.

Nowhere are the blockages of this passage, the lived limits to denying the power of the father as well as resisting the seduction of being a husband, more apparent than in the most influential of eighteenth-century romance fictions, *La Nouvelle Héloïse*, which sparked an epidemic of identity-exchanges, or, as Mary Wollstonecraft put it, of 'donations' of 'sentiments and feelings' from characters to readers and back again (Wollstonecraft 1975, p. 38). It is a novel worth considering in some detail, not just because here the familial conditions of advanced, contemporary intellectual production stand exposed but because, here, self-othering romance is transformed into art via the dual struggle against, and attraction for, patriarchy and nomadism. Furthermore, because the position of the reconciled father/husband is unattainable in *La Nouvelle Héloïse*, the novel clearly expresses the motive forces of modern primitivism. However unlikely it may seem, it begins to reveal the complexities of the interactions between European expansion and romance.

Rousseau's novel tells the story of Saint-Preux, a young man with no known family, thus with a self that, owing nothing to inheritance, is highly individuated and free. He becomes a tutor who falls in love with and seduces his young student, the Julie of the book's full title (*Julie ou la Nouvelle Héloïse*). His seduction, we can recall, is legally a rape punishable by death. Saint-Preux, who has no reason to live in one place rather than another, is kept close to Julie by his love – which is also a threat to the authority of Julie's unreasonable father, indeed a threat, potentially, to the authority of all patriarchs (though Rousseau has no character declare, as does Satin-Albin in Diderot's *Le Père de Famille*, 'Fathers, fathers . . . there aren't any . . . there are only tyrants' (Diderot 1990, 10, p. 233)). Against fathers, authority and conventions, the lovers appeal both to nature (to which their sexual love belongs) and to their capacity to exchange identities. Saint-Preux says to Julie: 'I am no longer in myself . . . my alienated soul is completely in you' (Rousseau 1960, p. 75) and, inversely, 'you penetrate my whole substance' (p. 122). These erotic transferences, which Saint-Preux's rape does not undo, intensify the effects of Saint-Preux's enlightened pedagogy which breaks down inherited roles and values so as to form new identities and ways of life. Teaching, male 'coming first' and romance all fuse.

In *La Nouvelle Héloïse*, it soon becomes clear that Saint-Preux cannot establish himself as a legitimate father because he has not sufficient money or inherited social status to provide independently for a family. 'Becomes clear' is a shorthand here, because once the lovers have had sex the narrative gains an extraordinary unpredictability and interest: anything at all can happen. In sociological terms it is an unpredictability based on readerly uncertainty as to whether an Enlightened intellectual, unwilling to work under the system of patronage and to marry a woman who is not his intellectual equal, can earn an independent living, find a home, so as to combine the role of the natural and sexualised lover with that of the head of a family, and thus be fully incorporated into modern society as a member of the public (a group of happy, privatised families). As it becomes clear that Saint-Preux cannot marry and produce legitimate offspring, he goes back to travelling, joining, if comfortably, the deracinated and homeless. Travelling here has a global sweep. Firstly, when he travels to Paris, he angers Julie by 'going native', by acquiring local manners to describe Parisian corruption and its indiscriminate mingling of the genders in public. Then he accompanies George Anson in his (historical if botched) circumnavigation of the globe, during which he is stranded on a South Seas island, living like a Polynesian, if not, this time, 'going native'. Finally he returns to tutor Julie's children – becoming, as it were, simultaneously their father and not their father, encouraging the next generation's autonomy. His return is possible because, during his travels, his self-othering has been restricted by his continual re-porting back to a domestic and stable centre – Julie herself. In writing to Julie, Saint-Preux begins to transform the life-conditions of the old travelling poor, their techniques of tactical self-othering, into a mode of modern be-coming another, that is, becoming a woman. By staying home, Julie provides the security by which Saint-Preux's self-othering is limited; in turn, Julie can live privately, absolutely outside the public sphere, because the world is represented to her through Saint-Preux's correspondence.

La Nouvelle Héloïse is a fiction which again re-figures certain conditions of its author's existence. Saint-Preux, with his nomadism, individuality and illegitimacy, is an idealised version of Rousseau (and his heirs). Rousseau abandoned his children, had left his father as a child; when young he had wandered from place to place, going so far as to undergo religious conversion to secure board; he worked as an assistant to an itinerant religious con-man, changed his name and so on. Later, despite his fame, largely because he had no access to an organised literary market, Rousseau remained mobile until old age. But what divides Rousseau's life (as narrated in *The confessions*) from his fiction is his imagining and speaking through Julie, that morally, if not sexually, 'pure' domestic woman. Here fiction allows Rousseau a means of becoming woman. Fiction also allows Rousseau to individuate himself as 'Jean-Jacques' the massively celebrated, and thus, public, private man – the man who can create (himself as) Julie. What also divides the fiction from the life is that this second kind of individuation is not permitted Saint-Preux, who does not himself write fictions and whose stability is guaranteed by Julie's fixity. It is as if in an ideal world there would be no public self-othering for purposes of self-individuation; in that ideal world, becoming woman would be routine for men, women merely providing the stability demanded by male becoming-another. Finally, though, what gives Rousseau's fiction a longer life than its author (and hence individuates its author all the more) is Julie's death. Why does Julie die? At one level, she dies because she loves the man who rapes her and because she cannot detach her paternalist husband, who was not her choice and cannot be loved, from her patriarchal father. She cannot utterly renounce Saint-Preux and ultimately cannot find her own home in the world, established with a man whom she has chosen, so that her death, narrated with much pathos, is not finally a belated punishment for having sex outside marriage but an index of the impossibility of her being simultaneously mother and lover, and Saint-Preux being father and lover. It is the narrative event that prevents paternal and familial values from either lapsing into or triumphing over nomadic or erotic ones. Yet a darker reading of the event is inescapable. Despite everything, Julie's death expresses a desire to annihilate that domestic, romantic woman who stands in the way of a return to patriarchy or to nomadism or to radical autonomy, who tie men to themselves and stabilise their self-othering. Her death, treated sentimentally, is the condition that permits Saint-Preux to remain on that border whose furthest reaches are the frontier of empire. More generally still, the pathos of Julie's end helps secure what Theodor Adorno called 'an identification with death' – an identification with what progress and Enlightenment can never overcome, Diderot's expansionist 'cruel energy' (Bloch 1988, p. 8). Given the logic of Enlightenment, it is by identifying with death that this romance attaches itself to art's temporal order, one which is unsurpassable. If this is not the 'same' death that western soldiers, traders and settlers were dealing out to indigenous peoples, it is at least an element in a wider cultural apparatus which had incorporated that particular massacre of innocents.

Notes

1 The French texts which had most influence in representing France as facing depopulation were Ange Goudar's *Les Intérêts de la France mal entendus* and the Marquis de Mirabeau's *L'Ami des hommes* – both published in 1756. An influential British literary expression of the same fear can be found in Oliver Goldsmith's *The deserted village*, which included a strong attack on emigration and colonial settlement. For the most influential, pre-Malthusian, contestation of the thesis that modernity was depopulated in relation to antiquity, see David Hume's essay 'Of the populousness of ancient nations', written around 1750.

2 For the *cahiers de doléances*, see Goubert and Denis 1964.

3 See Traer 1980, pp. 15ff. for a list of a father's powers in France.

4 It is pertinent to note that, as Michel Foucault and Arlette Farge have pointed out, it was precisely this kind of use of *lettres de cachet* which led to them becoming rarer after the late 1760s. See Foucault and Farge 1982.

5 For 'nomad' in this sense, see Mayhew 1968, vol. 1, p. 2.

6 An excellent account of the Hardwicke marriage act is to be found in Harth 1988.

7 The crucial text in circulating the theory and practice of contractual marriage during the eighteenth century was Le Ridant 1770, first published 1753.

8 Note also the importance of natural history and geography in the development of a new 'planetary consciousness' as Mary Louise Pratt calls it in Pratt 1992, p. 16. The proposer of the New South Wales colony, James Matra, was very conscious of the need to rebut the home underpopulation argument (see McNab 1908, vol. 2, p. 40).

9 For comparisons between European and Indian textile industries see Thorner and Thorner 1962. For a more general survey of the importance of technology to the 'ideology of western dominance', see Adas 1989.

10 For the emergence of the modern fashion industry and magazines, see Daniel Roche 1989, pp. 447–76.

11 For the *coureurs de bois* see Wolf 1982, p. 182, and Miquelon 1987, pp. 6–31.

12 See, for instance, George Cumberland's very successful comedy *The West Indian* (1771).

13 The 'women's only' debate attended by men took place at Carlisle House in May 1780. The most convenient source for information on these public debating societies is to be found in the third volume of Daniel Lysons's *Collectanea*, a collection of newspaper cuttings, at the British Library.

The locked heart: the creole family romance of *Wide sargasso sea*

PETER HULME

It's my belief that you remember much more than you pretend to remember. (Grace Poole's words to Antoinette, *Wide sargasso sea*, p. 149)

Local knowledge

In the Introduction to this book the editors discuss some of the problems raised at the Symposium about the term 'postcolonial'. One case to be argued in defence of the term would centre on its usefulness as a teaching tool, on how it quickly and not inaccurately marks out a terrain on which courses can be constructed in a way that both makes sense to students and puts on to the agenda questions of history, politics and canonicity. The term simplifies (as does every *single* term), but it does not, carefully used, do violence to the texts it designates. However, serious problems do arise when the term is pressed into service as an *analytical* tool, a point clearly made in Anne McClintock's chapter in this volume: in particular, the historical relationship supposedly suggested between 'colonial' and 'postcolonial' remains consistently undefined. *Wide sargasso sea* is a case in point: a novel published in 1966, at a time when the general decolonisation of the British Empire was well under way but before Dominica, the island of Jean Rhys's birth, had gained independence; a novel written by, in West Indian terms, a member of the white colonial elite, yet somebody who always defined herself in opposition to the norms of metropolitan 'Englishness'; a novel which deals with issues of race and slavery, yet is fundamentally sympathetic to the planter class ruined by Emancipation.

In a teaching context, *Wide sargasso sea* almost always appears alongside *Jane Eyre*, the postcolonial 'vindication' read after and against one of the novels which forms the imperialist canon.[1] This is how I teach the book, too, and there is no doubt of its effective presence along with other revisionary couples: *Robinson Crusoe* and *Foe*, *The tempest* and *Water with berries*. None the less, if this pedagogical opposition of the 'colonial' and the 'postcolonial' is allowed to become too fixed, too orthodox a way of organising research projects on books like *Wide sargasso sea*, then the critical enterprise risks becoming located at such a high level of generality ('postcoloniality') that the particular conditions that produced particular books can remain ignored, indeed even unavailable.

The need, as always, is for a properly historical criticism, and the problem, as always, lies in knowing just what 'historical' might mean in different circumstances. The recent exchange between Fredric Jameson (1986) and Aijaz Ahmad (1987) around the former's attempt to produce a general theory of 'Third World' literature is instructive in this respect, illustrating the point that 'history' is not some ready-made category which can be unproblematically introduced into the analysis of a piece of fiction. Ahmad's fundamental criticism is that Jameson has set out, quite properly, to 'historicise', but has historicised inadequately. The inadequacy has two dimensions. He has not historicised enough, defining the 'First' and 'Second' worlds in terms of their systems of production (capitalism and socialism) while the 'Third World' is defined exclusively in terms of the externally introduced experience of having suffered colonialism and imperialism. And he has historicised differentially, so that the non-western world is first differentiated from the west, and then homogenised, a procedure whose dangers Jameson recognises and then goes on to ignore. Homogenisation is precisely the point here. Terms such as 'Third World' (and – one could no doubt add – 'postcolonial') run the risk of imposing a single and simple (and usually metropolitan) label on an extraordinary variety of national and other traditions.

Postcolonial criticism does itself recognise this point. Helen Tiffin, for example, whose work has done much to popularise the ideas associated with the postcolonial, talks in terms of postcolonial strategies rather than of some homogeneous realm of the postcolonial:

> Postcolonial counter-discursive strategies involve a mapping of the dominant discourse, a reading and exposing of its underlying assumptions, and the dis/mantling of these assumptions from the cross-cultural standpoint of the imperially subjectified 'local' . . . *Wide sargasso sea* directly contests British sovereignty – of persons, of place, of culture, of language. It reinvests its own hybridised world with a provisionally authoritative perspective, but one which is deliberately constructed as provisional since the novel is at pains to demonstrate the subjective nature of point of view and hence the cultural construction of meaning. (Tiffin 1987, p. 23)

The strategies are plural and the standpoint 'local'. The argument here might begin to sound like, but should not be confused with, a Lyotardian valuation of *petits récits* over the supposedly impossible grand narratives. If it is indeed the moment to write some *petits récits* – and this article might be said to offer one – then it is not because the age of the grand narratives has been left behind on epistemological grounds, but rather that the grand narrative of decolonisation has, for the moment, been adequately told and widely accepted. Smaller narratives are now needed, with attention paid to local topography, so that the maps can become fuller. 'Local' knowledge in this sense of the word is situated, particular, 'native'. But the small narratives do not stand by themselves – as they would for Lyotard; they are local sentences in the chapter of the postcolonial world, to be distinguished from the egregiously restricted yet endlessly self-advertised postmodern idea of 'locality'.

To attempt to read *Wide sargasso sea* historically is then to confront a series of quite particular questions. What history are we talking about? Is the 'present' from which the book was written 1966 or 1957 (when the final version was started) or 1938 (when the first draft was apparently written and destroyed)? To what extent is the novel reworking material from childhood (1890–1907)? What of the historical period with which the novel deals (1834 onwards)? And is this a general 'West Indian history', or something more specifically Jamaican or Dominican?

These questions have been debated almost since the book's first publication. Although Rhys, born in Dominica, had left the Caribbean in 1907 aged sixteen and returned only once, briefly, in 1936, that lack of residence in the area did not prevent West Indian critics from claiming *Wide sargasso sea* as a significantly Caribbean novel. Wally Look Lai (1968) and Kenneth Ramchand (1983) both suggested the links; John Hearne, the Jamaican novelist, argued a strong case that *Wide sargasso sea* should be a 'touchstone' for West Indian fiction (1974, p. 323). And Louis James, in the first book-length study of Rhys, paid special attention to the West Indian context of her writing (1978).

However, less often recalled in the Rhys criticism is that Edward Kamau Brathwaite, the Jamaican poet and historian, took time out of his wide-ranging 1974 essay called *Contradictory omens* to contest the claims made for *Wide sargasso sea*. There are several different layers to his argument, but his central point is that white creoles cannot 'meaningfully identify or be identified, with the spiritual world' of the contemporary West Indies (1974, p. 38). That spiritual world is essentially the culture of the 'black ex-African majority' (p. 30), and Brathwaite does not want the articulation of that culture, now politically independent from Britain, confused by attempts to identify its 'essence' with the work of 'a white creole expatriate West Indian-born novelist' (p. 34) – whose protagonist, Antoinette, is similarly white, creole, expatriate and 'West Indian-born' – an unfortunate phrase which suggests that she is 'accidentally' rather than 'really' West Indian. Brathwaite's argument may be crude and essentialist, but at least he problematises any easy identification of *Wide sargasso sea* as a postcolonial novel – or makes us think more clearly about the true parameters of the term 'postcolonial'.

Other critics, among them Gayatri Spivak, alert to the kind of argument that Brathwaite presents, direct attention – properly enough – to the character of Christophine, Antoinette's black maid, seeing her as a kind of 'excess' that 'cannot be contained by a novel which rewrites a canonical English text . . . in the interest of the white Creole rather than the native' (1985, p. 253).

Spivak's argument is much subtler than Brathwaite's, but her use of the word 'native' suggests an underlying difficulty: in the West Indies the 'native' is either for the most part absent – if what is meant is indigenous – or 'creole' – if what is meant is 'born in the West Indies'. Claims to post-colonial authenticity, in India or Africa for example, will tend to ground themselves on that *native* terrain: to distinguish between black creole and white creole is already to blur the desired distinction. The term 'creole' seeps across any attempt at a Manichean dividing line between native and settler, black and white. Interestingly enough, the small indigenous population of the Caribbean does impinge on *Wide sargasso sea*, though it is that category of the creole which permeates the book's narrative and becomes the embodiment of its radical instability. Postcolonial theory, if it is to develop, must produce 'native' terminology; which is why I put at centre stage the Caribbean notion of the 'creole', the local name, if you like, for what the 'general' theory calls 'hybridisation' (see the second part of the quotation from Tiffin), but one which has the twin advantages of a long history in the Americas and a constant usage by Rhys herself.[2]

Remembering the family

What follows makes no pretence of being a full historical reading of *Wide sargasso sea*: one of the hallmarks of work at Essex has been the insistence that the historical work needs to be done, not invoked through anecdote as seems nowadays so often the 'new' approach to history. This then is a sketch of a project now under way to study how the 'materials' that went into the writing of *Wide sargasso sea* might be reconstituted so as to throw light on to the dense particularity of that novel. That these materials are 'historical', in the full sense of that word, rather than a merely anecdotal and familial adjunct to a 'proper' colonial history, is part of the point I want to make. *Wide sargasso sea* is a postcolonial novel, if that term is used carefully enough; it is counter-discursive, if the dominant discourse is taken as a kind of received Englishness, but attention to its local circumstances suggests that it also needs reading as a reworking of the materials from *Jane Eyre* inflected by the received traditions of a planter 'family history'.[3] In other words, literary production is viewed here less as a matter of individual creativity than as a trans-generational formation from 'event' to 'family memory' to 'literary text'.

On the first page of *Wide sargasso sea* Antoinette recalls hearing her mother talking to Mr Luttrell, her only friend, and saying 'Of course they have their own misfortunes. Still waiting for this compensation the English promised when the Emancipation Act was passed. Some will wait for a long time' (1968, p. 15). One of the families that waited in vain for compensation after the 1833 Emancipation Act was the Lockharts, Jean Rhys's mother's

family. Rhys's great-grandfather had bought Geneva, one of the largest plantations on Dominica at the beginning of the nineteenth century. Geneva never
recovered after losing its slave labour force, and was in genteel decay by the
time of Rhys's childhood at the turn of the century.

Wide sargasso sea, as a writing out of that family history, a kind of
extended autobiography or creole family romance, is offered as in some sense
a 'compensation' for the ruin of that family at the time of Emancipation, a
compensation, though, which also serves to occlude the actual relationship
between that family history and the larger history of the English colony of
Dominica. This chapter tries to comprehend something of that work of
occlusion.[4]

Rhys may have started writing *Wide sargasso sea* as early as the late 1930s,
soon after her return trip to Dominica in 1936. An early version may have
been destroyed (Angier 1990, p. 223). That return to the Caribbean in 1936
certainly seems to have initiated, or at any rate intensified, the collection of
West Indian material and memories which Rhys later refers to as 'Creole'.
The final stage in the writing of *Wide sargasso sea* began in 1957, although it
took nine more years for her to complete the book. In 1958 she wrote:

> For some time I've been getting down all I remembered about the West Indies as
> the West Indies used to be. (Also all I was told, which is more important). I called
> this 'Creole' but it had no shape or plan – it wasn't a book at all and I didn't try to
> force it.
> Then when I was in London last year it 'clicked in my head' that I had material
> for the story of Mr. Rochester's first wife. The real story – as it might have been.
> (Rhys 1985, p. 153)

By far the longest and most interesting of Rhys's letters about the composition
of *Wide sargasso sea* was written in April 1964 to Francis Wyndham, explaining how she had overcome the blockage which had prevented her completing the novel. It is an unusually long and full letter, which contains a
poem called 'Obeah Night': 'Only when I wrote this poem – then it clicked –
and all was there and always had been' (Rhys 1985, p. 262).

The poem is signed by Edward Rochester or Raworth (she was still toying
with the explicitness of the connection with *Jane Eyre*), as 'written in Spring
1842' – and therefore in England. The poem is awkward and not always easy
to construe, but focuses on the night of passionate and violent love between
Rochester and Antoinette following her administration of the 'love-potion'
supplied by Christophine:

> How can I forget you Antoinette
> When the spring is here?
> Where did you hide herself

After that shameless, shameful night?
And why come back? Hating and hated?
Was it Love, Fear, Hoping?
Or (as always) Pain?
(*Did* you come back I wonder
Did I ever see you again?)

No. I'll lock that door
Forget it. –
The motto was 'Locked Hearts I open
   I have the heavy key'
Written in black letters
Under a Royal Palm Tree
On a slave owner's gravestone
'Look! And look again, hypocrite' he says
   'Before you judge *me*'

I'm no damn slave owner
I have no slave
Didn't she (forgiven) betray me
Once more – and then again
Unrepentant – laughing?
I can soon show her
   Who hates the best
Always he answers me
   I will hate last

(Rhys 1985, pp. 265–6)

'History' is here in ways which take some untangling. Rochester seems to
suggest that he will (symbolically) lock his door against Antoinette's return,
before remembering her family motto written on the patriarch's gravestone.
('Corda serrata pando', 'locked hearts I open', was the motto of Rhys's
mother's family, the Lockharts, as she recalled in her conversations with
David Plante).[5] She will have ways of opening his heart again if she so
desires. But Rochester moves quickly to an imagined address he hears from
the gravestone, which seems to defend the slave-owning families against
the kinds of criticism that Mason and Rochester both voice in the novel.
Rochester chooses to make the connection with his wife, suggesting that she
is no 'slave' since she has betrayed him more than once. Two 'clicks in the
head' connect *Jane Eyre* with the personal memories and oral histories. This
is what makes possible the next stage of the composition. If one factor were
especially important, it might well be the coincidence of names: Edward was
the name of Rhys's grandfather, a significant figure in her family story, as
well as the name of Rochester, Brontë's hero in *Jane Eyre*.

My particular interest here, however, is in the significance of the *changes* which Rhys made to the chronology, topography and family relationships given by *Jane Eyre* once the decision had been taken to work with that narrative material. The crucial point about the chronological changes can best be gauged by quoting a letter Rhys wrote in 1962 when she sent the first two parts of *Wide sargasso sea* to her editor:

> The typed (and heavily corrected) part is the most important – it's the story of an old West Indian house burned down by the negroes who hate the ex-slave owning family living there. The time 1839, the white creole girl aged about 14 is the 'I'. (Rhys 1985, p. 214)

It was very unusual for Rhys to be that precise about dates. *Jane Eyre* is unspecific about its dates, although internal evidence would seem to set the West Indian episodes before 1820: they certainly take place before the watershed of Emancipation in 1833.[6] So, for all the extraordinarily close connections and parallels that exist between *Jane Eyre* and *Wide sargasso sea*, Rhys has adapted the chronology in order to bring it in line with her own family history: 1825 is, for example, the approximate birth-date of Rhys's great aunt Cora, one of the models for Antoinette (though the name Cora is transfered to Antoinette's aunt, who corresponds to Jean's great-aunt Jane). The dramatic events in her family history to which she wanted to relate *Jane Eyre* are post-Emancipation, so the time-scale is adjusted accordingly.

The topographical transpositions in *Wide sargasso sea* work in the same direction. That the first part of the story should take place in Jamaica is given by *Jane Eyre*. Rhys had never been in Jamaica: the Cosway plantation, which becomes the property of the Masons, is based upon the Lockhart plantation of Geneva, though in *Wide sargasso sea* given the name of Coulibri, the next estate along the south coast of Dominica. Mention of Spanish Town, then capital of Jamaica, is also given by *Jane Eyre*, but there are no attempts to 'transfer' the Dominican references that pervade the early part of *Wide sargasso sea*. The honeymoon island, home of Antoinette's mother, is also attended by Dominican references, although the island itself remains unnamed in the novel: the couple arrive at Massacre (a village just north of Roseau), there are persistent references to the Caribs, who are found only on Dominica; and Antoinette's house is clearly based on Rhys's father's estate, Amelia, though called in the novel Granbois, like Coulibri the name of a Dominican estate.[7] More circumstantially, the *surrounding* topography relates to Dominica which has, for example, plenty of traffic with Martinique, unlike Jamaica. When Rochester writes to the Spanish Town magistrate, Mr. Fraser, he gets a reply 'in a few days' (p. 118), which would be good going from Roseau, but inconceivable from Jamaica.

Let me use this example of the topographical references to try to clarify the argument. A fully 'autobiographical' reading – of the kind not being suggested here – would take all this as evidence that the 'Jamaica' of *Wide sargasso sea* is *really* Dominica. An aesthetic reading would say that it did not matter, that the 'Jamaica' of both novels exists in the parallel world of art, so that it makes no difference what topographical features are attached to it.[8] What I am suggesting is that proper attention to the production of *Wide sargasso sea* would investigate the intertwining of 'Jamaica' and 'Dominica' in the novel, the Dominican materials produced from memory and family history appearing under some of the toponyms provided by *Jane Eyre*.

In the West Indian family relationships the changes again involve alterations that inflect the materials closer to the Lockhart family history. In *Jane Eyre* the Mason family of Jamaica consists of husband and wife and three children, including Bertha. The black population of Jamaica is not directly mentioned, though arguably 'present' in some of the descriptions given by Jane of Bertha's 'thick and dark hair...' and 'discoloured face' (1934, pp. 282–3). In addition, Brontë's use of the term 'creole' – as in Rochester's 'Her mother, the Creole, was both a mad woman and a drunkard' (p. 291) – carries at least a hint of 'tainted' blood. What 'suits' Rochester, he says, must be the 'antipodes of the Creole', whom he now – as he tells Jane the story of his marriage – associates with 'the loathings of incongruous unions' (p. 311), a phrase that echoes the Book of Ezra's warning about the dangers of taking 'strange wives'. Rhys makes several changes to this story. The basic structure of two parents and three children remains, but this new family is a combination of two earlier family units, with the result that Antoinette (Bertha from *Jane Eyre*) is not a Mason by blood, Richard, her brother from *Jane Eyre* becoming her stepbrother, and her father in *Jane Eyre* becoming her stepfather in *Wide sargasso sea*. The dead father, Cosway, Antoinette's mother's first husband, is therefore introduced into *Wide sargasso sea*, and with him another set of at least possible relatives, Daniel and Alexander Cosway, presumably half-brothers to Antoinette – though she and others later challenge the relationship – and Alexander's son Sandi, a kind of half-nephew whom Antoinette calls cousin, and with whom she is presumed to have a (cross-generational) affair. The lack of clarity about these relationships is deliberate: Brontë's category of 'creole' is here being opened up and confronted. At one moment in *Wide sargasso sea* Rochester thinks that Antoinette looks like the servant-girl Amélie: 'Perhaps they are related, I thought. It's possible, it's even probable in this damned place' (p. 105). The 'reality' or otherwise of these family relationships remains unexplored in the text.

The significance of these shifts in the familial relationships is multiple. In one way they obviously connect with the change in the dating of the story, the Cosways becoming the old planter family destroyed by Emancipation, the Masons representing new capital from England, scornful of slavery but ignorant of the West Indies; a division entirely absent from *Jane Eyre*. As a result, Antoinette becomes a much more marginal figure even within her own society, a victim of historical forces rather than of inherited lunacy. The racial and cultural dimensions, ideologically dense in *Jane Eyre*, are unpacked in *Wide sargasso sea*. The white English 'norm' is still present, represented by Mason as well as Rochester, but the creole otherness to that norm is no longer the undifferentiated realm of the alien tropics – lunacy, sexuality, excess, so memorably articulated in the story that Rochester tells to Jane Eyre (Brontë 1934, pp. 307–8). Instead 'creole' is broken down into black, white and coloured, and further subdivided with Annette and Christophine coming from Martinique and being therefore alien to the 'English' creole of 'Jamaica'. Some interesting discussions of the novel have indeed turned on the character of Christophine, the black French creole. My suggestion is that the really troubling figures 'in the margins' of *Wide sargasso sea* are the coloured Cosways, Daniel and Alexander.

'Old' Cosway, Antoinette's father, has clear parallels with the old Lockhart whose portrait still hung in the dining-room at Rhys's family home. Like Cosway, old Lockhart's official family resulted from his second marriage. The founding father has his memorial in *Wide sargasso sea*, described in bitter tones by the illegitimate and coloured son Daniel: 'My father old Cosway, with his white marble tablet in the English church at Spanish Town for all to see. It have a crest on it and a motto in Latin and words in big black letters' (p. 101). The 'old' Lockhart (James Potter Lockhart d. 1837) was commemorated with just such a marble plaque until the hurricane of 1979 destroyed the Anglican church in Dominica.

Daniel's bitter words about the man he claims as father provide a troubling chorus to Rochester's doubts about the creole family relationships. Something of the highly mediated anxiety with which the offspring of these kinds of unofficial liaisons is invested can be gauged from the exchange between Rochester and Antoinette when they arrive for their honeymoon at Massacre, where Daniel Cosway lives. 'Who was massacred here?', Rochester asks, 'Slaves?' 'Oh no', Antoinette replies, 'Not slaves. Something must have happened a long time ago. Nobody remembers now' (p. 55). Antoinette, like Rhys, would have known very well that the 'massacre' here was the killing in 1674 of Indian Warner, the half-Carib son of one of the foremost English colonists in the West Indies, Sir Thomas Warner. Indian Warner and his Carib allies were killed by his half-brother, Philip, the legitimate son of Sir Thomas.[9]

These matters of race are negotiated by the novel in ways which take some unpacking. The dramatic events in the novel are those that deal with questions of race through confrontation, especially when the estate house, Coulibri, is burned down by black rioters, an event usually taken by Rhys herself, and by commentators on the novel, to be based on an incident from

Rhys's family history, the burning down of her grandfather's estate house in the years after Emancipation. As Rhys writes in her autobiography, with reference to Edward Lockhart: 'It was during my grandfather's life, sometime in the 1830s, that the first estate house was burnt down by the freed negroes after the Emancipation Act was passed. He was, apparently, a mild man who didn't like the situation at all' (1981, p. 33).

What interests me about this incident, and why it can become an emblem of the fraught relationship between literature and history, is that, because of *Wide sargasso sea*, this burning down of the estate house has passed into the history of Dominica as a fact. The argument has to be careful here because *Wide sargasso sea* is a fiction which makes no necessary historical claims itself: rather, readers and critics of the novel have wanted, too readily, to take Rhys's own remarks at face value and to install *Wide sargasso sea* as an 'authentic' and 'historical' response to the 'inauthentic' and 'fictional' version of West Indian creole life offered by *Jane Eyre*. What tends to be lost sight of in this view is the way in which *Wide sargasso sea* itself offers a certain kind of negotiation of its nineteenth-century materials, a 'vindication' in Rhys's own word, or perhaps better the 'compensation' referred to on the opening page of the novel as so slow in coming to the Dominican estate owners. In fact, one could say that the family history reworked in *Wide sargasso sea* already itself offers a negotiation of that material; so the work of production has at least two distinct stages to it.

The events to which the novel 'refers' were the 1844 census riots in which a series of disturbances ensued after the rumour took hold that the census was a prelude to the reintroduction of slavery. Threats were made to whites, a few stones were thrown, a few houses ransacked – but none burned down; as a result, the militia was called out, several protestors were killed and one had his head cut off and displayed on a pike to discourage others. Three hundred people were arrested, four were charged with capital offences, and one, Jean Philip Motard, executed after a trial in which the accused was given no defence. He was convicted of attempted murder for throwing a stone at a white planter; the planter received a graze on his forehead. These incidents brought the simmering personal and political tensions on the island to a boil. The Colonial Office pressed its local officials for clarification; the Anti-Slavery Society became involved and demanded an inquiry. As a result of this furore the intermittent rioting of these three days in June 1844 became known as the 'guerre nègre' and is recalled as one of the salient incidents in nineteenth-century West Indian history.[10]

Fire has symbolic power, as both *Jane Eyre* and *Wide sargasso sea* demonstrate, but there was no fire at Geneva: Mitcham House was stripped of its furnishings and some damage may have been done to its fabric, but none of the reports, either those sent to the Colonial Office or those kept in the local Minute Books, mention that the house was burned down. Statements of the value of property destroyed in the rioting, drawn up by William Elissonde of Stowe, Henry Bellot of St Patrick and Jane Maxwell Lockhart of Geneva, were forwarded to London by the local administrator, Laidlow. The Lockharts' list referred to furniture at Mitcham House: tables, chairs, glass-ware, pianos, books, pictures, and a jewel-case, to a total value of £202 19s 5d (House of Commons 1845, p. 119). It is inconceivable that a fire could have occurred and not been mentioned.[11]

So the Lockhart family memory produces a fire that – as far as can be told from written evidence – did not happen, but which becomes the key scene in a work of fiction, and is then reported by critics as an historical incident in nineteenth-century Dominica.[12] The 'memory' of something that did not happen is usually a screen-memory to occlude what did. It is clear from the documentation that Geneva Estate played an important part in the disturbances. Charles Leathem, its attorney, was, in turn, a proponent of violent response and a defender of the rights of the imprisoned peasantry (and in the course of this defence called Theodore Lockhart, probably the coloured son of James Potter Lockhart, as witness). It was on the road to Grand Bay (where the Geneva plantation was situated) that the incident occurred which led to the execution of Motard and, indeed, unusually, the execution was carried out at the scene of the crime, the better to impress its lesson upon the peasantry in the south of the island. The involvement of two Lockhart brothers was also substantial. William Brade Lockhart, Jean Rhys's great-uncle, does not appear at all within the family memories, but the initial Census Proclamation was issued in his name, and he played a significant role in the judicial procedures as Motard's executioner, claiming expenses for taking the tools of his trade by boat to Point Michel, the scene of the crime.[13]

Another brother, Edward, Rhys's 'mild' grandfather, was the subject of an investigation that went as far as the Colonial Office in London. Reports on the disturbances were dispatched by FitzRoy, Governor of the Leeward Islands, to Lord Stanley, the Colonial Secretary, in London. On 1 July 1844 FitzRoy's despatch enclosed the results of two particular investigations undertaken by Laidlaw, the acting Administrator and himself a prominent planter. The attorney for the Geneva estate, Charles Leathem, 'has been guilty of most wanton and outrageous acts of cruelty' (House of Commons 1844, p. 247). He had apparently apprehended two people who were both pinioned when he stabbed one in the groin with a bayonet and struck the other a violent blow on the head with a musket. Laidlaw reported to FitzRoy that proceedings would be instituted against this man by the Attorney-general. The other incident, referred to by FitzRoy as 'the matter of Mr. ——', he had to explain to Stanley because it referred to something not previously mentioned in the correspondence: a complaint made directly to FitzRoy by the labourers at Geneva that one of the census commissioners had 'wantonly broken into several of their cottages on finding them deserted by their owners' (p. 246). Laidlaw's comment on this case had been brief: he had had the charge investigated 'and I am happy to be able to acquit that young gentleman of any wilful intention of injuring them in the slightest degree' (p. 247). The 'young gentleman' was Edward Lockhart.

FitzRoy, under pressure from Stanley, was forced to pursue the matter of Edward Lockhart's behaviour. The two Justices of the Peace charged by Laidlaw to investigate the matter seem only to have collected an affidavit from Henry Hardcastle, schoolmaster of the Protestant school at Geneva (and therefore presumably an employee of the Lockhart family), who had been appointed enumerator for the census by Lockhart and who accompanied him on his rounds on 3 June. According to Hardcastle, Lockhart had merely rapped on three doors and windows with a small stick to see if people were home. Unfortunately the houses were so badly made that the doors and windows had fallen off. This may have convinced the JPs and Laidlaw, but it did not cut any ice with FitzRoy. He acquitted Lockhart 'of the charge of intentional violence on this occasion; but I cannot acquit him of having acted with very great indiscretion . . . I have, therefore, to request you [Laidlaw] will caution Mr. Edward Lockhart to act with greater consideration on any future occasion' (1845, p. 104). Stanley's response focuses on the behaviour of some of the commissioners 'and especially of Mr. Lockhart' as 'highly indiscreet' (p. 114). In the petition drawn up by many of the people imprisoned after the disturbances and supported by Leathem and by Charles George Falconer, the prominent radical politican, Lockhart's wanton forcing of the doors and windows 'of our little dwellings' is particularly mentioned. Most of the three hundred persons seized were guilty only 'of having fled in terror when they saw armed men coming towards their houses' (p. 123). A 'mild man' Edward Lockhart may have been; but not many British citizens in the West Indies received a personal rebuke from Lord Stanley for their role in breaking down the houses of the people whose census details they were supposed to be collecting: corda serrata pando, indeed. It is presumably no more than a coincidence that the manuscript original of *Jane Eyre* says that Mr. Rochester 'never was a mild man', whereas the printed editions amended this to 'never was a wild man' (Brontë 1969, pp. xxi).

Jean Philip Motard was executed for throwing a stone at the head of a white planter called Bremner. The following year (1845) Bremner's son married Cora Lockhart, daughter of the 'old' Lockhart who, as the original for Cosway, stands as father to Antoinette in *Wide sargasso sea*. During the burning of Coulibri in the novel, Antoinette's erstwhile black friend Tia throws a stone at her, cutting her head open. The compensations at work here, both discursive and psychological, are extremely complex, but they all work towards displacing the grotesque injustices of colonial violence with the story of an innocent childhood dream of friendship shattered by the realities of a racially-divided society. '*Even the dead* will not be safe', Walter Benjamin warned (1970, p. 257). The death of Jean Philip Motard, savagely and illegally executed in 1844, was hardly noticed at the time, so he could not exactly be said to have been 'forgotten'; but if a novel like *Wide sargasso sea* is going to be deprived of its 'locality' by the institution of Anglo-American literary criticism and made to replace and obscure a whole history of anti-colonial struggle in the smaller islands of the West Indies, then the effort of remembrance is necessary – for the better understanding both of colonial history and, ultimately, of *Wide sargasso sea* itself.

Across the seas

Wilson Harris, one of *Wide sargasso sea*'s most perceptive critics, makes the point, very much in line with what has been argued here, 'that Jean Rhys, intuitively rather than intentionally, is attempting to compensate a historical portrait of the West Indian creole' (1970, p. 10). Harris offers what he calls a 'limbo' perspective, using the name of the dance developed on the middle passage to suggest a 'gateway' or 'threshold', a 'dislocation' which allows the creole experience in its widest sense to be taken as 'a new corpus of sensibility that could translate and accommodate African and other legacies within a new architecture of culture' (p. 8). *Wide sargasso sea* is willy-nilly a West Indian novel from this perspective. For Harris, the colour of its author is irrelevant, as even is her intention in writing; indeed it seems as if *Wide sargasso sea* is West Indian to the extent to which regional myths have 'secreted themselves...unaware' (1980, p. 142) into the fabric of the novel:

> There exists in the narrow indirections of *Wide sargasso sea* that peculiar blend of opacity and transparency that alerts us to the force of the intuitive imagination in building strategies of which it *knows* yet does not *know*...The blend of opacity and transparency as figuration of groping consciousness backwards and forwards in time tends to be overlooked in fiction and in particular in a work such as *Wide sargasso sea*, which follows a deceptively straightforward narrative line broken by intrusions of abrupt fantasy populated by non-existences, non-existent voices, reappearing yet vanishing pathways and ruins pointing to the ancient estates within a succession of empires (Spanish, French, British), and to new wealth or legacies in great halls and museums of history in Europe across the seas. (1985, pp. 115–16)

The movement in this passage is exemplary: from individual consciousness and fantasy along pathways to ancient estates and finally to the museums of history across the seas. The local and the particular, even, I have suggested, the familial, should be validated as appropriate and necessary areas for post-colonial research: after all, if one of the strategies of colonial discourse is the homogenisation of cultural differences, then counter-strategies must include the affirmation of those differences, the insistence that the local and the particular do matter.

But once the local has been fixed, once the materials out of which a text has been made have been located and studied, the critical movement has finally to be outwards, towards the larger picture of which the locality forms only a part, for too easy a contrast btween *Jane Eyre* and *Wide sargasso sea* would risk missing that Charlotte Brontë and Jean Rhys do finally belong to the same world. Readings that focus on the counter-discursive strategies of *Wide sargasso sea vis-à-vis Jane Eyre*, though often carried out with impeccably radical motives, have tended to set the categories of 'colonial' and 'postcolonial' in stone, failing to see the multiple ways in which *Jane Eyre* is, in its production of its materials, already negotiating matters of West Indian slavery, even if the figure of Bertha is the only obvious textual residue of this negotiation. This is not to collapse differences but to argue for the need to understand the complex trafficking that exists between texts (and their authors) in the world, even ones that seem to invite consideration in terms of oppositions. It involves, for example, seeing the importance of the vast critical enterprise – starting in the case of *Wuthering heights* with Charlotte Brontë herself – which produced the novels of the Brontës as works of genius unconnected with the conditions of their production and sheered from the materials which went into the making of them, materials already shot through with colonial colours.[14] 'The Atlantic world' is a useful concept here, long a staple of slave-trade studies, recently given a cultural twist in Paul Gilroy's notion of a 'black Atlantic', and intriguingly already present in the deeply meditated title of Jean Rhys's novel, which names that which slows down (and therefore makes more palpable) the channels of communication which criss-cross the Atlantic: 'I thought of "Sargasso sea" or "Wide sargasso sea" but nobody knew what I meant' (Rhys 1985, p. 154).

Notes

I would like to acknowledge the helpful comments made on an earlier draft of this paper by the other participants in the symposium, and the assistance given me in beginning to trace Jean Rhys's 'local history' by Ena Williams, Lennox Honychurch, Patricia Honychurch, Janet Higbie, Daphne Agar – all of whom were interviewed in Dominica in November and December 1990 – and by Carole Angier, whose consistent encouragement and generosity with her own research materials are much appreciated.

1 Cf. 'The mad wife in *Jane Eyre* has always interested me. I was convinced that Charlotte Brontë must have had something against the West Indies and I was angry about it. Otherwise, why did she take a West Indian for that horrible lunatic, for that really dreadful creature? I hadn't really formulated the idea of vindicating the mad woman in the novel but when I was rediscovered I was encouraged to do so' (Jean Rhys, in Carter 1968, p. 5).

2 On creolisation, see Brathwaite 1971 and Glissant 1981.

3 What I refer to in this chapter as 'family history' means the stories that Jean Rhys herself recounts in her letters and autobiographical memoir (1981 and 1985); the information

contained in Carole Angier's biography (1990), which is drawn principally from Jean Beck (who had as *her* main source Jean Rhys's younger sister Brenda) and from a memoir written by Jean Rhys's brother Owen; and the family tree supplied by Norman Keith Lockhart in support of his claim for government compensation after Mitcham House was burned down in the political turmoil of 1932 (CO 152/438/9 and 444/10). This 'family history' therefore belongs to the generation born between 1883 and 1896, who would have learned about the family from their mother (or in Norman's case aunt) Minna (1853–1928), their aunt Brenda (1853–1934), and their great-aunt Jane (d. 1907), sister of Edward Lockhart's wife, Julia Woodcock. Additional information, some of which contradicts the 'family history', is drawn from a number of printed and manuscript sources, amongst the most important of which are the Morne Rouge *Register of Baptisms* (Dominica 1883–1952), papers laid before Parliament after the 1844 'disturbances' (House of Commons 1844 and 1845), transcriptions of monumental inscriptions (Oliver 1927), local records (Dominica 1844), and local newspapers. My contention – only sketched here – is that the contradictions between the two versions form a significant aspect of the local particularity needed to give a fully historical reading of *Wide Sargasso Sea*.

Recent criticism alert to matters of colonialism has been subtle in its readings of *Wide sargasso sea*: for example, O' Connor 1986, Emery 1990, Howells 1991. On memory in *Wide sargasso sea*, see Mezei 1987.

4 An important element in the postcolonial dispensation has been the re-writing of history that has gone on from school textbook to major new interpretations of the colonial period. One of the most prominent West Indian politicians at the time of independence, Eric Williams, was also the historian of his island, Trinidad, and of the whole Caribbean region. The materials to forge these new versions of the past are housed in the Special Collection rooms at the University of the West Indies campuses in Mona, Jamaica, and St Augustine, Trinidad, which provide, if not counter-discourses in any simple sense, then at least the documents supplementary or superfluous to the requirements of the metropolitan records in London, and which can therefore be used to assist the re-reading of the imperial story and the production of a narrative more appropriate to postcolonial times. In Dominica the 'national archive' is housed in the unlit cellar of the Police Traffic Department Offices, a room about six metres square. The archive is uncatalogued, unordered and virtually unusable, ravaged by weather, lack of attention and lack of resources. There is, in other words, a gross and material process of occlusion, which should not be lost sight of while attention is directed to the 'absences' that inform literary and historiographical production at the more minute, textual level.

5 Rhys MS b, folder 2. Rhys's great-grandfather was the cousin of the Lockhart who became Walter Scott's son-in-law and biographer. The story behind the family name is recounted in Scott's *Tales of a Grandfather*: 'there was one of the brave knights who was in the company of Douglas, and was appointed to take charge of the Bruce's heart homewards again, who was called Sir Simon Lockhard of Lee. He took afterwards for his device, and painted on his shield, a man's heart, with a padlock upon it, in memory of Bruce's heart, which was padlocked in the silver case. For this reason, men changed Sir Simon's name from Lockhard to Lockheart, and all who are descended from Sir Simon are called Lockhart to this day' (Scott 1851, p. 41).

6 See 'The chronology of *Jane Eyre*', in Brontë 1969, pp. 610–14.

7 'The place I have called Coulibri *existed*, and still does. It is now owned by a Syrian called Ayoub Dib (I'm not making this up – it's true). He is very fond of champagne it seems – and so am I. So I only grudge it a very little. . . . It was this Part II which was so impossibly difficult. I had no facts at all. Or rather I had one – the place. Again a real place. It was a small 'estate' my father bought. 'Coulibri' was, for Dominica, an 'old' estate – about 178-something (I rather think before that too) on sea level very fertile and so on. It had that

feeling too of that time: The place my father bought was way up – mountains, forest – oh incredibly beautiful but *wild* – I do not like writing about places much. Still – a great effort and I could be back there, remember – *be* there. The characters though had to be imagined – not one real fact' (Rhys 1985, pp. 176–7: letter to Francis Wyndham; and cf. Rhys 1981, p. 33).

8 Cf. the somewhat parallel argument about the setting of *The tempest* (Hulme 1986, pp. 106–7).

9 See the materials reproduced in Hulme and Whitehead, eds 1992, pp. 89–106. On the occasional but significant presence of the indigenous Caribs in Rhys's work see Hulme 1990. On Dominica the white Lockharts were also shadowed by their unacknowledged coloured relatives. One of old Lockhart's coloured sons was elected to the Dominica House of Assembly in 1846, the same year as Edward Lockhart, his half-brother and Jean Rhys's grandfather. His son was Alexander Lockhart, a prominent politician and journalist, who in name and relationship corresponds in *Wide sargasso sea* to Sandi Cosway, the man to whom Antoinette feels closest and who helps protect her from the threatening albino boy at the beginning of the novel. In all probability it was also this Alexander Lockhart who wrote to offer financial help to Rhys's mother following her husband's death in 1910, not long after Jean had left Dominica (Rhys MS a, p. 31). After Emancipation it was the coloured Lockharts who prospered, while the original white family sank into debt.

10 House of Commons 1844 and 1845. Any postcolonial history of Dominica has to be gleaned from the margins and footnotes of regional studies, and from reading against their grain the colonial records which, although chosen and cut according to certain criteria, are still far from monologic. In this instance, for example, the narrative that emerges from the papers laid before the House of Commons in 1844 and 1845 is by no means neutral, but it does consist of a polyphony of different voices and interests: the Dominica administration, the so-called 'mulatto ascendancy', the local colonial authorities, the Colonial Office in London, the Anti-Slavery Society and even, in heavily mediated form, at least some of the black 'rioters' themselves.

See also Nicholls 1893 for views contemporaneous with Jean Rhys's parents' generation (Nicholls was Rhys's father's superior); Honychurch 1984 and Chace 1989.

11 The jewel case is intriguing. During the fire at Coulibri Cora presumes that Annette has gone back into the house for her jewel case, when in fact she has gone back for the parrot (p. 35). In one of Freud's most famous case-histories Dora dreams of being woken by her father because of a fire: '*Mother wanted to stop and save her jewel-case; but Father said: "I refuse to let myself and my two children be burnt for the sake of your jewel-case"*' (Freud 1977, p. 99). Freud then explained the symbolic meaning of jewel cases to Dora (p. 105).

12 According to Louis James, 'Geneva estate was looted and burned' (1978, p. 47), an event Teresa O'Connor speaks of as 'recast in *Wide Sargasso Sea*' (1986, p. 20). The estate house at Geneva was burned down in 1932 during a period of unrest in which the incumbent Lockhart was very unpopular. This happened just four years before Jean Rhys returned to the island for a brief visit, and stories about the incident may have been transposed to the older family stories about the post-Emancipation riots.

13 A Minute Book of the 1844 House of Assembly records: 'That there be granted to W. B. Lockhart Esqr, Provost Marshall the sum of £13. 3. 4. sterling for extra expenses by him incurred in the Execution of a Criminal at a distance from the usual Place' (Dominica 1844, p. 27).

14 For recent work in this area, see Heywood 1987, Boumelha 1988, Chrisman 1990, Meyer 1991.

Different kinds of connection might also be made. One of very earliest pieces of Charlotte Brontë's writing to survive describes a childhood game in which she, Emily, and Branwell each chose an island and then decided who they would like to live there, tiny fictional utopias occupied by their favourite characters from the contemporary world. Emily's choices were Walter Scott, James Gibson Lockhart (his son-in-law and biographer) and Johnny Lockhart, Scott's grandson to whom the *Tales of a grandfather* were directed, including the story of how the Lockharts had got their name (Brontë 1987, p. 6). Rhys's family was already part and parcel of the Brontës' childhood.

The recalcitrant object: culture contact and the question of hybridity

ANNIE E. COOMBES

a willingness to descend into that alien territory ... may reveal that the theoretical recognition of the split-space of enunciation may open the way to conceptualizing an international culture, based not on the exoticism or multi-culturalism of the diversity of cultures, but on the inscription and articulation of culture's hybridity. (Bhabha 1988, p. 22)

hybridity, impurity, intermingling, the transformation that comes of new and unexpected combinations of human beings, cultures, ideas, politics, movies, songs. (Salman Rushdïe, cited in Wollen 1990, p. 57)

Since 1986 a new phenomenon has flowered in the cultural institutions at the heart of the western metropolitan centre: a series of exhibitions which claimed to disrupt radically the boundaries of that diad the 'west' and its 'other', the relationship of centre to periphery.[1] In fact each went even further and declared itself the harbinger, if not the representative, of a new 'post-colonial' consciousness.[2] In curatorial terms, a shared feature of all these exhibitions was the prioritising of transculturated objects, both as the ultimate sign of a productive culture contact between the western centres and those groups on the so-called 'periphery' and as the visible referent of the self-determination of those nations once subjugated under colonial domination.

More specifically, the cultural object was to be the primary signifier of a cultural, national and ethnic identity which proclaimed and celebrated its integrity and 'difference' from the centres of western capitalism. But it was also to be the sign of a mutually productive culture contact – an exchange. To accomplish this the curators deliberately selected cultural production which straddled a number of different taxonomies, objects designated at various moments as the domains of ethnography, science, popular culture and fine art.

This chapter explores some of the difficulties arising from the use of this particular curatorial strategy and the extent to which it actually offers a productive challenge to the eurocentrism of the western art establishment or simply a more complex revision of the primitivist fantasies of early modernism. I would like to add that my analysis is underwritten by a tacit recognition of hybridity as an important cultural strategy for the political project of decolonisation.[3] For me the problem is not to question the validity of hybridity, either as a strategy of oppositional identity ('roots revivalism') or as an instance of creative transactional transculturation. I take both as contingent and conditional. As Stuart Hall and Benita Parry have done elsewhere, I would argue for a strategic essentialism (Hall 1990; Parry below; see also Lloyd below). The focus of this chapter is rather to interrogate the ways in which 'hybridity' is transformed and to what effect, in the narratives of the western art and ethnographic museum, and to ask what relations of power and transgression it can still articulate there.[4]

One of the difficulties of appropriating 'hybridity' as a sign of post-colonial self-determination is that, as a cultural concept and as a descriptive term for the cultural object itself, it already has a particular pedigree in the discourse of both art history and anthropology as surrealist, pop, folk art or popular versions of historical cultural practices redefined for a commercial market. The meanings and values of each category shift of course, according to complex historical and social relations. Yet more often than not, such exhibitions demonstrate a curious resistance to addressing the implications of such potentially contradictory categories. Even the more obvious dialogical relation imposed by the distinct institutional contexts, the ethnographic museum on the one hand and the museum of fine art on the other, are not often seriously considered.[5] This is all the more remarkable in a curatorial project dedicated to a strategic reassessment of the relationship of the west and its 'other', since both sites are subject to different institutional and disciplinary histories directly implicated in both world capitalism and colonialism.

Successfully relocating the cultural object as a sign of processes of cultural assimilation, appropriation and transformation requires, perhaps, a more self-conscious acknowledgement of the ways in which this object, and, more specifically, cultural objects assigned to an 'other' (whether in terms of nationality, ethnicity, class or gender), are already circumscribed at any given moment. Not only in terms of the weight of meanings attributed to them through ethnography or anthropology, or the predominantly modernist paradigm of conventional art history, but also in terms of the competing definitions established by their presence in a variety of institutional and educational practices in the public sphere.

In Britain for example, during the stringent economic cut-backs characteristic of the 1980s, the local and national museum has ironically come into its own. Through transformations in marketing and policy, the museum has become both a vital component in the reclaiming and defining of a concept of collective memory on the local level and, on the national level, an opportune site for the reconstituting of certain cultural icons as part of a common 'heritage': a 'heritage' often produced as a spectacle of essentialist 'national' identity, with the museum frequently serving as the site for the nostalgic manufacture of a consensual past in the lived reality of a deeply divided present.[6]

Simultaneously, as the central argument against the restitution of cultural property, western museums proclaim the internationalism of museum culture as irrefutable 'proof' of their neutrality and objectivity and as justification for their self-appointed role as cultural custodians. Finally, multicultural educational initiatives from within the western metropolitan centres have heralded a new and possibly more self-reflexive conception for the ethnographic museum, despite debate on the relative merits of an intitiative which may well be multicultural without necessarily being anti-racist.[7] Resultant questions about constituency have been taken on by some anthropologists and ethnographers. These have revived a concern with the political implications of anthropological practice and the way anthropological knowledge is used that has been dormant since Kathleen Gough's and others' searing critiques of their own discipline at the height of American intervention in Vietnam.[8]

Any cultural object is of course recuperable to some degree. But in particular such ambiguity has always been intrinsic to western consumption of material culture from erstwhile colonies. Paradoxically however, this same material culture is simultaneously awarded the status of visible referent – the ultimate sign – of cultural and social value, replete with immanent meaning. Further complications follow once such objects are assigned an aesthetic value apparently commensurate with western standards, while at the same time they are declared as embodying other and different but equally valid criteria for determining cultural value. An ambitious project! Most recently these complexities have been neatly resolved by the liberal white curatorial establishment in terms of a recognition, celebration and reassertion of 'difference' through an apparently magnanimous acceptance of plurality and cultural diversity.

One of the difficulties with any exhibition which foregrounds hybridity is that while it may recognise and celebrate the polysemic nature of the objects on display, it often disavows the complexity of the ways in which this is articulated across a series of relations at the level of the social, not only in the culture of origin but also in the dominant culture of the host institution. I would argue that while the celebration of cultural diversity may well produce productive reassessments of certain racial and cultural stereotypes, the use of 'difference' and 'diversity' as analytical devices for the dissipation of grand narratives can ultimately produce a homogenising and levelling effect that has serious consequences.[9] As a curatorial strategy its fluidity actively undermines the potential of such exhibitions to explore and explode the means by which differentiation reproduces the experience of multiple but specific forms of social and political disempowerment.[10] More importantly, what this also means is that the ways in which the host institution and its ideal constituency is implicated in such discriminatory practices remain shrouded in mystery.

The celebration of 'difference' is a strategy which is particularly pernicious when mobilised in the sphere of visual culture precisely because of the way in which the site of its public consumption – the art or ethnographic museum – is predicated on a 'visibility' which reaffirms and naturalises the apparent transparency of meaning invested in the object. What might by now seem to be a commonplace observation – that the cultural object can never be an empty vessel waiting to be filled with meaning, but rather is a repository replete with meanings that are never immanent but always contingent – is evidently not to be taken for granted.

The ways in which such 'visibility' is mediated by an aesthetic considera-tion is especially significant in the post-colonial context. Of course the west's advocation of aesthetic criteria for evaluating material culture from the colonies or from independant nation states with a history of colonial sub-jugation is not, and never has been, an unqualifiedly progressive move.[11] While it has sometimes had the potential to disrupt and fracture certain assumptions of racial and cultural inferiority, it has always been fraught with more or less productive contradictions. When public ethnographic collections were established in Britain for example, at the end of the nineteenth century, their effectivity on a number of competing levels, indeed their very existence, depended precisely on promoting the material in the collection as simul-taneously fodder for the purportedly disinterested scientific and comparative study of culture, as visible 'evidence' of racial inferiority (and therefore as justification of colonial intervention), but also in their capacity as objects of aesthetic pleasure, exotic delectation and spectacle.[12]

The present historical conjuncture finds us at the crossroads of postmodern critiques of the alienating effects of commodity culture on the one hand and on the other the celebration of the liberating possibilities opened up by the subsequent demise of certain historical models now dismissed as hopelessly teleological. Perhaps this might be a good moment to reassess some of the more complex ways in which 'difference' is articulated across race, class and gender relations in highly specific ways. This is especially important if we are to avoid the uncritical celebration in museum culture of a hybridity which threatens to collapse the heterogeneous experience of racism into a scopic feast where the goods on display are laid out for easy consumption in ever more enticing configurations, none of which actually challenge or expose the ways in which such difference is constituted and operates as a mechanism of oppression.

In order to elaborate the intricate ways in which questions of aesthetic value, authenticity and racial purity (all of which the term 'hybridity' gives rise to) are formulated across a number of specific registers in relation to the colonial subject and are immediately implicated at the level of social and political experience, I want to go back to 1897, to a particular moment in the disciplinary history of British ethnography. It was a moment when debates over the assignation of aesthetic value to material culture from the colonies devolved around precisely the issue of 'hybridity' translated in terms of racial purity which masked at a much deeper level an intense anxiety over miscegenation.

The objects in question are the so-called Benin 'bronzes' which for some time now have shared centre stage with the 'Elgin' or, more accurately, 'Parthenon' marbles in the restitution debate.[13] In both Nigeria and Greece, this cultural property is constituted as an indispensable component in the formation of a national identity.[14] Successive British governments, on the other hand, have argued for their continued custody of this property on the basis of the 'internationalism' of museum culture, while at the same time asserting the bronzes' and marbles' significance as part of a 'British' national heritage (Coutts-Smith 1991, pp. 14–31). These objects then obviously fall into the categories of 'ambivalent', 'polysemic' and, less ambiguously and more importantly, politically and economically 'contingent'. The complex trajectory of these prestigious court objects whose significance continues to be fraught with contradiction and ambiguity, provides a useful means of exploring the peculiar ways in which museum ethnography and its attendant concern with questions of authenticity and cultural value, its preoccupation with taxonomic, disciplinary and institutional boundaries, has often been at the centre of definitions of race and national identity in the popular consciousness. In another sense also the bronzes and ivories from Benin are peculiarly appropriate since they represent the paradigm 'hybrid' or transculturated object and one which both narrativises the colonial encounter (in this case with the Portuguese), while also being a partial product of that contact.[15]

I

As late as 1908, anthropology in Britain was still in the process of making its debut as a discipline, a situation which made it expedient to court opinion on three fronts: the state, the general public and academia (Coombes 1988). The complex and often antagonistic national, institutional and disciplinary interests invested in the development of material culture studies in Britain, and the corresponding rise of anthropology as a professional domain between 1890 and 1920, ensured its ambivalent role, even in this early period, as both perpetrator and fracturer of certain racial stereotypes. Nowhere is this more clearly demonstrated than over the battle for the acquisition of the Benin ivories and bronzes, and the ensuing debate over the degree and nature of their aesthetic merit.

In September 1897 the British Museum put on public exhibition some three hundred cast brass plaques from Benin. Intrigued and perplexed that work of such technical expertise and naturalism had been found in such quantities in Africa, the national, local, scientific and middle-class illustrated press all postulated hypotheses to 'explain' the paradox. Indeed a factor which made the Benin incident such a perfect vehicle for anthropologists' campaign for academic and state validation was precisely its currency for a broad spectrum of the literate public in Britain.

On the one hand the discovery of the bronzes and ivories looted by the British from the royal court of Benin inspired such statements as: 'The discovery of these treasures resembles that of a valuable manuscript. They are a new "Codex Africanus", not written on fragile papyrus, but in ivory and imperishable brass' (Dalton 1898a, p. 419). On the other hand Benin society was summarily dismissed in altogether different terms: 'Although little authentic knowledge of the Benin people is current, the main character-istics of the surrounding tribes are thought to be theirs also in an intensified degree, finding expression in habits of disgusting brutality and scenes of hideous cruelty and bloodshed, ordained by the superstitions of a degraded race of savages'.[16] This chapter is about the conditions which enable(d) such apparently mutually exclusive appraisals to co-exist.

The emphasis on Benin as a 'degraded' race is an important feature of the representation of certain peoples prior to and during colonisation. It was a concept already familiar in Britain, in relation to the representation of what was euphemistically referred to as the 'Orient' (Said 1978; Nochlin 1991; Graham-Brown 1988). The terms 'decay', 'deterioration' and 'degradation' were mobilised in the Benin context, partly because they were a convenient means of undermining the all too substantial evidence of an ancient and thriving society in Africa which displayed all those signs associated with European definitions of civilisation. The popular narratives and 'first-hand' accounts of the punitive expedition enhanced this idea of Benin through a particularly potent juxtaposition of text and image. Though often not explicit, the correspondence between text and image in the middle-class illustrated press had the effect of implicitly reinforcing the sense of Benin as degraded and degenerate. Two aspects of this far-reaching preoccupation with 'degen-eracy' are worth going into in some detail – the representation of Benin women and of the city itself.[17]

II

Immediately after Benin forces ambushed and killed the Acting Consul-General Phillips and some of his entourage, the *Illustrated London News* for 23 January 1897 published an article denouncing Benin society as having 'a native population of grovelling superstition and ignorance'. Alongside was an apparently unrelated photograph entitled 'A native chief and his followers' showing a group of women sitting around the central figure of a man (fig. 1). The group of figures seems, from a contemporary European perspective, to be

Fig. 1 'A native chief and his followers'
Illustrated London news, 23 January 1897, p. 123

impassive and static. In the foreground two women are literally 'arranged' to 'frame' the image. The whole represents a posed ensemble which does not fit easily into the 'ethnographic' racial 'type' category nor yet a formal portrait. It is in fact a confusion of both taxonomies. While the 'native chief' is the central figure compositionally, it is the women who predominate and who arrest the eye. The nudity of the foreground women is both masked and accentuated because of their uncomfortable pose. This was partly because their objectification was reinforced by the fact that this was clearly not a 'natural' posture. They had evidently been 'put' there. To clinch this objectification their bodies signified as the human equivalent of the 'trophy' display which was so popular at this time with both ethnographer and big game hunter alike.

This is a recurrent feature of representations of not only Edo but other African women in the British illustrated press. Similar compositional devices were used in different contexts. A photograph in the *Reliquary*, a scientific publication with a readership of amateur and professional archaeologists, ethnographers and folklorists, employed the same motif ostensibly to illustrate bells on Benin women's girdles (fig. 2). To the viewer the bells must have seemed rather incidental since they are difficult, if not almost impossible, to make out (Quick 1900, p. 227). It is again the body, rather than the bells,

Fig. 2 'Benin girls with aprons of bells',
Reliquary, 6 (October 1900), p. 227

which is actually held up for inspection here. The 'scientific' aegis of the journal operated here is a specific way in relation to the image. Together with the same compositional framing device as the previous illustration, this photograph's additional status as 'document' rendered even more respectable such overt nudity and any sexual connotation implied, in much the same way that the familiar convention of mythologising the nude in western fine art supposedly masked the sexuality of the sitter sufficiently to render nudity inoffensive to bourgeois sensibilities.

In the context of the representation of Benin as a degenerate society, it is significant as it is banal that all the women in these close-up photographs are only partially clothed, while photographs in the illustrated press of those West Africans who had acknowledged British sovereignty were pointedly shown fully clothed.[18] This is not necessarily to suggest that the camera was not reproducing what was visible in some instances. Rather I want to emphasise that this is a reiteration of the old adage that while nakedness signified 'uncivilised', clothing was an obvious appurtenance of 'civilisation'. Consequently such juxtapositions reinforced this distinction. The fact that such assumptions could be made visible through the medium of the photograph lent a veracity that the old lithographs which had until recently been the mainstay of the illustrations in the popular press could not compete with.

Similarly, although the title of the first illustration suggests nothing about the relationship of the women to the central figure, it was presumed that they were his wives. While that favoured topic of orientalist paintings, the harem, was a familiar sign linking Islam with degeneracy, the practice of polygamy in African societies was not a ready-made genre. And yet as a sign it was irrevocably tied to African degeneracy. Debates and discussion on the topic of polygamy in African society were common in a variety of arenas. An attack on polygamy was often at the heart of arguments against the slave trade from the Anti-Slavery Society and the Aborigine Protection Society, particularly when Arab traders were involved, since this provided the perfect alibi for dual assault on slavery and Islam. Similarly the various missionary societies with interests in Africa (or indeed in India) never missed an opportunity to launch an offensive on Islam (or in the case of India, Hinduism), and polygamy was a key pawn in their defence of Christian values (Bolt 1971, pp. 112–13). At the same time others with the ear of different publics were busy defending the practice. Mary Kingsley, inveterate traveller, champion of British trading enterprise in West Africa, entomologist and self-styled ethnographer, was adamant about the cause of any degeneration on the West African coast. In a statement which echoed many West African 'patriots', she claimed, 'I know perfectly well that there is a seething mass of infamy, degradation, and destruction going on among the Coast natives. I know, humanly speaking, what it comes from . . . for it is the natural consequence of the breaking down of an ordered polygamy into a disordered monogamy.'[19] The practice of polygamy in representations of the colonised subject in Britain is more complex than I have space to deal with here. But it frequently functioned as an unspoken indictment of certain African societies while the additional comment in the text, 'the women develop, as usually in these regions, at a very early age', effectively positions the African woman ambiguously in the category of both victim of pagan practices and libidinous degenerate. Thus from the complacent vantage point of moral high ground the colonial gaze could scrutinise with impunity.[20]

Another feature of first-hand accounts is the way in which a degenerate topography is mapped for the city itself. T. B. Auchterlonie's narrative of a voyage to Benin City on New Year's Day 1890, delivered to the Royal Geographical Society in the wake of the 1897 expedition, starts by clarifying his use of adjectives such as 'New' and 'Old' or 'black' to describe different aspects of Benin. Old Benin was distinguished from 'New' Benin chiefly because of refusing British trading links. In common with most accounts of Benin City directly after the punitive raid, Auchterlonie introduces the sights and smells of human sacrifice early in the narrative, and refers to Benin as being in a state of crumbling decrepitude (Auchterlonie 1898, p. 7). On the other hand 'Old Calabar', Warri and Sapele, in what is called 'New Benin' were held up as examples of the prosperity which supposedly came with

British trade. The use of the adjective 'black' is of course a historically familiar device for emphasising the malevolent character of 'Old' Benin.[21] That it also happens to be the colour ascribed to the African's skin carried with it consequences which ensured the derogatory connotations of the term.[22] Similarly, in the *Illustrated London news* account of the lead up to the punitive raid, drawings of a European boat (the Hindustan Government hulk at Benin) together with the ordered ranks of 'loyal' African troops on the main deck of the *George Shotton* and at the British trade post Old Calabar juxtaposed with a rambling and dilapidated local town cannot escape comparison.

One reason for discussing some of the drawings and photographs published in the illustrated press is that their circulation extended beyond their own readership. Different versions of the same illustrations appeared in specialist and scientific journals to accompany eye-witness accounts or ethnographic studies. Through this repetition they gained particular currency as 'objective' visual documentation.[23] Consequently, these representations played a crucial role in providing a context for the Benin ivories and bronzes that were later displayed to a British public who had already consumed Benin through such reports and images.

III

While the popular narratives and first-hand accounts tend for the most part to use the concept of degeneration to reinforce a series of predictable stereotypes, the term takes on a rather different gloss in the aesthetic treatises concerning Benin culture produced by the anthropological community. Here degeneration plays a rather more ambivalent role in the representation of Africa to diverse sections of the British public, but one which was no less symptomatic of vested political interests – this time of an institutional and disciplinary nature.

Significantly the point at which ethnologists decided to intervene in the debate over the origin of the Benin bronzes was precisely at the moment when the paradox of technical sophistication and social savagery threatened a break with the evolutionary paradigm, which up to that time had also supplied the classificatory principles under which most collections of material culture from the colonies were organised. The concept of degeneration was summoned up as an aesthetic principle which would appease anxiety over these recalcitrant objects that refused to conform to comfortably familiar taxonomic solutions. And it is this articulation of the concept of degeneration, as part of a systematic evolutionary schema for explaining the origins of all art, which provides a nuance for the concept that exploits but also belies its immediate association with racial denigration.

In Britain, Lane Fox Pitt Rivers, Henry Balfour and Alfred Haddon were the earliest anthropologists who, operating in the more general public sphere as curators of large public ethnographic collections, also promoted the degenerationist thesis (as it came to be known), in terms of an aesthetic evaluation of material culture from the colonies (Haddon 1895; Balfour 1893). The theories laid out by these anthropologists were in direct opposition to most previous attempts to explain the 'origin' of art. These usually expounded a development beginning with geometric form and culminating in naturalism. The protagonists of the degenerationist school believed that, through carefully plotted sequences, they could 'prove' the opposite: the linear development of ornament from naturalistic to geometric and abstract.[24] Their method was characterised by a systematic analysis of the formal or stylistic elements of different objects in an attempt to produce a unified subject.

On the one hand this thesis represents a clearly overdetermined evolutionist account. On the other, the degenerationists were also at pains to point out that while the move to abstraction might be the result of unconscious variation (following the Darwinian model of 'accidental' evolution), this tendency might also be due to the producers' conscious decision and invention. Since both Balfour's and Haddon's examples were drawn from African and Papuan New Guinean societies, their arguments obviously offered the possibility of acknowledging an alternative aesthetic motivation currently denied to these societies. Crucially then, this attempt at producing a unified colonial subject which fitted neatly into the evolutionary mould was thwarted at every turn not only by the internal inconsistencies of the thesis itself but also because of the ambivalence of the term 'degenerate' as it was articulated across a range of discourses within Britain, from aesthetics to social policy. And it is paradoxically this gap that allows for both the possibility of a re-evaluation of material culture from the colonies and also its significance as a constituent of national culture within Britain.

One instance of the more progressive potential of this idiosyncratic thesis was that Haddon had already promoted it specifically as an antidote to the prevailing art historical view of art as a work of individual, inspired genius. According to Haddon's and Balfour's critics within the art historical establishment, 'in art there is no such thing as evolution but more or less isolated and veritable "creations" – for their [Balfour's and Haddon's] law cannot by searching be found out by men whose genius is true divinity' (Birdwood 1903). Haddon's retort would not be out of place in some current critiques of formalist art history:

There are two ways in which decorative art may be studied; these may be briefly defined as the 'aesthetic' and the 'scientific'. The former deals with all manifestations of art from a purely subjective point of view, and classifies objects according

to certain so-called 'canons of art'. These may be the generally recognised rules of
the country or race to which the critic belongs, and may even have the sanction of
antiquity. Or they may simply be due to the idiosyncrasy of the critic himself.
(Haddon 1894, p. 1)

Haddon and the other degenerationists proposed instead a comparative
analysis of all decorative art, both European and non-western, as a branch of
biology, mediated by environmental factors. The cultural relativism implied
by the suggestion that all art was subject to the same determining factors of
environmental conditions and material circumstances of production did more
than simply undermine the myth of individual genius.

One of the other effects of this debate was self-consciously to oppose art-
historical definitions of cultural value by qualifying anthropology's particular
contribution to the study of material culture – not only of the colonies but
also closer to home.[25] At a moment when anthropologists were fighting for
recognition as a scientific and academic discipline with a wide range of
applications and use-values, this could only count in their favour. Furthermore the biological basis of the degenerationist thesis, grounded as it was in a
theory of racial purity, had other important implications for more specific
debates around the nature of the Englishness of British art which were
currently resurfacing in the art-historical establishment.

Certain prominent critics and historians had already proposed that naturalism was somehow a precondition, if not an inherent property of true English
art – a property which was taken as irrefutable proof of the moral health of
the nation. Conventional or abstract tendencies, on the other hand, were
evidence of moral decline and degeneration. In this scenario, the morally
degenerate examples were drawn from the decorative art of various colonies
or from the celtic Irish tradition currently being revived as part of the cultural
nationalist movement within Ireland (Sheehy 1980; Dean 1988; Vaughan
1990, pp. 11–23). The relation of such xenophobia to the anxiety over
resurgent Irish nationalism needs no rehearsal here. The potential threat to
the moral integrity of English art posed by that aspect of Haddon's and
Balfour's thesis which suggested a more positive espousal of a non-European
geometric idiom, coupled with the indisputable 'fact' of naturalism in the
Benin bronzes themselves, is also clear in this context.

However, the degenerationist thesis had other features which further complicated its relationship to the idea of racial purity. In order for the theory to
work and fulfil the ultimate objective of most anthropological treatises on
aesthetics at this time (the elucidation of contemporary 'man's' creative
drive), it was deemed necessary to focus on those societies which conformed
to E. B. Tylor's earlier concept of a 'survival' (Tylor 1871; Burrow 1966). In
Balfour's book *The Evolution of Decorative Art*, two categories of 'survival'
are defined: primitive and degenerate. While certain societies are described as

'lowest on the scale of civilisation, whose condition of culture is in the most primitive of existing states', others are proposed as degenerate races. These were societies which, having 'in former times enjoyed a higher civilisation', now resided in a state of retrogression or degeneration – although interestingly enough this was a condition laid squarely at the door of the coloniser in this instance (Balfour 1893, p. 14). Aboriginal Australians and Tasmanians for example, were deemed truly 'primitive', since they had remained outside of the contaminating sphere of white contact until what is described in Balfour's treatise as 'their ruthless extermination by the savage methods of intruding civilisation, which resulted in their complete extinction in 1876' (p. 15).

However, such nostalgic reverie for the lost sanctity of originary unity was not always accompanied by so explicit a critique of colonial intervention. Haddon, for example, suggested that 'impurities' in race led to regrettable impurities in form: 'It will often be found that the more pure or the more homogeneous a people are, the more uniformity will be found in their art work, and that florescence of decorative art is a frequent result of race mixture' (Haddon 1894, p. 252).

Consequently, a thesis which in the context of art-historical debates had the power to rupture the xenophobic association of naturalism with moral stability as an intrinsic property of the English could, in the context of the discussions around the Benin bronzes, be mobilised to other rather less progressive ends. Back at the British Museum, the thesis provided the curators of the ethnographic material, Read and Dalton, with the opportunity of safely comparing the Benin mastery of the technically complex *cire perdu* process with the work of the Italian Renaissance and conceding that the castings were probably produced by a people long acquainted with the art of metal casting, while at the same time continuing to assign the Edo peoples to a state of savage degeneration. The apparent absence in most eye-witness accounts of any contemporary Benin work of similar naturalism, coupled with the apparent tendency towards 'florescence' of surface ornament in what were deemed later examples, ensured that there was no danger here of their interpretation transgressing the theory of degeneration in either its 'scientific' and aesthetic aspect (via anthropology) or the specifically racialised aspect already disseminated in the middle-class illustrated press.

One of the reasons why the more progressively disruptive potential of the degenerationist thesis could be disregarded, was precisely because of the way in which notions of racial purity had already acquired particular currency in another domain. The terms 'primitive' and 'degenerate' were familiar through their use in a context far closer to home. Discourses on health and racial purity produced through medicine, philanthropy and eugenics in the work of Francis Galton and, later, Saleeby and Pearson ensured the topicality of such theories. In this context the focus on racial purity was a symptom of anxiety over the degeneration of the 'imperial' Aryan race. Medical research and social surveys indicated an alarming decline in the state of health of the working classes, which in turn had generated concern by certain sectors over the social circumstances of the mass of the population (Booth 1892–1903; Rowntree 1901).

The ensuing debate, however, around the question of deterioration versus degeneration was exacerbated by the eugenists who were still mostly convinced of the inherited, rather that environmental determinants of such a decline in the nation's health. Consequently, while the findings provided the impetus for preventative health initiatives, they also provoked a public campaign for the surveillance and categorisation of those considered racially degenerate and unfit.[26] A. C. Haddon, and other anthropologists who were proponents of the degenerationist thesis applied to aesthetics, had already supplied expertise in physical anthropology and anthropometry techniques and statistics for Galton's work on systematic race regeneration and population control within the British Isles. Evidently then such terms as 'degeneration' had a particular resonance for certain ethnic, class and gender constituencies within Britain.

Another feature of this preoccupation with racial purity was the way in which evidence of this could supposedly be deduced from the physiognomy of the subject. Consequently the eighteenth-century principle that physiognomic characteristics were accurate indicators of intellect and morality acquired new potency in the early twentieth century through the eugenic movement's insistence on the visibility of moral, intellectual and racial degeneracy as physical traces left on the body and susceptable to mapping by the 'specialist' – be 'he' medic or anthropologist.

In the public domain, the ethnographic collection deliberately exploited this connection between eugenics, racial purity and the body. The body became the sign of the relationship between the inherited and cultural features of any race.[27] Consequently photographs, casts of the face or of the body, were almost always included to enhance the display of material culture from the colonies. In fact it was precisely because of the ambivalence of material culture as an index of race and culture, particularly once it had crossed into the register of the aesthetic, that the body becomes an essential component in fixing the object as a sign of racial purity or degeneracy. Small wonder, then, at the colonial fascination with the 'body' of Benin subjects and the neat topographic degeneracy mapped on to the city in both popular and scientific press.

It was this contradictory intersection of anthropological, medical and aesthetic discourse around the issue of degeneration, coupled with the exigencies of the demands for a professional status for ethnography, that precipitated the question of the origin of the Benin bronzes in the late nineteenth century into a national issue and transformed the bronzes into a symbol of national pride within Britain.

IV

In 1899 the British Museum's ethnographic curators, Read and Dalton, published a special presentation book entitled *Antiques from the city of Benin and other parts of West Africa in the British Museum*. This contained several significant shifts from their earlier argument regarding the origin of the bronzes. Both curators had initially rested their case on a Portuguese or Egyptian origin. By 1899, however, they were prepared to concede that although certain aspects of the ornamentation might be attributable to the Egyptians, the Benin material may well have preceded, or at any rate come into being independently of, Egyptian counterparts.[28]

What does the admissability of an African origin signify at such a moment? I would argue that the degree to which the Benin aesthetic is assigned an African origin corresponds partly to the stepping-up of pressure from ethnologists and anthropologists in the Museum for government recognition and financial support. Furthermore, the course of Read's and Dalton's argument for an African origin is inextricably linked to the fortunes of the Ethnographic Department within the British Museum.[29] Unlike the thriving department of Egyptology, ethnography was granted the status of an autonomous department only in 1941. It is within this context that the possibility of claiming an African origin for the bronzes becomes a viable strategy for both the Ethnographic Department's struggle in its bid for recognition within the Museum and for the Museum's bid for more government funds.

Initially the ethnographic curators assumed that the brass plaques on loan from the Foreign Office would become the property of the Museum through the Trustees' acquisition. By 1898, the year of Read's and Dalton's first publication, it was clear that a much smaller proportion of the loot remained in the Museum's possession than originally hoped. Over a third of the series had already been sold off as revenue for the Protectorate. The ensuing public auction aroused much bitterness amongst Museum staff with an interest in the affairs of the Ethnographic Department. To compound this frustration, Dalton visited Germany and in June 1898 published a report on the large-scale acquisition being made in African ethnography especially in Berlin, with the financial and moral support of the Kaiser. Following a detailed account of the facilities afforded museum ethnographers in Germany and a breakdown on annual government expenditure, Dalton observed that 'in almost every section . . . it leaves the Ethnographical Gallery at the British Museum far behind' (Dalton 1898b). His paper also stipulated that the Director of the Berlin Museum für Volkerkunde alone had already spent £1,000, chiefly in

England, on the very Benin material for which the British Museum was unable to get government funds.

The cry of 'national heritage' was taken up by the British press, which similarly couched its arguments in terms of British competition with Germany – a strategy calculated to inspire a sense of nationalist indignation. Details of the few 'fine bronze heads' (as they were now described) in the British Museum collection, were compared with the thirty or forty acquired for Berlin through the Kaiser's patronage. The German threat was also a card consistently played by anthropologists in their bid for popular and government support. And the insistency with which this competition was stressed is commensurate with the perceived increasing threat posed by Germany to Britain's imperial supremacy.[30]

Clearly while the ethnographic communities' hypotheses on the origin of the bronzes effectively produced knowledge that threatened to disturb the equilibrium of racial superiority that legitimised the colonial process, such knowledge was mediated by its function in the struggle for professional and institutional validation for the new 'science' of anthropology.[31] The Ethnographic Department was able to capitalise on the visibility of the Benin bronzes in the public domain as both evidence of barbaric savagery and artistic anomaly, in order to claim their retention as a matter of national urgency. This strategy had the additional benefit of enhancing the Department's own status in the eyes of both the government and the museum. The ethnographic curators' decision to assign an African (as opposed to Egyptian) origin to the 'bronzes' enabled them to foreground the importance of ethnography as opposed to the already well-endowed Egyptology department in the museum.

Similarly while certain aspects of the anthropological knowledge on Benin suggested definitions and values which contradicted some of those stereotypes promulgated in the popular middle-class illustrated press, the fact that Benin was consistently treated as an anomaly of African culture by anthropologists ensured that the more racialised sense of the term 'degenerate' popularised by the press accounts was always inherent in descriptions of Benin culture. Furthermore one of the effects of anthropologists' desire to be seen as indispensable to the colonial government, and thereby obtain both recognition for the establishment of the discipline and state funding, was that they used ethnography (and museums) as a way of broadening their popular appeal. This had, as in the case of Benin, particularly pernicious results. The popularisation of the science meant that a highly selective and doctored version of anthropological theory was appropriable by parties with distinct vested interests in colonisation. Paradoxically anthropology's accessibility speeded the disintegration of a division between the 'scientific' and 'popular' that it sought to maintain. At the same time it ensured that the popular stereotype of African, and in this case Benin, culture was able to derive more credibility through its relationship to the supposedly separate sphere of scientific knowledge.

V

At various moments in the history of western imperialism, different colonial powers have used the 'visibility' of the museum to set up initiatives which were as dependent on the rhetoric of equal access that we hear so much about now. In Britain in the 1850s, and again in the Edwardian era, for example, this was invoked in no uncertain terms. The museum was heralded as 'the most democratic and socialistic possession of the people. All have equal access to them, peer and peasant receive the same privileges and treatment.'[32] Museums occupied a territory apparently 'neutral' enough to provide what was seen as a 'common' meeting-ground for children from 'different class backgrounds' – the basis in fact of an objective education. Again in 1903 the ethnographic museums' potential as a 'scientific' and therefore 'objective' educational tool which cut across ethnic and national boundaries as well as those of class was affirmed through an initiative which aimed to bring children in different parts of the Empire in contact with one another and 'get them acquainted' with each other's lifestyles. Today, of course, in England and elsewhere, multiculturalism has other implications contingent on the different experiences of diverse social groups living in a white patriarchy. I would argue, however, that it is precisely under the banner of a form of multiculturalism that those exhibitions uncritically celebrating cultural 'diversity', through the primary strategy of displaying culturally hybrid objects from once colonised nations, can claim immunity from addressing the specificity of this experience. They ultimately invoke as misleading a rhetoric of equality as those earlier manifestations, laying claim to an impossible relativism that declares objectivity at the expense of a recognition of the multiple political interests at stake in such an initiative.

Evidently the preoccupation with originary unity and the emphasis on racial purity which characterised much of the aesthetic discourse around material culture from the colonies in the early part of this century have been challenged to some degree by the current celebration of hybridity.[33] Clearly it would be overdetermined to suggest a tidy continuum between the ideologies that marked the formation of anthropology as a discipline in the early twentieth century, and the present 'post-colonial' context. And yet the western curatorial establishment's predilection for a certain selective hybridised object smacks to me of some residual unease not unrelated to this earlier moment. Is it, I wonder, so far fetched to suggest that such an object functions in fact as a fetish, in the sense that it effectively displaces a continued anxiety over racial mixing – of miscegenation, and the social and political implications of this? In any case we need to be clear about the sort of shifts in significance which are possible for cultural objects with such a legacy once visual displays do acknowledge transculturation.

Again certain aspects of the professionalisation of anthropology, particularly in France and Britain, warrant elaboration. As a means of validating the expansion of ethnographic collections, the rhetoric most frequently employed was (and still is) the necessity of conserving and preserving the material culture in the museum's custody, in the face of what was taken to be the inevitable extinction of the producers themselves.[34] Paradoxically of course, anthropology's desire for government recognition as an academic discipline and its need for state funding, necessitated its aiding and abetting this extinction by proposing itself as an active agent in colonial subjugation. While speeding the inevitability of such destruction, anthropologists boosted the already multiple values assigned to the discipline's objects of study, thus enhancing the status of anthropological knowledge, while simultaneously ensuring that the producers maintained their position at the lower end of the evolutionary scale.

What we might then call the 'disappearing world' phenomenon is alive and well today and living in New York, London and Paris or in the cutting room of Britain's Granada TV. Of course, now as then, any analysis of the effects of this ideology is complicated by its adoption for ostensibly different ends in the discourses of both right and left, with organisations like Survival International working in tandem and often on the initiative of indigenous rights organisations. In the words of one critic of the Granada TV series which has done so much to popularise the concept: 'The structural need which Disappearing World has for a fragile exoticism (a world as yet unrepresented) demands . . . difference and . . . disappearance is the only way of maintaining that distance' (Pinney 1989, p. 27). Paradoxically, while the programmes are premised on the inevitability of this destruction usually as a result of contact with western capitalism (if not with the paraphernalia of film-making itself), it is precisely those moments where the inevitability implied by such 'documentary' veracity is rumbled that are edited out of the script permitted to the subjects of the Granada series (Woodhead 1987).

Crucially, critiques of the absences implicit in the 'disappearing world' syndrome have come from those whose experience is silenced through such representation. The example which immediately comes to mind is the protest made against the Museum of Mankind's 'Hidden Peoples of the Amazon' exhibition in 1985. Notwithstanding the use of the intractable interior of Burlington Gardens as an unlikely substitute for the Amazon Jungle, the exhibition itself provided a spectacle which represented the various Indian populations of the Amazon basin as productive, active and evidently in possession of an encyclopaedic knowledge of the complex ecology of their environment. The metanarrative of the exhibition however, if not already evident simply through both the actual and metaphorical 'containment' of diverse strata of Amerindian societies in three rooms of the museum, is made explicit in the accompanying guide, where, after cataloguing the threats to the very environment represented in the display, the writer continues: 'In the light of this, reservations such as the large Xingu Indian park set up in Brazil in 1959, must be seen as the most acceptable of alternatives for the protection of Indian interests in the welter of modern economic development.'[35] The tone of resignation and inevitability here is continuing proof of the way in which those discourses used to justify ethnographic practice during its historical formation as an 'officially' accredited 'profession' are continually invoked today.

However, on 8 August 1985, the museum was picketed by representatives from Survival International and two Indian representatives from different Indian rights organisations. What interests me here are the particular terms of their critique of the exhibition and the way it highlights some of the difficulties of addressing the issue of culture contact through the display of culturally 'hybrid' objects. The demonstration concerned not the absence of the evidence of culture contact, assimilation and adaptation in the display, but rather the absence of an acknowledgement of the dialectical and dynamic relationship of diverse Amerindian populations to such contact – not simply at the level of the hybridisation of material culture but at a much more fundamental social level. It concerned, in fact, the absence of any evidence of the ongoing struggle between the Indians and the Brazilian government – the absence of any signs of selective and strategic resistance – in short, the absence of any self-determination by those Indians represented in the exhibition. The Museum's concession to the contemporary situation was to put up a story-board advertising western aid campaigns against the decimation of the Amazonian rain forests and two photographs supposed to demonstrate a flourishing hybrid culture – a ceremonial house made out of recycled cans and a Panare Indian in 'traditional' clothing riding a yellow Yamaha bike on a cleared highway. The statement made by Evaristo Nugkuag, one of the leaders of an Indian rights organisation, neatly sums up the problem: 'It was as though we could have the white's machine without losing our land and our way of life.'[36]

Four years later, the Calgary exhibition 'The Spirit Sings: Artistic Traditions of Canada's First Peoples,' put on to coincide with the Winter Olympics in January 1988, became the centre of another controversy. The Lubicon Lake Cree organised a demonstration and boycott of the Olympic Games in order to draw attention to their forty-year-old land claim. The exhibition itself gradually became the focus of the boycott since its very existence was assured only as the result of a substantial grant from Shell Oil Canada Ltd – who also happened to be drilling in precisely the area of the land claim. In the words, of Bernard Ominayak, Chief of the Lubicon: 'The irony of using a display of North American Indian artefacts to attract people to the winter

Olympics being organised by interests who are still actively seeking to destroy Indian people, seems obvious' (cited in Harrison (1988, p. 6); see also
Fisher 1987). The curator's response was to play the old 'objectivity' card:
'Museums, like Universities, are expected by their constitutions, to remain
non-partisan.' In answer to the Lubicon's retort that Glenbow Museum had
already made a political stand by accepting Shell sponsorship, the astounding
response was that there was no 'evidence that the public confuses corporate
support for corporate policy' (Harrison 1988, p. 8).

Clearly those who apparently 'cannot represent themselves' are more than
able to do just that. In both the Tukano and the Lubicon Cree cases, their
intervention exposed not only the hidden agendas of corporate sponsorship
and 'objective' museum scholarship but also the inextricability of discourses
of cultural continuity and/or cultural transformation as a result of contact
with western capitalism, with other more problematic discourses around
the concept of 'tradition'. The 'disappearing world' syndrome – the west's
search for the authentic encounter with originary unity, which is constantly
threatened and passively awaited by those whose visibility rests on the
magnanimity of 'objective' scholarship (so the institution would often have us
believe) – was well and truly rumbled.[37]

Most importantly, both Amazon and Lubicon Indian rights groups have
made it clear that there are complex interests at stake in the representation of
culture contact in western museums. The 'context' which needs to be made
explicit in such displays is no longer solely the old functionalist call for
'mythic' and 'ritual' significance, or a reassessment of the validity of such
practices for the canons of the western art establishment, but the ways in
which such cultural activities are often framed within a specific engagement with global politics and certainly with local demands. The meanings
attributed and attributable to such practices are, in fact, politically contingent,
unstable and often strategic (Buchloch 1989).

The historical conditions for cultural appropriation by the west and the
critique of western modernism as posing some form of impossible universal
internationalism make it untenable to speak of shifting the binary oppositions,
for so long the structural principle in so much western appraisal of non-
European culture, by simply including in the display objects showing signs of
culture contact. Even if this does go some way towards disrupting the continuity of the search for authenticity it does little to disintegrate the problems
implicit in the continued suggestion of the inevitability of the cycle of corruption, change and modernity. After a discussion of the multiple meanings
produced by the evidence of such contact in the visual narratives of western
ethnographic museums and art galleries, not to mention other media, this
suggestion either has the ring of a naive voluntarism about it or takes on a
more pernicious aspect.[38]

Clearly we should recognise the positive way in which the 'disappearing world' phenomenon and the question of culture contact is today inflected with other knowledges and a recognition in some instances of a post-colonial context. The axes operative now may be more productive: 'traditional' versus tourist or airport art, popular versus high culture, local versus global (Brett 1987; Jules-Rosette 1984). But is there, in fact, any evidence of other types of display policy that would shift the implicit value-judgements of even these binaries – that would indeed provide the western viewer with the basis for acknowledging other, more complex, structural affinities and exchanges?

'Les Magiciens de la Terre' at the Beaubourg in Paris was one of the more notorious exhibitions to foreground hybridity as a condition of post-coloniality. It highlighted some of the problems in the kinds of binaries which are often reinforced notwithstanding the disavowal of any comparisons on the grounds of a spurious but supposedly self-evident 'similarity' between exhibitors from the western metropolitan centres and those from nation states with a more recent history of colonial subjugation. The irony here, of course, is that the one thing that most critics of the show picked up on was the major structuring device of racial and cultural 'difference': a 'difference' which is transformed here into a 'cultural diversity' – a contented global village, a highly selective 'difference' which includes African, Australian and Chilean artists, but has no room for the huge North African diaspora, the residents of the Beaubourg's neighbouring arrondissements.

This is where it might be valuable to consider the historical formation of the public museum as the transformation from private courtly collection to public collection, a moment represented in its starkest form by the foundation of the Louvre after the Revolution (Duncan and Wallach 1980). The subsequent invitation to participate in a supposedly shared culture – the address to the citizen – underwrites all public museums. In such spaces the viewer is necessarily interpellated as both citizen and individual, and the relationship between public and subjective identities and the values and exclusions implicit in both is crucial. In the context of 'Les Magiciens' for example the confusion invoked by such an address, and the contradictions between this and the actual address and conditions of access to cultural capital, might account for why the huge North African diaspora in Paris is a regular user of the videotech and library at the Beaubourg, but rarely, if ever, uses the exhibition space downstairs.[39] And this despite the fact that the Beaubourg is predicated on an almost monstrous visibility which declares through the 'transparent' functionalist architectural idiom a condition of permanent and open accessibility.[40]

If as Paul Gilroy has suggested, 'diaspora' makes possible a way out of a binary constituted across 'essentialism' versus 'difference', we need to recognise the significance of the fact that 'hybridity' and 'difference' in most of these exhibitions is articulated as a symptom of what is identified as 'post-colonial' (itself a rather dubious category) as opposed to 'diasporic' formations (Gilroy 1993). It is a coincidence which effectively marginalises diaspora – the 'other' within – a concept which is far more politically disquieting to western bourgeois hegemonic culture. Perhaps this also accounts for the disruptive and transgressive power (for all their failings) of exhibitions like Rasheed Araeen's 'The Other Story' at the Hayward Gallery and the earlier exhibition 'From Other Worlds' in London's Whitechapel Gallery.[41] Attentiveness to audience and constituency is all. Who is doing the looking, or, more precisely, who is being addressed, is of course a central issue. And perhaps for this very reason those exhibitions in the western metropolis which have turned an ironic and self-critical eye on the viewing subject and on the museological process of 'othering' have been most successful in pointing a way forward. In this respect the Museum of Ethnography at Neuchâtel under the direction of Jacques Hainard has been one of the most innovative precursors (Hainard and Kaehr 1985).

In exhibitions such as 'Les Magiciens de la Terre' the comparisons which serve to reinstate the binary divide are not between the signs of cultural assimilation or appropriation – the signifiers of 'difference' – in and between the work of Nancy Spero, Alfredo Jaar or Rasheed Araeen. The problematic and most striking comparison is between these self-consciously modernist and postmodernist artists and those like Cheri Samba or Sunday Jack Akpan, whose work grew out of a concern with and certainly use of the visual language associated with existing cultural practices initially transformed to create a new relevance and often for a popular local audience.

One of the questions this raises is whether or not the postmodern strategy of 'bricolage' (the organising principle for 'Les Magiciens') does in fact constitute a kind of counterpractice (Foster 1985, p. 202). Maybe one of the distinctions between modernist collage and postmodernist 'bricolage' lies precisely in the ability of the former to articulate the dialectical tensions which the latter tends to reproduce as a free-flowing confusion and flux, what becomes in fact, in-differentiation. Paradoxically it may be the ethnographic museum (traditionally the site of 'visibility' of colonial appropriation and terratorial expansion) where this dialectical relation is most likely, precisely because its 'visibility' was never the neutral in-difference of modernist universality – the claim to subjective individualism that is historically the project of the modern art museum.

In the same way that 'bricolage' superficially reproduces the qualities of 'collage' but smoothes over the fracture that 'collage' retains, 'difference' as an analytical tool can simply revert to the pitfalls of the older cultural relativist model, concealing the distances between cultures while affirming that all are equal. The chasm is too great between the actual experience of economic, social and political disempowerment and the philosphical relativism of postmodernism's celebration of flux and indeterminacy as the product of the mobility of global capital. We need an account of 'difference' which acknowledges the inequality of access to economic and political power, a recognition which would carry with it an analysis of class and gender relations within subaltern *and* dominant groups and would articulate the ways in which such differences are constituted, not only in relation to the western metropolitan centres. Maybe this would allow us to explore hybridity as a condition occurring within and across different groups interacting in the same society. García Canclini has usefully discussed the shortcomings of the cultural relativist model as a means of explaining the 'hybridity' of Latin American culture as one of conflictual groups with common or convergent histories which may no longer exist separately.[42] Lisa Lowe points to the divisions and identities within the Asian American community.[43] And finally, Homi Bhabha has spoken about the hybridity of all cultures – a suggestion which should encourage us to explore the specific conditions of this hybridity – the how and the who of it – which might then dispel the monolithic (despite postmodernist pretensions) repetition of hybridity as an encounter between the west and its other and the ultimate reassertion of a Manichean model (Bhabha 1988).

For culture contact to be an effective strategy in countering the implicit racism of primitivist discourses in museums then, it would require at least demonstrating a selective and self-conscious engagement with western consumerism – the knowing recognition of new markets, but also the vitality of a hybrid product that, crucially, speaks as directly to a thriving local market as it appeals now to a western tourist market. It would require a recognition of the cultural, economic and political infrastructure that already supports such activity on a local level and that existed long before the museum 'discovered' it. Such work is already inscribed within a complex critical discourse and does not depend on the western art establishment for its 'visibility'. In a sense, of course, the dialectical relationship that needs to be articulated in the cultural sphere – between the global and the local, the national and the truly international – is thwarted by the scarcity of exhibitions which raise any of these issues and the fact that each one that does is made to bear the entire burden of responsibility for redressing the balance. Nevertheless, one thing we should have learnt by now is that it is not enough to imagine the voluntarist disposal of the complex ideological frameworks which have existed for so long in western cultural and scientific institutions for the appraisal of non-western material culture, if the power relations which have facilitated such easy categories remain intact and unexposed.

Notes

My thanks to Avtar Brah, Laura Marcus and Michael Orwicz for generously sharing their critical insights on an earlier version of this text.

1 I have deliberately restricted my attention to large international institutions in western metropolitan centres rather than smaller local institutions since these museums still unfortunately maintain a hegemonic position in relation to the representation of other cultures.

For an interesting set of observations about the comparative function of what he calls 'majority' and 'tribal' museums, see James Clifford (1991).

2 Museum of Mankind (1986) 'Lost Magic Kingdoms and Six Paper Moons from Nahuatl', London; Museum voor Volkenkunde (1988) 'Kunst uit een Andere Wereld', Rotterdam; Beaubourg (1989) 'Les Magiciens de la Terre', Paris; Center for African Art and New Museum for Contemporary Art (1991) 'Africa Explores', New York.

3 Although my own chapter is framed as a critique of the kind of position on 'hybridity' articulated by Peter Wollen in his 'Tourism, language and art' (1991), he nevertheless usefully traces the adoption of hybridising strategies as models of resistance or nationalism in particular moments of Mexican, Irish and Jewish history.

4 See also Cornel West (1989, p. 91) where he writes: 'The issue here is not simply some sophomoric, moralistic test that surveys the racial biases of the interlocutors in a debate. Rather the point is to engage in a structural and institutional analysis to see where the debate is taking place, why at this historical moment, and how this debate enables or disenables oppressed peoples to exercise their opposition to the hierarchies of power.'

5 For example 'Les Magiciens de la Terre' at the Beaubourg, Paris 1989, 'Lost Magic Kingdoms and Six Paper Moons from Nahuatl' at the Museum of Mankind, London 1986. For a critique of the latter see Annie E. Coombes and Jill Lloyd (1986).

6 It is important to realise that the heritage boom is fraught with ambivalence. In Britain for example, there is a cruel irony in the tendency to set up museums of working life in once thriving industrial areas where unemployment has now decimated the workforce and shut down the very industries that are represented as 'living' displays in the heritage museums. On the other hand even the worst of these cannot avoid some reference to class and labour relations even of the most banal kind and have often provided an opportunity for local history groups to rediscover aspects of their collective pasts. For useful discussions on the implications of the heritage industry see: Patrick Wright (1985); Robert Hewison (1987); Robert Lumley (1988); John Corner and Sylvia Harvey (1991).

7 See for example, Ethnic Minority Rights Group, Education for all: the report of the Committee of Inquiry into the Education of Children from Ethnic Minority Groups (1985); A. Sivanandan (1983); Sneja Gunew (1985).

8 K. Gough (1968); P. Bandyopadhyay (1971); J. Clifford and George E. Marcus (1986); Edware Said (1989).

9 For a development of this argument see Avtar Brah (1992); Trinh, T. Minh-ha (1989); and Corner and Harvey (1991), p. 18.

10 Cornel West (1989) charts some of the pitfalls and difficulties with the concept of 'difference' but also its progressive potential.

11 Here I would take issue with James Clifford's positive espousal of the category of fine art as 'one of the most effective ways to give cross-cultural value (moral and commercial) to a cultural production' (Clifford 1991, p. 241).

12 For a development of these ideas see Annie E. Coombes (forthcoming).

13 Technically speaking, the term 'bronze' is a misnomer. Analysis has shown that these objects are not always bronze but may be zinc, brass or leaded bronze and are generally an alloy of copper, zinc and lead in varying proportions. The term 'bronze' is used here as a shorthand.

14 See P. Mauch Messenger (1989); and J. Greenfield (1989). At the time of writing this, Professor Anna Benaki, the new Greek Minister of Culture, was in London publicising a new museum being built at the foot of the Acropolis. As a protest the walls of the museum will maintain pointedly blank spaces until the return of the Parthenon Marbles to Greece.

15 For a history of British interference in Benin City see P. A. Igbafe (1979) and Alan Ryder (1977).

16 Illustrated London news, 23 January 1897, p. 123.

17 For a more detailed discussion of this in relation to Benin c. 1900 see Coombes (forthcoming).

18 *Illustrated London news*, 27 February 1897, p. 292.
19 Mary Kingsley to Frederick Lugard, 31 December 1897, cited in Dea Birkett (1992, p. 94). For a more detailed analysis of the relation between the discourse on degeneration in both West African nationalist writings and colonial texts see Coombes (forthcoming).
20 Nochlin (1991) makes this point in relation to the eroticism of nineteenth-century Orientalist paintings of the slave market specifically in relation to the representation of women.
21 Auchterlonie (1898, p. 11). The full implications of this use of the adjective become clear in the light of Auchterlonie's remarks that since the Oba's skin was not as black as most coastal tribes, he did not look like a killer.
22 For accounts of the ideological implications of colour in earlier periods, see Winthrop D. Jordan (1982); James Walvin (1982); Christine Bolt (1971). For contemporary analyses see Lawrence Errol (1982) .
23 See in particular Commander R. H. Bacon (1897), which was reviewed in *The Times* (19 April 1898) as an 'ethnographic' 'document'. Other reviews reiterated this attitude.
24 For a later formulation of a similar thesis see W. Worringer (1907).
25 See *Journal of the Anthropological Institute*, January 1900, where the presidential address was devoted entirely to the importance of anthropology's as opposed to art history's contribution to the study of culture.
26 See G. R. Searle (1976); C. Webster (1981); F. Mort (1987); J. Weeks (1981); A. Davin (1978).
27 For anthropologists' involvement in anthropometry over this period see Coombes (1985). For the significance of photography for eugenics, see David Green (1982).
28 For a development of the relationship between Egypt and Africa in European scholarship, see Martin Bernal (1987).
29 For a more detailed analysis of the development of the fortunes of the Ethnographic Department of the British Museum over this period, see Coombes (forthcoming).
30 After 1906 for example, a series of popular anthropological texts were published which all contained prefaces railing against the British government's indifference by comparison to the German government's expansive support and recognition for German anthropologists.
31 See, for example, Charles H. Read (1899). Apart from acknowledging a possible independent African origin for the Benin bronzes, the publication interviewed chiefs in the deposed Oba's retinue. These testimonials formed the basis of the history of the Edo narrated in Read's text. Consequently it established the existence of an ancient history and had the potential to validate an oral tradition as a legitimate source of information.
32 *Museums journal*, 7 (December 1907), p. 203.
33 See *Art in America*, July 1989, where Martha Rosler and James Clifford take up opposing positions on this issue.
34 For a contemporary example see the 1993 exhibition at the British Museum, 'Collecting the Twentieth Century' where the panel introducing the ethnographic department's collection states explicitly that this is the primary work of the department. The booklet which accompanies the exhibition, however, actually critiques this suggestion.
35 *The hidden peoples of the Amazon* (1985), p. 11.
36 *The observer*, 11 August 1985.
37 It is as a result of such acutely aimed and orchestrated protests from often disempowered indigenous peoples that the liberal white establishment is now being forced to take on board criticism that has become politically embarrassing. One such instance is the recent series on Channel 4 television, 'The Savage Strikes Back'. Instead of focusing solely on the 'inevitability' of extinction, this series, produced in direct consultation with local rights groups, highlighted the organised political struggles of a number of indigenous peoples to regain control over their lands and their lives. It is also interesting that the Chicago Field Museum have felt obliged to shut down their display of Hopi artefacts after protests by Hopi

representatives. I am grateful to Luke Holland, Lisa Tickner and Sandy Nairne for information on these points.

38 For an informed and critical view which analyses this issue in terms of the Australian context
and the recent celebration of Aboriginal cultural production, see Anne-Marie Willis and
Tony Fry (1988–9).

39 I am indebted to Michel Melot for this information.

40 For one of the most interesting critical assessments of the Beaubourg, see Cultural Affairs
Committee of the Parti Socialist Unifié (1978).

41 Whitechapel Art Gallery (1986) 'From Two Worlds'; Hayward Gallery (1990) 'The Other
Story'. See also 'The Decade Show' (1990), New York.

42 Néstor García Canclini (1988). Thanks to John Kraniauskas for bringing Canclini's work to
my attention.

43 Lisa Lowe (1991). Thanks to David Lloyd for bringing Lisa Lowe's work to my attention.

Anthropology and race
in Brazilian modernism

ZITA NUNES

Pouca saúde e muita saúva
Os males do Brasil sao.

With fewer ants and better health Brazil will lead the world in wealth. (Mario de Andrade, *Macunaíma*)[1]

The question, 'What is Brazil(ian)?', has informed much of Brazilian writing, be it political, sociological or historical. For literary critics and theorists, however, defining this identity has become, according to the critic Angel Rama, a patriotic mission, making out of literature the appropriate instrument for forging a national identity (Rama 1982, p. 13). Literature, then, is central not only to the reflection but also to the formation of a national identity. Most nationalisms base themselves on a return to a pure, homogeneous origin involving the repression of all that troubles the integrity and purity of that origin. This logic, which informed Brazil's discourse on race up to the beginning of the twentieth century and which also inhered in the quest to come up with a fixed identity, was threatened by the reality of miscegenation. I maintain that much of Brazilian literature relating to the question of national identity is an attempt to resolve the 'problem' of miscegenation.

During the course of the slave trade, Brazil received 37 per cent of the total number of Africans brought by force to the Americas (as compared to North America's 5 per cent (Curtin 1969). By the mid nineteenth century, according to Emilia Viotti da Costa, the population of Brazil consisted of 1,347,000 whites and 3,993,000 blacks and mulattos (da Costa 1989). Throughout the nineteenth century, debate centred on the necessity of creating the conditions which would allow Brazil to emerge not only as a nation but also as a participant in the movement of modernisation, progress and development taking place in Europe and the United States (see Barman 1988). After the abolition of slavery in 1888 did away with an institution that many abolitionists argued was an impediment to integration with the west, the increasing popularity of theories of biological and social determinism appeared to confirm the elite's anxiety about the inherent inferiority of the nation's largely black and mulatto population. The question became one of citizenship and the creation of a national myth. Any notion of a universal (white) subject became difficult to sustain; blacks, no longer Africans but subjects of the republic of Brazil (established in 1889), were perceived to be threats to stability of the 'self', the family and the nation (as for example in de Alencar's play, *O demónio familiar*) by an elite anxious to reproduce itself as 'Brazilian'.

Euclides da Cunha expressed this anxiety very clearly in *Os sertoes*, a book widely acknowledged to be one of the masterpieces of Brazilian letters. Early in the book, which chronicles the battle between government troops and followers of a charismatic leader in the interior of the north-east of Brazil, da Cunha inserts a chapter entitled 'An irritating parenthesis'. The mixture of races is harmful, he claims, because the resulting brief individual existence undermines centuries of natural selection and consolidation of a race. *Mestizos* are by nature unstable and incapable of reproducing themselves as they are, but only as approximations of one or the other of the component races. In da Cunha's conception, Brazil cannot claim a unity of race and, therefore, violates what he calls natural laws – instead of the nation originating from a race (as in the guiding myths of Europe), the nation must be constructed as a unity in order to allow the formation of what da Cunha calls a historic race (da Cunha 1966, pp. 166–8; Leite 1983). In this formulation the nation is a narrative of becoming fraught with ambivalence, and race a construct always in danger of coming undone (see Bhabha, ed. 1990). As will become clear, there is conflict between the elite's desire to reproduce itself within a context of a modern notion of the nation based on citizenship (where whites could continue to dominate) and the necessity of creating a unity based on a concept of mixture. The conflict was addressed through the elaboration of a myth of racial democracy.

It has become almost a cliché to call attention to the possibility of separating 'race' from 'biology' structured into Brazilian thinking on this issue. I am referring here to a Brazilian habit of claiming that race is not defined solely, if at all, in terms of biology. This tenet of racial democracy could appear to lend support to recent theoretical debates which rightly reveal race as a construct (see Degler 1971). Many have been misled, however, into thinking that Brazil has achieved a deconstruction of race; the irony is that race is being disavowed in the interest of protecting and ensuring the continuation of a highly racialised system. Paul Gilroy reminds us that while races 'are not simple expressions of . . . biological and cultural sameness', 'the brain-teasing perplexities of theorising about race cannot be allowed to obscure the fact that the play of difference in which racial taxonomy appears has extra-discursive referents' (Gilroy 1990, p. 264). In Brazil the very appearance of a deconstruction of race has permitted the obscuring of the fact that the statistical gap between whites and 'browns' (*pardos*) in terms of infant mortality, life expectancy and household income is consistently wide, while the statistical gap between 'browns' and blacks is consistently narrow (see Wood and de Carvalho 1988).

The issues which occupied the attention of politicians and intellectuals during the early decades of the republic continue to engage Brazilians. This is clear from debates that took place in 1989 during the campaign preceding the first direct presidential election in three decades. Soon after the election of Fernando Collor, the *Folha de São Paulo* one of Brazil's most prestigious newspapers, published a response by a widely known journalist to a com-plaint of racism received from a reader. In an earlier article, the journalist had described the new president as 'tall, handsome, white – white in the western mould'. The journalist defended himself against the charge of racism by claiming that in attaching a value to Collor's whiteness, he does nothing different from the vast majority of Brazilians[2] and that if this is sick, there are not enough doctors in Brazil to provide treatment. He writes that people of colour are as 'palatable' to him as any other but to consider Brazil a Third World country and to seek to forge links with Africa (as the other candidate, Luis Ignacio da Silva, had proposed) would require that 'we [Brazilians] turn away from our cultural heritage which is the West . . . [and] the United States' (Francis 1990, p. E–10).

In addition to demonstrating the continuity of a concern with defining a Brazilian identity particularly in relation to the rest of the world and with de-fining the representative Brazilian, this chapter calls attention to a metaphorics of the body which is a constant in discussions of race in Brazil and which has its roots in the modernist movement of the 1920s.

It would be impossible to overstate the impact of the modernist movement or its importance as a point of reference for subsequent generations. The Semana de Arte Moderna (Week of Modern Art) of 1922 is generally ac-knowledged to be the inaugural event of the modernist movement, an event that one of the organisers called 'o primeiro sintoma espiritual da trans-mutaçao de nossa consciência' ('the first intellectual symptom of the trans-formation of our consciousness') (Menotti del Picchia, cited in Pécault 1990, p. 27). Of the many events leading up to the Semana de Arte Moderna, one of the most important was a 1917 exhibition of art by the Brazilian painter, Anita Malfatti, who had just returned from a trip to Europe and the United States where she had been influenced by cubist and expressionist aesthetics and techniques. The exhibition drew together the writers, artists, journalists and scholars who would organise the Semana de Arte Moderna.

From 11 to 18 February 1922, the Municipal Theatre in São Paulo was the site of art exhibitions, dance and music performances, lectures and readings which explored or staged various aspects of modernism. The event launched a movement which proclaimed a rupture or a break with the past in order to subvert what were considered bourgeois methods of artistic expression. The modernists allied themselves with European vanguard movements such as surrealism and futurism. The writers published newspapers, journals and manifestos in addition to works of fiction, poetry and ethnography.

Although the speakers and performers were roundly jeered and heckled by the crowd that filled the theatre, a contemporary observer of the events noted that the Semana de Arte Moderna had been financed by many of São Paulo's most established business and social figures and supported by the *Correio Paulistano*, an organ of the governing PRP (Partido Republicano Paulista – Republican Party of São Paulo) party with the consent of Washington Luis, the republic's president (da Silva Brito 1970, p. 455).[3]

The decade of the 1920s in Brazil was marked by intense cultural and political unrest. The prevailing view is that during this decade the new generation of Brazilian artists who formed the modernist movement caused a profound intellectual upheaval by giving national values and themes precedence over foreign values and themes. One of the most prominent ideas to draw the fire of the modernists was that concerning the role and contribution of blacks to Brazilian society. By the 1930s a parallel socio-anthropological literature had appeared which emphasised (in ways that were paradoxical) that blacks were an integral element in Brazilian society as a result of their significant contributions to Brazil's history and development.

The most vibrant personality associated with this new school was Gilberto Freyre, who had returned to Brazil in 1925 after studying at Columbia with the anthropologist Franz Boas. Many Brazilians, as well as Americans and Europeans, have accepted as valid Freyre's luso-tropical assertions of racial tolerance.[4] Many scholars, however, have criticised Gilberto Freyre for dwelling on inter-racial liaisons while masking the basic economic and political realities of racial exploitation and oppression.

In an introduction to *The masters and the slaves* (*Casa grande e senzala*), a book that has greatly influenced the question of race and identity in Brazil, Freyre states that he based the method for his sociological–anthropological work on methods developed by Pablo Picasso in the realm of art, an approach which linked him (despite avowed differences) to the modernists in São Paulo. In addition, Freyre, like the paulista modernists, takes up the issues which had preoccupied Euclides da Cunha, particularly those related to perceived threats to Brazil's modernity.

In *Casa grande e senzala*, Freyre writes that there existed in the north-east a superstition that the blood of blacks (rather than the usual whale oil) mixed into the mortar would increase the strength of the foundation. It was rumoured that a plantation owner, anxious to guarantee the perpetuity of his domain, ordered that two blacks be killed and buried in the foundation of the Big House.

The irony, however, is that for lack of human potential this arrogant solidity of form and material was often useless: by the third or fourth generation, huge houses built to last centuries began to crumble, decayed by abandonment and lack of conservation [and] the inability of the great-grandchildren to save the ancestral heritage.

After recounting this anecdote which demonstrates how Brazil's foundation degenerates when the blood of Africans is (literally) mixed in, Freyre addresses the 'problem' of miscegenation. He states in the introduction that:

It was as if everything was dependent upon me and those of my generation, upon the manner in which we succeeded in solving age-old questions. And of all the problems confronting Brazil, there was none that gave me so much anxiety as that of miscegenation. (1946, p. xx)

Freyre continues:

Once upon a time, after three straight years of absence from my country, I caught sight of a group of Brazilian seamen – mulattoes and *cafusos* – crossing the Brooklyn Bridge. I no longer remember if they were from São Paulo or from Minas, but they impressed me as being caricatures of men, and there came to mind a phrase from a book on Brazil by an American traveller: 'The fearful mongrel aspect of most of the population.' That was the sort of thing to which miscegenation led. I ought to have had someone to tell me then what Roquette-Pinto had told the Aryanizers of the Brazilian Eugenics Congress in 1929: that these individuals whom I looked upon as representatives of Brazil were not simply mulattoes or *cafusos* but *sickly* ones. (pp. xx–xxi)

The discourse on race and miscegenation in Brazil is tied to a metaphorics of the body and an economy of eating, incorporation and sickness. The body politic has a sickness that it must rid itself of. The 'problem' with miscegenation is not miscegenation in and of itself, but with miscegenation as the perpetuation of a sickness. In this assessment blacks maintain the status of a foreign body. A healthy body is one which overcomes the weakening effects of an offending organism. Freyre's project of defining the relation of race to identity is grounded in this discourse:

Having considered these points [the ethnic groups to which Africans belong, physical characteristics, relative intelligence, etc.] which appear to me to be of basic importance in studying the African influence on Brazilian culture, character and eugenics, I now feel more inclined to undertake the task of discovering the more intimate aspects of this contagious influence. (p. 321)

The strategy for overcoming the contagious influence was so widely disseminated that even Roosevelt could summarise it: 'In Brazil . . . the idea looked forward to is the disappearance of the Negro question through the disappearance of the Negro himself – that is through his gradual absorption into the white race' (cited in Skidmore 1974, p. 68). Faced with the threat of miscegenation to the superiority of whites, Freyre transforms miscegenation into a narrative of assimilation. Of course, the absurdity of this formulation cannot be overemphasised given Brazil's population.

Freyre was certainly not the only scholar to link the notions of race, health and nation. Wilson Martins discusses at length how the athletics and robust health so important to writers such as Graca Aranha and Marinetti 'were themes directly and consciously connected with a concern for hygiene, public and private, and the problems of national defense' (Martins 1970, p. 90). Others who discussed the 'disadvantages' of miscegenation in these terms were Silvio Romero, Euclides da Cunha and Paulo Prado, whom Wilson Martins calls 'a physician or a surgeon who wishes to effect a cure' (p. 90). In *Retrato do Brasil*, Prado writes:

> The Brazilian mulatto has undoubtedly furnished notable examples of intelligence, breeding and moral value to the community. On the other hand, this population shows such physical weakness, such organisms which cannot defend against disease and vices, that it is natural to ask if this state of things isn't the result of the intense crossing of races and subraces... In Brazil, if there is harm in this, it has been done, irremediably. We wait in the slowness of the cosmic process for the uncoding of this enigma with the patience of laboratory researchers. (1931, pp. 196–7)

Prado adds in a footnote to this passage that already in the fifteenth century the mixing of European, American and African races had produced new sicknesses which proved to be veritable enigmas to doctors.

It is to Paulo Prado that Mario de Andrade, folklorist, poet and theorist of the modernist movement dedicates *Macunaíma* (1928), widely regarded as one of the comic masterpieces of Brazilian literature. Mario de Andrade said that one of his interests in *Macunaíma* was to deregionalise his creation while trying to 'conceive Brazil literarily as a homogeneous entity' (cited by de Hollanda 1978, p. 100). The modernists searched for a way to 'Brazilianise' Brazil. For them, however, this 'Brazilianising' was to be accomplished through artistic and literary efforts of which the aesthetics and techniques were almost entirely drawn from those of contemporary Europe. Let us remember that the cubists had already discovered the value of incorporating Africa.

The modernists' method was outlined by Oswald be Andrade in O *manifesto pau Brasil* (*The brazilwood manifesto*) and O *manifesto antropófago* (*The cannibalist manifesto*). This method consists of swallowing and absorbing what is useful in a culture and excreting what is not useful. The supposed cannibalism of the indigenous population served as a model for a different cultural relationship between Brazil and the outside world (defined largely as Europe) – a relationship where foreign influences would not be copied but digested and absorbed as a precondition to the creation of a new, more independent national civilisation. *Macunaíma* is one practice of the modernist project which has been upheld as a celebration of Brazil's 'indigenous past'. In fact, as we shall see, the indigenous past is merely a repository of possible paradigms and *Macunaíma* is localised in a metaphorics of the body where eating, incorporation and disease are foregrounded.

The story or 'rapsódia', to use Mario de Andrade's term, traces Macunaíma's origins in the Amazonian forest, his trip to São Paulo, and his return to the forest before ascending into the heavens to become the Big Dipper. In his letters and in the introductions to *Macunaíma*, Mario de Andrade describes how *Macunaíma* was composed mainly of found texts which he then exaggerated. In the Epilogue we learn how Macunaíma's story comes to be told:

> There in the foliage the man discovered a green parrot with a golden beak looking at him. He said, 'Come down, parrot, come down!'
> The parrot came down and perched on the man's head, and the two went along together. The parrot started to talk in a gentle tongue, something new, completely new! Some of it was song, some like cassiri sweetened with honey, some of it had the lovely fickle flavor of unknown forest fruits.
> The vanished tribe, the family turned into ghosts, the tumbledown hut undermined by termites, Macunaíma's ascent to heaven, how the parrots and macaws formed a canopy in the far-off times when the hero was the Great Emperor, Macunaíma: in the silence of Uraricoera only the parrot had rescued from oblivion those happenings and the language which had disappeared. Only the parrot had preserved in that vast silence the words and deeds of the hero.
> All this he related to the man, then spread his wings and set his course for Lisbon. And that man, dear reader, was myself, and I stayed on to tell you this story. (de Andrade 1984, p. 168)

Interestingly enough, this parrot is not a Brazilian parrot but a German one. Mario de Andrade came to his story of 'Brazil's indigenous past' and Brazil's hero via Europe.

He is very clear about his debt to Koch-Grunberg, a German anthropologist who travelled throughout Brazil between 1911 and 1913. Andrade relied particularly on volume II of *Von Roroima zum Orinoco* which contained the myths and legends of the Taulipang and Arekuna people. According to Mario de Andrade, the debt was not only one of inspiration but also of whole passages: 'I confess that I copied, sometimes word for word' (cited in Filho 1986, Introduction).

The name Macunaíma (Makunaima) was taken from Koch-Grunberg. According to Koch-Grunberg, Makunaima's name is made up of two words which join to mean the 'Great Evil' (*maku* = evil, *ima* = great) (1981). In the collection of myths and legends related to Koch-Grunberg, Makunaima is the hero of the tribe and the creator of the Taulipang people. He is the youngest of five brothers, two of whom, Ma'nape and Zigue, appear most often with Makunaima but not at the same time.

The birth of Makunaima is not described in Koch-Grunberg's collection. In Mario de Andrade's book, Macunaíma is born in the middle of the forest to an old woman of the Tapanhuma tribe. In the text it is claimed that the name of the tribe signifies 'black'. It is significant that Mario did not take the name of Makunaima's people offered by Koch-Grunberg, preferring instead to find the name of another tribe which, correctly or incorrectly, signifies black. Macunaíma, unlike Koch-Grunberg's Makunaima, 'was an oddity, his skin black as calcined ivory' (de Andrade 1984, p. 3). As a result of an encounter with an animal/spirit in the forest, Macunaíma grows a man's body but keeps his head of a child. Other important manipulations of the sources are, then, that Makunaima becomes black, ugly, lazy and an adult with a child's head.

After the death of their mother, the three brothers travel through the forest. They meet Ci, Mae do Mato, whom Macunaíma rapes with the help of his brothers. Macunaima and Ci have a child, the only child of the inter-racial relations of the book. Ci has one shrivelled breast, a sign that she belongs to the tribe of the *mulheres sozinhas* (solitary women). A Cobra Preta (the Black Snake) bites Ci's other breast, and her child is poisoned while nursing. In a letter to Manuel Bandeira, Mario claims that he chose the colour black for the snake by chance as he very easily could have closen the colour green. The choice hardly seems a coincidence given that Mario adheres closely to superstitions associated with the colour black. Manaape and Jiguê, for example, become sick with leprosy and die. Under their contagious influence, Macunaíma becomes sick but overcomes the disease by passing it to a mosquito, the seventh creature he bit. This is linked to a folk belief that a leper can be cured after biting seven children (Proença 1987, p. 224).

I began this paper with an epigram from *Macunaíma*. The sickness de-scribed in this couplet was associated with miscegenation at the time of the publication of *Macunaíma* (1928). Macunaíma's and Ci's child, Macunaíma's two brothers, Jiguê and Manaape, become sick and die. By the last third of the book, every black person, person of mixed race and indigenous person has become sick and/or died. Their illnesses must be seen in the context of the couplet that Macunaíma repeats throughout the book: 'Pouca saúde e muita saúva, os males do Brazil sao.'

For all the celebration of racial mixing that the cannibalist approach to writing implies, and contrary to the usual readings of *Macunaíma*, there is no racial mixture in this book. The three brothers are of three separate races.

The heat of the Sun had covered the three brothers with a scum of sweat, and Macunaíma was thinking of taking a bath ... Just then Macunaíma caught sight of an islet right in the middle of the stream in which there was a hollow the shape of a giant's footprint, full of water. They landed there. The hero, squealing because the water was so cold, washed himself all over. But this water was magic water, for the hollow was St Thomas' footprint, a relic from the time when he went around preaching and bringing the teachings of Jesus to the Indians of Brazil. When the hero had finished his bath he was white-skinned, blue-eyed and fair-haired; the holy water had washed away all his blackness; there was nothing left to show in any way that he was a son of the black tribe of Tapanhumas.

As soon as Jiguê saw this miracle he sprang into St Thomas' footprint. But by this time the water was very dirty from the hero's ivory blackness, so although Jiguê mopped himself like mad, splashing the water in all directions, he was left the color of freshly minted bronze. Macunaíma was bothered by this and to comfort him said, 'Look, brother Jiguê, you didn't become white, but at least the blackness has gone away. Half a loaf is better than no bread!'

Then Manaape went to wash, but Jiguê had splashed all the water out of the pool. There was only a cupful left at the bottom, so that Maanape could wet only the palms of his hands and the soles of his feet. That's why he remained black like a good son of the Tapanhuma tribe with only the palms of his hands and the soles of his feet pink after their washing in holy water. This grieved Macunaíma, who consoled him by saying, 'Don't be vexed, brother Manaape, don't let it get you down! Worse things happen at sea!'

The three brothers made a superb picture standing erect and naked on the rock in the sun; one fair, one red-skinned, one black ... (pp. 31–2)

In Legend 5, Koch-Grunberg relates how Makunaima created human beings but makes no allusion to race. Boddam-Whetham, however, records the following origin of races myth:

The Caribs in their account of creation say that the Great Spirit sat on a mora tree, and picking off pieces of the bark threw them in a stream and they became different animals. Then the Great Spirit – Makanaima – made a large mold and out of this fresh clean clay, the white man stepped. After it got a little dirty the Indian was formed, and the Spirit being called away on business for a long period the mold became black and unclean, and out of it walked the negro. (Boddam-Whetham 1879, p. 172)

J. R. Swanton records two other variants which follow the same pattern (white, Indian, black). He records a third variant where the hierarchy is Indian, white, black (Swanton 1929, p. 75). All of the Indian tales begin with white people who are transformed into people of other races. In Mario's version, however, all the brothers are black before the bath. Once again Mario turned away from his Indianist sources on a point having to do with race in order to produce an account consistent with Brazilian thinking.

Also important is the fact that Mario makes Macunaíma's enemy, the giant cannibal Piama, an Italian immigrant. During the period in which *Macunaíma* was written, the Brazilian government had a policy of encouraging immigration from European countries in order to speed up the process of *embranqueamento* (whitening). In 1921, the statesmen Fidelis Reis and Cincinato Braga drafted legislation to halt the immigation of non-whites in order to protect the ethnic (read racial) formation of the nation which had already suffered from the introduction of blacks. This project had the support of the National Academy of Medicine. (Reis 1931; the document from the Academia Nacional de Medicina is appended to the book).

In her book *Macunaíma: Ruptura e tradiçao* Suzana Camargo maintains that Rabelais' *Gargantua* is an intertext of *Macunaíma*. Using Bakhtin as a theoretical base, she analyses the relationship of *Gargantua* and *Macunaíma* to each other and to the body (Camargo 1977).

One aspect that *Macunaíma* and *Gargantua* share is that the grotesque body and eating are inscribed in both narratives. According to Bakhtin, 'the most distinctive character of the [grotesque] body is its open, unfinished nature, most fully revealed in the act of eating where the body transgresses its limits'.

> The encounter of the man with the world, which takes place inside the open, biting, rending, chewing mouth, is one of the most ancient, and most important objects of human thought and imagery. Here man tastes world, introduces it into his own body, makes it part of himself. . . . Man's encounter with the world in the act of eating is joyful, triumphant; he triumphs over the world, devours it without being devoured himself. The limits between man and the world are erased, to man's advantage. (Bakhtin 1968, p. 281)

If this incorporation works to man's advantage, it does not work to the advantage of all men – or women. What is seen as liberatory or subversive in Bakhtin becomes suspect, even oppressive, when race or indeed gender are factored in. The question becomes: 'Quem come quem' ('who eats whom')? It is important to note that the *mulata* plays a very significant role in the linking of race and nation, for it is through her body that *embranqueamento* takes place. In other words, 'o branco comeu a mulata' ('the white man ate the *mulata*' – in Brazilian slang *comer* (eat) means to have sexual intercourse); the couple is rarely a white woman and a black man. One implication of this is that the patrimony is European. Much is made in sociological literature of the father giving his name, education, historical and genealogical continuity to his children. This is in contrast with blacks in general and *mulatas* in particular who are identified with nature, sensuality and lack of family ties. The following citation from an essay by Gilberto Freyre is only one example among many of this:

> in the Orient, in Africa, in America, his [the Portugese] vigorous male body is multiplied in red, yellow and brown bodies; in new colors and new shapes of the human form, and these bodies communicate the qualities of the Portuguese or the Christian soul . . . The African, Asian and Amerindian mothers also are rendered Portuguese [*aportuguesadas*] by him most often in their souls and even, to a certain point, in the way they dress, adorn themselves and care for their bodies. This is reflected in the arts and literature of these people who through the Portuguese are in this way integrated into European civilization. (Freyre 1987, p. 239)

It should be noted that Macunaíma engages in his anthropophagist activities after having been miraculously transformed into a white man, and that the giant cannibal Piama is white.

According to Suzana Camargo, the theme of anthropophagy and its images of ingestion and absorption that so occupied Rabelais were taken up by Mario de Andrade to support the modernist maxim. Just as Rabelais manipulated *Les grandes croniques* simply to structure his story, Mario de Andrade manipulated the Indian legend (Camargo 1977, p. 100) Once again the African and the Indian have been incorporated into a (digestive) system. It appears that blacks and indigenous peoples are exploited for their transgressive shock value which derives from the modernists' ideas about the 'primitivism' of Africans and indigenous peoples. What is useful is extracted and the rest is excreted.

Although the philosophical trappings of anthropophagism would seem to imply a political vision of a democratic society, this is not the case. In fact, blacks have not been equal participants in a Brazilian 'mixture'. This is not the result of vulgar or individual prejudice; it lies at the heart of a notion of citizenship and is an enabling condition of a construction of a national identity. In the anthropophagist model, however, we discover that assimilation is unthinkable without the excretion. The law of assimilation is that there must always be a remainder, a residue – something (someone) that has resisted or escaped incorporation, even when the nation produces narratives of racial democracy to mask this tradition of resistance.

Notes

1 A more literal translation would be 'Little (or poor) health and many ants / are the problems of Brazil.'

2 This is an accurate assertion. When requested as part of an opinion poll to describe the ideal president, 89 per cent of the respondents agreed that he should be white (Atwood 1988).

3 For analysis of the ways in which the modernists contributed to and advanced conservative agendas see Pécault (1990), Holston (1989) and Miceli (1979).

4 'The fact should be stressed that among the Portuguese of the continent theological hatreds and violent racial antipathies or prejudices were rarely manifested. The same is true of the relations between whites and blacks: those hatreds due to class or caste extended and at times disguised in the form of race hatred such as marked the history of other slave-holding areas in the Americas, were seldom carried to any such extreme in Brazil. The absence of violent rancours due to race constitutes one of the particularities of the feudal system in the tropics, a system that, in a manner of speaking, had been softened by the hot climate and by the effects of miscegenation that tended to dissolve such prejudices' (Freyre 1946, pp. xii–xiii).

How to read
a 'culturally different' book

GAYATRI CHAKRAVORTY SPIVAK

One of the painfully slow results of the demand for a multicultural canon is the inclusion of global English on the college curriculum. The results of this uncertain victory are often dubious, because neither teacher nor student is usually prepared to take the texts historically and/or politically. This chapter is an attempt to walk a conscientious teacher through a limpid novel, R. K. Narayan's *The guide* (1980).

In the late 1950s, the term 'Indo-Anglian' was coined by the Writers' Workshop collective in Calcutta, under the editorship of P. Lal, to describe Indian writing in English. Although the term has not gained international currency, it is useful as a self-description.

The first question to be asked of a piece of Indo-Anglian fiction is the author's relationship to the creative use of his or her native language. This question is not identical with that asked by Ngugi Wa Thiong'o (1986).

The complexity of Ngugi's staging of the relationship between English and Gikuyu also involves the relationship between dominant *literature* and sub-ordinate *orature*. To draw that parallel in an admittedly asymmetrical way, we should have to consider the millennially suppressed oral cultures of the aboriginals of India. We have not yet seen an Indo-Anglian fiction writer of tribal origin; we are far from seeing one who has gone back to his or her own oral heritage. Indeed, anyone aware of the ruthless history of the expunging of tribal culture from the so-called Indic heritage, and the erasure of the tribal paraph – the authenticating flourish above or below the signature – from Indian identity will know that the case is difficult to imagine.

By contrast, literary activity is usually prolific in the mother-tongue of the writer of Indo-Anglian prose or poetry. The writer of Indo-Anglian literature might represent the dynamic base of regional public cultures as if it is no more than a medium of private exchange or a rather quaint simulacrum of the genuine public sphere. This artificial separation of public and private is, strictly speaking, a cultural class-separation. The relationship between the writer of 'vernacular' and Indo-Anglian literatures is a site of class-cultural struggle. This struggle is not reflected in personal confrontations. Indeed, the spheres of Indo-Anglian writing and vernacular writing are usually not in serious contact. By 'class-cultural struggle' is meant a struggle in the production of cultural or cultural–political identity. If literature is a vehicle of cultural self-representation, the 'Indian cultural identity' projected by Indo-Anglian fiction, and, more obliquely, poetry, can give little more than a hint of the seriousness and contemporaneity of the many 'Indias' fragmentarily represented in the many Indian literatures.

In fact, since the late 1960s, as metropolitan (multi)Cultural Studies began to establish itself through the good works of the Birmingham School, inaugurated by Richard Hoggart's *The uses of literacy*, and continued under the able direction of Stuart Hall, the Indo-Anglian writer began to acquire and transmit an increasingly 'post-colonial' aura of cultural self-representation. How does international cultural exchange of this sort operate? This question should be kept alive, not answered too quickly.[1] A too quick answer, taking the novels as direct expressions of cultural consciousness, with no sense of the neo-colonial traffic in cultural identity and the slow and agonising triumph of the migrant voice, would simply see them as repositories of post-colonial selves, post-colonial*ism*, even post-colonial resistance.

However difficult it is to fix and name the phenomenon, one might consider it carefully because its tempo is so different from the boomerang-effect of the cultural shuttle in fully telematic (computerised and videographic) circuits of popular culture. Consider merengue, the Caribbean dance music so popular in New York: the artists are in Santo Domingo, the market is supported by the dominicanos in New York, and the trend changes from the original 'pure' strain as fast as you can count.[2] Consider rap in South Africa, where the singers themselves acknowledge American influence, and remark on how African the US groups sound; the South African newscaster considers this a cultural re-appropriation of what originated in Africa; and the US group compliments the South African group on being so comprehensible in English, of having so little 'African accent'. Consider the Chicaricano 'border art' of the Mexican artist Guillermo Gomez Peña.

The only Indo-Anglian post-colonialist novel in this telematic tempo is Shashi Tharoor's *The great indian novel* (1989), inspired by Peter Brook's *Mahābhārata*, which prompted the author to read the *Mahābhārata* for the first time, in its condensed English version as the playscript for Brook's production of the epic.[3] The novel is an amusing verbal comic-strip series superimposing the struggle among the great nationalists of the Indian Independence movement upon the faimly feud at the heart of the ancient epic. Translation is immediate here. *Mahā* is literally 'great' and *Bhārata*, all complexities of history and geography forgotten, can be taken as identical with the contemporary (Hindi) name for India. *Mahā-Bhārata* = Great India; the post-colonial politicians' fantasy to make the present identical with the hallowed past; and thus win votes for a politics of identity at degree zero of history.

This example remains an anomaly. The spoof is inaccessible to the international readership of Commonwealth literature. And the Indo-Anglian novel is simply not a part of 'popular' culture on the subcontinent, whether global 'kitsch' or indigenous 'folk'. To think of the Indo-Anglian novel, even in its aggressively post-colonial manifestations as 'popular', is to think of *Sons and lovers* as a novel of the international working class. The tragedy (or the bitter farce?) of *The satanic verses* is that, precisely through electoral manipulation in India, it became available to, though not read by, the 'people' of whom it spoke.

By contrast, the general tempo of two-way traffic in the course of change in the Indo-Anglian novel in India and in its readership, institutional or otherwise, is less tractable. The change that we begin to notice in the early 1970s is an exuberantly mocking representation of the native language. In the wake of swiftly changing global cosmopolitan identities riding like foam on waves of diversified diasporas, what was an upper class, upwardly mobile or upwardly aspiring private relationship to a vernacular in national peripheral space is literally 're-territorialised' as the public declaration of ethnic identity in the metropolitan space of the newish migrant writer, borrowing his or her discursive strategy from the field prepared for the new immigrant by the only slightly less new.[4] Although *The satanic verses* might be the classic case of this, the landmark text, before the preparation of its readership, is Desani's *All about H. Hatterr* (1986), a virtuoso novel where 'English' attempts to claim its status as one of the Indian languages (belonging to a national underclass) through the technique of sustained literal translation of the vernacular rather than islands of direct monstrous speech in a sea of authorial Standard English.

Writers like R. K. Narayan (Nayantara Sehgal, Kamala Markandaya, Ruth Prawer Jhabwala, Mulk Raj Anand, Raja Rao *et al.*) predate this hyper-real scramble for identity on the move.[5] The 'internal evidence' for this is the stilted English of the dialogue in their novels, whenever it happens between the rural or underclass folk they often choose to represent; and of the representation of the subjectivity of such characters in so-called 'indirect free style'.[6] The situation of the underclass, or rural characters, or yet of the language of indirect free style, is dealt with quite differently in the vernaculars. With this earlier group of reportorial realist writers, then, one must be specially aware of the relationship with the vernacular.

The group started publishing fiction in English well before Indian Independence in 1947. Narayan's first book, *Swami and friends*, was published in 1935. If the emergence of a mode of production of identity recognisably 'post-colonial' by a younger group meant a setting wild of the private space of the mother-tongue, then negotiated political independence set this earlier group adrift, away from the current from which the post-colonial monstrous would emerge. They became novelists of the nation as local colour, the nostalgic rather than the hyper-real.

The representation of the temple dancer in *The guide* stands out in this miniaturised world of a nostalgia remote from the turbulence of post-colonial identity. The story, given in flashbacks, in between an autobiography, in the book's present, of the male lead released from prison and sheltering in an imageless temple, to a devotee who authenticates his felicity as a saint, can be summarised as follows.

With the coming of the railway station, Raju's father's shop moves up in class. With his father's death, Raju is able to respond to this upward move. He becomes not only a railway store owner but also a flashy and resourceful guide of conducted taxi tours of local beauty spots. On such a tour he meets Rosie/Nalini, daughter of a temple dancer (henceforth *devadāsi* – female servant of the Lord), the dancing in her blood strictly suppressed, firstly by a personal ambition that prompts her to take a Master's degree in political science, and secondly by an archaeologist/art historian husband. Raju the guide seduces her, she comes to live with him, his mother leaves home with his scandalised uncle, he makes immense amounts of money by setting her up as a dancer and being her agent, and goes to gaol for forging her signature in order to prevent re-establishment of contact between herself and her husband. She disappears from the scene. After a brief stint in prison, he emerges and takes shelter in the temple. He attracts one follower and then, as a result, an entire village full of devotees. When he is urged to fast and stand knee-deep in water for twelve days to end a regional drought, he starts telling his story to Velan, his follower.

The novel is not arranged in this straightforward way. It begins with Raju talking to Velan in the temple. We are not aware that the account is a confession, for two contradictory motives bleed into each other: avoidance of the hardship of fast and penance; avoidance of 'enforced sainthood' (Narayan 1989a, p. 167). We know these motives only towards the end of the book. In the meantime, some of the chapters begin to move out of the frame narrative as regular flashbacks. To put it in code, the reader begins to say 'yes' to Raju's past by inhabiting the roguish personality of a past character so unlike the present. That is the historically established power of the indirect free style of storytelling. The reader does not have to exercise his or her mind to get used to experiment. When the story makes no difference to Velan, the reader can say 'yes' to that indifference as well.

(Given primitive distinctions such as First World–Third World, self–other and the like, I tend to classify readers by slightly less crude stereotypes. In that spirit, and in the strict interest of decolonising the *imagination*, let it be proposed that, for the metropolitan reader or teacher reading or teaching Commonwealth literature, the limpid local colour prose of this style is quite satisfactory. For the rather special Indian readership of Indo-Anglian fiction, this class-distanced hyper-real is also satisfying, perhaps because it conveys a cosy sense of identification at a distance, thus identity-in-difference. The person who reads 'popular' vernacular literature for fun will not read *The guide*. The reader of 'high' vernacular literature will, if he or she reads English literature with the antennae up, be dissatisfied with the 'subjectivity' opened up by the free indirect style, precisely because the limpid prose would seem a bit 'unreal', a tourist's convenience directed toward a casual unmoored international audience.

Narayan tells us that the novel was written in a hotel room in Berkeley, California. There is a sizeable literature of displaced writers writing from abroad in the various vernacular literatures. *The guide* has no need to make use of that convention.

To classify readers in this way is a denial of contingency, which seems a particular loss when talking about literature. Deconstruction has taught us that taking contingency into account entails the immense labour of forging a style that seems only to bewilder.[7] If literary study is to work with established metropolitan colonial history, it seems best that one stay with the outlines of rational agency and give a hint of postcolonial heterogeneity according to the impoverished conventions of mere reasonableness.)

This fake saint then becomes a sacrifice. To what? Faith is not, after all, reasonable. And the line between virtue and the sustained simulation (making something happen by insisting it is so) of virtue is hard, perhaps finally impossible, to fix. So the book can suggest, in the end, that perhaps Raju *is* a miracle-worker, after all: 'Raju opened his eyes, looked about, and said, "Velan, it's raining in the hills. I can feel it coming up under my feet, up my legs –" He sagged down' (p. 220). A nice bit of controlled indeterminacy there, resting upon one of the most firmly established European cultural conventions: transition from Christian psychobiography to romantic imagination.[8] (In a broader field it is seen as the tranformation of Christianity into 'secular' ethics, theology into philosophy.) Michel de Certeau and Michel Foucault have, among others, speculated about the relationship between these changes and the turn to capitalism.[9] The dominant Hindu 'colonial subject' in India came to terms with his Hinduism with the help of the epistemic trick allowed (often clandestinely) by this shift. At the colonial limit, sacred geography thus became an interior landscape. The problem of irrational faith was interiorised into allegory in the narrowest possible sense. Religion as cultural allegory allowed the Indo-Anglian writer of the first phase to produce an immediately accessible 'other' without tangling with the problem of racism or exploitation. Raja Rao is perhaps the most striking example of this.

In the literary history of Britain, one reads this transition or transformation by way of the nineteenth-century project of rewriting Milton: by Blake, Wordsworth, Shelley. In Wordsworth's 'Hail to thee, Urania!' Imagination is supposed at last to be triumphant.

Alas, this high register, where literary production is in the same cultural inscription as is the implied reader, cannot be employed for the epistemic ruses of the colonial subject. No Indo-Anglian writer of Narayan's generation can speak of his education in English literature without self-irony, however gentle.

Narayan offers a vividly ironic account of his own education in English literature in chapters four to six of his *My days: a memoir* (1974). It would be difficult to imagine from this book that his conversations with his grandmother and the street-people might have taken place in his native Tamil. 'Thus ended one phase of my life as a man of Madras; I became a Mysorean thenceforth' (1974, p. 48). This meant a bilingual move – from Tamil to Kannada – for an adolescent. Can one surmise that the bilingualness of the move was not significant for largely English-speaking Narayan? Of course, from these Memoirs, or indeed from the self-contained small-town world of *The guide*, one would not be able to guess either that Tamil has one of the longest continuous literatures in India, and that both Tamil and Kannada were active in literary production and experimentation at the time of the writing of *The guide*.[10] For example, the literary and cultural–political universe inhabited by Anantha Murthy, the Kannadese novelist, is at many removes of 'concreteness' in terms of the weaving together of the fabric of national identity, torn from end to end in the current conjuncture. Native readers of Tamil and Kannada literature suggest that there might have been a surreptitious and unacknowledged one-way traffic between Indo-Anglian writing produced by Tamilian and Kannadese writers and the vernacular literatures in this case. This writer, whose mother-tongue is neither, cannot vouch for this judgement without extensive research, although she is *au courante* in her own.

In Narayan's own estimation at least, the novel's core is the predicament of the male lead (1974, pp. 168–9). Rosie/Nalini is therefore merely instrumental for the progress of the narrative.

My method of considering this instrumentality will be 'allegorical' in the most ordinary sense (one-to-one correspondence, as we used to say), or semiotic in the most formulaic way (this 'means' that). This may be the only way in which the literary critic can be helpful for the study of culture and for the historical study of the aftermath of colonialism and the post-colonial present. It is an enabling limitation, a *découpage* for the sake of the disciplines.[11]

Rosie/Nalini is, then, the remote instrument of Raju's enforced sanctity. How does Narayan represent her so that the narrative of Raju's transformation may be revealed? Let us notice, first of all, that she is absent at the actual transformation, the present of the frame-narrative. She is instrumental only in getting him to gaol. Release from that chain of events, release from imprisonment, is release into the road to sanctity.

The story is not just a boy–girl story, however. It is also a decently muted tale of access to folk-ethnicity (protected by that nice indeterminacy already mentioned). Here the main burden of the frame-narrative is that Raju transforms Rosie into Nalini or lotus. But that is represented as not an authentic entry into folk-ethnicity. The author makes clear that that attempt was the vulgarisation of culture in the interest of class-mobility. Raju transforms Rosie into Miss Nalini, and, as her impresario, becomes besotted by his access to money and the attendant social power. Within the miniature field of Indo-Anglian fiction this authorial judgement is the celebration of tradition over modernity that its readership can devoutly wish, *at a tasteful distance*. And, since Raju's obsession interferes with his obsessive love for Rosie, it resonates on the boy–girl register as well. It is by a neat and accessible irony that his forgery, prompted by 'love' (he wants to keep Rosie from further contact with her husband), is mistaken for 'love of money'.

Rosie has tried to lift herself from the patriarchal ethnos by going the route of institutional western education. But dancing is in her blood. If the railway train as a harbinger of progress and class-mobility is a cliché of the literature of imperialism, the nautch (dance) girl is a cliché of the imagining of British India. Raju is first taken by her in a passage indicating the rhythm in her blood:

> He [a derelict cobra man] pulled out his gourd flute and played on it shrilly, and the cobra raised itself and darted hither and thither and swayed. . . . She watched it swaying with the raptest attention. She stretched out her arm slightly and swayed it in imitation of the movement; she swayed her whole body to the rhythm – for just a second, but that was sufficient to tell me what she was, the greatest dancer of the century. (p. 58)

But Raju the entrepreneur cannot bring Nalini to life. It is her husband the gentleman-archaeologist who wins her back, at least in spirit. There is a bond between them in their passion for their cultural labour. Narayan has the modernist literary tact not to conclude her story, and Raju's last word on it shows his inability to grasp the mysterious bond. Reporting to him in prison, his secretary

> Mani explained that the only article that she carried out of the house was the book [her husband's book about the caves – a counter-*Guide* that we never get to read]. . . . Mani said, 'After the case, she got into the car and went home, and he got into his and went to the railway station – they didn't meet.' 'I'm happy at least about this one thing,' I said. 'She had the self-respect not to try and fall at his feet again.' (p. 205)

She is not needed in the last phase of the book: the phase of ethnicity over culture. India *is* folk-kitsch. E. M. Forster had written the 'Temple' section (1952, pp. 283–322).

Although (or perhaps precisely because) the dancer is not central to the novel, a feminist reader or teacher in the USA might wish to know a little more about the temple dancer in order to grasp the representation of Rosie/Nalini.

The source book most readily available to her is Frédérique Marglin's *Wives of the god-king* (1985).[12] Although for most metropolitan teachers of Commonwealth literature, the terrain of *The guide* exists as 'India', the reader might have specified it to herself as southern India from internal and external signals.[13] The state where Marglin did her field-work is not Narayan's south, but Orissa, where the south-east meets the north-east. How does the Orissan *devadāsi* (or *dei*), imprisoned in her own temple-community of women in a gender-hierarchy that mixes 'tradition' and 'modernity' in its unique blend, communicate with her counterpart in the south, in Mysore or Bangalore? Certainly not in their mother-tongue. In fact, it is unrealistic to think that there *can* be actual situations of communication between them. These are subaltern women, unorganised pre-capitalist labour, and it is not yet possible to think of them as *Indian* collectivities of resistance, although the Indian constitution appropriately thinks of them collectively as victims and thus offers a redress that has never been fully implemented in the individual states. Indeed, current feminist activism around this issue, dependent upon the direction and organisation of the women's movement in various regions, is much more forceful and visible in the states of Maharashtra, Karnataka and Tamil Nadu (roughly Narayan's area) than in Orissa, Marglin's field of work. The language barriers that allow the Indo-Anglian writer precisely to represent one of them as our implausible Rosie keeps her locked in isolated communities. The patriarchal system that informs *The guide* so that Raju can finally occupy the temple as saint makes the temple her prison.

(There are a very few rags-to-riches stories of the daughters of temple dancers becoming great *artistes*, but Narayan's focus on Rosie is too slight for us to feel that this is the point of her representation. To emphasise that point, Rosie's entry into secondary and post-secondary education would have had to be dramatised.)

Is literature obliged to be historically or politically correct? Because it is not, this sort of literary criticism is a category mistake, derided as 'politically correct'. But it should be considered that literature is not obliged to be formally excellent to entertain, either. Critical evaluation is dismissed as 'pedantic' by the real consumers of popular culture. Here again is class-negotiation. This way of reading, pointing at its cultural-political provenance, can be useful in the specific situation where the heterogeneous agency of the colonised in post-coloniality cannot be imagined, although the details of colonial history are known professionally.

As the feminist reader moves into *Wives of the god-king*, she notices a peculiar blandness in the reporting of the *devadāsi*'s prostitution. This curious apologetic finessing of judgement, invariably called cultural relativism, has

become an unavoidable mark of the field-investigator who has become sensitive to the risks of neocolonial knowledge, but will compromise with it. This
is perhaps exacerbated by the investigator who learns the social practice as
artistic performance (in this case *Odissi* dance), now the property of the
middle and upper middle classes.[14]

The transmogrification of female dance from male-dependent prostitution
to emancipated performance helps the indigenous colonial elite to engage in a
species of 'historical (hysterical) retrospection' which produces a golden
age (Baudrillard 1983b, p. 16). Raju in *The guide* enters the hallucination
without any particular historical thickening.

Dr Marglin's traffic with a great many Indian men, acknowledged in her
book, is coded as exchange with a student of the *devadāsi*-system or a
student of *Odissi*, eager cultural self-representation in response to altogether
laudable white interest in our heritage; rather different from the traffic
between men and women described in her chilling prose. It would be impossible to suspect from this account that feminists have internationally
battled and are today battling (not the least in India) against this view of the
role of the woman in reproduction:

> The chastity of the wives of the temple brahmins is crucial not because it is they
> who transmit the characteristics of the caste and the *kula* to their children, but to
> ensure that only the produce of that species of seed that has been sown in it is the
> one that will be reaped and not the produce of some other species of seed. A
> woman, like a field, must be well guarded, for one wants to reap what one has
> sown and not what another has sown, since the produce of a field belongs to its
> owner. Such an idea was expressed long ago by Manu.... This theory by the
> ancient law-giver certainly corresponds well to what is the case today in Puri....
> Women are like the earth, and the earth is one, although it is owned by many
> different types of men ... the woman palace servant (*dei*) told me that her mother
> answered her query [about menstruation rituals] ... in the following way: ... 'God
> has taken shelter' (in you).... 'You have married and you'll do the work of the
> god ...'. The 'work of god' and 'the shelter of the god' she said referred to the fact
> that from that time on she would start her rituals in the palace and would become
> the concubine of the king. (1985, pp. 67, 73)

Wives of the god-king is a thoroughly vetted and rather well known book.
It is hard to imagine that it was published in 1985! The author takes at face
value the invocation of the golden age by Orientalist and bourgeois alike. The
usual anti-Muslim explanation of the decay of Indian (read Hindu Aryan)
culture under the Muslim rule, and hence the deterioration of the *devadāsis*
into prostitutes, draws this from the author:

> This view is representative of many if not most English-educated Indians today.
> The historical research necessary to confirm or refute the above statement was
> beyond my abilities, even if the records were available, which is highly doubtful.
> My training has prepared me to do ethnography, which happily the particular
> historical circumstances of Puri made possible. (p. 11)

'Ancient sources' are so regularly proclaimed that our inquisitive feminist literary critic will probably be daunted away; especially since there are repetitions of post-colonial piety and the claim that if Dr Marglin had been born a hundred years ago, her views would have coincided with those of Annie Besant, the noted Theosophist. Would the feminist investigator check this claim by consulting Mrs Besant's biography? Amrit Srinivasan has given a fine analysis of the relationship between the Theosophist interest in saving the dance rather than the dancer and the establishment of western-style residential schools for dance, like *Kalākshetra* (lit. the artistic field) in Madras by the indigenous elite.[15]

There seems nothing to link the women in Marglin with the world of *The guide* except to imagine that the daughters of one of these hapless women had been able to enter the educational system with nothing but her mother's good wishes as her resource.

And if the Indian colleague or friend who is the US feminist's 'native informant' happens to be a not untypical woman from the emancipated bourgeoisie, the work of her own uneven emancipation will have been undertaken by the slow acculturation of imperialism that is, in its neo-colonial displacement, the topic of our discussion. If this imaginary informant happens to be a careful student of the dance form, she has learned the entire social ritual *as* ritual reverently museumised in an otherwise 'modern' existence. She might see the dance as directly expressive of female resistance in its very choreography. The result of this innocent ethnic validation is Cultural Studies as alibi.

Vigilance, then, about class as we read the novel and look for background. Impatient non-major students of required English courses often mutter, Can we not just read for pleasure? Their teachers were taught to offer a consolation from US New Criticism, Knowing the rules of the game does not detract from pleasure. But reading in the style of Cultural Studies, looking into the class provenance of form and information, may not enhance pleasure. The most it can do is to give a clue to the roadblocks to a too-quick enthusiasm for the other, in the aftermath of colonialism, even as it attempts to offer untrained resistance to the arrogance of the discipline.

One of the most tedious aspects of racism as the science of the everyday is the need to refer every contemporary act of life or mind performed by the cultural other to her cultural origin, as if that origin is a sovereign presence uncontaminated by history. In order to stem that tide *vis-à-vis* Narayan's novel, some brief and inexpert comments on the so-called 'ancient texts' are offered below. My gratitude to Dr Mandakranta Basu, who has helped locate the texts.

There are no known direct references to dancing *in the temple* in the oldest books of dance theory and trade talk on dance practice, *Nātya Śāstra* and *Abhinaya Darpana*. (The current debate seems to be between where the limits of dance and drama are fixed.) There is a passage in the *Nātya Śāstra* (second or third century AD) on how to transform the body into a space of writing and turning. The yoking of dance to the body is in order proficiently to lead toward what is signified by the body as a collection of *aksara* or letters. 'Leading towards' – *abhinaya* – is crudely translated 'drama' by English translators, so that even without the *devadāsi* we fall into the Aristotelianised problematics of mimesis. There is no mention of temple dancing in this early text, though an interesting distinction between the improper and proper use of the signfication-representing body, in consecrated lust and in the consolidation of attraction respectively, is made (Kavi, ed. 1926, I, V, pp. 103–25).

A millennium later, the *Nātya Śāstra* is being legitimised as holy knowledge or *Vēda* in the *Sangītaratnākara* (Apte, ed. 1897, VII, pp. 3–16). *Lāsya* or carnal affection is being recuperated into theogony. The word relates to the root *las*, which, at its most rarefied, means 'to appear in shining'.

It is not surprising that the *Sangītaratnākara* also gives a list of *social* rather than interpersonal occasions where dance is appropriate: coronations, great feasts, voyages, valedictions to divine images after periodic festivals, marriages, meetings with the beloved, entries into the city, the birth of a son. Dance enhances the auspiciousness of all these activities. No temple dancers yet. *Lāsya* can still mean only dance, which belongs to the ceremonial life of kings and well placed householders.

The first mention of temple dancing is located in the medieval collection of stories called *Kathāsaritsāgara* (*The sea of stories*).[16] Aparna Chattopadhyay offers a theory of west and central Asian provenance and offers connections with Corinth and Phoenicia. Legitimation by 'Vedic' origin becomes all the more interesting.

Of particular interest is the twelfth-century *Kuttinimatam* (*The art of the temptress*) by Damodargupta. Here the stylisation of seduction through body movements is taught as a practice by an older prostitute to a younger.[17]

Who knows exactly how *lāsya* changes into the art of lust? Muslim conquest is about as useful as the International Jewish Conspiracy. Words change meaning bit by bit, here-excess, there-lack. We find fossils of 'earliest use' and strain this intimate mystery of linguistic change at east from the incomprehensible social field of manifestation and concealment and sublate it into one line of a dictionary.[18] Any history that tries to imagine a narrative of the subaltern woman's oppression *must* imagine that familiar lexicographical space, that line in the dictionary, into the uncanny, the strange in the familiar. That space is the mute signature of the process by which the woman becomes a ventriloquist, beginning to act as an 'agent' for *lāsya*. If this painful invitation to the imagination does not produce the disciplinary writing of history, then, as an apologetic outsider, I would submit that it might strengthen the discipline to recognise it as a limit.[19]

As part of preliminary on-site research, I viewed documentary footage shot by Dr Veena Sethi when she travelled with the Indian National Commission on Self-employed Women in 1987. I discovered the existence of this footage on a research trip to India in December 1990. In that material, there is a discussion, in the presence of the temple pimps, between the *devadāsis* and the activists. Some resistance to rehabilitation can be sensed in that conversation. This may be due to the presence of the pimps, to the class-separation between activist and subaltern, to the bitter awareness of the absence of follow-up to keep 'the new way of life in place', and/or to patriarchal ventriloquism.[20]

If the *devadāsi* cannot speak *to* an unreconstructed subalternist history, and *in* the entrpreneurial fantasy of Indo-Anglian fiction, she also cannot speak by way of capital logic.

Shramshakti (*Labour-power*), the impressively heavy report of the Commission, published in 1988, mentions the encounter with the *devadāsis* in a few paragraphs in the prefatory material and moves on to 'regular' prostitutes:

> Another group of women represented at this Pune meeting were the Devadasis, of whom there are many here. Most of them are girls of poor, landless, low caste families who dedicate their girls to the service of God. Their 'services' are taken for granted by upper class men. Although this practice is sanctioned by tradition and religion, these women usually end up in prostitution or begging. There is no one to look after them when they grow old, and no source of income. Some of them develop diseases which remain untreated. In this meeting, they requested education for their daughters, old age homes, and some income generation programme. A blind woman asked for reservation for the blind in jobs, and special training in telephone exchanges, chalk making, or cane making. At the Kolhapur Devadasi Vikas Centre, there were 50 devadasis present. Shantibai said that she was dedicated to the Devi because her father had promised (God) to do so if he got a son. Now her father is old and blind, and that son is in jail. The Commission heard numerous similar cases: they had been dedicated to God in exchange for a son. Chhayabai and Ratnabai said they were made devadasis purely because of poverty. 'There was not enough at home to feed everyone.' So they lived in the temple and got fed there. At the age of 13 they started serving the devi with men, and started bearing children. In all cases, the men do not stay with the devadasi or the children. Then the devadasis have to resort to begging. On Tuesday and Friday near temples they have some income out of begging alms. But generally they have lost their capacity to earn by hard honest labour. Their priority is education for their children, which is problematical. Because the father's name is not given, the children are often not admitted. (*Shramshakti* 1988, p. liii)

This report was published three years after Marglin's book. The tenor of the conversations seems somewhat different. The reader is convinced of the contrast between the US anthropologist and the Indian activist. (Although a single example does not prove a case, a single counter-example makes human generalisations imperfect.) I am none the less arguing that even an effort as thoughtfully organised as SEWA's cannot allow the agency of the *devadāsi* to emerge, because she is not written in the idiom of organised or unorganised labour, self-employment or other-employment (autocentrism versus extraversion in broader registers; namely capital logic).[21]

In the body of the report, the 'occupation' *devadāsi* does not emerge in the many tables. The master-list, included in the chapter headed 'Demographic and economic profile', includes thirty 'types of skill'. The last two are 'others' and 'no skill'. The percentage distribution is Rural: 0.97 and 89.69; and Urban: 3.26 and 69.48. How would the *devadāsi* be docketed? Is *lāsya* – the convincing representation of lust – still her skill?

There is no reason at this point not to credit the tiny but significant report of their agency (out of which comes demand): 'Their priority is education.' There can be no doubt that education is perceived by them as a way out of the vicious impasse of female proletarianisation (reduced to nothing but your body) outside of capital logic. It is not difficult for R. K. Narayan to put his finger on this pulse. But we are concerned with another story: that at the utterly remote other end of the trajectory denoted by 'education' (international conferences), one must still engage in the question of 'decolonising the imagination'. I should be able to say right away that one of the important tasks of the local women's movements in the *devadāsi* areas is to fight in an organised way against the lethal requirement of 'the father's name'. The novel can ignore this hurdle and present the query as coming from Raju's Mother, and immediately deflected by Raju himself – a proof of his masculine ingenuity. But we, decolonising *our* imagination, must admit that, even if this first barrier is crossed, and justifiably, in the imagination of these hapless infirm *devadāsis*, education is an instrument of upward class-mobility. These women are correct in perceiving that it is class-jumping that gives the woman 'freedom' in patriarchy (and access to feminism as a matter of choice).[22] If their daughters and granddaughters emerge for the 'New Europe' as objects of domination and exploitation only when they emerge *in* the 'New Europe' as migrant labour, this obscure moment of the agency of the infirm *devadāsis* ('their priority is education for their children') remains a negligible part of a minor agenda, rather than the most serious necessity for educational reform 'originating' out of a subltern or sub-proletarian priority. This is the question not of militant centres of localised 'pedagogy of the oppressed', but of overhauling the presuppositions in general national education. If the subaltern – and the contemporary *devadāsi* is an example – is listened to as agent and not simply as victim, we might not be obliged to rehearse decolonisation interminably from above, as agendas for new schools of post-colonial criticism. But the subaltern is not heard. And one of the most interesting philosophical questions about decolonising remains: who decolonise, and how?

Let us get back on the track of our feminist teacher. She will encounter a debate about the 'real' *devadāsi*: Was the 'real' *devadāsi* a 'free woman, an artist'? Is her present condition a result of the collusion between colonial and nationalist reformists, supported by men of her own community who stood to gain by her fall?

Amrita Srinivasan advances an affirmative answer to this question. She offers a challenge to the critical imagination when she 'anthropologises' colonial reform and asks us to consider the ways in which it rewrote its object: 'If sacrificial infanticide and *sati* had been banned earlier as "murder", then by the late nineteenth century temple-dancers were being presented as "prostitutes", and early marriage for women as "rape" and "child-molestation"' (Srinivasan 1988, pp. 178–9). She situates the Theosophist impulse mentioned by Marglin: 'The British government officials and missionaries were not slow to play up non-Brahmin suspicion of Indian nationalism, coming as it did from the largely Brahmin-dominated Theosophical circles and Congress alike' (p. 197). Marglin treats Orissa, Srinivasan treats Tamil Nadu (R. K. Narayan's Madras). And she is on target about the appropriation of the dance form by the elite:

> By 1947, the programme for the revival of *sadir* [the name of the dance-form of the Tamil *devadāsis*] as Bharatanatyam, India's ancient classical dance, was already well underway with the patronage and support of Brahmin dominated Congress lobbies of elite Indians drawn from all parts of the country. (p. 197)

Her analysis of the pre-colonial *devadāsi*'s controlling position within 'the efficacy of the temple as a living centre of religious and social life, in all its political, commercial and cultural aspects' (p. 184) is indeed an attempt at decolonising the imagination, however difficult it might be to agree that

> the conscious theological rejection [on the part of the *devadāsi*?] of the harsh, puritanical ascetic ideal for women in the bhakti sects, softened for the devadasi the rigours of domestic asceticism in the shape of the widow, and the religious asceticism in the shape of the Jain and Buddhist nun. (p. 191)

If one must see conscious agency here, one might think of Marx's suggestion that the capitalist carries the subject of capital. For although it is no doubt true that in Tamil Nadu the *devadāsi* was free of marriage and domestic duties, Srinivasan herself shows us that there can be no doubt that the *devadāsi*'s exceptional sexual status was tightly and gender-divisively controlled in the interest of economic production:

> In the *nāgeswaram* tradition the women of the group were scrupulously *kept* out of public, professional life. . . . Married girls were not *permitted* to specialise in the classical temple dance and its allied music. . . . The devadasis represented a badge of fortune, a form of honour managed for civil society by the temple. . . . The

devadasi acted as a conduit for honour, divine acceptance and competitive reward at the same time that she invited 'investment,' economic, political and emotional, in the deity. (pp. 186, 183; emphases mine)

In this context, to claim that

the devadasi stood at the root of a rather unique and specialised temple artisan community, which displayed in its internal organisation the operation of pragmatic, competitive and economic considerations encouraging sophisticated, professional and artistic activity (p. 192)

might be to emphasise social productivity isolated from forces and relations of production. Perhaps in reaction against the colonial–nationalist elite collaboration, Srinivasan has created a bit of a static utopian past as well. She is surely right in noticing the interest of the men of the group in pushing through colonial reforms so that the *devadāsis'* economic 'power' could be broken. But to perceive these forces as supervening upon a freely functioning structure seems unconvincing. In fact the *devadāsi* structure was subsumed in a general patriarchal structure. As Gail Omvedt puts it: 'Can any special section of women be free of patriarchy in a patriarchal society?' (Omvedt 1983, p. 17).

Srinivasan's utopian solidarity for these competitive, robustly celibate prostitutes (her Indo-centric re-definition of 'celibacy' is her boldest attempt at unsettling our imagination) is combined with a contempt for contemporary popular culture which must also be examined:

In the midst of new forms of vulgarity surrounding the dance profession today, such as the commercial cinema, it is the devadasi tradition alone which is propagated by the elite schools as representative of the ancient and pure Bharatanatyam.... If the devadasi's dance was a sacred tradition worth preserving and the legislation (justified though it was on the grounds of anti-prostitution) came down with a punitive hand not on prostitutes in general but on the devadasi alone – why did the devadasi need to go? (1988, p. 198)

This question cannot be asked alone but must be put in the context of broader questions: Why did pre-capitalist institutions disappear under imperialism? Why can the *devadāsi* not be fully captured in capital logic today? Srinivasan's own economic argument would suggest that this pre-colonial economic institution was 'supplemented' by capital-formation. The *devadāsi* had to go not only because she was the member of a non-Christian female artists' community who challenged notions of female chastity (Srinivasan's argument) but because the structure of competition and production in the community was pre-capitalist (also her argument). Because of her functionalist utopianism, she cannot see that the commodification of woman's body in art in the commercial cinema is not different in kind from its imperfect commodification in the commercial temple. They are two links on the chain of displacement of capitalist/colonial production.

Let us attempt to project this sequential displacement on to a cross-section of class-stratification.

(1) As Gail Omvedt suggests, the contemporary predicament of the *devadāsi* is a social tradition pressed into the service of capitalism ('pimps from the Bombay prostitution industry pay for the dedication ceremony, and often pay something to the girl's parents, in order to directly recruit the girl for a commercial brothel in Bombay').

(2) The *devadāsi* dance-forms of *Odissi* and *Bhāratanātyam* have, as their felicitous goals, the commodification of superstars in 'high' cultural performances. (On the authority of a male dancer, reputedly the son of a *devadāsi*, now a regular teacher of classical dance in Puri, the actual performance of the *devadāsis* was much more improvisatory; the various stages of the dance were not as fixed.)

(3) The *devadāsi* dance-forms in the convention of the musical film commodifies women's bodies in 'popular' cultural performance.

With this projection, the debate about the *devadāsi* would be as fully inscribed in women's class-stratification as the sources of metropolitan information about the cultural other.

Do *devadāsis* visit the commercial cinema? What have they thought of the film version of *The guide*? It seemed impertinent, indeed absurd, to put the question to the oldest living *devadāsi* in Puri, a woman ravaged by poverty and disease, one of Marglin's informants.

The film is an indigenous translation of Narayan's novel. It is part of the immensely popular internationally distributed and prolific Bombay film industry. Here *The guide* is lifted on to an altogether broader canvas. Almost every detail of the film recorded below is absent in the novel and in contradiction with its spirit.

Folabo Ajayi, a renowned dancer from Nigeria, said recently to Sanjukta Panigrahi, an internationally renowned cultural performer of *Odissi*, that she had been partially prepared for Ms Panigrahi's live performance by the many filmic representations of Indian dance that she had seen.[23] Thus the 'popular', scorned by the Indo-Anglian novelist, and treated with amused contempt by his or her Indian readership, can mediate the relationship between practising artists.

The film thus speaks *for* India, as does Indo-Anglian fiction. The translation of the absent Tamil–Kannadese specificity into Hindi makes nonsense of the material situation of the *devadāsi*. The terrain of the film is now Rajasthan, an area which allows the regulation long-skirt costume popular in Hindi film.

Narayan is apart from 'the people', a ruefully apologetic but affectionate commentator. 'He never misses an eccentricity of Indian English', offers *The times* of London as jacket blurb. *The guide* in the Hindi film version is the condition and effect of the *vox populi*. As such, the film brings into bold relief the multiculturalism of (the now-precarious) official Indian self-representation, the religious tolerance of the Hindu majority that was still ideologically operative in the Nehruvian atmosphere of the 1960s, and the protected subject/object status of the woman in love and performance ('Your caste is the same as Uday Shankar's and Shantha Rao's', says the film's Raju, mentioning two famous Indian dancers the histories of whose production are about as different as can be). These cultural generalisations catch a moment in post-colonial history that still hung on to the shreds of the dream of decolonisation immediately after Independence, especially in the first two areas. The violence of the translation of the English novel into the national language (not the appropriate vernacular) forces into the open the relay between empire and nation, English and Hindi, and the rivalry between.

At this stage, the American girl-reporter is still the boorish outsider. The sequence of the reporter questioning the dying and saintly Raju is repeated in *Gandhi*, but of course one dare not say that Attenborough cites *The guide*.

The novel *is* in English, the film fights *with* it (in both senses), and neither scenario captures the different beat of Indian literatures. The film mocks the ugly American and gives shelter to vernacular heterogeneity in certain brief moments, under the paternalist arm of the multicultural nation. It is possible to suggest, although such suggestions are always debatable, that – since the Emergency of 1975, the de-emphasising of the federal structure, the manipulation of electoral politics, the attempt at centralising power and the emergence of the new politics of fragmentary consolidation(s) of opposition, as well as the rise of Hindu fundamentalism – the presentation of multiculturality and Hindi as protector of the vernaculars is not part of the current 'task of the translator' in India. The first item, re-programmed within dominant global capital, has now moved to the space of migrant post-coloniality. *The satanic verses* opens with the citation of a song from a 1960s film, *Shri 420*, where the invocation of unity in diversity is even broader in scope (Aravamudam 1989).

At the beginning of the film of *The guide*, we have a scene where a betel-leaf vendor rattles off a list of the places from where the ingredients of the little betel-leaf pack of spices (*pān*) have come: the nuts from Mysore, the leaves from Calcutta, the limewash from Bikaner, the caoutchou from Bombay. And Raju answers back: you seem to be fostering national unity from your *pān*-stall alone. In the very next sequence, Raju the guide is shown managing at least two Indian languages and English with some degree of flair.

These two invocations of national unity stand at the beginning of the film, to 'set the mood', as it were. The fight *with* English, however, plays an integral part in making the heavily moralised story come across to the reader. When Raju is first established as a holy man, two village priests challenge him with a Sanskrit *sloka* or couplet. Raju is of course clueless in Sanskrit. After an electric pause, he comes back at them in English: 'For generations you've been fooling these innocent people. It's about time you put a stop to this!' The priests are bested, for they do not know English. The villagers rejoice. Raju is legitimised.

Of course Raju is himself a fraud as well. He *has* to be if the story is to remain a transformation story. But the seriousness of the message in English cuts across the mere story-line and indicates a major theme: the new nation will get rid of religious bigotry through the light of western reason. The west is now to be used as an equal rather than a subordinate. This is the promise of decolonisation; immediately broken by that other relay race: between colonialism and neo-colonialism, and the rise of isolationalist fundamentalism which stages the west only as violator.

A metropolitan focus on popular history sometimes denies this first confident hope of decolonisation. It can also be argued that it is the denial of this hope by global capital and racism in post-coloniality and migrancy, and its popular dissemination, that has brought us to the general scene of superstate powers versus guerrilla counter-warfare and particular scenes of domestic confusion and violence.

Let us review the situation schematically. (1) The gendered subaltern woman, the contemporary *devadāsi*, can yield 'real' information as agent with the greatest difficulty, not the least because methods of describing her sympathetically are already in place. There is a gulf fixed between the anthropologist's object of investigation and the activists' interlocutor. She slips through both cultural relativism and capital logic. (2) The 'popular' film forces the issues of the immediate post-decolonisation nation up into view because it speaks to *and* from the 'people' as it constitutes itself for representation and self-representation as the Constitutional subject; it also transforms itself into its asymmetrical opposite through the circuit of distribution – as commodity it performs the function of representing the nation to an international (though *not* inter-national) audience. (3) The Indo-Anglian novel in the colonial mode puts the lid on (1) and (2) by its apparent accessibility.

And an 'Indian' commentator is not necessarily helpful. To think the contrary is to fetishise national origin and deny the historical production of the colonial subject. Indo-Anglian fiction as well as Commonwealth literature have now been disciplinarised in Indian English departments. The history and management of the university in the colonies are by and large conservative. Here for example is a Reader in English at a reputable Indian university, sounding like the usual unproblematic Reader's Guide:

The next important novel of our study should be *The Guide* (1958), which is perhaps the most widely discussed of Narayan's works. The book, *which has all the ingredients of a commercial film* (indeed it was made into one), both on the maturity of the comic vision and in the novelist's artistic sophistication shown in the treatment of his theme (a sophistication which was lacking in the earlier novels), *transcends* the limits of a seemingly bizarre story. The *authenticity* in the treatment of Raju, an ordinary tourist guide with no extraordinary qualities except a certain cunning with which he plays on the gullibility of the village folk and Rosie the dancer, shows Narayan's artistic restraint in projecting Raju as a saint. It is this restraint which makes Raju's character and Narayan's art look credible. (Srinath 1986, pp. 7–8; emphases mine)

Upon being questioned, the author of this passage dismissed the film as not faithful to the novel.[24] True and false, of course. In this passage the making of the film is parenthetical, and perhaps what one is discussing in the present essay is the relationship between the text and that parenthesis.

At the end of the film, English is withheld by the saintly and triumphant Raju. He is fasting, waxy, bearded and swathed – in some shots deliberately made up to look like a standing photograph of the nineteenth-century popular visionary Sri Rama Krishna, one of the most recognisable icons of liberated Hinduism. The reconciled Rosie – here the film diverges wildly from the novel – holds him up and an immense crowd is gathered. An American reporter appears. She is in safari clothes. She asks a few inane questions: Do you believe in science? Have you been in love? etc. The moribund saint answers in Hindi through an interpreter, and surprises her with an English-language answer in the end. The American answers with a delight that is, alas, still typical: You speak English! The journalist too denies history by conveniently mistaking the progressive bourgeoisie for the primitive.

Another important theme de-subtilised by the film is: Woman with a capital W. Rosie is a failed enterprise in the modernisation of culture in the novel. In the film she appears in the house of an unreally opulent good-whore *devadāsi* mother who inserts her into the mainstream through marriage. (Rumour has it that the star Waheeda Rahman – a Muslim – who plays the role was rescued by the actor–director Guru Dutt from the red-light district of Bombay.)

In response to the stylistic requirements of the morality play of decolonisa-tion, the greatest identity-change is undergone by Rosie's husband, who becomes the lascivious instrument of the *devadāsi*'s daughters's social libera-tion. In the novel he is rather an odd obsessive archaeologist who is troubled by his wife's dubious profession. He is privately christened 'Marco' by Raju because his obsession puts Raju in mind of 'Marco Polo', a cliché figure for the small-town guide. In the film he becomes that anomalous and detested thing, a Eurasian Indian (a reminder that we were not always 'equal to the West'), whose last name becomes 'Marco'. Rosie is Rosie Marco before she becomes Miss Nalini.

Both Raju and Nalini become more and more like fashionable Delhi and Bombay undergraduates and young executives as their love progresses. Indeed, although the end of the film is ideologically most satisfying in terms of the new nationalism, this love-story is the part that, in context, is trend-setting.

This is also where 'form' and 'content' split apart to put into the field of vision the fault lines in the self-representation of the nation, precisely in terms of the woman as object seen. For this genre of musical film, especially in the 1960s, is always an elaborately staged frame for song and dance. These are Bombay musicals actively transforming the filmic conventions of the Hollywood musical and re-coding the myth of India in the process. What are remembered across classes, genders, nations – years afterward, in other countries – are the songs by famous artistes lip-synched by famous actors and actresses and, in *The guide*, the spectacular solo and group dance numbers. Here the cultural good is most visibly de-authenticated and re-territorialised. In the strictest sense of commodity (a product produced for exchange) the three classical dance traditions of India, and multiple folk forms, are put into a hopper, swirled around with free-form musical structuring to produce a global 'India'.

One of the most cliché items routinely noticed in Indian classical dance is the *mudra* – or the range of expressive hand–head–eye gestures. The Sanskrit word *mudra* is also 'coin' – a common concept-metaphor straddling the money-form and the simple semiotics of stylised gesture, capable of considerable elaboration, but incapable of incorporating contingency. It is also, characteristically, the word for engraving, imprint. It is not by chance, then, that it is through this already in-place value-form that the expressive repertoire of the Hollywood musical rushes in, culture-marked with the proper name 'India', ready for exchange.

The film is plotted in easy doubles. If Raju is purified through jail and drought, Nalini is purified through her search for and discovery of Raju. In usual patriarchal fashion, that process is not shown but implied. Let us consider it through a few moments of the 'real' time of our film, rather than the flashback temporality of the narrative.

At the jail gate, six months after Raju's good-conduct release, Raju's mother and Nalini arrive polarised, the former on foot from the village, the latter by car, just back from London. Their reconciliation starts the flashback in response to the mother's question: 'If you were going to step out, why did you marry?'

In the flashback, her dance-impulse is opened up at her own request. One of the film stills, framed by the bare legs of the rural snake-dancer, shows us the couple caught in the gaze of the dancer, whose graphic symbol is shaped like the female sex. The focus of the riveted gaze of the couple is indeterminate.

But dancing as such is not important to the film's Rosie. It is revealed through a conversation between Rosie and Mr. Marco (where the juxtaposition of sculptured dancers and Rosie makes the point that he is not in touch with life) that Rosie needs to dance because Marco cannot give her a child. Thus the cultural politics of the film do not allow the commodity-value of the dance-woman to be anything more than a splendid distraction which gives national information outside the nation, unaffected by the forces fabricating 'national identity' out of progressivism and nostalgia. The function of the novel (giving information without attention to its historical production) has more in common with the dynamic kitsch of the film's frame than one would suspect; it is just that the target-audiences are different.

The transformation of the classical *mudra* (money-form of expressive equivalence) into the vocabulary of the musical comes to a climax in the final dance, ending this central part of the film, where Waheeda Rahman's eyes, arms and hands combine an expressive (or free) understanding of gesture with vestiges of the (bound) traditional lexicon of the *mudra*, visible through the crescendo of music and tempo as she brings the refrain to its repeated conclusion: *hai, hai re hai, sainya be-iman* (alas, alas, (my) lover (is a) traitor). Whatever the eyes do, the mouth is fixed in a rictus that signals the separation of the dance from the direct expression of anguish or anger. From a complex set of perspectives, this is the *devadāsi* as living doll, stunningly expert in her art. Here the representation of *lāsya* is indeed again a skill, distanced by the work of the screen.

The first version of this chapter was written in Princeton, New Jersey. The circulating library of videotapes in a Princeton shopping mall where I obtained a videotape of the film is one of thousands spread across the United States and indeed all countries where there is a sizeable Indian immigrant presence. The value of the film in class-heterogeneous migrant subcultures has globalised the film differently from its ealier popular international presence, which continues on its own course. It has already been suggested that the current situation of the fabrication of 'national' identity in India makes of the film an anachronism. This new globalisation brings it clear out of the nation-theatre, into the space of cosmopolitan diasporic culture, at the other end from the radical cacophony of *The satanic verses*. At the end of the opening sequence of the central movement of the film (Miss Nalini's dancing career), where she is shown as receiving a prize, the film cuts to Raju's gloating face. In the place of the original fadeout, we read the following message:

> World Distribution
> Esquire Electronics Ltd.
> Hong Kong

There seems to be an appropriate if obscure typographic felicity that 'Esquire' is in the copyright typeface of the US-based men's magazine.

If the gendered subaltern, the young Maharashtrian *devadāsi* encountered by the SEWA group is at one end of the spectrum, this message on the screen, inside as well as outside the film, points at the immense network at the other end. The space in between is not a continuity. It offers a cross-section where the travestied premodern marks the failure of modernisation into the circuit of postmodernity. In the meantime, the muted modernism of the novel is in the classroom that moulds the traditional disciplinary dominant in the pluralist academy.

The film accommodates two minor and completely outdated gestures toward Hindu-Muslim secularism quite absent in the novel. As Raju lies in the arms of his mother and Nalini, Gaffur (the Muslim taxi-driver from his days as a guide) arrives, drawn by rumour. The villagers will not let him enter. Raju insists. They embrace. And, on a more atmospheric level, a popular folk-song, praying for rain, from what was then East Pakistan (now Bangladesh), is played in the film's otherwise Hindi song-track. Since Bangladesh is a Muslim-majority area of the subcontinent, the prayer is addressed to Allah, and the Bengali is Urdu-ised enough for one line of the song to pass as Hindustani. Only one word needed to be altered and in the syllabic space released is inserted the name of Rama, the Hindu god-king who was Gandhi's totem, and in whose name India is being 'ethnically cleansed' of its Muslim population in the 1990s. If, in the embrace of Gaffur, the nineteenth-century Rama Krishna is glimpsed, the coupling of Allah and Rama in song brings the Mahātma himself to mind. In the contemporary context of religious strife, these overdetermined moments would have to be either suppressed or elaborated.

If we remain within the taxonomic impulse, it may be submitted that the film translates the novel from elite colonial to popular national; from English to Hindi. Nowhere is this more apparent than the end. The novel makes miracle tastefully indeterminate as mental allegory. The film, in a bravura move, leaves Raju's body dying and discovered dead by a fully Indianised and respectable Nalini. Raju's spirit splits in two, the fashionable anglicised Raju dressed in the hip clothing of mid-film, and a resplendent Hindu Raju swathed in light, wrapped in a saffron-gold toga. The film's four final moments: lightning, then rain; the people dancing, the mother weeping; western Raju squirms and dies, Indian (secularist Hindu) Raju stands tall and smiling, with this to say to his other self: *tum ahamkār, main ātmā hum* (you are the ego, I the spirit). The corporeal Raju lies similingly dead, mourned by his beloved. This portion is uncontaminated by song, no lip-synching here, the connection between voice and consciousness intact; at the same time, the centre of the film, the woman's place of song and dance, retains its outline as commodity.

To conclude: the itinerary from colonial through national to post-colonial and/or migrant subjects is complex, diverse, many-levelled. This chapter has tried to plot a few way-stations on that itinerary by reading a text of cultural self-presentation. The method of reading has kept to the representation of agency. These representations are gender-divided. The medium of the male agent's self-representation in this case is the *devadāsi*. Such readings in the sub-discipline of Cultural Studies cannot claim the attention of the disciplinary historian of the aftermath of colonialism. They can timidly solicit the attention of the teacher of multicultural literature courses so that he or she can remain aware of the differences and deferments within 'national identity' and 'ethnic minority', and not take the latter as the invariable starting-point of every decolonisation of the mind.

Notes

1 See, for example, Richard Hoggart (1970) and Stuart Hall (1980b). Work produced from a black British subject-position, such as the early and influential *The empire strikes back* (Centre for Cultural Studies, eds 1982), has a singularly different aura from its effect on postcolonial self-representation in Indo-Anglian writing.

2 For an extended discussion of the role of popular music in this telematic cultural field, see Jean Franco, 'The sound of music', in her *Border patrol* (forthcoming).

3 This information is provided in the biographical blurb on the inside back cover.

4 Dipesh Chakrabarty notes the divide, but does not account for it: 'Until the Salman Rushdies arrived on the scence and made the intellectual ferment of modern India more visible to the outsider' (1992, p. 541).

5 For 'hyper-real', see Jean Baudrillard (1983b), p. 2.

6 Volosinov proposed a classification of literary form in terms of the reporting of speech (1973, pp. 115–23). I have commented on the problems of bilingual representation of subjectivity with reference to Nadine Gordimer's *July's people* (Spivak 1993, pp. 152–3).

7 In this respect, the visible 'difficulty' of Derrida's *Glas* (1986) is less 'bewildering' than the philosophical prose of his *Of spirit: Heidegger and the question* (1989), where he 'follows' every principle of style developed in his thought so implicitly that an uninstructed or too-quick reading can and often does interpret his grave denunciation of Heidegger's betrayal of himself in his later politics as an apology!

8 The best-known elaboration of this argument is to be found in Abrams (1971).

9 This is one of the suporting arguments in that part of Foucault's work which is interested in a chronological narrative of discursive formations. The argument is most persuasively made in Michel de Certeau (1988, pp. 147–205).

10 Narayan is thus able to make this sweeping generalisation, worthy of a Macaulay: 'all imaginative writing in India has had its origin in the *Rāmāyana* and the *Mahābhārata*' (1989b, p. 14). The problem of 'English In India' becomes a jolly safari arranged by some better-bred version of the India Tourist Board. Is Narayan naive or ironic in the following passage? 'In the final analysis America and India differ basically though it would be wonderful if they could complement each other's values ... One may hope that the next generation of Indians (American grown) will do better by accepting the American climate spontaneously or, in the alternative, by returning to India to live a different life' (p. 30). It is significant that only on the Raj is he uncompromisingly dismissive: 'The Raj concept seems to be just childish nonsense, indicating a glamorized, romanticized period piece, somewhat phoney' (p. 31). His word on decolonisation is back on the track of general niceness (perhaps we should allow for the fact that this piece was first published in the US *TV guide*): 'With all the irritants removed [at Independence], a period of mutual goodwill began between the two

countries' (p. 33). It is possible that, as a result of this general avoidance of conflict, Narayan is a preferred author in the underclass multicultural classroom in Britain (information received from Badar Nissar Kaler, Oxford).

11 For *découpage* see Derrida (1984), p. 28.

12 This book has been criticised by Indian scholars, but the politics of that criticism is itself a text for interpretation.

13 Narayan would like this not to be so (1989b, p. 32), and the Malgudi novels might have some unspecified regional specificity. *The guide* does not carry specific regional signals.

14 Making dancing acceptable as a fully-fledged career, inserting *Odissi* into the classical repertoire, has its own 'feminist' histories, in quite a different space from subalternity. My conversations with Sanjukta Panigrahi, an *Odissi* dancer of my own generation and class, brought this home to me yet once again. This history must not be allowed to take first place. And the role of the quiet proto-feminist mothers of this generation who, working with immense innovativeness behind the scenes, made their daughters' career-freedom possible must not be obliterated in the accounts of the daughters' struggles.

15 See Srinivasan (1988). One wonders how seriously one should examine Marglin's claim of solidarity with Mrs Besant. Annie Besant (1847–1933) was a brilliant woman of extraordinary enthusiasms and unremitting activism: for Christianity, atheist secularism, socialism and Theosophy/India. It is well-known that her aim for India was 'Self-Government within the Empire' (in Kumar 1981, p. 139). Indeed, her Thesophist millenarianism 'was to bring about a universal, theocratic state under whose firm, wise rule men could not but behave as brothers' (Taylor 1992, p. 277). As Taylor comments further, her 'historical account of India's spiritual past [was] heavily biased towards Hinduism. . . . Indians as well as Europeans blamed her for inciting race hatred and caste hatred. . . . "A democratic socialism controlled by majority votes, guided by numbers, can never succeed," she wrote as early as 1908; "a truly aristocratic socialism, controlled by duty, guided by wisdom is the next step upward in civilisation"' (pp. 311, 327, 313). Her attitude towards Indian women was consonant with her conviction that 'knowledge of British ways and political methods [would lead] to India's strengthening' (Kumar 1981, p. 102), and with her 'approval [of] a proletariat in the condition of a child, ready to be governed, ready to admit the superiority of its elders' (Taylor 1992, p. 313). I recommend a browse through a document like Besant's *Wake up, India* (1913) for a sense of her attitude to Indian women's education. It is no underestimation of her commitment, but a recognition of her historical inscription, to acknowledge that 'Victorian and Edwardian feminists collaborated in the ideological work of empire, reproducing the moral discourse of imperialism and embedding feminist ideology within it' (Burton 1990, p. 295). If Marglin's throwaway claim had been serious, her own invocation of a century's difference between herself and Besant would have led to considerations of the relationship between imperialism and neocolonialism, liberal humanism and cultural relativism. Who decolonises? And how?

16 See Chattopadhyay (1967). The famous reference in Kalidāsa's *Meghadūta* is not necessarily a reference to the institution.

17 See Bose (1990). I am grateful to Dr Bose for allowing me to summarise unpublished material.

18 'Sublate' is a newish translation of *Aufhebung*, usually translated *overcoming* or *superseding*, words that do not keep the colloquial German aura of preserving in a higher way while destroying the lower way.

19 The technique of analogising from individual pathology through the history of the language to the history of culture can perhaps do no more than figure forth the impossibility of ever performing this task successfully. For a bold excursion into this area, one might consult Freud's essay on the word 'uncanny', which still stops short of the cultural history of gendering (Freud, 1961).

20 Gyan Prakash (1990) has theorised this resistance in terms of pre-capitalist/pre-colonial and capitalist/colonial/postcolonial discursive productions (without reference to gender). Recognition of this resistance makes Kamala Kumar's unpublished report (1987) an unusually valuable source-document. Activists in the field interpret this resistance in various ways. From a distance it gives rise both to theories about the 'natural' inferioriy of ethnic/racial groups, classes and genders, as well as to cultural relativism. A certain variety of armchair resistance refuses to recognise its reality as well as its critical potential.

21 For more on SEWA (Self-Employed Women's Association), see Sheila Allen and Carol Wolkowitz (1987), p. 149.

22 'I am using "feminism" here in a loose sense. a) Work for the removal of social practices based on and perpetuating expoitation of women; b) follow-up support so that implementation of a) does not in fact become impossible through masculist and class reprisal; and c) education so that men and women want to be free of gender-bias and not consider the consequences of gender-freedom demeaning to themselves as men and women, and necessarily destructive of the social fabric' (Spivak 1991).

23 Discussion of Panigrahi's performance, Conference on Inter-cultural performance, Bellagio, Italy, 18 February 1991. Ms Ajayi's questioning was most perceptive, and revealed the difference in approach between performer and academic theorist. The bit about the film is the only part that relates to my argument.

24 The author of the novel would endorse this sentiment (Narayan 1989b, p. 32).

Post-apartheid narratives

GRAHAM PECHEY

Not all people exist in the same Now. They do so only externally, through the fact that they can be seen today. But they are thereby not yet living at the same time with the others.

World history . . . is a house which has more staircases than rooms. (Ernst Bloch, *Heritage of our times* (1935))[1]

This chapter took shape thanks to two images dredged from my memory of being on the South African student left thirty years ago. The first of these quotations from the left-hand margin of the social text of post-1948 South Africa is the letterhead symbol adopted by the National Union of South African Students in 1959 to epitomise its struggle against Pretoria's segregation of the English-medium universities: a jackboot of giant size smashing a fluted Ionic column in half, trampling culture underfoot. The second is verbal rather than graphic: it is the expression 'pillar structure' which was then regularly used in the Congress Alliance to describe the relationship of its constituent parts, whereby the four 'racial' congresses along with the South African Congress of Trade Unions imagined themselves as so many columns fronting a classical temple. Barbarism treading down culture; and the custodians of non-racial democracy under apartheid tyranny figuring their own internal relations under the sign of a line of verticals of equal height: what unites these columnar images is that they are both classically, quintessentially *modern*. Both, that is to say, draw on that architectural icon of a noble equality in terms of which the modern project of emancipation has been imaged over the last two hundred years. Why when modernity articulates its emancipatory narrative iconically it should typically freeze that story in a stone structure rather than flesh and human form is not a matter that concerns us here: no doubt it emblematises a claim for the impersonality of reason, the notion of rights as inhering in the individual rather than conferred by another person hierarchically placed over the latter. The foot in the boot belongs to the brute body of fascist power, and its sacrilege is the greater for being committed on that which transcends mere self-interest and arbitrary *Diktat*.

However that may be, consider the historical moment from which these images spring. South Africa had in the 1950s emerged, along with the other victorious allies, from an anti-fascist war; its prime minister Jan Smuts had been a member of the British war cabinet and had later been one of the foremost 'architects' (note that image again) of the Atlantic Charter. Having helped to beat fascism, South Africa within three years was itself set on a quasi-fascist course. The trauma for the classes of the colonised majority and for white democrats, whose hopes had been raised in the war years, could not have been more severe: when at last it seemed that 'their' polity would join the march to modernity in good order, getting in step with history, the terrible countermarch of apartheid began.

Or so it seemed: apartheid was anti-modern only on the outside, though it suited liberal discourse to paint it as anti-modern to the core, as an atavistic frontier phenomenon at odds with the logic of capital. Britain had after all pioneered in southern Africa the old colonial practice of modernisation by military force – what else was the Anglo-Boer War but that? – and now it had fallen to the Boers to perfect the legislative violence of apartheid to the same ends. This too came later to be seen as an edifice in its own right: a 'grand design' whose most visionary exponent was the 'granite' Hendrik Verwoerd, and whose 'pillars' are certain laws that are now said to be in process of demolition.

I

These memories and my reflections on them should by now have hinted that my concern here is to ask whether 'post-apartheid' is anything distinct from 'postcolonial' and whether it and the postmodern have anything to say to each other. Put rather more bluntly, it is also to ask how far the demolition of the edifice of apartheid has now put on the agenda the selective decon- struction of those *anti*-apartheid discourses under the sign of which that structure has been heroically, if often in a certain sense collusively, refused and opposed. Some brief preliminary definitions would seem to be called for.

'Postcolonial' has a banal sense which might apply equally to South Africa after 1910 and India after 1947: the sense of formal political 'independence', of having gone through a transfer of power, or of belonging to the period after that transfer. The reality of course is that 'postcolonial' is only too often a polite expression for states that are both economically and culturally *neo*colonial. Indeed – if we except the early one-off case of Liberia – South Africa might be called the first neocolonial state in Africa. It all depends on where you stand, where you are looking from, what you choose to look at. That this statist or centralist meaning of 'postcolonial' is a weak sense of the term is clear when one reflects that from the standpoint of most of its citizens

South Africa is anything but postcolonial, plunged as they were after 1948 into that worst of all forms of colonial subordination: the plight of finding themselves forcibly written into somebody else's narrative of redemption-after-long-persecution; in the condition (just when it seemed they would enjoy the fruits of the victors) of being what Edward Said has called, with reference to the Palestinians, the 'victims of victims'.[2] The stronger sense of 'postcolonial' emerges when we consider this seeming paradox: that it takes anticolonial struggles to produce neocolonial conditions. The postcolonial condition is the perspective one enters when one has resolved that paradox, relished that irony of history, and moved on. Postcoloniality in this sense is not confined to any particular kind of geopolitical space: it applies equally to the experience of diasporic and autochthonous communities, settler colonies no less than to territories of indirect rule, South African apartheid no less than to Indian democracy. Resisting any simple periodising correlations, the postcolonial condition is not one of power secured and centrally exercised in certain times and places. It is rather a dispersal, a moving field of possibilities which everywhere carry within them the mutually entailing, intimately cohabiting negative and positive charges of both power and resistance.

'Post-apartheid' – as we would expect, given that it is a species of the genus 'postcolonial' – is similarly open to different uses. South Africa's ruling party today would regard the post-apartheid condition as something already empirically in place, on the ground that segregationist ideology had been officially discarded and that some of the forms of legal exclusion and separation legitimated by it were being 'dismantled'. Business circles and the whole middle ground of white politics would concur in pronouncing the adjective with the same optimistic intonation and the same ends of keeping things as far as possible as they were. Against this banality of usage, the sense of 'post-apartheid' I am invoking here defines a condition that has contradictorily always existed and yet is impossible of full realisation: always existed, because apartheid as a politics of permanent and institutionalised crisis has from the beginning been shadowed by its own transgression or supersession; impossible of realisation, because the proliferating binaries of apartheid discourse will long outlive any merely political winning of freedom.

'Merely political': the phrase is meant to be provocative. I want to suggest that the privileging of politics is to be identified with the modern project as such, and that the self-scrutiny of the political we now see on many sides is one of the clearest signs of our ineluctable postmodernity. Feminism, for example, has been understood on the one hand as the finishing of an unfinished modern agenda of emancipation, and on the other as a postmodern revision or extension or even transcendence of politics. To be postmodern in politics today is to be ready to listen to the unconscious of modern political reason and to engage with the difficult, not always welcome (but always 'negotiable') return of its cultural and spiritual repressed. The post-apartheid condition is only one of the more striking contemporary instances of this coming-home-to-roost of lost histories.

What I have just said of feminism could be applied to the whole complex, 'uneven', many-sided struggle in South Africa today. Any consideration of that struggle must begin with what it is against: if the post-apartheid condition is a variety of postcoloniality, what kind of colonialism is apartheid? In 1962 the South African Communist Party proposed that apartheid was 'colonialism of a special type', or 'internal colonialism'.[3] This analysis informs the strategic perspectives of the African National Congress; it is rejected by the ultra-left and by Black-Consciousness-oriented movements. Briefly, this is the thesis that in South Africa colony and metropolis are co-extensive – not separated geographically, but (as it were) one on top of the other in the same territory. All classes organised around the oligarchy have an interest in its maintenance, while all classes within the majority have an interest in its overthrow. The sphere of the metropolis enjoys bourgeois democracy, civil society (of a sort), access to capital, social mobility. The people of the colony whose cheap labour helps to deliver these advantages of a democratised polity and a modernised economy themselves enjoy none of them.

Now this is a subtle thesis, and it has every appearance of modifying (albeit in an orthodox Leninist way) the classical 'class' analysis, inasmuch as it is a sensitive reading of the very specific historical experience of South Africa. The revolution in that territory, so it argues, is a complex dialectic of 'class' and 'national' forces; class antagonism by itself cannot either explain that revolution's course or dictate its strategies. At the same time, the thesis remains within the highly problematic discourse of (objective) 'interests' as a spring of action to which (subjective) 'consciousness' may or may not correspond. Its language is not unlike that of the 'labour aristocracy' thesis, a language of the long-term and short-term calculations of 'homogeneous' class-subjects with 'positive and non-contradictory' identities (Laclau 1990, p. 91). Indeed it is in a sense that thesis turned inside-out, theorising as it does sectional self-sacrifice rather than the pursuit of sectional advantage. Being co-subjects of the 'colony' along with the proletariat, the African bourgeoisie are predisposed to put the 'national oppression' of the whole before a class interest in economic exploitation that would ordinarily align them with the white ruling bloc. The effect of this analysis is to trap the agents of South African history in a logic which offers no ground beyond mystification on the one hand and clarification on the other, in a narrative which foresees the defeat of a reactionary nationalism by a revolutionary nationalism, giving to the latter the task of clearing the space for a finally clarified battle. It is a case, in other words, of class analysis not modified at all but only suspended. Theory has already clarified what history will eventually clarify for its agents (and for some of whom, the subjects of mystification especially, that process will take painful forms). Theory disguises its *hubris* by displacing its insights upon a future in which freedom will be the recognition of a necessity no longer hidden to all save the enlightened vanguard, but universally revealed. To adapt Freud on the ego and the id: where theory is, there history shall be.

This thesis of 'internal colonialism' needs not so much to be rejected out of hand as *re-read*. In such a re-reading or rewriting the peculiarity of this history would no longer be a matter of territory and the economy; no longer a merely local instance of 'combined and uneven development' offered as a particular inflection – a sublatable interruption, as it were – of what is in the end a metanarrative of world history; it would instead be a way of understanding the distinct and yet coinciding temporalities lived by South Africa's communities as they have journeyed together, belatedly but relatively rapidly, towards modernity. We need to see that what coincides in South Africa are not two 'superstructural' spheres on one 'infrastructure' but rather so many 'nows' lived alongside each other (Bloch 1977, pp. 22–38; 1991, pp. 97–116), and we need to place *discourse* at the centre of our concern rather than those categories that treat discourse as a mere epiphenomenon of bodiless social contradictions. In doing this we will wrest back from the alienations of a theoretical conceptuality the multifarious ways in which collectivities and subjectivities actually constitute and reconstitute themselves, those 'intensely believed' and solidly effectual 'serious fictions' of the social imagination (Clifford 1988, p. 98). The 'internality' of this colonialism can then be understood metaphorically as a redescription of 'South Africa' that bypasses the grand categories of the geopolitical and the world-historical in a new emphasis upon the *dialogue* that underlies all antagonism, the competing utopias that speak to each other inwardly even as their narrators outwardly turn laws and guns on each other. The history of South Africa is less the simple triumph of one such narrative of collective identity over another than an irreducible plurality of imagined communities that are not as deaf to each other as their manifest mutual contradiction might give out.

There are then, I am suggesting, singularities in the force field of South African politics that will always resist the totalisations either of grand theory or of grand history, areas of communal micropolitics unamenable to any macropolitical subsumption. Any anti-apartheid discourse that ignores this complex of singularities risks reproducing the distortions it sought to correct: there is no guarantee that a realised anti-apartheid universalism will avert the perils of the 'grand design' any better than the reactionary particularism of apartheid itself. The project of apartheid could be seen as an attempt to binarise the diverse times lived by South Africa's communities and to translate these times into (grossly unequal) spaces, freezing a heterogeneous history in the stasis of a Manichean racial geography. Apartheid modernises by imposing premodern cultural identities upon those it dominates; it reifies communities and it legitimates its domination by projecting its own particularism upon the dominated. Who is to say that the western narrative of emancipation in its 'pure' form will do any better?

That is one side of the argument; the other side to it is that no situation more fully justifies the emancipatory project of modernity than South Africa's: that if a universalist humanism has its dangers for some, South Africa's oppressed have no reason to fear them as an alternative to what they know of one of the world's most unjust particularisms; that what life there is in that project is certainly to be found in the likes of South Africa. Postmodern critiques of totality seem to be a metropolitan irrelevance – indeed to be themselves symptoms of a covert neo-universalism, an imperialism of theory which seeks to remake the world in its own image. Aren't we by exporting abroad our scepticism about universalising discourses ourselves replicating their very gesture of speaking for everyone, guilty (in short) of totalising in practice our theoretical detotalisations? Postcoloniality has some sobering lessons for the too-eager celebrants of postmodernity.

Just how much of the modern project still has weight and purchase in South Africa is no better demonstrated than by the Freedom Charter, the most powerfully mobilising document of the country's leading democratic movement (Cronin and Suttner 1986, pp. 262–6). Adopted in 1955, the Charter proposes a vision of a future South Africa by programmatically negating the prior negations of apartheid, translating into the terms of a manifesto that fragile and threatened utopia of non-racial collaboration in Congress and in the cultural field which was so notable a feature of those years. Its precursor texts, beginning with the great revolutionary declarations of late eighteenth-century Europe and America, would make a roll-call of all those documents in which the discourse of rights has been articulated, those textual holy places of secularised modernity in which the values of 'freedom' are (as they say: another architectural image) 'enshrined'. Collectively produced, it is also collectively received, rewritten by its readers, endlessly re-inflected in different class and communal contexts – in trade unions no less than in the 'new social movements'.[4] No text in the country's history has organised so many so variously behind a vision of how South Africans might one day live. The constituency it addresses and holds together is not racially defined: the blacks who reject it do so mainly on nativist and separatist grounds; the whites who do so for other than right-wing reasons are usually supporters of the ultra-left. Answering to the heterogeneity of its origins is the heterogeneity of those it helps to empower and enable. Implicitly bound up in a pragmatics of address, knowing none the less that it cannot (yet, or ever truly) perform the acts it names, this peculiarly hypothetical 'performative' utterance that is the Freedom Charter constitutes its readers as those who have the will to bring about the 'happiness conditions' in which its promises will be realised.

In a sense, then, the Charter resonates with its own unfolding context in so far as it combines in both production and reception distinctively modern and (equally distinctively) postmodern dimensions. Classically 'anti-apartheid' as to its historical occasion – the reality of consolidating segregation and repression in the 1950s to which it defiantly opposes its positives is to be felt in its every clause – the Charter is a post-apartheid text in more than just the grammatical sense suggested by the fact that all of those clauses are couched in the future tense: it is also and more profoundly 'post-apartheid' in its constant recreation of the freedom and equality it promises. The Freedom Charter takes its character from South Africa's extreme 'concentration of world history' (Derrida 1985, p. 297), from a context of the 'non-synchronous' mixing of historical processes and human possibilities that the west has long forgotten or not yet imagined, and it is in this context that its work is carried forward. 'Modern' in its paraphrasable content, it is, as Russell Berman has recently argued, none the less thoroughly postmodern in the rich and always unfinished political and cultural textuality it brings forth wherever it is read or cited (Berman 1988, p. 171).

II

While it has always existed in African translations, the Charter's authorised version is in English. This obviousness flowing from a known colonial history bears looking into. A liberated South Africa will doubtless follow India's example and set up English as the language of the state and the courts, while constitutionally recognising Afrikaans along with the (other) major African vernaculars. English has of course long been the *lingua franca* of the territory; and with auguries aplenty of a restored 'British' connection as apartheid goes, we need to ask what English and Englishness have hitherto signified in that context.[5] This will mean spelling out the stories and values which its transplantation there as a language of imperial power has carried in suspension and which, with its later transformation into a language of resistance, have not so much been displaced as skilfully refunctioned.

The official self-image of English in South Africa has been one of neutrality and anonymity. This habit of shyness about naming itself openly reminds one of Roland Barthes's remarks in *Mythologies* on the same characteristic in the very class with the rule of whose British contingent English first came to South Africa in 1806 (Barthes 1972, p. 138). Belief in this image has been the stronger thanks to a clutch of closely related historical contingencies, in a complex overdetermination.

Firstly, English is spoken as a native language by such a small minority of South Africans; probably as few as one in twelve. Secondly, the economic interests which English has historically accompanied have been since 1910 represented at the apex of state power by compliant Afrikaners. Thirdly, since 1948 the economically dominant English community has been displaced into relative political powerlessness by the militant Afrikaner foes of collaboration with Empire. Finally, unlike Afrikaans, English arrives homogenised and fully formed, its history as a language having taken place elsewhere and long ago, and its dialectal variety in speech having been effaced with the first generation to grow up in the colonies. The impotence that thus seems to hedge English about has had its compensations in an appearance of innocence amidst manifest wickedness, and in the fact that no other language in the land so evidently approaches the condition of money: that of universal (discursive) equivalence.[6] Its status is rather like that of Latin in early modern Europe, in that most of those who communicate in it speak some other tongue at home, and most of these users can also read. Fluency in English is virtually synonymous with literacy in a context where orality still determines the consciousness of millions. All but a few of the daily newspapers that circulate in South Africa are in English, and – with one (state-sponsored) exception in *The citizen* – they have always opposed the ruling party. The necessary language of any politics that is going to justify itself before the world is the language of a community excluded from power at home. As one North American ethnographer has astutely observed (Crapanzano 1986, p. 26), it is a community which typically enacts that very exclusion in the readiness of its members to discourse at length upon the characteristics of any other community besides their own. To read or speak or write English is, then, for most South Africans to look at themselves with the eyes of a global other, beyond the atactic intimacies of inner speech and the solidarities of the 'understood' in communication with a fellow speaker of one's own language.

Perhaps the clearest way of putting this is to say that English in South Africa is the language of full sentences and of contexts that cannot be assumed. Such contexts, where they are not implicitly universal, will need to have their particularity explicitly spelt out. Speaking English is for many rather like modulating from the spontaneity of everyday speech to that quasi-dramatic expository mode in which one explains oneself to an outsider. Writing it as the medium of poems and novels and plays is for many South African writers a difficult act of translation into a language that none the less presents itself to her or him as the necessary language of making oneself heard by an alien audience. For the African majority English is the 'natural' means of 'secondary resistance', not only unifying and mobilising for the struggle speakers of many different vernaculars but also determining by its very adoption the ends for which it is used. The weapons of 'primary resistance' – that is, the early military response to colonial conquest – could serve quite neutrally the ends of reversing dispossession and restoring premodern relations and institutions. The gun and the spear are interchangeable as means. English commits even its would-be nativist users to ends which cannot be other than culturally hybrid and politically modern.

Afrikaans is another matter altogether. From an anti-apartheid perspective

Afrikaans appears to be (in Gramscian terms) inherently repressive; English by contrast appears to be (counter-)hegemonic. In other words, anti-apartheid discourse sets up an asymmetry: Afrikaans is the language of domination by pure force, the mere unregenerate instrument of the refusal of dialogue, language which answers nobody and forbids an answer; English is the language of domination by consent (however limited or managed) and can therefore become a language of liberation. A post-apartheid perspective would complicate this schematic asymmetry with a welter of past ironies which need to be rescued from forgetfulness if they are ever to be compelled into future possibilities of freedom.

In the first place, the script of twentieth-century South African history – which began as we have seen with an episode of modernisation by sheer military force – was written in English. The fact that British capital disappeared behind its own creation after this fatal act of writing, pushing collaborators from among the defeated Boers onto the stage, should fool nobody. The happy outcome of all this is that when the colonial order embryonically imagined by John Buchan at the end of *Prester John* learned to call itself 'apartheid', it used an Afrikaans word. From the standpoint of those who coined this term it is of course *English* that is perceived as repressive, and with some justice, given the brutally enforced anglicisation of the period 1902 to 1910, when the humiliation of the battlefield and the concentration camp was replicated in the schools. And then of course the Afrikaners' own struggle after 1902 was (notwithstanding the armed rebellions against the war effort in 1914 and after 1939) almost classically counterhegemonic, a highly resourceful cultural struggle crowned with political success in 1948. Behind this irony is another, long suppressed in an unconscious collusion of antagonists. On the one hand, the petty-bourgeois Afrikaner intellectuals who fashioned Afrikaans as a literate idiom of modernity sought to purge it of its associations with poverty, servitude and illiteracy. Meanwhile the 'English' and the Dutch-speaking upper and middle classes of their own community agreed in denouncing Afrikaans as a 'kitchen dialect' (Hofmeyr 1987, p. 97). What neither could easily be brought to admit was that the language around which this (white) nationalist battle was conducted was a 'brown' language in its formation, as it was later to become in the racial composition of its actual speech community. A Dutch creole that grew out of a pidgin or 'contact language' used to communicate with slaves by settlers at the Cape (themselves speakers of several metropolitan dialects), Afrikaans is now in the situation where its typical native speaker is neither white nor even (necessarily) Christian: many of the 'coloureds' who are now a clear majority of its speakers are Muslim. Well into the nineteenth century the word 'Afrikaner' signified a person of mixed race; and it is now a commonplace that among the first printed texts in Afrikaans was a nineteenth-century Islamic sacred text published in Cairo.

If English, then, can appear anonymous and historiless, Afrikaans wears its history very much on its sleeve, having become a recognised grapholect in what is still living memory for its older speakers. There is all the difference in the world between a process of pidginisation–creolisation–standardisation that began a thousand years ago in the interaction of Danes and Saxons and Norman French on a remote island in another hemisphere (for English shares this history with Afrikaans) and one which culminated only yesterday for those who can still remember having to write and read the Bible in Dutch. No use of standardised Afrikaans can therefore be anything other than deeply and more or less openly politicised. To speak or write the *vernederlandsde* (Dutchified) Afrikaans of the Akademie – contemporary Dutch speakers find Afrikaans more 'Dutch' in its lexis than the freely borrowing Dutch of today – is to reaffirm a complex historic act of refusal: of the 'High Dutch' of Church and state before 8 May 1925; of the imperial vernacular legislated into equality with the latter; and of the 'Cape Dutch' *patois* of the mixed-race underclass among whom the creolising process has never really been arrested and still goes on.

Notwithstanding the heroising pathos of a nationalist myth which would seek to unify the language and confiscate it for a single racially defined community, Afrikaans always threatens to reveal its heterogeneity and its inescapable non-identity with itself. Afrikaans today is not so much a language as a spectrum of signifying possibilities running all the way from the stiffest 'official seriousness' to the most thoroughly carnivalised speech genres one can imagine (Bakhtin 1968, *passim*). The language on which Brown and Gilman drew in 1958 for evidence of what they called the 'power semantic' is no less rich in instances of the semantic of 'solidarity'.[7] This range of possibilities – of forms of subjectivity inscribed less in the formalities of its lexis and syntax than in its intonations, its creolised intensification-by-repetition, its fondness for diminutives – this range open to all of its speakers ceaselessly recalls the early history of Afrikaans in the age of slavery as the medium not only of overt and dominative master–servant relations but also of sexual liaisons and of peer-group interaction in play between children of owners and owned. It is a mark of the crisis of Afrikanerdom today that whereas this spectrum from the law-governed to the libertine once seemed to correlate exactly with a continuum of darkening complexion, those older correlations now no longer hold. As cultural legislators lose their grip on the *volk*, the revolt of middle-class Afrikaner youth has found expression in acts of deliberate 'recreolisation', and nowhere more publicly and audibly than in the lyrics of the 'Boer reggae' and rock groups that have sprung up of late.[8]

Now it is against this linguistic background that South Africa's other 'official language' emerges in all its reticent prominence as the one vernacular that rises free of all the others – that is to say, free of the taint of the compromised literacy of standard Afrikaans, while still graciously helping the mainly oral cultures of the majority to speak to each other and to the world at large. English in South Africa is the language of what Jürgen Habermas calls *Öffentlichkeit*, the 'public sphere' promised in liberal discourse but not (as yet) realised there. English is the potentiality of a mature civil society in South Africa because it seems to offer itself as the one language into which all the rich variety of the territory's idioms and meanings can be translated, and by means of which all of its diverse times can (at least hypothetically) be made to synchronise. It is because of this universalising *authoring* function, as the privileged medium of the monologue of modernity, that English has always been the language of anti-apartheid struggle.

Here is an area where what I have called the post-apartheid condition challenges that struggle and the whole conception of politics that it exemplifies. For the homogeneity that English seems to project is, needless to say, far from the truth of its actual – until recently only *oral* – variety. What has cowed that variety of Englishes into denying itself is a linguistic culture in which British norms dictate all written discourse and still determine the speech of professionals and 'communicators'. Decolonised Englishes flourish in popular performance – in, for example, the poetic declamation that accompanies every meeting within the counter-hegemony, and alongside music in the 'secondary orality' (Ong 1982, p. 136) of the electronic media. British norms of writing are also being challenged in the alternative press that has burgeoned in the 1980s, with the code-switching that has long been a habit of speech in many urban subcultures and linguistically liminal communities entering journalistic discourse as a cultural signifier of political difference from the established press of anglophone liberalism.[9] All in all, we could say that the linguistic flux that first colonial and then apartheid rule kept from knowing itself and from the world's knowledge has now come out into the open. For writers this means that writing in both grapholects can no longer address stable constituencies, no longer bracket-out the other uses of those languages which are now making themselves heard. Though English in our conditions of spreading literacy and a domesticated globality will never gel into coherent regional creoles as Dutch did in its isolation from Europe all those years ago – let alone become a new written standard – it will certainly go on generating hybrids, becoming ever more palpably heteroglot within the real South African polyglossia that an official diglossia has always occluded.

III

If a positive tone has up to now largely prevailed in this account of how South Africa's dominant languages are beginning to yield up the truth of their complex histories, then that tone now needs to be qualified by the recognition that along with an openly diversifying field of discourse there has gone an eerily analogous proliferation of the forms of violence. The forms of what is precisely the pathological negation and denial of discourse have multiplied as a terrifying undertow to its healthy growth. Through the 1950s the force of the state was met by the force of (defiant) language; after 1961 the liberation movements began to answer back with the language of (armed) force. Despairing of shaming the oligarchy into a moral literacy it didn't have, they began to speak the only language it could understand.[10] That polar simplicity of state violence on the one hand and revolutionary counterviolence on the other has gone for good. As the locked binaries both of apartheid discourse and of its antagonists self-deconstruct, not everything that is thus released is welcome, still less redemptive or healing, in its effects. As the principals in the current drama of negotiation exchange the niceties of diplomatic English, other members of their communities act out older narratives: some ride horses and carry guns and the flags of long-vanished republics; others are seen bearing the assegais and cattlehide shields of early battles against conquest. Others, again, are re-inventing the 'Great Trek' of the 1830s in projects of all-white survivalism in remote areas that hope in time to turn themselves into states.[11]

What are these but the old stories of desperate resistance to forceful modernisation coming back? At the end of *The colonizer and the colonized* we find the argument that the coloniser resorts to segregation because both of the alternatives – assimilation of the colonised, or their extermination – have a logic that would bring about the end of colonialism itself (Memmi 1990, pp. 214–19). Perhaps it was inevitable that when the apostles of segregation in South Africa embraced assimilation (as they now have), rival exterminisms should rush in to fill the vacuum. The space that has enabled some South Africans to open their mouths in dialogue with each other has stimulated others to get at each other's throats. Nineteenth-century cultural reflexes of 'fight' and 'flight', long relegated to the status of metaphors in an urbanised and modernised South Africa, are now being literalised. Armies of neo-fascist whites and armies of protofascist blacks are part of the price of entering the post-apartheid condition, with all its insights and its possibilities. They are the murderously negative outcome of master narratives that had always already failed of absolute mastery (they always do). In them we have the painful proof that beyond all illusions of normality and continuity unfolding in 'homogeneous, empty time' (Benjamin 1970, p. 263) the modern history of South Africa has without exception been a process of 'continuous catastrophe' (Habermas 1979, p. 38).

For writing in South Africa has always existed in, and been implicitly or explicitly informed by, a certain relationship to fighting. The only English analogue for this condition is to be found in texts like *The pilgrim's progress*, when in a still 'developing' England the passage to modernity still bore the marks of a communal ordeal by civil war that had been its most spectacular act to date, and a poor man (the first of his line to be literate) claimed for his class the right to imagine community beyond that terrible division. It is small wonder that this text – proffered in mission contexts as the devotional classic it had by then become, translated early on into the African vernaculars – should be so eagerly taken up by the first African writers as the record of a socio-political experience that spoke so directly to their own. That experience has in South Africa been speeded up from a process unfolding over ten or more generations to the experience of a single life: indeed it is the distinction of twentieth-century South African experience that it has been for so many the almost intolerable condensation of otherwise abstract historical processes into the concretely and subjectively *lived*.

It is then as the pacific alternative to fighting – specifically, for the contending nationalisms, its continuation by other means – that twentieth-century South African writing comes into being. If writing for those communities has been the effort of characters to become authors of their own narratives, writing in English by anglophone whites has been the fictional enactment of ever more liberal authorial modes, alternative styles of 'authoring' South African history offered by members of an already quasi-authorial linguistic community. This is the situation after the early fighting ended: for Afrikaners after 1902; for Africans after 1906. That act of cavalier imperial authorship called the Act of Union threw down a challenge to these two subaltern communities, and their writing and their politics must be read as a response to that event.

After 1961, this discursive *alternative* to fighting had to adjust to becoming its *accompaniment*, as the revolutionary counterviolence of the majority who were still 'characters' answered the violence of the new 'authors' of apartheid. All the writing since around 1960 is in some sense the infinitely various record of this adjustment. It is then of course complicated not only by the difference of communal perspectives but also by successive historical phases, situations that could be given shorthand descriptions by decade as 'the 1970s' and 'the 1980s'. The manifest failure of the early armed struggle, with its 'modern' binary logic, was followed around 1970 by the first wave (itself groping and failing as a workable project) of South Africa's postmodern politics. I refer to Black Consciousness, in which young intellectuals of the majority sought to existentialise and detotalise the struggle against 'internal colonialism' and whose *locus classicus* is Steve Biko's: 'the most potent weapon in the hands of the oppressor is the mind of the oppressed' (Biko 1988, p. 108). Black Consciousness is itself a fascinating instance of writing trying to launch itself into the world as a communal micropolitics – as pedagogy, as self-help, and as political theatre. It is to Black Consciousness that we are indebted for a deconstruction of the binary of 'physical' versus 'moral' coercion, and for an at least provisional settling-of-accounts with attempts to realise abstract 'equality' and the whole European discourse of rights in South Africa. In place of Mill or Marx, the young black intellectuals of the 1970s studied Frantz Fanon, Paulo Freire and Augusto Boal; liberation theology rather than the secular discourse of radical liberalism was their inspiration.

South African history shows itself here – as in so many other places – to be a quarry of collective stories and reflexes, of roles or modes of agency always ready for reversal or exchange. Where the Africanism of the Pan-Africanist Congress (the ANC schismatics of 1959 and after) was a latter-day attempt to reinvent the spontaneous nativism of early anticolonial battles in a myth of the return of the stolen land, Black Consciousness reruns and updates the cultural-separatist narrative of that intermediate moment when primary resistance was on the way out and pan-ethnic secular mobilisation had not yet got off the ground. This turn-of-the-century motif was realised in the 'Ethiopianism' of those independent African Churches which started out as attempts to indigenise European spirituality and which Benita Parry in her paper (in this volume) includes among other types of 'native disaffection', 'modes of refusal' that belong to groups other than the native elites. This proto-nationalist move subjected the universalism of Christian discourse to a spontaneous denial in practice; while the nationalist discourse that later mobilised millions embraced that very universalism and turned it against colonial injustice. (The Churches, which now run into the thousands, were to descend later into quietist accommodation with settler power and open collaboration with apartheid.) Thanks to this reinvention by Black Consciousness of an older separatism, underpinned no doubt by an unconscious emulation of the early phase of Afrikaner nationalism, the skills of patiently building a counter-hegemony passed into the collective wisdom of the South African resistance.

The rising of 1976 registered both the (contingent) failure of this politics and also its ineffaceable contribution: in the placing of psycho-cultural and spiritual issues – of discourse and consciousness – firmly on the agenda of any politics of the future. The old simplicities of collective identity ('class', 'nation') would never be the same after this searching problematisation they had undergone in practice. Both politics and its continuation by other means, the whole modern spectacle of parties and armies, of 'left' and of 'right', would henceforth be qualified by the arrival on the South African stage of quite new kinds of movement for change. Black writing had been renewed, wakened out of its state-inflicted amnesia; white writing in English was shocked into the production of a J. M. Coetzee and a radicalised Nadine Gordimer. The 1980s saw a regrouping, a reinvention of national mobilisation which none the less took into itself the heterogeneous social identities of differently oriented movements. Writing in the same period has echoed that diversity in the rich polyphony of its forms and modes. At the same time, it has more and more tended to negotiate the heightening militancy of the struggle: either, on the black side, to thematise 'fighting' in cathartic stories of recent struggles and in 'battle hymns' (Gordimer 1989, p. 293); or, on the white side, to let violence have its effects in the formal dislocation of its texts and in its vivid imaging of a chaotic apocalypse still to come (which some may think is already with us in the diversely privatised mayhem since the late 1980s).[12]

Summing up, we might say that black writing in the 1980s was just starting to recover from the long-drawn-out shock of a modernisation brutally instrumentalised by apartheid – for the first time fashioning its own ways of psychically resisting and living through that nightmare, becoming ever more confidently the author of its own narratives. White writing meanwhile has been afflicted by shock of a second-order and more mediated kind: shock at the demise of liberalism, at the failure of modernity's noble aims to counter that potential terrorism of modernisation which a Theodor Adorno would say was built into the quantifying logic of reason from the beginning. Upstaged and marginalised, the extremity of their twofold alienation – from the majority by privilege as well as from their own communities by their dissidence – has been met by extreme gestures, including a rounding-upon the category of history itself and a deep suspicion of 'commitment'. Coetzee of course represents this Adornian move; Gordimer the Benjaminian (Habermasian?) alternative.[13]

Does post-apartheid writing, then, bifurcate into a modernist or postmodernist white writing on the one hand and a neo-realist black writing on the other? Firstly, it needs to be said that these metropolitan aesthetic categories have a very different valency in colonial contexts like South Africa's: modernism, set against such a manifestly discontinuous social text, might seem to be a species of 'realist' reflection; whilst realism, in a context where community has had to be figured formally and 'fictionally' for as long as it has never been truly realised in life, might seem to partake more of hypothesis and reflexivity. Beyond this, I would want to suggest that South African writing has never been anything other than postmodern (as a whole practice, as an institution), though not always (technically, in the sense of its internal textual relations) postmodern*ist*. What is in any case certain is that South African writing in all its postmodern diversity usefully rumbles the Eurocentric assumptions of much modernist criticism, and none more so than the Marxist (post)structuralism of Pierre Macherey, some of whose concepts are very searchingly reviewed by Peter Hulme elsewhere in this volume. Can one so easily pronounce that the literary work is the 'imaginary solution of implacable ideological contradictions' (Macherey 1978, p. 8) where writing is so plainly the place where marginalities of *all* kinds can meet and be positively valued, where writing always shadowed by violent death is so plainly the one healing alternative to fighting? Only a hubristic confidence in the all-explaining, all-resolving power of theory and history (or in the Party constituting itself as the 'imputed' consciousness of the class) could produce a formula so grotesquely irrelevant to the experience of millions outside western Europe, who have lived the Stalinist and imperialist 'solution of contradictions' in reality only as slavery or genocide. The formula is, moreover, an insult to the human imagination itself: without whose social projections and introjections there would be no 'contradictions' to resolve in the first place.

We may more usefully look at the question with the help of Benjamin's *rettende Kritik*, as his distinctive way with texts or objects has been called (Habermas 1979, pp. 30–59). Where South African writing has been more than the mere inertia of metropolitan discourse reproducing itself in an exotic place (as in the case of those early anglophone birds of passage like Rider Haggard who wrote ripping yarns), its narratives have always in effect been allegories of community, strenuous efforts of memory or anticipation that contest by their own example theory's privileging of the present as the 'hegemonic moment of historical time' (Aronowitz 1981, p. 121). This writing has since the extraordinarily prefigurative example of Olive Schreiner's *The story of an African farm* been for a century at least the critical custodian of the lost or imagined times of communities that have been forced by the galloping dynamic of bourgeois modernity to fetishise land and its ownership, space and its occupation. The project of righting the wrongs of South Africa has now at last caught up with a writing that has always been beyond (or before) both racism and humanism, those rival discourses of its perverse modernity. Neither the freezing of difference into metaphysical opposition nor its universal dissolution, this writing has always been the site of an irreducible and plural difference. 'Beyond' *is* 'before' in the case of Schreiner's novel: the consciously self-valorising discontinuity of that protomodernist text of 1883 resists by way of form a totalising process that was then still to come (or only beginning), a story whose culmination was the 'marriage of maize and gold' in the unified settler state (Pechey 1983, pp. 65–78). The early documents of South Africa's troubled encounter with capitalist modernisation (Sol Plaatje's *Mhudi* is another) speak to our time not as expressions of liberal ideology more or less ignorant of their own conditions – objects of our suspicion – but as radiant fissures in the continuous text of our history, priceless resources in our own 'moment of danger' (Benjamin 1970, p. 257).

We are all now, whatever our age and wherever we live, children of 1976. The actors pushed forward by that moment were the youth: those whose time is the future (Bloch 1977, p. 23; 1991, p. 98). The coalitions of the 1980s wove together a range of times and positionalities; the 1990s have opened with a new crisis of transformation which shows that the age of parties and armies is far from over in South Africa: in its very success the politics of coalition has fed a polarisation into murderously threatening sects driven by monopolistic narratives from the past. But the writing of the 1980s

– driven by nothing more than its own unsubsumable, unsublatable difference from and within itself – has preserved that moment of rupture precipitated by the urban youth, using it as an optic for the rescue of earlier moments, constructing with it a common 'address to the future' (Clingman, in Trump, ed. 1990, p. 43). Gordimer's *July's people* and Coetzee's *Life and times of Michael K* are exemplary texts of this orientation. Gordimer's writing life spans the history of apartheid that it has redeemed by living from the inside out a process that has mutilated millions with its invasion of their inmost lives, thereby 'fictionally' compelling heteronomy into autonomy.[14] Unlike Gordimer, who co-leads the Congress of South African Writers, Coetzee has eschewed politics and concentrated instead on a pitiless quarrying and parodic reworking of the whole gamut of colonial narratives, latterly taking his exploration of 'white writing' as a global phenomenon back to its *Ur*-text in *Foe*. In his belief that fiction's relation to history should be one not of 'supplementarity' but of 'rivalry', he is only generalising in English the earlier move of his fellow Afrikaner dissidents who write in their own language: namely, contesting the nationalist epic of Afrikaner history by rewriting it as a novel, a story whose characters are transgressive anti-heroes of the picaresque (Brink 1983, pp. 20–1). Coetzee takes this particular scepticism and predicates it across history as such, so that history becomes nothing but 'a certain kind of story people agree to tell each other' (Attwell 1990, pp. 102–3).

Over against these 'postliberal' modes of white writing is a new 'postnationalist' black writing that breaks with the stance of 'protest', insisting that the endlessly rehearsed pathos of injustice and its redress starves the social imagination of the oppressed, and advocating instead a conscious 'rediscovery of the ordinary' (Ndebele 1986, pp. 143–57). In his *Fools and other stories*, Njabulo Ndebele puts this programme into action with protagonists who are middle-class township children, and with a focus displaced away from the polar conflicts and towards the inner differences of autonomous urbanised communities, where the modern and the premodern co-exist (harmoniously or otherwise) on terms neither dictated by the state nor fully understood by its liberal opponents. Ndebele saves his world from these 'soft' and 'hard' heteronomies alike by letting its various times speak to each other, outside any enforced synchronisation.[15]

In this, as in all of its modes, South African writing is a dialogue of creoles of all 'colours' overheard by the world – 'overheard' rather than heard because it is quite capable of positing its own 'superaddressee' (Bakhtin 1987, pp. 126–7), and because the story's pace and path are determined by nobody but the participants themselves. If it is, then, a sort of collective and dialogical autobiography, the subject of that auto-narrative is neither of those *a priori* collectivities posited by a universal history: neither nation nor class; nor indeed any 'unevenly developing' combination of nations and classes working teleologically through the ruse of historical reason towards the ultimate abolition of difference.[16]

Which brings us back to the 'social text' that I began by 'quoting'. Modernity in the epoch of late capital, in the self-scrutinising moment that Zygmunt Bauman has called its 'coming of age', does after all have an icon that is other than architectural, a *person* whose stature matches those classical capitals and pediments. As Simon During has recently written, 'the most charismatic living figure of the enlightenment is a black South African: Nelson Mandela' (During 1989, p. 37). This icon is a breathing hero in whom the values of modernity are incarnated, agonistically lived rather than cognitively articulated. As the last colonial territory of Africa goes, it throws up from its marginality a figure of such spiritual power that everyone in the centre wishes to be seen standing in his aura. The promise of an absolutely homogeneous time is carried by a man actually hedged around by many times, who in himself condenses the divergent temporalities of the young and the old in his own country. It is possible for the world to consume the spectacle of Mandela in a self-confirming way; it is also possible to look beyond him, to honour the auratic and authentic in him and yet to let the post-apartheid condition (which surrounds and deeply qualifies his every word or move) deliver its critical verdict upon the whole late-modern world.

Postscript

That is where the first draft of this paper ended. In revising it, I can now see how much it is a text of its moment: of 1990, or at least of 1990 as it was lived and 'read' by someone who cut his political teeth in the now almost unimaginably different and distant world of 1960. The crisis of transformation we thought we were going into then was actually much longer in coming; that 'interregnum', replete with all of its 'morbid symptoms', had by 2 February 1990 decisively arrived. It fell out that de Klerk's speech to the Cape Town parliament coincided with the first publication in South Africa of an address by Albie Sachs to an ANC in-house seminar, in which this respected and authoritative voice echoed Njabulo Ndebele's call for an end of the art of 'fists and spears' and for a democratic culture that was freed at last from 'the multiple ghettoes of the apartheid imagination' (Sachs 1991, p. 8). The year 1990 also saw Rian Malan's *My traitor's heart*, an extraordinary offering in the genre of the 'new journalism' which recorded the impotence of all theoretical paradigms deriving from the enlightenment to explain the 'tales of ordinary murder' that make up so much of the texture of South African life (Malan 1990, pp. 105–334). Finally, it was the year in which Steve Hilton-Barber's photographic exhibition on African initiation schools raised a storm of protest when it opened in Johannesburg, and when a range of democratic organisations (including the ANC itself) lined up to explain their policy on traditional circumcision.

When the words proclaiming normalisation were spoken from above, the circumstances in which they were spoken couldn't have been more different from 1960, with its high-minded constitutionalist discourse pitted against a recognisable evil centred in the state: what had happened? Either politics had swallowed everything, exploding outwards to the furthest horizons, down into the deepest recesses of the unconscious, and back into a premodern past that was still with us; or all of these had swept into the space left after the terminal implosion of that lucid region that was 'the political' as 'we' had always known it. Or perhaps South Africa was simply displaying in practice that revenge of politics on the false objectivity and totality of 'the social' for which Ernesto Laclau has called in theory. Years of fighting the 'irrationality' of racism with your own rationality (for we were all closet liberals in our everyday consciousness) are no preparation for an encounter with the non-rational that undoes and escapes that old complicity of opposites. Whatever it was, this ambiguous extension–extinction of politics will have consequences on the ground in South Africa: more will have to be 'negotiated', more delicately and for far longer, than any agreement of mere parties could enforce. And, of course, consequences for theory: we who had spent our best years speaking of culture as the repression of politics might now want to turn that formula on its head, as I have done here.

The question of the repression of 'ethnic' identities (culture) by world-historical narratives (politics) surfaced at the Symposium in discussion of the role of the postcolonial intellectual, and at most length in Neil Lazarus's paper. His (and Said's) notion of that role as one of the irreplaceable 'crystallising of memories and experiences' resonates strongly with my own claims for writing as carrying a Blochian 'utopian surplus' with real effects in the redemptive (re)composition of the social text itself. At the same time, his inflection of this case has helped me to see the dangers of even seeming to suggest that the postcolonial is in any simple sense to be identified with the one-sided valorisation of the local or marginal over the global: thanks to imperialism, 'experience and social identity' are now ineluctably and always already global, 'world-historical in their constitution', and globalism is not only more needed but has also 'intensified' in recent years. Speaking-for-everybody is now to be the task of the hitherto always spoken-for. Perhaps after all the little narratives of the margins are only ever hybridisations of the grand narratives of the centre; perhaps even 'nativism' is a naive parody of nationalism; 'liberationism' its subtler, 'disidentifying' counterpart. In post-colonial intellectual practice indigenising theory and globalising experience are two names for the same move.

Notes

1 The translation of these epigraphs from Bloch is that of Neville and Stephen Plaice (Bloch 1990, pp. 97 and 114); another translation may be found in *New German critique* (Bloch 1977, pp. 22 and 36). Their context is of course the Nazi period; later, in the period of decolonisation (in 1963 to be precise), Bloch's attention takes in far more than the history of Europe: 'The firmer the refusal of a purely Western emphasis, and of one laid solely upon developments to date (to say nothing of discredited imperialism), all the stronger is the help afforded by a utopian, open-ended and in itself still experimental orientation. Only thus can hundreds of cultures flow into the human race; and that only then takes shape in non-linear historical time, and with an historical direction that is not fixed and monodic' (Bloch 1970, pp. 140–1).

2 I cannot trace a reference for this phrase in the writings of Said to which I have access; it is likely then that I have remembered it from a televised interview.

3 The thesis was first enunciated in the programme of the reconstituted SACP (formerly CPSA) entitled *The road to South African freedom*. A modified version is to be found in *The path to power*, the new programme adopted by the party in 1989. The ANC document on 'Strategy and tactics' from the Morogoro conference in 1969 signals its adoption by the wider movement; for further information see Joe Slovo's 'South Africa – no middle road' (Davidson *et al.* 1976, pp. 106–210).

4 In South Africa the trades unions *are* 'social movements' rather than the defensive associations only of workers at the point of production; adoption of the Freedom Charter by a number of COSATU unions in the late 1980s signalled an awareness of this broader role within the community at large. Stanley Aronowitz has drawn international parallels and described the unions as 'characterized by a whole network of cultural affinities' (Aronowitz 1989, pp. 60–1).

5 Exemplary indices of these reviving British links include: the decision by the BBC in 1990 to begin broadcasting on medium wave in South Africa; the now almost certain return of South Africa to the Commonwealth; the rush to drop sanctions and reinvest there; and the Tory government's offer to train future South African bureaucrats at the Civil Service College.

6 The phrase 'universal equivalent' to describe the peculiar commodity status of money is of course Marx's, from volume 1 of *Capital*. My metaphor is not extravagant or fanciful: arguing for English as the sole medium of education in South Africa, a prominent member of its English Academy has observed that 'thought, like money, has no colour' (Butler 1986, p. 169). For an excellent critique of the 'innocence' and 'neutrality' of English in this context, see Ndebele (1987), pp. 217–36.

7 See Brown and Gilman, 'The pronouns of power and solidarity' (1972), pp. 252–82. J. M. Coetzee's heroine Magda in *In the heart of the country* has this to say of Afrikaans: 'A language of nuances, of supple word-order and delicate particles, opaque to the outsider, dense, to its children, with moments of solidarity, moments of distance' (Coetzee 1977, p. 30). Her author interestingly cites Brown and Gilman in his critical work *White writing* (Coetzee 1988, p. 180), suggesting that these echoes of their terms in the novel are not fortuitous.

8 I am thinking here of two groups in particular: the reggae band led by Bernoldus Niemand; and Johannes Kerkorrel en die Gereformeerde Blues Band. Kerkorrel – his name means 'church organ' – has spoken publicly of his aim of furthering the linguistic promiscuity that first gave birth to Afrikaans.

9 The relevant comparison here would be the *Weekly mail*, founded in 1985 to succeed the *Rand daily mail* by a collective of younger journalists from the latter. Left-liberal and social-democratic (rather than 'mining-house' liberal) in orientation, the *Weekly mail* has from the start cultivated a deliberate South Africanism in its language, notably on its cultural pages, where township *patois* and the odd Afrikaans word or phrase rub shoulders with

(post)Marxist and post-structuralist vocabulary. For their part, radical Afrikaans journals like the *Vrye weekblad* and *Die Suid-Afrikaan* have broken with conservative journalistic norms by not straining to avoid English. Thus 'the struggle' regularly translates not as *die stryd* but as *die struggle*.

10 'Defiant' in this passage alludes to the Defiance Campaign of 1952 in which 'volunteers' of all races openly broke apartheid laws governing places of public resort, and were gaoled for doing so. My point is that the shift to armed struggle was a potential already implicit in the metaphoric discourse of civil disobedience; tenor and vehicle change places as we move from a (constitutionalist) language of moral force to the (Fanonist) claim that violence is the only language the oppressor understands. Nelson Mandela's speeches of the 1950s are a rich source of the former; for the latter we have only to look at his speech from the dock in 1962 (Mandela 1965 pp. 162–89).

11 Verwoerd's son and son-in-law have launched separate schemes of this kind in recent years, so far without much success, in the north-west Cape and the eastern Transvaal.

12 These post-1976 fictions of struggle include Mongane Serote's *To every birth its blood*, Sipho Sepamla's *Ride on the whirlwind* and Mbulelo Mzamane's *Children of Soweto*. For a study of these and other novels see Sole (1988), pp. 65–87 and Trump (1990), pp. 161–85.

13 Some of the ideas in this paragraph and in the argument that follows were formulated after a reading of Neil Lazarus's very stimulating essay (Lazarus 1987, pp. 131–55). I would like to record here an indebtedness to this piece which I expressed privately when I met the author himself at the Symposium and benefited further from his impressive grasp of Frankfurt School theory. For more on the problematic postmodernity of South African writing, see also Carusi (1989).

14 This rather tortuous sentence which tries to render the specificity of Gordimer's achievement cannot be allowed to pass without a reference to the book that traces her work patiently and expertly through this whole history (Clingman 1986).

15 See Vaughan (1990), pp. 186–204 for a discussion of Ndebele's stories that develops very well their status as 'cultural' alternatives to the categories of a 'theoretical' knowledge of his community.

16 See Pechey (1990) for a review of some recent South African fiction which extends this case by recommending a writing of the struggle that refuses the 'positive heroism' of 'movement' history. Menán du Plessis's *Longlive* (1989) is contrasted in these terms with Mandla Langa's *A rainbow on the paper sky* (1989).

Resistance theory / theorising resistance or two cheers for nativism

BENITA PARRY

it is not the literal past, the 'facts' of history, that shape us, but images of the past embodied in language... we must never cease renewing those images, because once we do, we fossilise. (Brian Friel, *Translations* (1981, p. 66))

I

That the colonised were never successfully pacified is well known to the postcolonial study of colonialism and the long and discontinuous process of decolonisation.[1] But proposals on how resistance is to be theorised display fault-lines within the discussion that rehearse questions about subjectivity, identity, agency and the status of the reverse-discourse as an oppositional practice, posing problems about the appropriate models for contemporary counter-hegemonic work. An agenda which disdains the objective of restoring the colonised as subject of its own history does so on the grounds that a simple inversion perpetuates the coloniser/colonised opposition within the terms defined by colonial discourse, remaining complicit with its assumptions by retaining undifferentiated identity categories, and failing to contest the conventions of that system of knowledge it supposedly challenges. Instead the project of a postcolonial critique is designated as deconstructing and displacing the Eurocentric premises of a discursive apparatus which constructed the Third World not only for the west but also for the cultures so represented.[2]

The performance of such procedures does display Richard Terdiman's contention that 'no discourse is ever a monologue; nor could it ever be analyzed intrinsically... everything that constitutes it always presupposes a horizon of competing, contrary utterances against which it asserts its own energies' (Terdiman 1985, p. 36). However, the statements of the theoretical paradigms, where it can appear that the efficacy of colonialism's apparatus of social control in effecting strategies of disempowerment is totalised, are liable to be (mis)read as producing the colonised as a stable category fixed in a position of subjugation, hence foreclosing on the possibility of theorising resistance. Even if this is a crass misrepresentation of the project, the colonised's refusals of their assigned positions as subjected and disarticulated are not – and within its terms cannot be – accorded centre stage.

The premise to modes of criticism within the postcolonial critique which are attentive to those moments and processes when the colonised clandestinely or overtly took up countervailing stances is that no system of coercion or hegemony is ever able wholly to determine the range of subject positions. For although the colonial is a product of colonialism's ideological machinery, the formation of its differentiated and incommensurable subjectivities is the effect of many determinants, numerous interpellations and various social practices.[3] A postcolonial rewriting of past contestation, dependent as it is on a notion of a multiply (dis)located native whose positions are provisional, and therefore capable of annulment and transgression, does not restore the foundational, fixed and autonomous individual; what it does resort to is the discourse of the subject inscribed in histories of insubordination produced by anti-colonial movements, deciphered from cryptic cultural forms and redevised from vestiges perpetuated through constant transmutation in popular memory and oral traditions.

There is of course abundant evidence of native disaffection and dissent under colonial rule, of contestation and struggle against diverse forms of institutional and ideological domination. Inscriptions and signs of resistance are discernible in official archives and informal texts, and can be located in narrativised instances of insurrection and organised political opposition. Traces of popular disobedience can also be recuperated from unwritten symbolic and symptomatic practices in which a rejection or violation of the subject positions assigned by colonialism is registered. Here the modes of refusal are not readily accommodated in the anticolonialist discourses written by the elites of the nationalist and liberation movements. Since they were not calculated to achieve predetermined political ends or to advance the cause of nation-building, the anarchic and nihilistic energies of defiance and identity-assertion, which were sometimes nurtured by dreams, omens and divination, and could take the form of theatre, violated notions of rational protest.[4]

If we look at the work of contemporary critics recuperating figures of colonial resistance, not from the rhetorical strategies of the dominant dis-courses but by revisiting dispersed and connotative informal sources, these projects do not appear as preoccupied with victimage, or as enacting a regressive search for an aboriginal and intact condition/tradition from which a proper sense of historicity is occluded – charges which have been made against such undertakings. As an instance of a resistant mode available to the colonial Caribbean, Wilson Harris cites limbo dancing, a practice stemming from Africa and reinterpreted on the slave ships of the Middle Passage, and which although indebted to the past – as is voodoo – is not an imitation of that past but rather 'a crucial inner re-creative response to the violations of slavery and indenture and conquest' (Harris 1974, p. 14). Such a strategy is not the total recall of an African past since that African past in terms of tribal sovereignty or sovereignties was modified or traumatically eclipsed with the Middle Passage and with generations of change that followed. Limbo was rather the renascence of a new corpus of sensibility that could translate and accommodate African and other legacies within a new architecture of cultures. (Harris 1974, p. 10)

Does revisiting the repositories of memory and cultural survivals in the cause of postcolonial refashioning have a fixed retrograde valency? Such censure is surely dependent on who is doing the remembering and why: certainly as Rashmi Bhatnagar suggests, in some situations the mythologising of beginnings can be suspect 'in that it can unwittingly serve the reactionary forces of revivalism. Nowhere is this danger greater than in the Indian context, where the search for the source of Hindu identity in Vedic times has almost invariably led to a loss of commitment to our contemporary plural/ secular identity' (Bhatnagar 1986, p. 5).[5] A very different impulse towards recuperating a very different history marked by discontinuities and erasures is attested by Edouard Glissant whose repeated references to the Acoma tree intimates that the need to renew or activate memories is distinct from the uncritical attempt to conserve tradition: 'One of the trees that has disappeared from the Martinican forest. We should not get too attached to the tree, we might then forget the forest. But we should remember it' (Glissant 1989, p. 260). In his aphoristic and fragmentary critical writings Glissant urges a postcolonial construction of the past that, far from being a desire to discover a remote paternity, is an imaginative reworking of the process of *métissage* or an infinite wandering across cultures including those of Africa. Because the slave trade snatched African-Caribbeans from their original matrix, erasing memory and precluding the ability to map a sequence, Glissant contends that it is the function of a contemporary counter-poetics to engender that tormented chronology:

> For history is not only absence for us. It is vertigo. The time that was never ours we must now possess. We do not see it stretch into our past and calmly take us into tomorrow, but it explodes in us as a compact mass, pushing through a dimension of emptiness where we must with difficulty and pain put it all back together. (Glissant 1989, pp. 161–2)

Since these are definitions of a discursively produced resurgent subjectivity that is volatile, polyglot and unconcerned with discovering the persistence of an original state, it would seem that critics who continue to valorise the identity struggle, and to reclaim forms of situated agency asserted in the struggle over representation, do so without returning to the notion of an ahistorical essential and unified self. In this vein Stuart Hall has braved the reprobation directed against ethnic identitarianism, to make a carefully

modulated case for decoupling ethnicity from its equivalence with nationalism, imperialism, racism and the state as it functions in the dominant
discourse, and appropriating it for a different usage in the current post-
colonial discussion: 'The term ethnicity acknowledges the place of history,
language and culture in the construction of subjectivity and identity, as well
as the fact that all discourse is placed, positioned, situated, and all knowledge
is contextual' (Hall 1988c, p. 29). Now although Hall is wary of postmodernism's 'absolutist discourse', since he considers that 'the politics of
absolute dispersal is the politics of no action at all', he defines subjectivity as
'a narrative, a story, a history. Something constructed, told, spoken, not
simply found' (Hall 1987, p. 45), and identity as an invention 'which is never
complete, always in process, and always constituted within . . . representation'
(Hall 1990, p. 222).

Hall is quite aware of the colonial subject as the product of multiple
constitutions, of the contradictions and overdeterminations of postcolonial
ideological positions – having written of these as always negotiated and
negotiable – and of ethnic and cultural difference as sites of articulation. He
has all the same directed attention to the indispensable role played in all
colonial struggles by a conception of '"cultural identity" in terms of one
shared culture, a sort of collective "one true self" . . . which people with a
shared history and ancestry hold in common'. This, he adds, 'continues to be
a very powerful and creative force in emergent forms of representation
amongst hitherto marginalized peoples . . . We should not . . . underestimate
or neglect . . . the importance of the act of imaginative rediscovery which this
conception of a rediscovered essential identity entails' (Hall 1990, pp. 223,
224). And before we pillory Hall for reviving the myth of an organic com-
munality, we should note that he emphasises the impossibility of its indivisible,
homogeneous meaning, recognising this to be an 'imaginary reunification',
imposing an 'imaginary coherence' on the experience of dispersal and frag-
mentation, and acknowledging that its other side is rupture and discontinuity.

Because in another register Henry Louis Gates Jr has reclaimed the *ethnos*
from vilification as false consciousness (Gates 1990), it could appear that
there is a move to restore affect to the fiction of identity, and rather than the
toleration extended to its expedient use in political mobilisation, we see it
embraced as a pleasure, and one that is all the greater because identity is now
perceived as multi-located and polysemic – a situation that characterises
postcoloniality and is at its most evident in the diasporic condition. An
uninhibited statement of the gratification of inhabiting many cultures and
identifying with all oppressions and persecutions, while electing to be affiliated
to one's natal community, comes from the artist R. B. Kitaj, in whose
paintings Rosa Luxembourg and Walter Benjamin are emblematic figures
of that particular and permanent condition of diaspora in which he is at
home:

> The compelling destiny of dispersion . . . describes and explains my parable pictures, their dissolutions, repressions, associations, referrals, their text obsessions, their play of difference . . . People are always saying that the meanings in my pictures refuse to be fixed, to be settled, to be stable: that's Diasporism . . . Diasporist art is contradictory at its heart, being both internationalist and particularist . . . The Diasporist's pursuit of a homeless logic of *ethnie* may be the radical core of a newer art than we can yet imagine . . . the Jews do not own Diaspora, they are not the only Diasporists . . . They are merely mine. (Kitaj 1989, pp. 35, 37, 39, 21)

There are moreover critics who testify to the possibility that the identity struggle of one community can serve as a model for other resistant discourses, since the self-definition articulated by, say, the black or the Jew in defiance of received representations can be communicated to different situations of contest against the authority of the dominant by marginals, exiles and subjugated populations. (see Diawara (1991) and Grosz (1990)).

II

When we consider the narratives of decolonisation, we encounter rhetorics in which 'nativism' in one form or another is evident. Instead of disciplining these, theoretical whip in hand, as a catalogue of epistemological error, of essentialist mystifications, as a masculinist appropriation of dissent, as no more than an anti-racist racism, etc., I want to consider what is to be gained by an unsententious interrogation of such articulations which, if often driven by negative passion, cannot be reduced to a mere inveighing against iniquities or a repetition of the canonical terms of imperialism's conceptual framework. This of course means affirming the power of the reverse-discourse[6] by arguing that anticolonialist writings did challenge, subvert and undermine the ruling ideologies, and nowhere more so than in overthrowing the hierarchy of coloniser/colonised, the speech and stance of the colonised refusing a position of subjugation and dispensing with the terms of the coloniser's definitions.

The weak and strong forms of oppositional discursive practices have been designated as counter-identification and disidentification (Pêcheux 1982), and re/citation and de/citation (Terdiman 1985). For Pêcheux a 'discourse-against' is that in which the subject of enunciation takes up a position of separation 'with respect to what "the universal subject" gives him to think . . . (distantiation, doubt, interrogation, challenge, revolt) . . . a struggle against ideological evidentness on the terrain of that evidentness, an evidentness with a negative sign, reversed on its own terrain'. Disidentification however 'constitutes a *working* (transformation-displacement) of the *subject-form* and not just its abolition' (Pêcheux 1982, pp. 157, 159). In Terdiman's terms, the technique of re/citation seeks 'to surround the[ir] antagonist and neutralize or explode it'; whereas de/citation, a total withdrawal from the orbit of the dominant, strives 'to exclude it totally, to expunge it' (Terdiman 1985, pp.

68, 70). Neither writes off the force of the counter-discursive, and Terdiman, who concedes that reverse-discourses are always interlocked with and parasitic on the dominant they contest – working as opposition without effacing the antagonist, inhabiting and struggling with the dominant which inhabits them – maintains that they function to survey the limits and weaknesses of the dominant by mapping the internal incoherences: 'From this dialectic of discursive struggle, truths about the social formation – its characteristic modes of reproduction and its previously hidden vulnerabilities – inevitably emerge' (Terdiman 1985, p. 66).

A recent discussion of nativism condenses many of the current censures of cultural nationalism for its complicity with the terms of colonialism's discourse, with its claims to ancestral purity and inscriptions of monolithic notions of identity cited as evidence of the failure to divest itself of the specific institutional determinations of the west. Although allowing the profound political significance of the decolonised writing themselves as subjects of a literature of their own, Anthony Appiah's critique, which is principally directed against its current forms, extends to older (all?) articulations. In exposing the operation of a 'nativist topology' – inside/ outside, indigene/ alien, western/traditional – it installs a topology of its own, where the coloniser is dynamic donor and the colonised is docile recipient, where the west initiates and the native imitates. Thus while the reciprocity of the colonial relationship is stressed, all power remains with western discourse. For example: 'the overdetermined course of cultural nationalism in Africa has been to make real the imaginary identities to which Europe has subjected us' (Appiah 1988, p. 164); the rhetoric of 'intact indigenous traditions' and the very conception of an African personality and an African past are European inventions; the Third World intellectual is Europhone, immersed in the language and literature of the colonial countries. These statements could be modulated without underplaying or obscuring a necessary registration of western discursive power: Europe's fabrications of 'Africa' were deflected and subverted by African, Caribbean and African-American literary discourses; 'African identity' is the product of refusing Europe's gaze and returning its own anti-colonialist look; Europhone colonials transgress their immersion in European languages and literatures, seizing and diverting vocabularies, metaphors and literary traditions.

The occasion for Appiah's case against nativism is *Toward the decolonization of African literature* – whose authors, Chinweizu, Jemie and Madubuike, invite censure for taking an unqualified position on cultural autonomy – but its object is a critique of cultural nationalism's entrapment in a reverse-discourse:

Railing against the cultural hegemony of the West, the nativists are of its party without knowing it. Indeed the very arguments, the rhetoric of defiance, that our nationalists muster are . . . canonical, time tested . . . In their ideological inscription, the cultural nationalists remain in a position of counteridentification . . . which is to continue to participate in an institutional configuration – to be subjected to cultural identities they ostensibly decry . . . Time and time again, cultural nationalism has followed the route of alternate genealogizing. We end up always in the same place; the achievement is to have invented a different past for it. (Appiah 1988, pp. 162, 170)

The effect of this argument is to homogenise the varieties of nationalisms and to deny both originality and effectivity to its reverse-discourses. Such a contention is disputed by Partha Chatterjee's study which, despite a subtitle (*A derivative discourse*) encouraging selective citation in the interest of re-legating nationalist thought as mimetic and while recognising the inherent contradiction of its reasoning within a framework of knowledge serving a structure of power it seeks to repudiate, is concerned to establish its *difference*: 'Its politics impel it to open up that framework of knowledge that presumes to dominate it, to displace that framework, to subvert its authority, to challenge its morality' (Chatterjee 1986, p. 42).

Some of the implications of arguments according a totalising power to colonialist discourses emerges in Rosalind O'Hanlon's discussion of current research concerned to emphasise the British 'invention' of nineteenth-century caste as a challenge to 'the notion of an ageless caste-bound social order', but which maximises the effectivity of 'colonial conjuring', and by occluding the 'complex and contradictory engagements with colonialist categories . . . often produces a picture of Indian actors who are helpless to do anything but reproduce the structures of their own subordination' (O'Hanlon 1989, pp. 98, 104, 100). In this connection Ranajit Guha's eloquent inventory establishing the presence of an 'Indian idiom of politics' discernible in the many languages of the subcontinent, demonstrates that the modes of subaltern colonial resistance, far from being determined by forms and vocabularies borrowed from the dominant culture, were rearticulations of pre-colonial traditions of protest (Guha 1989).[7]

Mindful of Robert Young's caution that the search for a 'nativist alternative' may simply represent 'the narcissistic desire to find an other that will reflect Western assumptions of selfhood' (Young 1990, p. 165), I will argue that something quite different animates those modes of postcolonial critique concerned to reconstruct a story from tales, legends and idioms which are themselves transcriptions and improvisations of dissent that was never formally narrativised, and to produce an uncensorious but critical interrogation of colonial resistances when they were. It will be evident that the interest of such readings is to retain in the discussion that realm of imaginary freedom which these histories prefigured or configured, as well as to register decolonising struggles as an emancipatory project despite the egregious failures these brought in their wake. Although the assumption here is that the discourses or discursive retracings of past dissidence come to us already encoded with the elements of a counter-narrative (which diminishes the critics' claim to be performing the insurgent act), it is we who by appropriating it to our theoretical purposes alter the material, in the process making visible its erasures, suppressions and marginalisations, evident for example in the fore-grounding of male figures of praxis and authority.

Elleke Boehmer's discussion of narratives of nationalist recuperation, identity reconstruction and nation formation shows how images of the female body were used to embody ideals of the wholeness of subjectivity, history and the state. Thus, while reversing colonialist iconography figuring penetration, pillage and dismemberment – 'repression upon the objectified, enslaved, colonised body' – such invocations of the female body 'rest[s] upon the assumption of predominantly masculine authority and historical agency', nationalism's core concepts nesting in the metaphor of the maternal body. Because, Boehmer argues, postcolonial discourses of self-determination 'have a considerable investment in nationalist concepts of "selving" and of retrieving history, the gender specifics of nationalist iconography are accepted, or borne with, or overlooked', the deconstructions of such configurations only now being effected in postcolonial literatures (Boehmer 1991). In a related register, Ella Shohat writes that 'Anticolonial intellectuals, though not particularly preoccupied with gender issues, have ... used gender tropes to discuss colonialism', Césaire and Fanon implicity subverting representations of rape by violent dark men and cultures, and fantasies of rescuing virginal white and at times dark women, 'while at the same time using gendered discourse to articulate oppositional struggle' (Shohat 1991, pp. 56, 57).[8]

Such modulated attention to the retention of patriarchal positions in anticolonialist discourses points up the inadvisibility of using the sources to write an optimistic narrative of liberation struggles as 'ideologically correct'. But in order to do justice to their histories – to borrow a phrase from Jonathan Dollimore[9] – it is surely necessary to refrain from a sanctimonious reproof of modes of writing resistance which do not conform to contemporary theoretical rules about discursive radicalism. Instead I would argue that the task is to address the empowering effects of constructing a coherent identity or of cherishing and defending against calumniation altered and mutable indigenous forms, which is not the same as the hopeless attempt to locate and revive pristine pre-colonial cultures.[10] It is an unwillingness to abstract resistance from its moment of performance that informs my discussion of Césaire and Fanon as authors of liberation theories which today could stand accused of an essentialist politics. For, as I read them, both affirmed the invention of an insurgent, unified black self, acknowledged the revolutionary energies released by valorising the cultures denigrated by colonialism and, rather than construing the colonialist relationship in terms of negotiations with the structures of imperialism, privileged coercion over hegemony to project it as a struggle between implacably opposed forces – an irony made all too obvious in enunciations inflected, indeed made possible, by these very negotiations.

III

These remarks are a prelude to my considering whether those articulations of cultural nationalism I examine can be disposed of as a reverse ethnocentrism which simply reproduces existing categories, performing an identical function and producing the same effects as the system it contests. My route will be to Fanon via Négritude, an unsafe road since, despite its heterogeneous languages and its interrogations of western thought, this body of writing is routinely disparaged as the most exorbitant manifestation of a mystified ethnic essentialism, as an undifferentiated and retrograde discourse installing notions of a foundational and fixed native self and demagogically asserting the recovery of an immutable past. Perhaps this would account for the current tendency to ignore Fanon's voyage into and then around Négritude or to dismiss it as a detour not mapped onto his theories. However, as the path of his project passed through the thickets of uncertain affiliation and irresolute withholding before emerging as unequivocal denunciation, this suggests that the appointment of Fanon as exemplar of anticolonialist theory liberated from identitarian thinking should perhaps be qualified.

In his unsententious critique of decolonising discourses Edward Said suggests a progression from nativist through nationalist to liberation theory. While acknowledging the transgressive energies of the former in deranging the discourses of domination ranged against the colonised, and recognising the achievement of nationalist movements in winning statutory independence for the occupied territories, it is liberation writing which is credited with producing a politics of secular illumination, articulating a transformation of social consciousness beyond ethnicity and reconceiving the possibilities of human experience in non-imperialist terms (see, for example, Said 1988, 1993). Not only are the stages less disjunct than the periodisation suggests – messianic movements and Pan-Africanism were utopian in their goals, Nkrumah's nationalism was not exclusively Africanist, acknowledging as it did the recombinant qualities of a culture which had developed through assimilating Arabic and western features, and so on – but the liberation theory of Fanon and Césaire was more impure than is here indicated, nativism remaining audible despite the strenuous endorsements of a post-European, transnational humanism as the ultimate goal.

Négritude's moment of articulation and reception – before the nationalist movements in Africa and the Caribbean had gained momentum, but after Marxist critiques of colonialism had been developed within the Indian independence struggle – may testify to both its originality as a cultural-political position and its limitations as an ideology. Many of the contemporary objections to Négritude came from those who had welcomed its inception, and were delivered from a Marxist standpoint. These can be arranged into the following categories: systemised mystification construing 'black being' as irrational and 'black culture' as genetically determined, unified and transnational, thus fostering the universalising myth of a unified black identity in the face of its multiplicity and diversity; political error in failing to represent the anti-colonial struggle as the national liberation of all classes, or to acknowledge the specificities of each national culture in the colonised world and, in the case of the Caribbean, in driving a wedge between African and other oppressed communities; theoretical error in distorting African worldviews and overlooking that the synthesising of indigenous with foreign elements in the colonised world had issued in complex and particularised modes of *mestizaje* or creolisation[11] – sometimes, though rarely, this fusing being differently represented as the reconciliation of the African with the western, or even complete cultural acclimatisation to the west.[12]

What is notable is that many critics of Négritude were prepared either to concede its liberating effects in fostering new modes of consciousness[13] or to offer alternative means of constituting reconceived identities. To counter the mystifications of Négritude, the Haitian writer Jacques Stéphen Alexis in the 1950s proposed 'marvellous realism' as a literary practice appropriate to producing the fantastic reality of the Caribbean's broken histories, different temporalities and creolised cultural identities (Dash 1973). In another register, René Depestre, who dissociated himself from Négritude's indifference to the diverse material conditions of cultural constitution and national character, emphasised the 'syncretic elaboration of cultural elements taken from Africa and Europe', offering an alternative and not dissimilar programme of ideological '*cimarronaje*' as the means for Caribbeans to resist depersonalisation: 'This cultural escape is an original form of rebellion which has manifested itself in religion, in folklore, in art and singularly in Caribbean literatures', the people in search of their identity becoming aware 'of the validity of their African heritage latent in our society' (Depestre 1976, pp. 62, 63).[14]

The sustained attack on Négritude as an irrational ideology which perpetuated western stereotypes came during the 1960s from a new generation of African philosophers and intellectuals concerned to expose the errors in notions of Africanism and the African personality. Scholars such as Stanislas Adotevi, Marcien Towa and Paulin Hountondji attacked notions of the African as an intuitive being, of a fixed black essence and a static African culture, and dismissed 'ethnophilosophy' for failing to distinguish between cultural anthropology and philosophy's critical activity when attempting to demonstrate the existence of a distinctive African mode of philosophical thinking (Irele 1986, Mudimbe 1988). According to Irele, Hountondji refuses to concede 'any positive significance to the effort to rehabilitate African culture', asserting that the relationship between Négritude and the ideology it intends to combat revealed 'a peculiar ambiguity, a pathetic correspondence between the terms of African affirmation and the opposite system of ideas or representations proposed by the colonial ideology in its image of Africa' (p. 147). The revolutionary socialist Towa, however, despite his repudiation of a cultural nationalism that seeks to resuscitate a heritage of past values irrelevant to the modernising preoccupations and goals of contemporary Africa and his hostility to the state Négritude of Senegal and the Cameroons, acknowledges the inspiration of Césaire and has referred to him as the prophet of the revolution of black people: 'he announced the freedom of the Black [Nègre], he prophesied with his great voice the "Beautiful City", a world in which the Black could be himself, master of his destiny' (cited in Arnold 1981, p. 172).[15]

The presence of absolutist denunciations of Négritude makes it necessary to recall its historical juncture and to differentiate between the articulations subsumed under its rubric. As a structure of feeling and a seizure of the means of self-representation by a rebellious elite, Négritude was anticipated by the Haitian literary movement of the nineteenth century and in the United States by the Back to Africa Movements and later by Dubois's Pan-Negroism and Pan-Africanism.[16] The definitive articulations of Négritude are however usually attributed to the activities of students, writers and intellectuals from the French colonies, who were closely associated with African-American expatriates in Paris during the early 1930s, the prime movers being Senghor from Senegal, Césaire from Martinique and Léon Damas from French Guiana. (The subsequent dissemination of the movement was promoted by Alioune Diop's *Présence Africaine* which began publication in 1947.) Irele (1970) has characterised Négritude as the francophone equivalent of Pan-Africanism and a distinct current in African national consciousness and cultural nationalism. All the same, the extent to which Négritude was embraced by the African-Caribbean diaspora is significant both to the willed construction of Africa as a country of the mind, rather than a representation of a geohistorical place, to the notion of 'Africa' as the homeland of dispersed populations in search of solidarity, and to the construing of black identity as creolised and dislocated. Here it could be noted that if there were exponents prone to definitions of an intrinsic black nature and a unified black culture centred on an eternal Africa, others deployed 'black' as a multi-inflected signifier of oppression and resistance, energising a discursive stance from which colonialism's most eloquent creatures interrogated the essentialising definitions foisted on peoples of African origins. In this mode, exemplified by Césaire's poetry, Négritude is not a recovery of a pre-existent state, but a textually invented history, an identity effected through figurative operations, and a tropological construction of blackness as a sign of the colonised condition and its refusal.

Commentators on Négritude tend to distinguish between Senghor's bio-
logically determined notion of blackness as a distinctive mode of being and a
collective identity in which emotion and intuition are located as the essential
attributes of the race (though Senghor did insist on the actuality and desir-
ability of cross-cultural fertilisation), and Césaire's historical/cultural concept.
Arnold (1981), however, suggests that at the outset their views approxi-
mated, both having been influenced by the obscurantist ethnological notions
of the subsequently discredited Frobenius, and by anti-rational philosophers
such as Spengler and Bergson. But by the 1940s Césaire, at the time a
member of the Communist Party, with which he broke in 1958,[17] was concerned, in his analysis of colonialism as economic exploitation and cultural
aggression, to establish a theoretical rather than a metaphysical basis to
Négritude, hence rejecting the attempt to essentialise an African world-view
or to define it as a closed system. The perspective in his *Discourse on
colonialism* is resolutely transnational and, while honouring an ante-European
past, looks to a post-European future, the dossier on the west's sham humanism anticipating Fanon's execration in *The wretched of the earth*:

> The Indians massacred, the Moslem world drained of itself, the Chinese world
> defiled and perverted for a good century; the Negro world disqualified; mighty
> voices stilled forever; all this wreckage, all this waste, humanity reduced to a
> monologue, and you think that all this does not have its price? The truth is that
> this policy *cannot but bring about the ruin of Europe itself*, and that Europe, if it is
> not careful, will perish from the void it has created around itself... what else has
> bourgeois Europe done? It has undermined civilizations, destroyed countries, ruined
> nationalities, extirpated 'the root of diversity' (Césaire 1972, pp. 57, 59)

Where Césaire is sure to be faulted by those who deplore nativist nostalgia is
in his lament for what colonialism has destroyed:

> the wonderful Indian civilizations – and neither Deterding nor Royal Dutch nor
> Standard Oil will ever console me for the Aztecs and the Incas... [for] extraordi-
> nary *possibilities* wiped out... For my part I make a systematic defense of the non-
> European civilizations... They were communal societies, never societies of the
> many for the few. They were societies that were not only ante-capitalist... but also
> anti-capitalist... I systematically defend our old Negro civilizations; they were
> courteous civilizations. (Césaire 1972, pp. 20, 22, 23, 31)

An explicit reconstruction of Négritude's beginnings can be found in
Césaire's 1967 interview with the Haitian writer and political activist René
Despestre, where he speaks of the programme as a collective creation of
Africans, North Americans, Antilleans, Guianans and Haitians who came
together in Paris during the 1930s to give expression to their struggle against
alienation and the politics of assimilation:

> We adopted the word *nègre* as a term of defiance . . . We found a violent affirmation in the words *nègre* and *négritude* . . . it is a concrete rather than an abstract coming to consciousness . . . We lived in an atmosphere of rejection, and we developed an inferiority complex . . . I have always thought that the black man was searching for his identity. And . . . if what we want is to establish this identity, then we must have a concrete consciousness of what we are – that is of the first fact of our lives: that we are black; that we were black and have a history . . . . [that] there have been beautiful and important black civilizations . . . that its values were values that could still make an important contribution to the world. (Césaire 1972, pp. 74, 76)

This concrete coming to consciousness was realized by Césaire as a poet; and because many of the writings of Négritude are open to some or all of the charges made against it as an ideological tendency, any argument that as a literary practice it performed a textual struggle for self-representation in which the indeterminacy of language ruptured fixed configurations, invented a multivalent blackness, and wrenched 'Africa' out of its time-bound naming and into new significations, is most readily made by referring to his over-determined and polysemic poetry. Although made possible, as he concedes, by surrealism, this exceeded the influence of European modes and violated its forms in what Arnold calls a 'sophisticated hybridization, corrosion and parody' of western traditions.[18]

In an essay on Césaire, James Clifford argues for uncoupling his coinage of Négritude from the 'elaboration of a broad black identity' and attaching it to 'very specific affirmations and negations', citing the passage in *Notebook* beginning 'my negritude is not . . .'(see below, p. 185). However Clifford's selective citation of 'The verb "marronner" / for René Depestre, Haitian poet' suggests that the trajectory of his case is directed at dissociating Césaire from Négritude. The poem, written in 1955 and subsequently published in numerous revised versions, was Césaire's response to Depestre's ready compliance with the Communist Party's decree against surrealism and for accessible and committed verse. Clifford's reading is appropriately concerned with how 'Césaire makes rebellion and the remaking of culture – the historical maroon experience – into a . . . necessary new verb [that] names the New World poetics of continuous transgression and cooperative cultural activity' (Clifford 1988, p. 181). But what is occluded is, as Arnold argues, that the poem appeals to Depestre not to abandon his Négritude – 'Courageous tom-tom rider / is it true that you mistrust the native forest . . . is it possible / that the rains of exile / have slackened the drum skin of your voice?' – entreating him to 'escape the shackles of European prosody' (Arnold) just as in the past slaves had escaped from bondage, to this end coining the neologism 'marronner': 'shall we escape like slaves Depestre, like slaves' (in an earlier version this read: 'Let's escape them Depestre let's escape them / As in the past we escaped our whip-wielding masters') (Césaire 1983, pp. 369–71).

It is possible to disregard Césaire's account of his intentions when he speaks of his poetry as a way to break the stranglehold of accepted French form in order to create a new language, 'an Antillean French, a black French . . . one capable of communicating the African heritage' (Césaire 1972, pp. 66 and 67). However, we cannot overlook that poetry which adapted the structure of some African languages, and drew on African folklores and cosmologies, does effect an identification with Africa – 'from brooding too long on the Congo / I have become a Congo resounding with forests and rivers' (Césaire 1983, p. 51) – and does construct an imaginary Africa as signifier of the legacy shared by Africans of the continent and the diaspora. The 'Guinea' of his 'Ode to Guinea', written before the name was adopted by a post-independence territory, is the mythic land of the Caribbean creole languages – the 'Africa' or 'Guinea' that is the heaven of black peoples – and the 'Ethiopia' of 'Ethiopia . . . / for Alioune Diop' embodies what Eshleman and Smith call 'the dignity lost to other African peoples', a location occupying a special place 'in the personal mythology of Négritude writers'.[19] By rewriting the stories of Africa's long oppressions – see 'All the way from Akkad, from Elam, from Sumer' and 'Africa' – Césaire derives an ethos common to all blacks, out of which an anti-colonial and ultimately an anti-capitalist identity can be constituted, as in 'A salute to the Third World / for Léopold Sedar Senghor' where connections between the Caribbean dispersal and the African motherland are forged before gesturing towards a larger and more inclusive solidarity.

Arnold's attention to the shifting values produced by images of blackness in *Notebook of a return to a native land* convinces that this is indeed 'The epic of Négritude' and a classic in the literature of decolonisation. What Arnold traces is how through the creation of a new style, the transformation of black consciousness and the self-construction of an African–Caribbean identity is enacted, the neologism 'Négritude' occurring both to hail past glories in Haiti and to signify abjection before its 'third and decisive statement of negritude' as reconciled to itself:[20] 'my negritude is not a / stone, its deafness hurled against the clamour of the day . . . / my negritude is neither tower nor cathedral / it takes root in the red flesh of the soil / it takes root in the ardent flesh of the sky' (Césaire 1983, pp. 67, 69). As an instance of what Ella Shohat calls the use of gendered discourse in articulating anticolonialist struggles, she cites Césaire's remark about adventurers violating Africa 'to make the stripping of her easier' (Shohat 1991, p. 57). Yet although his poetry does invoke Africa as inscribed on the woman's body (see 'Ode to Guinea', 'Hail to Guinea', 'Africa', 'Ethiopia' and 'A salute to the Third World'), and while the authoritative voice is masculine, the figure of suffering and endurance is not invariably the woman, and in *Notebook* the trope of Négritude is doubly gendered: 'all our blood aroused by the male heart of the sun / those who know about the feminity of the moon's oily body / the reconciled exultation of antelope and star / those whose survival travels in the germination of grass! / Eia perfect circle of the world, enclosed concordance' (Césaire 1983, p. 69).

The multivalencies of Césaire's Négritude pre-empts both closure and fixity, making it available to rearticulations covering other modes of oppression. It has since been reinvoked by national liberation movements and continues to be renewed in unforeseen ways within the postcolonial critique – as when James Snead, while acknowledging the necessity of preserving the specificity of historical experience, commends a 'broad-based, even militant usage of the term black as a unifying metaphor', and an object of cultural identification and ideological bonding (Snead 1988, p. 48); or when Kobena Mercer looks back to the redefinition of black identity in Britain during the early 1980s as 'an empowering signifier of Afro-Asian alliances' (Mercer 1990, p. 77). What was it then in Négritude that caused Fanon to recognise it as liberating and resist it as mystifying before launching a concerted attack which was at pains to signal that its hold on his thinking had been relinquished?

IV

The somewhat schematic summary which Mudimbe (1988), in an otherwise modulated account of the movement, gives of Fanon's relationship to Négritude – namely that an initial affiliation gave way to a position based on situating African ideologies of otherness as the antithesis to colonialist constitution, the synthesis to be realised in political liberation – tends to smooth over the persistent instabilities in Fanon's writings where proclamations of a future beyond ethnicity continue to be intercepted by affirmations of the immediate need to construct an insurgent black subjectivity. In another register, what Abiola Irele neglects when he claims that Césaire's poetry provided 'the essential ground-plan for Fanon's phenomenological reflection on black existence' in Black skin, white masks (Irele 1986, p. 138) is that, despite its many salutations to Césaire's liberating influences and its moments of unstable identification, the study effects the problematization of Négritude. Fanon may well have perceived his mode of thinking as dialectical; however, the language of his flamboyant writing (he wrote a number of plays which he chose not to publish) is witness to the conflicting predications remaining disjunct. Although such incommensurability is especially marked in Black skin, white masks, where Marxism co-exists with existentialism and psychoanalysis, scholarly citation is juxtaposed to anecdote, and the torsions of self-analysis are precariously balanced against the poised interpretation of a historical condition, none of his writings – with the exception of the last section of The wretched of the earth – is without the discord of incompatible testimony. Hence I will argue that Fanon's writings function at a point of tension between cultural nationalism and transnationality, without 'resolving' the contradiction and without yielding an attachment to the one or the aspiration to the other.

It is this 'historical Fanon' who never quite abandoned 'all fixity of identity', an ironic figure who resists recuperation as the paradigmatic figure of liberation theory that is recognised by Henry Louis Gates Jr (Gates 1991). Thus when Fanon moved from the many different first-person-singular voices deployed in the psycho-autobiography of an assimilated and insulted Martinican tempted by Négritude to the 'we' of Algerians and unspecified African communities in polemical writings proclaiming a new international community, he continued to concede the importance of valorising pre-colonial histories and cultures that had been systematically disfigured and devalued by colonialism:

> it was with the greatest delight that they discovered that there was nothing to be ashamed of in the past, but rather dignity, glory and solemnity. The claim to a national culture in the past does not only rehabilitate that nation and serve as a justification for the hope of a future national culture. In the sphere of psycho-affective equilibrium it is responsible for an important change in the native. (Fanon 1968, p. 170)

As I read it, both an intellectual apprehension of blackness as a construct ('what is often called the black soul is a white man's artifact' (1986, p. 16)) and a visceral attachment to the powerful fiction of black identity are always evident in *Black skin, white masks*, the language of criticism repeatedly interrupted by articulations of empathy with the impulse. What I will try to trace is how the precise statements of intention as laid down in the Introduction – i.e. a clinical study of the attitudes of the modern Antillean Negro and a psychopathological explanation of the state of being an Antillean Negro – mutate into the multivocal enunciations of the essays that follow, and where the stated brief is exceeded when specified Negroes are displaced by 'the Negro' in the white world. (All existing translations of Fanon use this term for the black person of African descent.) At the start, which appears to have been written first and does not attempt to elide the ensuing contradictions, Fanon outlines his project as the attempt to effect the disalienation of the depersonalised Negro by offering a psychological analysis of the massive psychoexistential complex produced through the juxtaposition of the white and black races. Although a passage from Césaire's *Discourse on colonialism* serves as the epigraph, and the importance of social and economic realities is acknowledged, no further reference is made to colonialism as the specific situation of the pathological juxtaposition. What is given space in an address directed at white and black brothers is the perspective of transcending the present and an insistence that if the existing structure is to be eliminated and the Negro extricated from his universe, then unilateral liberation is insufficient.

So here we find the vision of a condition beyond ethnicity already in place – 'I believe that the individual should tend to take on the universality inherent in the human condition' – while the attempt of blacks 'to prove to white men, at all costs, the richness of their thought, the equal value of their intellect' (p. 12) is designated as a symptom of that vicious circle where whites are sealed in their whiteness and blacks in their blackness. To break out of this entrapment, fervour is eschewed, and digging into one's flesh to find meaning is scorned, the narrative voice in 'The fact of blackness' distancing itself from its portrayal of the desperate struggle of the educated Negro, 'slave of the spontaneous and cosmic Negro myth . . . driven to discover the meaning of black identity', who 'with rage in his mouth and abandon in his heart . . . buries himself in the vast black abyss' (p. 16).

The incommensurable enunciations of *Black skin, white masks* produce a dissonance that is something other than ambivalence, for the adoption of heuristic procedures in order to establish Négritude as a pathology involves the speaking subject voicing opposing stances with an equally passionate intensity – the process of discovering a black identity and history registering intimacy with that impulse simultaneously with recoil from the extravagance of its rhetoric and its recourse to the paralogical (see especially Fanon (1986), pp. 113, 115, 122, 123–7). The graph of this learning process – if this is what it is – continues when the speaker adopts the stance of one who turns to antiquity in order to establish black creativity and achievement. Up to and including this moment, and let us suppose always in forensic mode, the strategies of affirming blackness, embracing unreason and reclaiming the past had been explored and found wanting, every move having been determined and countermanded by the white world's demands and reactions: 'Every hand was a losing hand for me' (p. 132). But how are we to read the protest against Sartre which is delivered in a register of unalloyed identification when the speaker takes up the position of that black person who had determined 'on the level of ideas and intellectual activity to reclaim my négritude', only to find that 'it was snatched away from me . . . Proof was presented that my effort was only a term in the dialectic . . . I felt I had been robbed of my last chance' (pp. 132, 133).·

This is a reference to Sartre's *Black Orpheus*, which appeared in 1948 as the preface to Senghor's *Anthology of new Negro and Malagasy poetry*, and which Fanon designates as 'a date in the intellectualization of the *experience* of being black' when challenging its mistake not only in seeking 'the source of the source' but in blocking that source (p. 134).[21] Sartre's essay applauded the act whereby the oppressed seized a word hurled at them as an insult and turned it into a means of vindication, while at the same time relegating the movement as 'the weak stage of a dialectical progression'. In his schema, the theory and practice of white supremacy is the thesis, and Négritude the moment of negativity and thus dedicated to its own destruction: 'it is passage and not objective, means and not ultimate goal' (p. 60), this being the passing into the objective, positive, exact notion of the proletariat. Despite which

Sartre commended the fashioning of a black subjectivity and the invention of an 'Africa beyond reach, *imaginary* continent' (p. 19), grasping as others since have not always done the revolutionary project carried out by poets of Négritude who, in 'degallicising' the oppressor's language, shattered its customary associations.

Is Fanon wearing one of the many masks he dons for exegetical purposes when he accuses Sartre of attributing Négritude to the forces of history? 'And so it is not I who make a meaning for myself, but it is the meaning that was already there, preexisting, waiting for me' (p. 134). This anger appears to be sustained when he censures the born Hegelian for forgetting that to attain consciousness of self, to grasp one own's being, 'consciousness has to lose itself in the night of the absolute' (p. 133). In destroying black zeal, what Sartre had failed to understand was that 'I needed to lose myself completely in Negritude ... in terms of consciousness, black consciousness is immanent in its own eyes. I am not a potentiality of something, I am wholly what I am. I do not have to look for the universal ... My Negro consciousness does not hold itself out as a lack. It is its own follower' (p. 135).[22]

If this could appear to be a vindication of Négritude's project, then in the last chapters, specified in the Introduction as an attempt at 'a psychopathological and philosophical explanation of the state of *being* a Negro' (p. 15), Fanon again disavows not only the Antillean Negroes' attempt to be white but the effort to maintain their alterity – 'Alterity of rupture, of conflict, of battle' (p. 222). By the time of the Conclusion, the impulse to discover a black past is unequivocally repudiated: 'In no way should I dedicate myself to the revival of an unjustly unrecognized Negro civilization' (p. 226), the denunciations moving towards a lofty detachment – 'I do not have the right to allow myself to be mired in what the past has determined. I am not the slave of the Slavery that dehumanized my ancestors ... The body of history does not determine a single one of my actions. I am my own foundation' (pp. 230–1) – before rising/collapsing into the utopianism of his ultimate desire: 'That it may be possible for me to discover and to love man, wherever he may be. The Negro is not. Any more than the white man' (p. 231).

The 'drama of consciousness' performed in *Black skin, white masks* can be read as Fanon directing a scenario in which the players are alienated Antillean blacks learning or being weaned from the errors of both assimilation and Négritude, and hence as charting the move from the reactional, in which there is always resentment, to the actional (p. 222). But perhaps it traces the path of the author effecting his own cure within the space of its pages – Négritude marking the transgressive moment of emergence from the colonised condition, and the transition from Négritude to universal solidarity signalling disalienation and the transcendence of ethnicity. The problem here is that subsequent writings replay the dilemma of fashioning/disavowing black identity. Some years later in 'West Indians and Africans' Fanon continued to affirm Césaire's positive influence in valorising what West Indians had rejected, teaching them to look in the direction of Africa, and instead of identifying with and mimicing the white world, recognising themselves as transplanted children of black slaves. But now, writing in the third person about the West Indian, Fanon detaches himself from what he had proclaimed in the first person as a transformation of consciousness, by denying the existence of a Negro people, deriding the Africa of the West Indian imagination – 'Africa the hard and the beautiful, Africa exploding with anger, tumultuous bustle, splash, Africa land of truth' (1967, p. 26) – and pronouncing that 'It thus seems that the West Indian, after the great white error, is now living in the great black mirage' (p. 27).

The retreat from a wavering empathy with Négritude becomes an ambiguous critique in Fanon's address to the First Congress of Negro Writers and Artists in Paris in 1956. In his disobliging account of the meeting, where he intimates that the agenda was incoherent and the platform much given to demagogy, James Baldwin (1961) observes that what Césaire left out of his eloquent speech reviling the colonial experience was precisely that it had produced men like himself. Since this is now something of a platitude, it is notable that Fanon did not dwell on his own colonialist formation, concentrating instead on colonialism as expropriation and spoliation matched by 'the sacking of cultural patterns', the natives having been induced by the overwhelming power and authority of the oppressor to repudiate their original forms of existence (1967, p. 33). Having earlier protested at Sartre's relegation of Négritude to a minor term, Fanon now essentially follows his model, and while like Sartre he commends black affirmations in the face of white insult, the negative/positive evaluations of cultural revaluations interrupt each other in a double-voiced critique of the native intellectual's abrupt movement from ardent assimilation to the swooning before tradition:

> This culture, abandoned, sloughed off, neglected, despised, becomes for the inferiorized an object of passionate attachment ... The culture put into capsules, which has vegetated since the foreign domination, is revalorized. It is not reconceived, grasped anew, dynamized from within ... The past, becoming henceforth a constellation of values, becomes identified with the Truth. (1967, pp. 41, 43)

But at the moment when a reader could assume that this predicates a total rejection of Négritude's project, the perspective again shifts when cultural affirmation is marked as a necessary moment in the realisation of a combative position:

> This rediscovery, this absolute valorization almost in defiance of reality, objectively indefensible, assumes an incomparable and subjective importance ... the plunge into the chasm of the past is the condition and source of freedom. (1967, p. 43)

Fanon's argument characterises native culture under colonialism as inert, stultified, lethargic, rigid, uncreative, with the natives reduced to despising their indigenous modes of existence – assertions for which much countervailing evidence can be adduced. However, for Fanon it was only when the movement for decolonisation was set in motion that there occured a qualitative leap from stagnation to modernity, from passivity to insurgency. It is this 'zone of occult instability where the people dwell . . . that fluctuating movement which they are just giving a shape to' (1968, p. 182) that remains unknown to those native writers and artists who, lagging behind the people and going against the current of history by seeking to revive abandoned traditions, forget 'that the forms of thought and what it feeds on, together with modern techniques of information, language and dress have dialectically reorganized the peoples' intelligences' (1968, p. 181). Hence his eloquent defence of the natives' discovery of the past as a means of rehabilitation is countermanded when, and as it were in the same breath, disdain is directed at the recovery of old legends that will be 'interpreted in the light of a borrowed aestheticism and of a conception of the world which was discovered under other skies . . . the poetic tom-tom rhythms breaking through the poetry of revolt' (1968, pp. 179–81). In Fanon's argument the condition of possibility for producing a literature of combat is that writers take up arms on the side of the people, since only such writings will mould the national consciousness 'giving it form and contours and flinging open before it new and boundless horizons' (1968, p. 193). That he could be formulaic in his appreciation of the arts is apparent in his comments on the blues as the black slave's lament, 'offered up for the admiration of the oppressor', and his prophecies that the 'end of racism would sound the knell of great Negro music' (1967, p. 37), or that as soon as the Negro comes to an understanding of himself, the jazz howl that whites perceived as an expression of nigger-hood will be replaced by 'his trumpet sound[ing] more clearly and his voice less hoarsely, (1968, p. 195).[23]

Fanon's writings on National Culture can be read as a response to Césaire's Address to the First Congress in 1956 where, in countering Senghor's metaphysical version of Négritude, he had argued that whereas a culture must be national, a civilisation can be supranational, and that whereas specific African cultures had been decimated by enforced dispersal and colonial aggression, important elements of an African civilisation had persisted ('Culture and colonization', cited in Arnold 1981, pp. 185–7). By this time Fanon's disenchantment with the official cultural nationalism of the newly independent African states had been exacerbated by the apostasy to the cause of the national liberation struggles of its most eloquent exponents – Senghor had underwritten De Gaulle's proposed Franco-African community and withheld Senegal's support for the Algerian liberation struggle; Césaire had backed the constitutional referendum on the Fifth Republic whereby Martinique would become as an overseas department of France, and Jacques Rabemananjara of Malagasy had voted against the Algerian people in the General Assembly of the United Nations (I will evade any questions of whether a theorist's public acts can be held to invalidate the theories he or she espouses). Fanon now took the position that any notion of a continental African culture, of 'Negroism', was a blind alley, stressing instead the heterogeneity of Negro and African–Negro cultures and the different concrete problems confronting specific black populations, and insisting that solidarity was forged not in declamations of a common culture but in political struggle. In his statement to the Second Congress of Black Artists and Writers in Rome in 1959 (1968), Fanon declared that culture is necessarily the expression of the nation, just as the nation is the condition of culture, once again pointing to the error of the native intellectual's ways, whether assimilationist or 'Negroist'. Distinguishing between national consciousness and nationalism, Fanon maintained that the former was the most elaborate form of culture, and declared that the national period was the necessary space for the growth of an international dimension and of universalising values.[24]

To the end there are signs of Fanon's links with the Négritude movement – the title of his last essays taken from *The Internationale* had previously been adapted by Jacques Roumain in a poem calling for a black revolt against the bourgeois white world, and he remained in touch with the editors of *Présence Africaine*.[25] Yet his repudiation of Négritude in his 1959 Address to the Congress is unqualified: like Trotsky, who scorned the notion of a proletarian culture since the proletariat would be abolished on the attainment of classless society, so Fanon now rejected black culture as an abstract populism: 'To believe that it is possible to create a black culture is to forget that niggers are disappearing, just as those people who brought them into being are seeing the break-up of their economic and cultural supremacy' (Fanon 1968, pp. 188–9). This optimism of the intellect is what Albert Memmi addresses when he remarks that for Fanon 'the day oppression ceases, the new man is supposed to appear before our eyes immediately' (Memmi 1969, p. 88), although it should be noted that Fanon predicated this leap into the future, this instant emancipation on the transformative powers of a principled decolonising struggle: 'After the conflict there is not only the disappearance of the colonized man ... This new humanity cannot do otherwise than define a new humanism for itself and others. It is prefigured in the objectives and methods of the conflict' (Fanon 1968, p. 197).

The verso of these epiphanies to a future transcending ethnicity and nationalism is a measured demystification of Europe's 'spiritual adventure' undertaken at the expense of the rest of the world, and a call that the oppressed should slough off enslavement to its values by recognising the failure of its claims: 'Let us try to create the whole man, whom Europe has been incapable of bringing to triumphant birth' (Fanon 1968, p. 253). Here Fanon's writings appear as prematurely postcolonialist and are reminiscent of what Anthony Appiah, in discussing Ouologuem's 'post-realist' novels, describes as writings of delegitimation that inscribe a post-nativist politics and a transnational rather than a national solidarity: 'they reject not only the Western *imperium* but also the nationalist project of the postcolonial national bourgeoisie... the basis for that project of delegitimation cannot be the postmodernist one: rather it is grounded in an appeal to an ethical universal' (Appiah 1991, p. 353). In turning away from Europe as a source and model of meanings and aspirations, Fanon's last writings look not to the fulfilment of the Enlightenment's ideals within the existing order but to decolonisation as the agency of a transfigured social condition; hence holding in place that vision of the anti-colonial struggle as a global emancipatory project and projecting the radical hope of an oppositional humanism. What is less certain is whether the time for transnational politics had come when Fanon was writing, whether it has now, and whether the prospect of his post-nativist 'whole man' is one that wholly delights.

Notes

1 For Fanon, the colonised prior to modern movements for national independence were passive, stultified, unproductive. Presumably this characterisation applied only to the Caribbean and sub-Saharan Africa, since Algeria is credited with sustained military and cultural resistance against the French occupiers (1967, p. 65).

2 This position is elucidated and underwritten by Robert Young (1990).

3 These issues are addressed by amongst others Paul Smith (1988), Diana Fuss (1989) and, in a colonial context, Rosalind O'Hanlon (1988; see especially pp. 204–5). The framing of the agon of structure and agency has been questioned by Anthony Appiah (1991).

4 Instances are the upsurge during the late nineteenth century of messianic movements and Ethiopian or Zionist Churches in sub-Saharan Africa which Thomas Hodgkin (1956) has described as precipitating a clash between colonial and prophetic power; maroonage or the flight of slaves from the plantation and post-plantation systems of the Americas to an outlaw life in the mountains and forests or to other territories; the concealment of meaning from master and overseer in creole and carnival; the parodic inversions of the coloniser's images in song and dance; non-cooperation with projects of 'social improvement'; adherence to traditions the occupiers sought to reform; idleness and malingering to circumvent and undermine the demands of enforced and indentured labour regulations; and – if one is tempted to adapt the schema of silent majorities devised by Baudrillard (1983a) to specify inertia as opposition to a contemporary condition saturated by information technology – silence as a weapon against political authority. The problem here is that silence can be read either as a sign of resignation to subjugation – being reduced to silence, as marking the refusal to speak or be heard within the oppressor's system of meanings, or as a form of non-speaking subjectivity; it can also register an exclusion operated by the text – the hole in the narrative. Some of the modes listed above have been problematised by David Theo Goldberg, who maintains that 'The discourses promoting resistance to racism must not prompt identification with and in terms of categories fundamental to the discourse of oppression'. As examples of the failure to make this distinction, he cites the black separatist movement and the tactics of resistance used by plantation slaves: 'slow work and malingering undermined

the plantation economy but reinforced the stereotype of laziness; self-mutilation increased labour costs but steeled the sterotype of barbarism' (1990, pp. 313 and 318 n. 58). The terms of this strong reservation impinge on the argument for the effectivity of a reverse discourse pursued in this essay.

5 Ranajit Guha however has maintained that 'the appropriation of a past by conquest carried with it the risk of rebounding on its conquerors. It can end up by sacralizing the past for the subject people and encouraging it to use it in their effort to define and affirm their own identity' (1989, p. 212).

6 A case for the power of the reverse-discourse which uses the same categories and vocabulary as the texts of social control it contests is made by Jonathan Dollimore, citing Foucault's argument in *History of sexuality*, vol. 1: 'Deviancy returns from abjection by deploying just those terms which relegated it to that state in the first place – including "nature" and "essence" ... A complex and revealing dialectic between the dominant and the deviant emerges from histories of homosexual representation, especially from the homosexual (later gay) appropriations of nature and essence' (1991, pp. 95–6).

7 See Guha: 'peasant uprisings variously called *hool, dhing, bidroha, hangama, fituri, etc*; ... *hizrat* or desertion *en masse* of peasants or other labouring people ... ; ... *dharma* or protest by sitting down in the offender's presence with the pledge not to move until the redress of grievance; ... *hartal* or the general suspension of public activity; ... *dharmaghat* or withdrawal of labour; ... *jat mara*, or measures to destroy the offender's caste by refusal to render such specialist services as are required to insure him and his kin against pollution; ... *danga* or sectarian, ethnic, caste and class violence involving large bodies of the subaltern population' (1989, p. 267).

8 Where Shohat seems to be overstating her case is in suggesting that stories of sexual violence against Third World women are 'relatively privileged' over those of violence toward Third World men.

9 See Dollimore who argues for avoiding a 'theoreticist' writing-off of the histories of 'essentialist politics' (1991, pp. 44–5).

10 But nor should the cost of the 'hybridity' effected by colonialism's invasions be uncounted: glossing Edward Brathwaite's definition of creolisation 'as one's adaptation to a new environment through the loss of parts of oneself and the gain of parts of the Other', Manthia Diawara adds that 'one must be aware of the fact that in fusing Whiteness with the seductiveness of hybridization, one is also sacrificing not only a part of Blackness, but certain Black people' (Diawara 1990–1, p. 82). These 'certain Black people', inhabiting extant although neither static or intact autochthonous cultures, emerge in Caroline Rooney's reading of a story by Ama Ata Aidoo where she draws attention to a narration which legitimates 'a culture that predates and is not erased by colonial founding fathers, who are not then an originating point of reference', and criticises the amnesia of those who, having embraced the metropolitan culture, renounce their natal communities (1991, p. 222).

11 In the late 1940s African writers and political activists close to the Communist Party – Gabriel d'Arboussier, Albert Franklin and Abdoulaye Ly – attacked Négritude for failing to give expression to the anti-imperalist revolution as a national liberation struggle fought by all classes, dismissing it as a mystification which placed the accent on the irrational aspects of African life and claimed the existence of a unique Negro culture – charges of which Césaire was exonerated (Hyams 1971). Cf. Wole Soyinka (1976) who faults Négritude for negative and contradictory definitions, distortions of the African world-view and reinstalling blasphemies about the African as a non-analytic being.

12 During the 1950s and 1960s black writers who were the step-children of an Anglophone oppression tended to emphasise their western formation – see, for example, Baldwin (1961) and Mphahlele (in Hyams 1971) – or to stress the fusion of African strains with other lines in the making of African American identity (see Ellison 1967).

13 Mphahlele (Hyams 1971) allowed the historical fact of Négritude as both a protest and a positive assertion of African cultural values, and Soyinka conceded that 'it had provided a life-line along which the dissociated individual could be pulled back to the source of his material essence and offered a prospect for the coming into being of new black social entities' (1976, p. 64).

14 Depestre was subsequently to put a greater distance between his stance and that of Négritude, attributing its 'original sin ... and the adventures that destroyed its initial project' to 'the spirit that made it possible: anthropology', a criticism which Mudimbe reads as referring to techniques of ideological manipulation (cited by Mudimbe 1988, p. 187).

15 Towa's article 'Aimé Césaire, prophete de la révolution des peuples noirs' was published in *Abbia* (Cameroon) no. 21, 1969; see Bjornson on *Abbia*, founded in 1962 by William Eteki whose influential policies/politics attempted to reconcile Négritude with scientific knowledge in constructing a new African philosophy (1991, pp. 173–4).

16 There was apparently some continuity in Haiti where during the 1920s the journal *Revue indigène* was established, while in the 1930s a group of intellectuals and writers calling themselves Les Griots (a name borrowed from an African term for the profession of poet – historian – musician) coined the word *nigrité* to signal a rejection of assimilation and the reconstruction of an African identity. Similarly there were moves by literary coteries in Puerto Rico, Cuba and Brazil to locate the black communities of the territories within an African continuum and effect a bond of solidarity with other products of the African dispersal – as there were in the Harlem Renaissance.

17 Césaire's *Letter to Maurice Thorez* (1956) criticised the Communist Party's position on the Caribbean dependencies, questioned the applicability of orthodox Marxist analysis to Martinican conditions, rejected the thesis that the urban proletariat, which scarcely existed in Martinique, was necessarily the vanguard of revolution, and reiterated his adherence to Négritude (cited by Arnold 1981, p. 172). Two years later Césaire, apparently at the behest of André Malraux, supported De Gaulle's constitutional referendum whereby Martinique became an overseas department of the Fifth Republic.

18 So novel are language, syntax and trope that commentators have in glossing his poetry been moved to their own displays of stylistic pyrotechnics: 'A poem of Césaire ... bursts and turns on itself as a fuse, as bursting suns which turn and explode in new suns, in a perpetual surpassing. It is not a question of meeting in a calm unity of opposites but rather a forced coupling into a single sex, of black in its opposition to white' (Sartre 1976, p. 36).

19 See Eshleman and Smith, Introduction to Césaire (1983, p. 11) and Arnold (1981, p. 218).

20 Cf. Irele: 'Césaire's poetry ... becomes quite literally an affect; a drama of consciousness, a sloughing off of processes by which the complex of negative associations through which the black subject has been forced to perceive himself is overturned and transformed into a mode of mental liberation and ultimately of self-acceptance' (1986, p. 137). In their introduction to Césaire's poetry, Eshleman and Smith refer to French usages of words to designate things or persons belonging to the black race: the euphemistic 'Noir', the derogatory 'negro', and the more neutral; 'nègre': 'it is in this light that one must read Césaire's use of the word "nègre" and its derivatives "négritude", "négrillon" and "négraille": he was making up a family of words based on what he considered the most insulting way to refer to black. The paradox, of course, was that this implicit reckoning with the blacks' ignominy, this process of self-irony and self-denigration, was the necessary step on the path to a new self-image and spiritual rebirth' (Césaire 1983, p. 27).

21 For Mudimbe and Irele, Sartre's contribution was to have shifted Négritude from an ethnic to an historical concept and a revolutionary project, Mudimbe crediting Sartre with transforming it into a major political event and a philosophical critique of colonialism, while at the same time subjugating 'the militant's generosity of mind and heart to the fervour of a political philosophy' (1988, p. 84).

22 The movement of Fanon's argument resembles the tropological production of blackness's different registers in *Notebook of a return to the nativeland*.

23 The cultural agenda proposed by Fanon, in which an 'upward springing trend' is required in writing, dancing and singing, iterates the desiderata heard before and since in the programmes for the arts drawn up by radical political movements, bringing to mind Césaire's ironic reprimand to Depestre for supporting the then party line on poetry: 'Comrade Depestre / It is undoubtedly a very serious problem / the relation between poetry and Revolution / the content determines the form / and what about keeping in mind as well the dialectical / backlash by which the form taking its revenge / chokes the poem like an accursed fig tree' (1983, p. 371).

24 Writing on cultural resistance, Amilcar Cabral looked forward to the emergence of a *'universal culture'*, while calling for 'a spiritual reconversion of mentalities, a *re-Africanization* that will aim at the development of a people's culture and of all aboriginal positive cultural values' (1980, p. 153). In his Memorial Lecture for Eduardo Modliane, 'National liberation and culture', Cabral, who calls national liberation 'an act of culture', steers a course between concessions to and rejections of Négritude, advocating that a people freeing themselves from foreign rule must 'recapture the commanding heights of its own culture' and reject 'any kind of subjection to foreign culture', while repudiating the 'rather byzantine discussion of which African cultural values are specific or non-specific to Africa' (1974, pp. 15–16). All the same he writes of the armed war of liberation as an 'expression of our culture and our African-ness. It must be expressed when it comes, in a ferment signifying above all the culture of the people which has freed itself' (p. 17). In the editorial, Cabral is cited as denouncing a notion, held even by the left, 'that imperialism made us enter history, at the moment when it began its adventures in our countries', substituting instead 'We consider that when imperialism arrived in Guiné, it made us leave history – our history.'

25 Peter Worsley suggests that 'It is more than possible that Roumain's poem rather than the Internationale, was the source of Fanon's title. It is a poem that saw the revolt of colour and the revolt of class as overlapping ... Roumain, after a "furious embittered rhapsody on the sufferings of the Negro", stops himself short with a POURTANT in capital letters – "And yet / I only want to belong to your race / workers and peasants of all countries"' (1972, p. 197).

National consciousness and the specificity of (post)colonial intellectualism

NEIL LAZARUS

This paper is drawn from the second chapter of a book in progress. Entitled *Hating Tradition Properly*, the book deals with questions concerning cultural production and reception in the contemporary (capitalist and postcolonial) world-system. It opens with a chapter, 'Doubting the new world order: Marxism, realism, and the claims of postmodernist social theory', in which I offer a materialist critique of postmodernist thought.[1] This critique is premised on two principal assertions. Firstly, that the globalism of postmodernist social theory amounts to an unwarranted generalisation from the specific experience of a class fraction of the western (or western-centred) bourgeoisie.[2] Secondly, that, indispensable though postmodernist theories might be in criticism of the dominant ideological formations of empiricism, rationalism, objectivism, scientism, etc., they typically throw out the baby with the bath-water. By constructing the dominant (but attenuated) ideological formations as the only formations, and the only ones imaginable, postmodernism tends to discard reality along with empiricism, rationality along with rationalism, objectivity along with objectivism.[3] All forms of realism are extrapolated to empiricism, all forms of science to scientism. In this respect postmodernism emerges as the dark underside of bourgeois thought. For both, what has happened historically is the only thing that could have happened. But where bourgeois thought (as witness the recent publicity surrounding Francis Fukuyama) finds this conception a cause for celebration, postmodernism views it with a baleful, jaundiced eye. For postmodernism, such overarching philosophical categories as Enlightenment, modernity, progress and revolution loom as indefensible: they are to be disavowed because they have realised themselves (this is taken for granted); and because their self-realisation is deemed not to have proved emancipatory. The suggestion that modernity might best be regarded as an unfinished project, that it might be precisely in the name of Enlightenment, modernity, progress, and revolution that what has in fact happened historically can be most rigorously criticised, is either ignored or else cynically dismissed by postmodernist theorists.

What is true of such concepts as modernity in this respect might also, it seems to me, be true of the concept of nationalism, at least in the context of anti-imperialist struggle. For obvious reasons, an examination of nationalism has once again become unavoidable for social theorists today. In common with many other people, I have been struck by the overlap between dominant (western-centred) disparagements of nationalism and deconstructive readings of the phenomenon in current theories of colonial discourse (the phrase is Benita Parry's). In this chapter, I would like to begin to look again at anti- (or, for that matter, post-)colonial nationalism and its contemporary theoris- ation, by way of suggesting the continuing indispensability of national consciousness to the decolonising project. An obvious place to start is with the writings of Frantz Fanon.

I

In his essay on 'The pitfalls of national consciousness', written at the height of the Algerian war of independence, Fanon drew a distinction between two kinds of nationalist ideology in the context of anticolonialism. On the one hand, there was bourgeois nationalism; on the other, there was a liberationist, anti-imperialist, nationalist internationalism. The former tendency rep- resented the interests of the elite indigenous classes, and was aimed at the (re)attainment of nationhood through means of the capture and subsequent appropriation of the colonial state. The latter tendency was represented in the Algerian arena by the Front de Libération Nationale, the radical anticolonial resistance movement to whose cause Fanon had committed himself. Fol- lowing Anouar Abdel-Malek, we might describe the politics and ideology of the FLN as 'nationalitarian' in outlook:

> [The] nationalitarian phenomenon . . . has as its object, beyond the clearing of the national territory, the independence and sovereignty of the national state, uprooting in depth the positions of the ex-colonial power – the reconquest of the power of decision in all domains of national life . . . Historically, fundamentally, the struggle is for national liberation, the instrument of that reconquest of identity which . . . lies at the centre of everything. (1981, p. 13)[4]

From the nationalitarian vantage point, Fanon argued, bourgeois national- ism was 'literally . . . good for nothing' (1968, p. 176). Its specific project was 'quite simply . . . [to] transfer into native hands' – the hands of bourgeois nationalists – 'those unfair advantages which are a legacy of the colonial period' (p. 152). The social aspirations of bourgeois nationalists were geared toward neocolonial class consolidation: this meant that their 'historic mission' was to constitute themselves as functionaries, straddling the international division of labour between metropolitan capitalism and the subaltern classes in the peripheries. The 'mission' of the national elites, Fanon wrote, 'has nothing to do with transforming the nation; it consists, prosaically, of being the transmission line between the nation and a capitalism, rampant though camouflaged, which today puts on the mask of neo-colonialism' (p. 152).

'The pitfalls of national consciousness' was written as an admonitory essay. With his eye on the unfolding of anticolonial struggles, especially in Africa, Fanon warned that if, at independence, leadership were to come to rest in the hands of the elite classes, the whole momentum of the struggle for liberation would be jeopardised. He argued, accordingly, that it was necessary for radical anticolonialists to oppose bourgeois nationalism as resolutely as they opposed imperialism:

> In underdeveloped countries, the bourgeoisie should not be allowed to find the conditions necessary for its existence and its growth. In other words, the combined effort of the masses led by a party and of intellectuals who are highly conscious and armed with revolutionary principles ought to bar the way to this useless and harmful middle class. (pp. 174–5)

For Fanon, bourgeois nationalism could not be opposed effectively by any exclusively local politics of the people. Popular consciousness needed both to be disciplined (this was the role of the party) and generalised (the task of intellectuals). Transformed through these means into a nationalitarian force, however, the movement for national liberation could not be resisted. Fanon valorises nationalitarianism, in these terms, as a form of national consciousness that does not merely mobilise 'the people' but that actively registers and articulates their aspirations. Nationalitarianism represents 'the all-embracing crystallization of the innermost hopes of the whole people' (p. 148). Fanon insists that the relationship between the FLN and the masses of the Algerian people has been rendered 'profoundly dialectical' by the exigencies of the liberation struggle. It is not only that the party envisions itself less as 'an administration responsible for transmitting government orders' than as 'the direct expression of the masses', their 'energetic spokesman and . . . incorruptible defender (pp. 187–8). It is also that after generations of dispossession, subjugation and forced depoliticisation, the Algerian people have through the struggle become 'an adult people, responsible and fully conscious of its responsibilities' (p. 193). As such a people, they 'are no longer a herd; they do not need to be driven. If the leader drives me on, I want him to realize that at the same time I show him the way' (p. 184). In its resourcefulness and its resilience, its ability to withstand the brutality and terroristic violence of the massive French colonial force, the nationalitarian movement prefigures 'the Algeria of tomorrow'. As Fanon puts it,

> The Algerian people, that mass of starving illiterates, those men and women plunged for centuries in the most appalling obscurity have held out against tanks and airplanes, against napalm and 'psychological services,' but above all against corruption and brainwashing, against traitors and against the 'national' armies of

General Bellounis. This people has held out in spite of hesitant or feeble individuals, and in spite of would-be dictators. This people has held out because for seven years its struggle has opened up for it vistas that it never dreamed existed. (p. 188)

Despite its soaring political idealism, this evocation in Fanon's work of a revolution in the making is deeply problematical. In *Resistance in post-colonial African literature*, I discussed some of the difficulties associated with Fanonism, under the rubric of the category of messianism. I argued that Fanon's tendency to project a unity and co-ordinated political will on to the masses of the Algerian population in the late 1950s could not withstand close historical scrutiny. It is impossible, on Fanon's reading, to account for the wholesale demobilisation and disenfranchisement of 'the people' in the years immediately following the acquisition of independence in Algeria in 1962, after an anticolonial war that had lasted for eight years and claimed a million Algerian lives. Such a development cannot be reconciled with Fanon's evocation of a disciplined and progressively unified population coming closer and closer to self-knowledge as the struggle against the French colonial forces intensified. For it seems inconceivable that, having been decisively and world-historically conscientised during the anticolonial struggle, this population would have permitted itself to be so easily and so quickly neutralised after decolonisation. Against Fanon, therefore, one is tempted to conclude with Ian Clegg that

> [t]he involvement of the population of the traditional rural areas in the independence struggle must be clearly separated from their passivity in face of its revolutionary aftermath. The peasants were fighting for what they regarded as their inheritance: a heritage firmly rooted in the Arab, Berber, and Islamic past. Their consciousness was rooted in the values and traditions of this past, and their aim was its re-creation. (1979, p. 239)

Clegg's account of the political consciousness of the Algerian peasantry during the war of independence is couched in the language of a more or less orthodox Marxism. It is clear that Clegg sets little store by Fanon's distinction between nationalism and nationalitarianism. What matters to him, on the contrary, is the distinction between nationalism and *socialism*. Because Fanon addresses himself in such detail to the question of *national* liberation, he emerges for Clegg as a nationalist – no matter how progressive – rather than as a socialist revolutionary. Opposing himself to Fanonism, Clegg emphasises the centrality of class struggle and the indispensability of an explicitly socialist ideology to the radical project of anti-imperialism. He insists that while the Algerian peasantry might well have committed itself to a chauvinistic struggle for the restitution of its 'homeland', as a class it lacked the ideological resources to transform this struggle into a full–fledged social revolution: '[r]evolution, as a concept, is alien to the peasant consciousness, while the peasants' relationship to the environment remains one of passive endurance rather than active transformation' (p. 239).

In one respect, at least, it is easy to demonstrate the insufficiency of this sort of reading. Ethnographic and social–historical scholarship produced since around 1980 has tended pretty thoroughly to demolish the supposition that peasants' relationship to their world can be characterised in terms of passivity. Moreover, in his failure to problematise his own standpoint, Clegg discloses an elitism that does not inspire in us any great confidence that his own reading of the Algerian scene is likely to be more reliable than Fanon's. It is in this context, indeed, that Christopher Miller has recently challenged the Marxist claim 'to possess the only fully integrated political ... vision' (1990, p. 32). Marxism, Miller writes, 'lacks relativism'. Operating with a universalising optic, it gestures conceptually toward a 'totalizing unity' and, in the name of this unity, tends to 'overlook or "liquidate"' difference, that which it cannot assimilate or subsume (p. 64).

The irony of invoking Miller at this point is that, like Clegg, he also criticises Fanon for his nationalism. Where Clegg opposes Fanon from the standpoint of Marxism, however, Miller takes Fanon's commitment to the question of the nation to be indissolubly linked to his commitment to Marxism. Arguing in general that 'the Marxist approach tends too much toward projection of a Eurocentric paradigm onto Africa, a continent in reference to which terms such as "class struggle" and "proletariat" need to be rethought' (p. 32), Miller claims to find the same irreducible Eurocentrism in Fanon's use of the concepts of nation and national liberation:

> by placing the word at the center of his concern for evolution, without questioning the complexities of its application to different geographical and cultural environments, Fanon winds up imposing his own idea of nation in places where it may need reappraising ... Far from being 'natural national entities' or cohesive nation-states, the modern nations of black Africa must make do with borders created to satisfy European power brokering in the 'scramble for Africa,' borders that often violate rather than reinforce units of culture ... In Fanon's essay on national culture, there is no analysis of what a nation might be, whether it is the same in reference to Algeria as it is in reference to Guinea, Senegal or, most notoriously, the Congo (now Zaire). The single most important fact of political existence in black Africa, the artificiality of the national borders and the consequent problem of cultural and linguistic disunity, receives no attention. (p. 48)

One must start by conceding the validity of much of what Miller says here. It is indeed true that Fanon fails to question the purchase of the idea of the nation on African hearts and minds. In this respect he simply takes for granted the unforgoability and even the world-historical 'appropriateness' of what has been imposed upon Africa by the colonial powers, privileging the nation as the primary unit of anti-imperialist struggle. Certainly, his commitment to internationalism is such that he does not theorise the acquisition of nationhood as an historical terminus: on the contrary, he insists that 'the building of a nation is of necessity accompanied by the discovery and encouragement of universalizing values' (Fanon 1968, p. 247). But this is only to underscore Miller's general observation that Fanon's thought follows the predominant course of post-Enlightenment western reason in subordinating 'history ... to History, particular to universal, local to global' (Miller 1990, p. 50).

It is also clear that Fanon's conceptualisation of the nation is derivative of the discourse of romantic nationalism in Europe. In his essay 'Nationalism: irony and commitment', Terry Eagleton has argued that

> [t]he metaphysics of nationalism speak of the entry into full self-realization of a unitary subject known as the people. As with all such philosophies of the subject from Hegel to the present, this monadic subject must somehow curiously preexist its own process of materialization – must be equipped, even now, with certain highly determinate needs and desires, on the model of the autonomous human personality. (1990b, p. 28)

It is relatively simple to demonstrate the applicability of this formulation to Fanon's nationalitarianism. Fanon's discourse is full of references to the self-realisation of the Algerian people-as-nation through their struggle against colonialism. And in 'The pitfalls of national consciousness', he moves explicitly to figure the relation between individuality and nationhood in the essentialist Hegelian language of particular and universal:

> Individual experience, because it is national and because it is a link in the chain of national existence, ceases to be individual, limited, and shrunken and is enabled to open out into the truth of the nation and of the world. In the same way that during the period of armed struggle each fighter held the fortune of the nation in his hand, so during the period of national construction each citizen ought to continue in his real, everyday activity to associate himself with the whole of the nation, to incarnate the continuous dialectical truth of the nation and to will the triumph of man in his completeness here and now (p. 200).

Yet Miller's fundamental argument against Fanon is less that his discourse is derivative of European theory than that it is inapposite – not to say, hostile – to African realities. He writes that Fanon 'leaves no room for local knowledge': his nationalitarianism commits him to viewing 'precolonial history as no history at all' (p. 50). This reading strikes me as being not only ungenerous but also willfully selective. Miller fails to consider numerous passages in *The wretched of the earth*, and elsewhere, in which – even though his focus falls fairly unremittingly on *colonial* culture – Fanon does clearly move to address the specificity and interior adequacy of precolonial social and cultural forms. It seems to me that one could legitimately criticise

Fanon's analysis in these passages on the grounds that it severely underestimates the resilience and vitality of precolonial cultural forms in the colonial era. But to do this would not by any means be to say, as does Miller, that Fanon had nothing but contempt for precolonial African cultures, or that he regarded the social universe which they registered and to which they constituted a response only as 'a primitive stage to be transcended, or . . . "liquidated"' (Miller 1990, p. 49).

But Miller goes even further than this. He suggests that Fanon's ignorance about and arrogance towards pre-colonial African history is reminiscent of that of Hegel or Hugh Trevor-Roper (p. 50). The claim is perverse and tendentious. Yet Miller does not commit himself to such an extreme statement accidentally. On the contrary, having introduced us to a conception of 'ethnicity' – tentatively defined as 'a sense of identity and difference among peoples, founded on a fiction of origin and descent and subject to forces of politics, commerce, language, and religious culture' (p. 35) – he insists that Fanon's *imposition* of the category of 'nation' upon African cultures organised ideologically around 'ethnic' modes of self-understanding has to be accounted an act of epistemic violence, of such colossal proportions as to invite comparison with the violence of colonial discourse itself. 'What matters most, what is most impressive in reading Fanon', he writes, 'is the sheer power of a theoretical *truth* to dictate who shall live and who shall be liquidated' (pp. 50–1). Miller constructs an image of Fanon fully compatible with bourgeois nightmares of Robespierre or Lenin or Mao. When, for instance, Fanon calls for the 'liquidation of regionalism and of tribalism' and, addressing himself to the collaborative role often played by local chiefs (the deliberate wooing of whom by colonial regimes, in an attempt to facilitate the pacification of local populations, is well documented), suggests that '[t]heir liquidation is the preliminary to the unification of the people' (Fanon 1968, p. 94), Miller draws the conclusion that: 'Fanon's response to local resistance is to call out the firing squad' (Miller 1990, p. 50). The statement *reverses* the logistics of power in the colonial context. It was not the national liberation movement but the colonial state that tended to use firing squads; and it was not 'local resistance' but the official *suppression of local resistance* that mandated the liberation front's 'response'.

Miller's implication of Fanon in the execution of poet–politician Keita Fodiba in Sekou Toure's Guinea in 1969 is similarly dehistoricising, and not only because Fanon himself died in 1961. Rhetorically, Miller's question as to whether 'the fact that Sekou Toure wrapped himself in Marxist and Fanonian discourse ma[kes] Fanon responsible for the reign of terror in Guinea' is answered in being asked at all. Miller is careful to affect scrupulousness: he states that Keita Fodiba's execution cannot be read as a '*necessary* outgrowth of either Marxism or Fanon's theories' (p. 62; emphasis added). But this circumspection is surely compromised by being positioned between an earlier observation that, when alive, Fanon had often cited Toure as 'a practitioner of what...[he] preache[d]' (p. 52), and the subsequent suggestion that Fanon's 'discourse on liberating violence inevitably [leads] to thoughts on the violence of discourse' (p. 63). In constructing Sekou Toure's Guinea as a model of Fanonism realised, Miller completely ignores an important feature of Fanon's analysis of 'the pitfalls of national consciousness'. In his essay, Fanon had spoken with extraordinary prescience of the evolution of precisely such a leader as Sekou Toure, a 'man of the people' who might have had 'behind him a lifetime of political action and devoted patriotism', but whose objective historical function it would become in the postcolonial era to 'constitute a screen between the people and the rapacious bourgeoisie' (Fanon 1968, pp. 167–8). No matter how progressive the role he played prior to independence might have been, Fanon argued, this populist leader, positioned between 'the people' and the elite, would find himself thrust, in the postcolonial era, into the position of a pacifier of 'the people':

> For years on end after independence has been won, we see [the leader] incapable of urging on the people to a concrete task, unable really to open the future to them or of flinging them into the path of national reconstruction, that is to say, of their own reconstruction; we see him reassessing the history of independence and recalling the sacred unity of the struggle for liberation...During the struggle for liberation the leader awakened the people and promised them a forward march, heroic and unmitigated. Today, he uses every means to put them to sleep, and three or four times a year asks them to remember the colonial period and to look back on the long way they have come since then. (pp. 168–9)

Far from being 'responsible' in any way for the direction taken by Sekou Toure as the leader of Guinea after independence, Fanon had already foreseen its likelihood and tried to warn against it. Miller points to the contradiction between Toure's 'ostensibly socialist ideology' and the fact that 'his Guinea was always dominated by multinational corporations', as though this tells in some way against Fanon and Fanonism (Miller 1990, pp. 60–1). Fanon, however, does not need the lesson; before it had even entered the political vocabulary, he had already subjected 'African socialism' to a blistering critique.[5]

Miller paints Fanon in the colors of despotism in order to suggest that his anticolonialism exists only as a would-be hegemonic counterpart to colonialism. Miller's claim is that Fanon's nationalitarianism is predicated upon a will to power that cannot, in ethical terms, be distinguished from the will to power materially exemplified by the dominant discourse of colonialism itself. A European-derived import, it is without autochthonous roots in African soil, and can be imposed upon Africa only by force. Between colonialism and Fanonism, on this reading, there is little to choose. Because nationalitarianism is a totalising discourse, there can be no dialogue between it and the 'local' discourses of 'ethnicity'.

II

In an influential and challenging recent essay, Benita Parry has drawn attention to a 'disparaging of nationalist discourses of resistance' in much of the current scholarship on (post)colonialism, especially that emanating from a broadly post-structuralist standpoint. Miller's commentary on Fanon obviously provides an example of this tendency. But similar examples could also readily be found in the work of such writers as Homi Bhabha and Trinh Minh-ha. (Trinh's recent film *Surname Viet, given name Nam*, for instance, is especially marked in its hostility towards the discourse of nationalism in the Vietnamese context.) Writing with specific reference to the work of Gayatri Chakravorty Spivak, Parry suggests further that this 'disparaging' of nationalist discourse is often 'matched' by an 'exorbitation of the role alloted to the post-colonial... intellectual' (Parry 1987, p. 35).

Parry's idea, that in the work of various contemporary theorists of (post) colonialism there is a relation between a 'disparaging' of nationalism, on the one hand, and an 'exorbitation' or exaltation of intellectualism, on the other, seems suggestive, and I shall return to it in due course. Firstly, however, I should state that I am not convinced that a consistent case can be made against Gayatri Spivak in this respect. Parry's reading of Spivak's position on nationalism strikes me as being somewhat reductive. The problem derives, perhaps, from the fact that Parry evidently interprets Spivak's theory of subalternity in the light of a post-structuralist 'translation' of *agency* into the language of *interpellation,* such that the colonised come to be cast 'passively' as constituted subjects—objects of colonial discourse rather than 'actively' as colonialism's self-conscious resisters. Thus Parry charges that Spivak 'gives no speaking part to the colonized, effectively writing out the evidence of native agency recorded in India's 200 year struggle against British conquest and the Raj' (p. 35). In fact, Spivak's theory of subalternity does not seem to me to be a theory of 'native agency' at all, but a theory of the way in which disenfranchised elements of the 'native' population are *represented* in the discourse of colonialism. The subaltern is for Spivak not a colonised person but a discursive figure in a battery of more or less integrated dominant cultural texts. Since historians of the colonial period, especially, are often obliged to rely centrally on these texts in pursuing their research, it is clearly important that they should not confuse the social practices and forms of consciousness of the classes and groups of people they are investigating with the (mis-, or even non-)representation of these practices in the available colonial documents. In her essay 'Feminism and critical theory', accordingly, Spivak urges (post)colonial theorists to analyse the production of subalternity at the same time as they research various forms of 'native agency'. Theorists today, she writes, need to study 'not only the history of "Third World Women" or their testimony but also the production, through the great European theories, often by way of literature, of the colonial object' (1987, p. 81).

Unfortunately, Spivak herself often fails to live up to this injunction, from the 'other side' as it were. While she clearly offers the examination that she calls for, of the mechanics underlying the 'production . . . of the colonial object', it seems to me that an investigation of the 'history of "Third World Women"' is too often deferred in her own writings. She states explicitly that

> [r]eporting on, or better still, participating in, antisexist work among women of color or women in class oppression in the First World or the Third World is undeniably on the agenda. We should also welcome all the information retrieval in these silenced areas that is taking place in anthropology, political science, history, and sociology. (1988, p. 295)

In her own work, however, the deconstructive interrogation of subalternity is typically given precedence over the radical historiographical account of native agency. This has implications for Parry's critique of Spivak, and for our evaluation of that critique. I have suggested that, in assuming that the discursive category of the subaltern models for the disenfranchised subject of colonialism in Spivak's thought, Parry seems to misread Spivak. To complain that Spivak 'gives no speaking part to the colonized' is in this light no objection at all, since Spivak is entitled to respond that *she* can hardly be held accountable for what *colonial discourse* has wrought. Yet Spivak's intellectual production on the question of colonialism *is* so unmediated in its emphasis upon subalternity, and so saturating in its claims for colonial discourse, as to have prevented her, apparently, from turning her attention in any sustained fashion to an examination of the kinds of issues – concerning native agency in its insurgent aspects – that not only Parry but also, para-doxically, Spivak herself deem of fundamental importance. There is, therefore, a significant truth to Parry's charge that Spivak 'effectively writ[es] out the evidence of native agency recorded in India's 200 year struggle against British conquest and the Raj', as there is, too, to her suggestion that 'the lacunae in Spivak's learned disquisitions issue from a theory assigning an absolute power to the hegemonic discourse in constituting and disarticulating the native' (p. 34). But this truth emerges only on the grounds that we construe Parry's qualifier, 'effectively', in a very strict sense: Spivak, that is to say, does *not* write out the 'evidence' of native agency; but much of the time it is *as though she did*, since in her own work she characteristically defers any detailed presentation of the mass politics of the colonised. (One remarks in passing that this is not always the construction that Parry herself gives to the term 'effectively'. On the contrary, her claim that there is in Spivak's work a 'deliberated deafness to the native voice where it is to be heard' (p. 39) seems to suggest a much stronger – and, I believe, unsupportable – reading: that Spivak willfully fails to register, even suppresses, the fact of colonised peoples' resistance to colonial domination.)

I believe that the validity of Parry's claim against Spivak needs to be qualified in other ways too. From any radical standpoint, her evocation of 'India's 200 year struggle against ... the Raj' seems immediately compelling, and even obviously appropriate. And yet the more one thinks about the terms of Parry's formulation, the more fraught they begin to seem. Take, for instance, the proposition that 'evidence of native agency' is 'recorded' in the history of the colonial era in India. An obvious question in this context is what such 'evidence' is in fact evidence *of*. For Parry, apparently, the answer is clear: 'native agency' betokens Indian resistance to British colonialism. This, however, is to take the (elite) Indian nationalist representation of 'native agency' too much for granted; thus Parry deploys the term 'recorded ' as though it did not suggest a mediation, an ideological intervention, between the actuality of an event and the meaning(s) that it comes to assume in various historical narratives. But the nationalist representation of (anti) colonialism cannot be uncritically affirmed. There is now an abundance of scholarship to suggest that in colonial India, as elsewhere in the colonial world, local struggles and everyday forms of peasant resistance were often entirely divorced from and unassimilable to the 'vertical' political concerns of elite anticolonial nationalists. And even if we were to restrict ourselves to such manifestly 'historical' events as peasant insurgencies, strikes, protests, rebellions, insurrections, acts of sabotage, etc., there would still be good reasons to problematise the elite representation of them as struggles for national liberation. It is true that peasant insurgency is never 'spontaneous' but, on the contrary, always 'a motivated and conscious undertaking on the part of the rural masses', as Ranajit Guha has pointed out with reference to such diverse instances in the Indian context as the 'Rangpur *dhing* against Debi Sinha (1783), the Barasat *bidroha* led by Titu Mir (1831), the Santal *hool* (1855) and the 'blue mutiny' of 1860 ... the revolts of the Kol (1832), the Santal and the Munda (1899–1900) as well as ... the jacqueries in Allahabad and Ghazipur districts during the Sepoy Rebellion of 1857–8' (1986b, pp. 1–2). But as Guha himself makes clear, it does not follow from this that the colonial order is necessarily the antagonist in such events; nor, ideologically, that elite nationalism is necessarily implicated in their prosecution. On the contrary, Guha speaks of a 'politics of the people', arguing that

> parallel to the domain of elite politics there existed throughout the colonial period another domain of Indian politics in which the principal actors were not the dominant groups of the indigenous society or the colonial authorities but the subaltern classes and groups constituting the mass of the labouring population and

the intermediate strata in town and country – that is, the people. This was an *autonomous* domain, for it neither originated from elite politics nor did its existence depend on the latter. (1986a, p. 4)[6]

Peasant insurgents in India during the colonial era, that is to say, did not necessarily think of themselves as Indians, and they did not necessarily believe themselves to be fighting for the liberation of India. Parry does not provide us with an explanation as to why, under these circumstances, the acts of native agency to which she refers should automatically be thought of as moments in *India's* struggle *against the Raj*.[7]

It is, moreover, in precisely this context that Spivak's critique of nationalist discourse seems especially insightful. One of Spivak's insistent contentions, after all, is that the 'genuinely disenfranchised' among the colonised are represented as subaltern not only in the texts of empire but also in 'the great narratives of nationalism, internationalism, secularism, and culturalism', whose unfolding marks the trajectory of anticolonialism (1990a, p. 102). Reading Mahasweta Devi's story 'Douloti the bountiful', for instance, Spivak urges us to 'realize that, in the context of this fiction, "Empire" and "Nation" are interchangeable names, however hard it might be for us to imagine it' (1990b, p. 107). The burden of this argument, if I understand it correctly, is to suggest that to cast 'the colonised' as such, and only as such, in a historical narrative, is to privilege a certain kind of native agency – a certain kind of subjectivity and of 'speaking': that of the *colonised subject* who 'speaks' *as an Indian nationalist* – and to homogenise and bracket as irrelevant all other kinds. Spivak suggests that in arrogating to itself the authority to represent the aspirations of all Indian people and movements, Indian nationalism not only posits the concept of 'India' ideologically, as an 'imagined community' to which all classes and groups of people in the society have equal access and to which they all share the same allegiance, but also serves to render 'subaltern' a variety of forms of self-understanding, social practice and struggle in India – forms that do not articulate themselves in the language and syntax of national consciousness.

It is for this reason, presumably, that Spivak bids us, as postcolonial intellectuals and/or theorists of (post)colonialism, to 'watch out' as keenly in the presence of nationalist discourse as in the presence of imperialist discourse 'for the continuing construction of the subaltern' (1988, p. 295). This is not in my view as difficult a task as Spivak seems to suppose. Yet it remains an indispensable task, and unless it is responsibly shouldered any speculation about the vexed questions of nationalism, internationalism and anti-imperialism in colonial and postcolonial societies is likely to find itself imitating the elite nationalist propensity for appropriation, for unselfconscious projection of its own quite specific needs, fears and aspirations on to the population at large.

Parry, however, reads Spivak as maintaining that it is up to the postcolonial intellectual to 'plot a story, unravel a narrative and give the subaltern a voice in history', a conception that she criticizes as corresponding to an 'exorbitation' of the postcolonial intellectual's role (1987, p. 35). Yet I would want to argue that just the reverse is true: for I read Spivak not as hypostatising or otherwise exalting the work of intellectuals but as claiming too little for it. Spivak concludes her celebrated essay, 'Can the subaltern speak?' with the observation that '[t]he female intellectual as intellectual has a ... task which she must not disown with a flourish' (1988, p. 308). The formulation seems to promise a negotiation with the specificity and potential progressivism of intellectualism as a form of social practice. Yet – to restore the ellipsis – what Spivak actually writes is '[t]he female intellectual as intellectual has a *circumscribed* task ...' (emphasis added); almost invariably when she comes to talk about intellectualism, the weight of Spivak's emphasis tends to fall on the question of circumscription, on the checks and constraints governing intellectual practice and on the severe limitations of what intellectuals – especially radical intellectuals in the context of imperialism – can hope to achieve politically as intellectuals.

Spivak recognises the irreducibility of (post)colonial intellectualism, but underestimates its socially transformative capabilities, which – I would want to argue – are a function of the ability of intellectuals to represent the aspirations of others, to speak for them. It is interesting in this respect to consider the way in which Spivak responds to the work of Ranajit Guha. In his essay 'On some aspects of the historiography of colonial India', Ranajit Guha writes of 'the failure of the Indian bourgeoisie to speak for the nation' (1986a, p. 5). This failure emerges for him as an inability on the part of the Indian elite during the colonial era to forge an articulated national ensemble out of the relatively autonomous domains of elite and popular politics. The bourgeoisie were unable to win the consent of the people, whose interests they failed to recognise, let alone represent: 'There were vast areas in the life and consciousness of the people which were never integrated into the ... hegemony [of the Indian bourgeoisie]' (pp. 5–6). Moreover, the political dominance of the dominant classes could not be challenged effectively by any counter-hegemonic alliance of workers and peasants:

> the initiatives which originated from the domain of subaltern politics were not, on their part, powerful enough to develop the nationalist movement into a full-fledged struggle for national liberation. The working class was still not sufficiently mature in the objective conditions of its social being and in its consciousness as a class-for-itself, nor was it firmly allied yet with the peasantry. As a result it could do nothing to take over and complete the mission which the bourgeoisie had failed to realize. The outcome of it all was that the numerous peasant uprisings of the period, some of them massive in scope and rich in anticolonialist consciousness, waited in vain for a leadership to raise them above localism and generalize them into a nationwide anti-imperialist campaign. (p. 6)

Although Guha's suggestion, that elite Indian nationalism failed to represent the interests of the people, becomes a central inspiration for Spivak's
own critique of elite nationalist discourse, her position is revealingly different
from his. For on Guha's interpretation, the social 'mission' that the Indian
bourgeoisie failed to realise – the 'mission' that the Indian working class for
its part was too weak to appropriate and bring to fruition in 'anything like a
national liberation movement' – is to be characterised as a 'historic failure of
the nation to come to its own' (p. 7). The distinction drawn here by Guha,
between the practical ideology of the 'nationalist movement' and the ideology
that might have characterised a working-class-led 'nationwide anti–imperialist
campaign', finds an echo in Edward Said's distinction, in an essay on 'Yeats
and decolonization', between the 'insufficient' moment of 'nationalist anti-
imperialism' and 'liberationist anti-imperialist resistance' (1990b, p. 76). Like
Said, Guha emerges in his work as an open advocate of the project of
national liberation; this commits him to a nationalitarian politics – that is, to
a discourse of representation predicated upon the assumption that it is indeed
possible for a movement or alliance or party to 'speak for the nation'.

It is at this claim, I believe, that Spivak tends to balk. She seems reluctant
to follow Guha or Said in drawing nationalitarian conclusions from her
critique of the pretensions of bourgeois nationalism. An air of hesitancy tends
to mark her response to any claim for political representation – representation
in the sense of *Vertretung* as she analyses it in 'Can the subaltern speak?'.
Despite the declaration in that essay to the effect that '[r]epresentation
has not withered away' (1988, p. 308), Spivak continues to grant a very
sympathetic hearing to arguments for a post-representational politics; and,
conversely, she continues to evince a real disinclination to affirm the assumption of representation on the part of politico-intellectuals, even where –
as in the case of anti-imperialist struggle – her ideological solidarity with
them is freely admitted. Spivak's ability to juxtapose the claims of nationalitarianism and post-representational discourse, to read each in terms of the
other, is exhilarating. Ultimately, however, it is a holding action; and if, as
we have seen, it is not strictly correct to maintain, as Parry does, that in
Spivak's work a rigorous ideological critique of nationalism has passed into a
wholesale 'disparaging of nationalist discourses of resistance', there is nevertheless a clear and present danger that this holding action is in the process of
ossifying into a *standpoint*.

III

I find it interesting, in this respect, that Christopher Miller should conclude
his chapter on 'Ethnicity and ethics' – in which he has presented his critique
of Fanon's nationalitarianism – with a call for a new cultural relativism,
'retooled as contemporary critical anthropology' (1990, p. 66). Appealing to

the (western) intellectual to unlearn his or her privilege, to re-imagine universalising thought as 'local knowledge' (p. 65), Miller goes to considerable lengths to disclaim any privilege for this intellectual, above all where the representation of Africa and Africans is concerned. Similarly, in Trinh Minh-ha's work, the manifest 'disparaging of nationalist discourses of resistance' seems to be accompanied not, as Parry had speculated, by a compensating exaltation of intellectualism but, on the contrary, by what I would call an *intellectualist anti-intellectualism*, a post-Foucauldian disavowal of the problematic of representation, such that the very idea of speaking for others comes to be viewed as a discredited aspiration, and secretly authoritarian. Trinh argues, thus, that any attempt to distinguish in social terms between intellectuals (or members of the elite), on the one hand, and 'the people' or 'the masses', on the other, already contains an implicit justification of class-division:

> Like all stereotypical notions, the notion of the masses has both an upgrading connotation and a degrading one. One often speaks of the masses as one speaks of the people, magnifying thereby their number, their strength, their mission. One invokes them and pretends to write on their behalf when one wishes to give weight to one's undertaking or to justify it . . . Guilt . . . is always lurking below the surface. Yet to oppose the masses to the elite is already to imply that those forming the masses are regarded as an aggregate of average persons condemned by their lack of personality or by their dim individualities to stay with the herd, to be docile and anonymous . . . One can no longer let oneself be deceived by concepts that oppose the artist or the intellectual to the masses and deal with them as with two incompatible entities. (1989, pp. 12–13)

What truth there is in Trinh's statement is a function of the insight that self-proclaimedly radical intellectualism is often an exercise in bad faith, and that expressions of solidarity with 'the masses' should therefore be scrutinised carefully. Theodor Adorno expressed much the same idea in *Minima moralia* when, in a particularly tough-minded statement, he observed that '[i]n the end, glorification of splendid underdogs is nothing other than glorification of the splendid system that makes them so' (1985, p. 28). But the conclusions that Adorno drew from his argument were quite different from those drawn by Trinh, and I believe that they point to one of the weaknesses of Trinh's position. For Adorno, certainly, 'guilt . . . is always lurking below the surface'. Since intellectualism is predicated upon privilege, that is, upon class domination, this guilt is unforgoable. But where Trinh moves to advocate the *theoretical* dissolution of the socially instituted division between intellectuals and 'the masses', Adorno insists that any such dissolution can be secured only through means of the transformation of *society* – and that until that hypothetical time any disavowal of privilege (or its guilt) is strictly ideological. To be sure, the relation between intellectuals and 'the masses' should not be figured in terms of 'incompatible entities'. Between them, rather – as Adorno and Max Horkheimer wrote with respect to the relation between 'light' and 'serious' art – 'the division itself is the truth' (1987, p. 135). But this socially-instituted division-in-unity cannot be *theoretically* redeemed or wished away.

The work of such theorists as Trinh and Miller also seems to me to be susceptible to criticism in terms of what it says about the representation of 'the masses' in the discourse of intellectuals. As we have seen, Trinh argues generally that 'to oppose the masses to the elite is already to imply that those forming the masses are regarded as an aggregate of average persons condemned by their lack of personality or by their dim individualities to stay with the herd, to be docile and anonymous'. Miller makes the same claim about Fanon's intellectual practice in particular. Returning to *The wretched of the earth*, however, we find Fanon reiterating, time and again, that the relationship between 'the masses' and 'intellectuals who are highly conscious and armed with revolutionary principles' is *not* to be viewed from the standpoint of elitist assumptions about leaders and led, seekers and followers, shepherds and sheep. 'To educate the masses politically' Fanon writes,

> does not mean, cannot mean, making a political speech. What it means is to try, relentlessly and passionately, to teach the masses that everything depends on them; that if we stagnate it is their responsibility, and that if we go forward it is due to them too, that there is no such thing as a demiurge, that there is no famous man who will take the responsibility for everything, but that the demiurge is the people themselves and the magic hands are finally only the hands of the people. In order to put all this into practice, in order really to incarnate the people, we repeat that there must be decentralization in the extreme. (1968, pp. 197–8)

It is easy to be cynical in face of such formulations as these. Miller states that '[e]veryone gives lip service to dialectics' (1990, p. 64). Doubtless, there is something to this complaint. But not everybody who evokes dialectics is a hypocrite, or merely giving lip service to it. And in a remarkable passage in 'The pitfalls of national consciousness' Fanon points to the implications that follow from his understanding of the relation between intellectuals and 'the masses' as dialectical:

> If the building of a bridge does not enrich the awareness of those who work on it, then that bridge ought not to be built and the citizens can go on swimming across the river or going by boat. The bridge should not be 'parachuted down' from above; it should not be imposed by a *deus ex machina* upon the social scene; on the contrary, it should come from the muscles and the brains of the citizens. Certainly, there may well be need of engineers and architects, sometimes completely foreign engineers and architects; but the local party leaders should be always present, so that the new techniques can make their way into the cerebral desert of the citizen, so that the bridge in whole and in part can be taken up and conceived, and the responsibility for it assumed by the citizen. In this way, and in this way only, everything is possible. (1968, pp. 200–1)

Miller and Trinh would, of course, seize on the characterization of the citizens' intellect in this passage as a 'cerebral desert'. Although I believe that, in context, the objectionability of this metaphor is considerably reduced, I do not wish to overwrite or ignore Fanon's ethnocentrism in this respect. There is, as I have already conceded, a good deal of justice to Miller's claim that Fanon was profoundly Eurocentric in his evaluation of 'local knowledges'. Yet taken as a whole the passage is remarkable for its *refusal* to sanction the idea of imposing epistemologies or technologies upon any people who have not first 'internalised' or appropriated them, who have not first made them their own. The very thing that Miller accuses Fanon of doing, in fact, turns out to be the one thing that Fanon refuses on principle to do! Even if the citizens' intellect does amount to a 'cerebral desert', even if the citizens are – from the point of view of the cosmopolitan intellectual – intransigent, narrow-minded, stubborn, wrong, nothing can proceed without them. The 'fighting' intellectual can 'shake the people' or try to 'turn...himself [*sic*] into an awakener of the people' (Fanon 1968, pp. 222–3). Ultimately, however, 'he' 'must realize that the truths of a nation are in the first place its realities' (p. 225). And these realities neither necessarily follow, nor can they forcibly be made to follow, 'his' script.

One finds these Fanonian emphases also in the work of Amilcar Cabral. In his essay 'National liberation and culture', initially delivered in 1970, Cabral spoke of the need for revolutionary intellectuals and leaders of the national liberation movement to live with and among 'the masses' as the liberation struggle unfolded:

> The leaders of the liberation movement, drawn generally from the 'petite bourgeoisie' (intellectuals, clerks) or the urban working class (workers, chauffeurs, salary-earners in general), having to live day by day with the various peasant groups in the heart of the rural populations, come to know the people better. They discover at the grass roots the richness of their cultural values (philosophic, political, artistic, social and moral), acquire a clearer understanding of the economic realities of the country, of the problems, sufferings and hopes of the popular masses. The leaders realize, not without a certain astonishment, the richness of spirit, the capacity for reasoned discussion and clear exposition of ideas, the facility for understanding and assimilating concepts on the part of population groups who yesterday were forgotten, if not despised, and who were considered incompetent by the colonizer and even by some nationals. (1973, p. 54)

Writing a decade after Fanon's death, Cabral clearly cannot be represented as undervaluing the richness and sophistication of pre-colonial African sociality. He refers explicitly to the 'richness of the...cultural values' of the 'rural populations', and notes, in a separate passage, that 'the accomplishments of the African genius in economic, political, social and cultural domains, despite the inhospitable character of the environment, are epic – comparable to the major historical examples of the greatness of man' (p. 50). Animated by his hostility toward nationalism, and by his fetishisation of intellectualism, however, Christopher Miller nevertheless contrives to read Cabral precisely as he had read Fanon. He quotes an observation of Cabral's, to the effect that although the peasantry, as the overwhelming majority of the population of colonial Cape Verde and Guinea Bissau, were indispensable to the armed struggle against Portuguese colonialism in those territories, the national liberation movement did not find it easy to mobilise them to arms: *'we know from experience what trouble we had convincing the peasantry to fight'* (cited by Miller 1990, p. 44). Miller then proceeds to gloss this observation as follows:

> Any revolution in Africa must have the support of the so-called peasants, who make up the vast majority of the population, yet the peasants do not lead but must be led ... The Marxist leader must stand in a transcendent relation between the peasant and History. The peasant's destiny will be revealed to him by the leader, in a relation of active to 'passive,' literate to 'illiterate,' progress to tradition, knowledge to 'ignorance.' (p. 44)

It becomes apparent that, for Miller, Cabral's fault is that he sought to 'convince' the Guinean peasantry to take up arms against Portuguese colonialism. Initially encountering among the peasantry views that were dissimilar to his own, Cabral ought, it seems, as a good, respectful cultural relativist, to have accepted their legitimacy and abandoned forthwith his own aspirations to struggle for the overthrow of colonial rule! Miller reads Cabral's word 'convince' as meaning to 'impose'. The fact, therefore, that Cabral was so successful in persuading the Guinean peasantry to take up arms against their colonisers that they were able, within a space of fifteen years, to topple the colonial regime is interpreted by Miller as revealing only the degree to which the PAIGC (Partido Africano da Independencia da Guine e Cabo Verde) was able to inflict a 'new' colonialism upon an already colonised people. It seems not to occur to Miller that the Guinean peasantry's struggle against the Portuguese might have reflected their own identification – however belated – with the PAIGC's cause; nor, indeed, that the PAIGC's ideology might itself have been a barometer of popular aspirations.

In these terms, the hostility to nationalism exemplified in the work of Miller, Trinh and others comes into focus, ultimately, and despite itself, as a kind of radical elitism. Nationalism is viewed as a derivative discourse of the Europe-oriented colonised middle classes, and is disparaged, as such, for its externality and, indeed, alien-ness, to the majority of the colonised population. The central weakness of this vision, however, is that it is incapable of accounting for the huge investment of 'the masses' of the colonised in various kinds of nationalist struggle – the 'involvement', as Ranajit Guha has put it, in the context of India, of the Indian people in vast numbers, sometimes in hundreds of thousands or even millions, in nationalist activities and ideals' (1986a, p. 3). Disregarding the ideological difference between bourgeois nationalism and nationalitarianism, theorists like Miller and Trinh follow the trajectory of liberal scholarship in tending to cast *all* forms of national consciousness as impositions upon more or less disunited 'ethnically' (or 'local knowledge') identified communities. In Guha's words,

> What ... historical writing of this kind cannot do is to explain ... nationalism for us. For it fails to acknowledge, far less interpret, the contribution made by the people *on their own*, that is, *independently of the elite* to the making and development of ... nationalism. In this particular respect the poverty of this historiography is demonstrated beyond any doubt by its failure to understand and assess the mass articulation of this nationalism except, negatively as a law and order problem, and positively, if at all ... in the currently more fashionable terms of vertical mobilization by the manipulation of factions. (1986a, p. 3)

IV

Even with respect to nationalitarianism, it remains essential to 'watch out for the continuing construction of the subaltern'. As Gayatri Spivak has shown, to insist on this is not 'an idealist red herring'. On the contrary, to ignore the question of the production of the subaltern 'is an unacknowledged political gesture that has a long history and collaborates with a masculine radicalism that renders the place of the investigator transparent' (1988, p. 295). One thinks here, for instance, of recent work by such theorists as Abdul JanMohamed and Patrick Taylor, which, for all its validity and genuine insightfulness in other respects, is distinctly homogenising in its representation of the colonised masses.[8] Elitism remains a danger for nationalitarian discourse. Even in the context of a radical movement for national liberation, it is necessary for intellectuals to remain cognizant at all times of the danger that they might have ceased to speak *for* or *with* and begun to speak *to* 'the masses'. Making such determinations is not always easy, since in the ebbs and flows of nationalitarian struggle the consciousnesses of both intellectuals and 'masses' undergo continual transformation. We have seen Cabral comment on the 'realisations' and 'discoveries' (about themselves and about 'the people') that the leaders of the liberation movement make in their interaction with 'the various peasant groups in the heart of the rural populations'. But Cabral focuses, too, on the transformations wrought on the consciousness of 'the people':

> On their side, the working masses and, in particular, the peasants who are usually illiterate and never have moved beyond the boundaries of their village or region, in contact with other groups lose the complexes which constrained them in their relationships with other ethnic and social groups. They realize their crucial role in

the struggle; they break the bonds of the village universe to integrate progressively into the country and the world; they acquire an infinite amount of new knowledge, useful for their immediate and future activity within the framework of the struggle, and they strengthen their political awareness by assimilating the principles of national and social revolution postulated by the struggle. They thereby become more able to play the decisive role of providing the principal force behind the liberation movement. (1973, p. 54)

I am particularly interested, here, in the idea of a movement from 'local knowledge' to knowledge of 'the principles of national and social revolution'. This, of course, is the desired consequence of the articulation of intellectuals and 'the people'. It reveals, therefore, not only exactly what it is that intellectuals (can) bring to the struggle against imperialism, but also why the moment of nationalism (and, behind and beyond it, of internationalism) should emerge as decisive to this struggle.

Readers will no doubt recall that Fredric Jameson opens his controversial article 'Third-world literature in the era of multinational capitalism' by casting himself, oddly, as an eavesdropper on 'recent conversations among third-world intellectuals' (1986, p. 65). The empirical weaknesses and questionable conceptual assumptions of Jameson's article have been very widely discussed: and I am sure that they do not need rehearsing here.[9] What Jameson 'overhears', of course, is that 'a certain nationalism is fundamental in the third world'; and this 'mak[es] it legitimate' in his view, 'to ask whether it [nationalism] is all that bad in the end' (1986, p. 65). One would have wanted a much more precise formulation, obviously; yet the 'information' that Jameson relays to us remains valuable, nevertheless. For it seems to me that 'a certain nationalism' *is* fundamental in the 'Third World'. It is fundamental, arguably, because it is only on the terrain of the nation that an articulation between cosmopolitan intellectualism and popular consciousness can be forged; and *this* is important, in turn, because in the era of multinational capitalism it is only on the basis of such a universalistic articulation – that is, on the basis of nationalitarian struggle – that imperialism can be destabilised.

The discourse of national consciousness is a derivative discourse. Miller is quite correct to point this out. But he commits himself to an essentialism in presenting his dissenting case for 'ethnicity'. He does not allow for the possibility that, in adapting the discourse of nationalism to the ends of anti-colonialism, even bourgeois nationalists might have had to refunction it, in order to make it bear the burden of their particular political needs. This, however, is precisely the argument advanced by Partha Chatterjee in his impressive study *Nationalist thought and the colonial world*. Conceding that bourgeois anti-colonial nationalism was ineluctably derivative of European nationalist ideologies, Chatterjee nevertheless argues that, merely by virtue of its specificity as *anti-colonial* nationalism, it was obliged to go beyond them:

Pitting itself against the reality of colonial rule ... [anti-colonial] nationalism succeeds in producing a *different* discourse. The difference is marked, on the terrain of political–ideological discourse, by a political contest, a struggle for power, which nationalist thought must think about and set down in words. Its problematic forces it relentlessly to demarcate itself from the discourse of colonialism. Thus nationalist thinking is necessarily a struggle with an entire body of systematic knowledge ... Its politics impels it to open up that framework of knowledge which presumes to dominate it, to displace that framework, to subvert its authority, to challenge its morality.

Yet in its very constitution as a discourse of power, nationalist thought cannot remain only a negation; it is also a *positive* discourse which seeks to replace the structure of colonial power with a new order, that of national power. Can nationalist thought produce a discourse of order while daring to negate the very foundations of a system of knowledge that has conquered the world? How far can it succeed in maintaining its difference from a discourse that seeks to dominate it?

A different discourse, yet one that is dominated by another: that is my hypothesis about nationalist thought. (1986, pp. 40, 42)

What is true of bourgeois nationalism in this regard is true too of nationalism as a mass configuration. Referring to the colonial era, Ranajit Guha argues that even in those cases in which 'the masses' were mobilised very self-consciously and wilfully by the bourgeois nationalist elite, they 'managed to break away from their control and put the characteristic imprint of popular politics on campaigns initiated by the upper classes' (1986a, p. 6). *Especially* if we follow Cabral (or, ironically, Miller), in believing that '[w]ith certain exceptions, *the period of colonization* was not long enough, at least in Africa, for there to be a significant degree of destruction or damage of the most important facets of the culture and traditions of the subject people' (Cabral 1973, p. 60), we should be willing to concede that 'the people' could or would not have spoken the language of nationalism without transforming it at least to some degree into a discourse capable of expressing their own aspirations.

Following Chatterjee, I have spoken of nationalism as a 'derivative discourse'. I do not mean by this that it is an 'ambivalent' discourse, at least not in the sense that that term has been deployed by Homi Bhabha. Predicating himself upon the work of Fanon, but reading Fanon 'back to front', as it were – that is, from *The wretched of the earth* to *Black skin, white masks* – and thereby disavowing the testimony of Fanon's own evolution as a theorist, Bhabha seems to me to overstate dramatically the ideological and cultural effects of colonialism, mistaking dominance for hegemony.[10] In 'Of mimicry and men', he introduces us to the notion of 'colonial mimicry', defining it as

the desire for a reformed, recognizable Other, as *a subject of a difference that is almost the same, but not quite.* Which is to say, that the discourse of mimicry is constructed around an ambivalence; in order to be effective, mimicry must continually produce its slippage, its excess, its difference. (1984, p. 126)

'*Almost the same but not white*', he puns a few pages later: 'the difference between being English and being Anglicized' (p. 130). As a reading of colonised elitism – of the figure of Frantz Fanon as he presents himself in *Black skin, white masks*, perhaps – Bhabha's work strikes me as being suggestive. In these terms I would agree with Benita Parry, who suggests that Bhabha is able to render 'visible those moments when colonial discourse already disturbed at its source by a doubleness of enunciation, is further subverted by the object of its address; when the scenario written by colonialism is given a performance by the native that estranges and undermines the colonialist script' (Parry 1987, p. 42). Yet Bhabha's theory of mimicry parades as a *general* theory of the constitution of subjectivity under colonialism. And as such a theory, I believe, it fails at a very fundamental level to engage with the vastly differential thrusts, effects and modes of domination/subjection of colonialism as practised at different times by different powers in different parts of the world, or even within single but 'unevenly developed' colonies.[11]

In his essay 'Yeats and decolonization', Edward Said helps us to theorize the particular connection between nationalism as a derivative but different discourse and the specificities of (post)colonial intellectualism. He writes that

> [i]t has been the substantial achievement of all of the intellectuals, and of course of the movements they worked with, by their historical interpretive, and analytic efforts to have identified the culture of resistance as a cultural enterprise possessing a long tradition of integrity and power in its own right, one *not* simply grasped as a belated reactive response to Western imperialism. (1990b, p. 73)

The significance of this passage, arguably, is that it enables us to envision the accomplishments of (post)colonial intellectualism as irreducible. For Said, it seems, what intellectuals have been able to contribute to the anti-imperialist struggle – the opening up of horizons, the crystallising of memories and experiences as legitimate aspects of a cultural heritage, the globalising of resources, etc. – could not have been provided by any other form of labour-power, by any other social practice, in any other arena. Elsewhere, Said has commented on the immense significance of the role that literature, as one specific medium of intellectual production, has been able to play in advancing the cause of anti-imperialism in the post-1945 era:

> in the decades-long struggle to achieve decolonisation and independence from European control, literature has played a crucial role in the re-establishment of a national cultural heritage, in the reinstatement of native idioms, in the re-imagining and re-figuring of local histories, geographies, communities. As such, then, literature not only mobilised active resistance to incursions from the outside, but also

contributed massively as the shaper, creator, agent of illumination within the realm of the colonised. (1990a, pp. 1–2)

Obviously, some writers, some intellectuals, could have 'contributed massively' to the decolonising effort on the basis of their work as trade unionists or party officials or co-ordinators of armed struggle. (One thinks for example of such figures as Sergio Ramirez or Ghassan Kanafani or Jose Luandino Vieira.) But Said's point seems to be that intellectuals have contributed most decisively to decolonisation on the basis of their specific labour as intellectuals: by writing, thinking, speaking, etc.[12] It is in these terms alone that they have been able to constitute themselves as 'agent[s] of illumination within the realm of the colonised'. Nothing, therefore, could have replaced this kind of practice, whose effects have been both unique and, perhaps, indispensable.

It is in this connection that I would like, in closing, to urge (post)colonial theorists to think again about the potentialities of intellectualism. Of course I have in mind Lenin's asseveration that '[w]ithout revolutionary theory there can be no revolutionary movement', an idea, as he put it, that 'cannot be insisted upon too strongly at a time when the fashionable preaching of opportunism goes hand in hand with an infatuation for the narrowest forms of practical activity' (1969, p. 25). But it also seems to me that in the context of the contemporary capitalist world system, the need to construct a 'counternarrative . . . of liberation' (Gates 1991, p. 458) is especially pressing. Such a counternarrative would necessarily be derivative of the narrative of bourgeois humanism, with its resonant but unfounded claims to universality. But it would not need to concede the terrain of universality to this Eurocentric projection. On the contrary, where postmodernist theory has reacted to the perceived indefensibility of bourgeois humanism by abandoning the very idea of totality, a postcolonial strategy might be to move explicitly, as Fanon already did in concluding The wretched of the earth, to proclaim a 'new' humanism, predicated upon a formal repudiation of the degraded European form:

> Leave this Europe where they are never done talking of Man, yet murder men everywhere they find them, at the corner of every one of their own streets, in all the corners of the globe . . . When I search for Man in the technique and style of Europe, I see only a succession of negations of man, and an avalanche of murders . . . For Europe, for ourselves, and for humanity, comrades, we must turn over a new leaf, we must work out new concepts, and try to set afoot a new man. (1968, pp. 311–12, 316)

From the standpoint of postcolonialism, it is today impossible to think about politics without invoking the category of universality. For in the postcolonial world-system, experience is multiply overdetermined, and not least by imperialism itself. Social identity has become world-historical in its constitution.

'To understand just one life, you have to swallow the world', Salman Rushdie has his narrator, Saleem Sinai, observe in *Midnight's children*. Hence, arguably, the specific role of postcolonial intellectualism: to construct a standpoint – nationalitarian, liberationist, internationalist – from which it is possible to assume the burden of speaking for all humanity.

Notes

1 Versions of this chapter can be found in Lazarus (1990b, 1991).

2 For other statements of this general position, see Callinicos (1989), Rustin (1989), Sangari (1987) and Tiffin (1991).

3 The obvious reference here is to the work of Habermas (1987), but see also Eagleton (1990a) and Norris (1990).

4 See also Cabral (1973), p. 52: '[T]he chief goal of the liberation movement goes beyond the achievement of political independence to the superior level of complete liberation of the productive forces and the construction of economic, social and cultural progress of the people.'

5 For a critique of African socialism explicitly animated by Fanon's reading, see Armah (1967).

6 In this connection, see also Guha (1983).

7 It is worth noting that my critique of Parry's formulation of mass politics in 'Problems in current theories of colonial discourse' seems to follow the trajectory of her own thinking on this subject. Parry's comments on subalternity and mass politics in her recent essay 'Resistance theory / theorising resistance' (in this volume) indicate a decisive turn away from any uncritical endorsement of nationalism.

8 See JanMohamed (1983 and 1986) and Taylor (1989).

9 Aijaz Ahmad's (1987) critique of Jameson, among the first to be published, is still arguably the most thorough.

10 See Guha (1989) for a discussion of the concepts of 'dominance' and 'hegemony'.

11 The tendency to generalise unwarrantedly, to globalise, from particular instances is characteristic also of Bhabha's recent theorisation of nation-ness as a diasporic configuration, today written pre-eminently from the margins of the nation state. See Bhabha (1990).

12 The title of one of E. San Juan, Jr's essays captures this point brilliantly: 'The responsibility to beauty: toward an aesthetics of national liberation'. In this essay, San Juan offers a suggestive analysis of Roque Dalton's extraordinary essay 'Poetry and militancy in Latin America'. Quoting directly from Dalton's essay, San Juan writes as follows: 'Retrospectively noting the "painful scars" left by his Jesuit education, his irresponsible lifestyle nurtured in the "womb of the mean-spirited Salvadoran bourgeoisie", Dalton's career exemplifies the predicament of the Third World artist bifurcated by his "long and deep bourgeois formative period" and his "Communist militancy". His text registers the hesitancies, reservations, misgivings and scruples of this hybrid genealogy. The writer engages in self-criticism not by jettisoning the past, but by subsuming it in a dialectical mode of absorption/negation: he believes that far from exhausting its potential, the bourgeois outlook offers "creative possibilities", so by discarding its essentially negative aspects, the artist can "use it as an instrument to create ideal conditions for the new people's art that will spring up" in the process of Salvadorans fashioning a new autonomous life for themselves' (1988, p. 90).

Ethnic cultures, minority
discourse and the state

DAVID LLOYD

In 1987, Abdul JanMohamed and I sought to elaborate, by way of introductions to two collections of essays published in *Cultural critique*, some
theoretical considerations on what we had termed 'minority discourse'
(JanMohamed and Lloyd 1990). In the few years following their original
publication these essays have evoked some criticism, and the present chapter,
learning from such criticism, is not so much a defence as an attempt at
further elaboration and clarification of the concepts involved. I will attempt
to sharpen the distinction that seems increasingly necessary between a concept
of 'ethnic culture' and that of the 'minority', whether it refers to an individual,
a group or a discursive formation. In addition, out of this distinction I hope
to elaborate the political consequences, for practice within and without the
university, of the dynamics of ethnic and minority discourses.

This chapter, then, seeks to transform the concept of minority discourse so
that it can generate a critique of its conditions of existence. But that will
demand clarifying the distinction between individual ethnic cultures and
minority discourse itself in a way which was not fully achieved in our initial
formulations. And secondly, it will demand a recognition of a tension, and a
tension which is constantly registered in the writings of minority intellectuals,
not only between minorities and the state they confront in various institutional forms but between the minority and the ethnic subject. This tension
exists in a double mode: around the relation of the minority subject to the
ethnic community and in the long-standing political problem of articulating
the bases for solidarity between distinct groups while respecting the specificity
of their own histories and projects. Both kinds of tension are the source of
painful affect and political difficulty, but exactly in so far as they derive from
contradictory formations have the capacity to become the ground for a far-
reaching critique of the state formation itself. Around this antagonistic relation
between ethnic cultures and the state formation, a further theoretical intervention becomes possible through which the practice of ethnic studies critically
engages the received function of culture, as a concept and as an institution, in
and for the state. It is, in turn, only through a fuller elaboration of this
function of culture that the differential space designated by 'ethnic cultures'
can be grasped.

We can summarise the distinction between ethnic culture and minority discourse that I shall return to more fully later by remarking that where an ethnic culture can be conceived as turned, so to speak, towards its internal differences, complexities and debates, as well as to its own traditions or histories, projects and imaginings, it is transformed into a minority culture only along the lines of its confrontation with a dominant state formation which threatens to destroy it by direct violence or by assimilation. Minority discourse is articulated along this line and at once registers the loss, actual and potential, and offers the means to a critique of dominant culture precisely in terms of its own internal logic. An ethnic culture, strictly speaking, is inassimilable; minority discourse forms in the problematic space of assimilation and the residues it throws up.[1] The distinction is variously narrated in different ethnic literatures as a transitional moment or movement that marks, as we shall see further, the retrospective constitution of the ethnic: it is, for example, succinctly captured in Villareal's *Pocho*, where the young Richard becomes conscious of his *ethnicity*, his 'people', as opposed to the internal contradictions or debates of his community with which the novel had been concerned, in confrontation with and under interpellation by a white police officer (Villareal 1970, pp. 157–64). As I hope to make clearer, such a distinction (even if other terms may be chosen) is crucial to the critique of current liberal pluralist attempts to assimilate ethnicity in the cultural sphere.

Liberal pluralism, adopting as its motto 'E pluribus unum', continues to legitimate the assimilation of minorities by abstracting ethnic cultural phenomena, whether food or music or literature, from the material grounds of their existence and appropriating them on the model of what I will term aesthetic culture: namely, as belonging in a separate, recreationary sphere whose political significance derives precisely from its apparent autonomy from either economic or political considerations. The work of rationalisation and homogenisation continues apace in these spheres, while culture preserves itself in a sphere apart. The work of pluralism in the era of late capitalism is strikingly like that of fascist ideology, which, as Benjamin once put it, 'attempts to organize the newly created proletarian masses without affecting the property structure which the masses strive to eliminate' (Benjamin 1970, p. 243). In the present moment, however, the objects of liberalism are not so much new proletarian masses as minorities who must be affirmed at the level of culture while being assimilated into a dominant society which at every level but that of recreation denies their cultures of *Herkunft*.[2] That this is leading to increasingly aggravated contradictions between these groups and less relatively privileged minorities, and, more significantly and dangerously, white proletarians who also suffer from the property system, is increasingly evident and a particularly troubling effect of pluralism's own incoherence. It is for this reason that any alliance we make with liberal projects such as affirmative action can at best be provisional and tactical. A fuller minority political project is drawn to a further reaching critique of liberal solutions for liberal institutions. As Lisa Lowe has put it, this mode of multiculturalism 'reestablishes the stability of existing relations, and in this reestablishment makes acceptable the larger system of inequalities and exclusions' (Lowe 1992, pp. 6–7). Any minority political or cultural project that stops at this point sells short the struggles of those minorities in whose name it pretends to speak.

I

The oppositional usage of the concept of ethnicity involves such a radical transformation of both conservative and liberal terminology.[3] The history of Ethnic Studies programmes and departments in American universities, which are at once products and crucial spaces for the further articulation of this transformation, is at once one of struggle for the right to self-representation and of continuing marginalisation. This history indicates the extent to which, in itself, an insistence on the intrinsic importance of ethnic cultures as a proper object of study, as of ethnic subjects as *producers* of the studies, is problematic for the present structure of the universities, and specifically for universities as state institutions. At the same time, the huge effort of scholarship and research that has been undertaken within these departments has made them among the very most important and innovative areas of knowledge production as the current debates on education rather back-handedly acknowledge. But more important than the already invaluable archival work that has been carried out in these programmes is what often goes virtually unremarked, the fact that it is a given of Ethnic Studies that they should cut constantly across disciplinary boundaries. We must insist here, however, that the interdisciplinary nature of Ethnic Studies is not the reflection of a recent trend but is based on the crucial recognition that 'cultures' are inseparable from their material conditions. This is also the point of intersection of Ethnic Studies with Cultural Studies. That intersection, however, is not merely one of reciprocity but enforces a specification of the concepts of culture to be deployed.

We can schematise broadly three distinct but related conceptions of culture at work in the contested field of Cultural Studies. The first is that which I have elsewhere designated 'aesthetic culture', that is, a concept of culture which assumes the autonomy of aesthetic forms as belonging to a separate sphere differentiated from the economic and political. Its ideological function can be derived from its claim to autonomy as the condition at once of the production and reception of aesthetic work, as opposed to those other domains of human practice which are defined by the heteronomy of need and interest. Its autonomy grounds the assertion that human freedom is most fully realised in aesthetic culture since the absence of constraint, of heteronomy, permits the free and harmonious development of the individual in conformity to a universal concept of the human.[4] This conception of culture structures conservative versions of the study of culture in the form of liberal education.

The conception of the autonomy of culture has long been critiqued or challenged by two distinct counter-conceptions. The first, which has been most fully elaborated in the Marxist tradition, variously counters the claim to autonomy with the analysis of the socio-economic determination of aesthetic forms, whether in terms of their expressive determination by relations of production or in the more complex forms, derived from Althusser, for which relatively autonomous cultural objects are subject to economic 'determination in the last instance'.[5] The second is broadly speaking derived from anthropological discourse, and can be characterised, with only slight reductiveness, as the conception of 'culture as everything'. That is, culture is conceived as the totality of practices that constitute the life-world of a given society or social grouping. Within this model, whether structuralist or functionalist, the differentiation of aesthetic culture as not only distinct but as monopolising the concept itself is at the least problematic. The universalist claims of aesthetic culture are challenged in turn by a principle of cultural relativism that subordinates value to function or structure (cf. Hall 1980, p. 26).

Neither of these versions of culture, critical as they are of the aesthetic tradition, is entirely adequate to ground a cultural theory for Ethnic Studies though both have been influential on the development of Cultural Studies in its principal current forms. The reasons for this are several and divergent. Paradoxically for the Marxist approach, it has been their common tendency to reduce the play of contradiction within cultural practices themselves. For functionalist anthropology especially, the determination of practices in terms of their regulated and regulating role for a given society virtually precludes the positing of cultural contradictions. The society is effectively conceived as a closed and integral totality. Structural anthropology similarly requires that even differentially signifying practices resolve rather than stage contradiction. Within the Marxist tradition, the very assertion of the determination of cultural forms, while emphasising their ideological function, has tended to posit simultaneously their distinct existence as a given, even to the extent of maintaining the transhistoricity of the aesthetic as a category of human experience.[6] One effect of this tradition on materialist aesthetics (though it is often neither historical nor materialist) has been to relegate the cultural forms of the oppressed to pre-aesthetic status, precisely on the grounds of their lack of autonomy, a tendency surprisingly clear in Raymond Williams's foundational *Culture and society*:

> 'working class culture,' in our society, is not to be understood as the small amount of 'proletarian' writing and art which exists. The appearance of such work has

been useful, not only in the more self-conscious forms, but also in such materials as the post-Industrial ballads, which were worth collecting. We need to be aware of this work, but it is to be seen as a valuable dissident element rather than as a culture. The traditional popular culture of England was, if not annihilated, at least fragmented and weakened by the dislocations of the Industrial Revolution. What is left, with what in the new conditions has been newly made, is small in quantity and narrow in range. It exacts respect, but *j*t is in no sense an alternative culture. (Williams 1983, p. 320)

The analogy with the historical situation of ethnic cultures as equally products of historical damage and susceptible to a like relegation is evident and will lead us to remark on the need for a different grasp of the dynamic of cultural forms. Another effect is that while contradiction is a crucial term for materialist aesthetics, recently influential theoretical work has placed the space of contradiction either between the work and its historical moment or in its gaps and silences, its 'political unconscious', that is, in what it does not or cannot represent. Though the aesthetic work in such theories may be restored into a relation with history, the radical historicity of contradictions does not belong to the constitution and texture of the work itself. What needs to be emphasised, however, is that ethnic cultures and their productions are thoroughly determined in contradictions, in contradictions of a highly over-determined nature to which no resolution may be offered or even attempted.[7] Excellent analyses of the specific contradictory formations of both working-class and ethnic cultures have been carried out of late – the work of Stuart Hall in Britain and George Lipsitz in the United States being exemplary here, especially in their attention to intersections of race and class (see especially Lipsitz 1990a and Hall 1988a). My intention here is not to discount such work but to supplement it by elaborating the theoretical framework within which the significant difference of ethnic cultures, and not least in their heteronomous and contradictory dynamics, dismantles the cultural formation of the political subject for the state.

To propose resolution to contradiction would, indeed, be to think ethnic cultural work as a repetition of aesthetic culture, as a space, that is, abstracted from the heteronomy of everyday existence in order to prefigure the moment of freedom and reconciliation. Conceived in such a manner, ethnic cultural narratives would merely reproduce contradiction at another level, since the reconciliation of the ethnic to the dominant, or to history as it is given, can occur only at the expense of subordinating the specific culture which is to be thus reconciled. But if it is problematic to define ethnic cultural *products* by analogy with aesthetic cultural works as possessing an even relative autonomy, it is none the less problematic to conceive them on the ethnographic model as functional social wholes, that is, concentrating on them as 'forms of living' rather than by reference to a set of specifically cultural products. This is so for several reasons. In the first place, ethnic cultures are always already determined not only by heteronomy, by historical damage and domination, but also by an effective differentiation of spheres – the religious, political, economic and, indeed, cultural – which have at once an interrelated internal development and a distinct set of relations to the same spheres as they have developed elsewhere, in dominant society or in other ethnic groups. Thus, for example, despite the continuing existence of relatively autonomous economic formations in Chinatown or in the black community, such formations can never be entirely independent of the national or global political economy. The same remark can be made of specifically 'cultural' works and institutions. But if we follow Williams in rethinking the concept of 'base' as itself a dynamic and contradictory space of processes, constituted by social relations of production (Williams 1980, pp. 32–7), we can perceive ethnic cultures to be always under a double and contradictory mode of determination, subsumed within the dominant base yet able simultaneously to draw on oppositional sites of alternative determinations. This perception is, of course, the ground of the conceptual distinction between ethnic cultures and minority discourse as well as an assertion of their logical interdependence and will lead us to critique the developmental structure of Williams's own thinking concerning the temporal relations of what he terms residual, dominant and emergent formations (Williams 1980, pp. 40–2 and Williams 1977, pp. 121–7).

Beyond this aspect of the non-totalisable character of the ethnic culture, however, lie the theoretical problems of the 'culture as everything' model. The first of these is methodological and, simply stated, regards the semiotic focus of Cultural Studies: the intervention of Cultural Studies as such, even at the purely hypothetical point where no distinction would be possible between the economic and the cultural, none the less addresses social phenomena as signifying practices as, for example, economic analysis strictly speaking does not. Cultural Studies, that is, constitutes its objects as a quasi-discipline precisely by reproducing the very differentiations of sphere that have historically determined the emergence of culture as concept. The second theoretical problem is distinct but profoundly related. Ethnographic discourse emerges in distinction from sociology around the division between societies with the state and those without or, in Pierre Clastres's phrase, *against* the state (Clastres 1987). Its models cannot, accordingly, be extended to ethnic communities that are historically constituted in relation to the state formation. For ethnic cultures are, as we shall see further, in the perpetually contradictory position of being constituted by the state as the very forms which it is its logic to annihilate. This insistence of the state in its relation to culture is decisive in constituting the space of Cultural Studies in any form.

It is for this reason that, despite the theoretical inadequacy of given models of Cultural Studies, we cannot dispense with attention to the *differential* significance of the cultural sphere. This is not, as with Williams's earlier work, to re-establish the normative nature of aesthetic culture at the expense of subordinated 'non-cultures' nor to accept the transhistorical self-evidence of aesthetic judgement as a special faculty. On the contrary, it is in the historicity of the concept of culture alone that its ideological function can be deciphered, a point well understood by thinkers from Schiller to Arnold for whom, in the latter's terms, 'culture suggests the idea of the State' (Arnold 1984, p. 96). We will return to this crucial political function of aesthetic culture shortly, pausing here to indicate how its emergence as a sphere in the gradual process of differentiation permits a dynamic rethinking of Cultural Studies in its relation to Ethnic Studies. The point here will be reciprocally to clarify the significant difference of ethnic cultural formations and to deploy that difference in a reconceptualisation of Cultural Studies itself.

Within the traditional discourse on the aesthetic, the differential space of culture defines it as that through which the full potential of the human as universal subject is to be achieved and relates it accordingly to a trans-historical disposition of the subject. This ethical disposition is *for* the state, in so far as it is defined as the representative of universal rather than divided and interested humanity. A double differentiation can be deciphered here: synchronically, the aesthetic is defined both against other spheres of practice, the economic and political in particular, opposing 'culture' to 'society', and against other recreationary forms which constitute low or non-autonomous culture; diachronically, aesthetic culture stands as the apex, i.e., as the exemplary and prefigurative moment, of a universal narrative of human development. This combinatory axis allows us to grasp the domain of aesthetic culture as precisely that in which the *political* judgement of the inadequacy of ethnic cultures is articulated as a falling short of the state formation to which, none the less, they are subject. Where, as a consequence of historical damage, ethnic cultures are held not to have developed a fully autonomous cultural sphere, they are regarded as historically inadequate, under-developed rather than differently developed. This is the logic which underwrites the common practice of regarding ethnic writings as ethnographic sources or as reactive protest. Where, on the contrary, selected instances of ethnic cultural production are seized as autonomous works, it is by virtue of formalisation out of their material conditions of emergence or their dialogical relation to a given community. This in turn underwrites the liberal pluralist version of inclusion: the ethnic subject is assimilated precisely in proportion to (his or her) imitation or repetition of canonical cultural values. The correspondent curricular practice is the inclusion of one or two ethnic works at the end of an historically organised syllabus, as if, finally, the 'other' had been acculturated and grown literate. The critique of aesthetic culture as the ground of political judgements requires accordingly a simultaneous articulation of the historical emergence of the concept and institution in its dynamic relation to subordinated social groups and the affirmation of alternative histories against the normative claims of developmental history. That is to say, neither the traditional Marxist critique of the autonomy of culture nor the generalisation of the concept to signify 'forms of living' is fully adequate to analyse the ideological effectivity of the differential sphere of culture in the subordination of ethnic minorities. They are adequate, that is, neither to Ethnic Studies as currently practised nor to Cultural Studies as a political as well as a disciplinary intervention.

It follows that the political significance of Ethnic Studies as a paradigm for Cultural Studies lies not simply in the revaluation of formerly marginalised works or traditions, nor in the mere expansion of the field of possible objects in the name of greater democracy, but precisely in the elaboration of the signifying difference of the ethnic space. To return for a moment to the remark of Williams on the non-existence of working-class culture, it is clear now that the conceptualisation of what is found lacking, a simulacrum of high culture in working-class life, obscures the very different terms of what is there, namely, modes and assumptions of social organisation which more or less explicitly challenge the divisions of labour, politics and recreation that ground the cultural narrative.[8] The same holds for the dynamic and critical relation of the objects of Ethnic Studies to the dominant cultural tradition: resistance to cultural subordination is articulated in the history and formation of alternative conceptions of social organisation.

II

Intrinsic to this critical rearticulation of the concept of culture is the dialectic of ethnic and minority identity, a dialectic which constitutes the non-totalisable and anti-representational structures of minority discourse. For the desire for totality and for representativeness, terms structured within the narrative of culture, has a peculiarly contradictory status within this dialectic. Figurations of the ethnic community, bounded from, often indifferent to, but never unrelated to the dominant which presses in on it, abound in the literature of ethnic cultures. One thinks of the dying *abuelita* (grandmother) in Moraga's *Loving in the war years* as a vivid representation of the integrity of the Mexican community even in its migrations:

> And what goes with her? My claim to an internal dialogue where el gringo does not penetrate? Su memoria a de noventa y seis años going back to a time where 'nuestra cultura' was not the subject of debate. *I write this book because we are losing ourselves to the gavacho. I mourn my brother in this.* (Moraga 1983, p. iii)

Yet one crucial aspect of that integrity is the internal rather than exotic diversity, the internal heterodoxy of the communities which are divided and complicated by gender, sexual, class and even ethnic differences and hierarchies within and across which criticism and transformations are constantly in play. It is this internal heterodoxy which produces the non-totalisable nature of the community – and the aesthetic – and simultaneously a specific problematic of representation:

> Riding on the train with another friend, I ramble on about the difficulty of finishing this book, feeling like I am being asked by all sides to be a 'representative' of the race, of the sex, the sexuality – or at all costs to avoid that. 'You don't speak for me! For the community!...'
>
> 'Ah, Chavalita,' she says to me. 'Tú necesitas viajar para que veas lo que en verdad es la comunidad. There's really no such thing as community among politicos. Community is simply the way people live a life together...' (Moraga 1983, p. vi)[9]

The concept of the generic minority, the typical Mexican American or Black, is one imposed from the outside and encountered by ethnic subjects in the transition from the community into dominant culture. Zora Neale Hurston captures the moment beautifully where she writes in 'What it feels like to be colored me', in what is surely an ironic reflection on the conditions of writing such an essay at all, of how she never knew she was black until entering into the white world (Hurston 1979). As in Villareal and Moraga, 'ethnicity' from this perspective becomes a retrospective hypothesis, a reconstruction of that which, outside its relation to dominant culture, knows no such terms.

These developmental metaphors must be treated with caution, since they temporalise a structure of distinctions which is virtually always in play and forms a topology rather than a temporal curve. None the less they do define a movement from individual to subject that is quite deliberately envisaged as an ethical, and therefore exactly developmental process from the perspective of domination.[10] But a description of the social topography of that movement, which is principally the passage of the individual through the state apparatuses which interpellate him or her as subject, redirects attention to the power relations at stake. For the movement 'out' of the terrain of an ethnic culture is constructed as a passage into a mainstream within which one has diminished voice by virtue of being constructed as a minority. As I have tried to suggest above, however, it is not that the ethnic culture is in any literal sense bounded but that it is constructed as such, as local and limited, in the same moment at which the individual subject becomes a minority. The concept of the minority emerges in time with that of the ethnic and their simultaneous positing constitutes together a localised and strictly speaking inassimilable ethnic culture and an always unevenly or inadequately interpellated minority subject.

The constitution of the minority can take place in any of the spaces which Althusser designates rather extensively as 'ideological state apparatuses' (Althusser 1971). Probably the most significant, however, are the educational institutions, which enact simultaneously the topographic and developmental schemas we have been discussing. These institutions are crucial to the formation of subjects in the democratic state and it is within the formally democratic nation state alone that the concept of the minority makes sense.[11] For the democratic nation state, legitimated by a concept of participatory popular government, must gain consent by hegemony rather than direct coercion. Its hegemony, in turn, can operate only through individuals constituted as citizens, that is, as formally equivalent subjects whose private interests are put in abeyance in free subordination to the will of the majority. What is perhaps less evident is that this process requires conformity to a singular form of public sphere so that the process of re-formation of the individual into citizen demands equally the effective dissolution of alternative cultural formations. It is not simply that minority individuals are separated in the political or economic sphere from their own cultural formations, but that those formations, conceived now as sites of at least latent resistance, are denied legitimacy. The movement from one sphere into the other simultaneously assumes a temporal movement by which the ethnic culture must be 'superseded' or left behind. Hence, for the minority, as indeed for the colonial subject, schooling involves not merely passage from family (in which one is constituted as individual) to school but also passage from an ethnic group into the dominant culture. This factor constitutes the contradictory and irresolvable relation of dominant culture to its minorities: it seeks to dissolve cultural formations in order to assimilate individuals from that culture as subjects, yet at the same moment produces those individuals as generic representatives of their cultures of origin.[12]

This contradiction in the double formation of the minority as at once individuated and generic points equally to the determining assumption of the state, namely that its legitimacy resides in the formal equivalence of individuals who are posited prior to any material conditions of existence: the self-evident truth that all men are born equal.[13] Hence the deep and continuing antagonism of the state to the ethnic communities whose very survival questions the terms of its legitimacy. One of the forms in which that antagonism is most consistently articulated is in the conversion of a virtual 'war of positions' between alternative cultures, one dominant, the other subordinate, into the temporal narrative outlined above. The resistance of a subordinate culture is recast as a stage in human development which must be superseded. According to this narrative, although the identical human subject is latent in every human being, it must be 'educed' from its subjection to the heteronomous forces of nature or barbarity in a deliberate process of cultivation. The end of this process is the production of a public sphere which is grounded in the interactions of ethical subjects and assumes their autonomy, freedom from interest and formal equivalence. What it achieves in relation to subordinate communities is at once to primitivise them and to transform their collectivity into an index of heteronomy, of lack of individuality. The first of these tendencies is captured in the semantic resonance of the very term 'minority', which connects numerical or demographic subordination to the legal concept of immaturity which deprives one of the right to self-representation. In this perspective, minorities are the underdeveloped who have yet to attain the capacity to participate in representative structures, rather than those whose numbers have been systematically controlled by exclusion or genocide. The second tendency legitimates the dissolution of alternative communities by casting the process as the extension of freedom, a freedom which can be the economic freedom from natural needs or the moral freedom from group pressures, conformities or, in its most common form, the constraints of local and limited horizons. (It must be said that forms of this narrative have not been without influence on the self-representation of minorities, as many autobiographies suggest, but generally speaking these representations dialogise the relation between the community and the individual self in ways which express ambivalence at the least towards the dominant narrative, as for example Richard Wright's *Black boy* or Sandra Cisneros's *The house on Mango Street*.)

It has, of course, long been recognised that the formal equivalence of citizens in the political domain at once masks and legitimates, through a discourse of rights which are founded in rights of property, the material inequalities of the economic sphere.[14] It is also the case that the possibility of conceiving of formally equivalent citizens requires the simultaneous and paradoxical emergence of individuals as units of abstract labour within capitalist relations of production. As many since Marx have noted, capitalism creates the conditions for the 'unleashing' of the individual from the specificity of traditional ties, though at the cost of simultaneously dissolving the material contents of individuality into formality and abstraction. To the capitalist reorganisation of relations of production corresponds a public sphere equally antagonistic to inassimilable specificities, localised communities, alternative modes of social organisation and equally devoted to the production of abstract equivalence, though in the political and cultural spheres.[15] The American narrative of immigration provides one account of this process which quite neatly conjoins the two spheres. It casts immigration as a process in which the local is exchanged for the universal in the same process as traditional social relations are exchanged for the conjunction of freedom and capitalism within abstract labour relations which are the ground of self-making. It cuts therefore necessarily against any culture which would place collective values before individualism though it may preserve certain cultural differences precisely in the sphere of their commodification.

To remark this, however, demands also that we stress the logical unevenness and contradictoriness of the processes involved. One way to conceive this is to grasp the perpetual 'decodings and recodings' of capitalism as constant negotiations with the pre-existent desires of individuals and com-

munities (their 'imaginaries', in one version) in the interests of commodification and market expansion. Capitalism, in other words, cannot function
without the processing and reformation of materials, psychic and desiring as
well as 'raw'. But this fact also necessitates the often resistant as well as
merely utopian spaces in which all kinds of 'subcultures' (and not only ethnic
ones) find the means to adapt and transform commodity culture in relation to
desires and projects which answer to specific and not necessarily conformist
social needs.[16] By the same token, as dialectical materialism has always
argued, capitalism produces its contradictions. Traditional Marxism has
always viewed this in terms of the necessary production of a proletariat
whose systematic exploitation leads to class conflict and revolutionary consciousness. More recent thinking, derived in theory largely from Gramsci and
Althusser, as well as from reflection on the struggles of non-class-based
groups such as, notably, those of feminist, gay/lesbian and minority groups,
has placed more emphasis on hegemony and on the formation of counter-
hegemonic formations and blocks resistant to domination.[17] Valuable and
critical as this work has been, it has often run the risk of reducing differents
to equivalents, lacking a basis other than analogy for making distinctions
between the conditions of possibility and modes of struggle of specific group
formations. Consideration of the relations of minority groups to the capitalist
formation allows us to sketch a necessary distinction here between class and
minority politics as a basis for their rearticulation.

III

Traditional Marxist accounts of class struggle envisage it as emerging within
the parameters of the capitalist state as a consequence of contradictions
internal to capitalism itself. It is equally, despite the internationalist dimension, in the first place a struggle conducted within the nation state, as
Gramsci stressed constantly. Though the end of the struggle is the transformation of the property relations which ground exploitation, the process of
struggle has generally been seen as one of gaining control of the state
institutions, repressive and ideological, in Althusser's formulation, which
protect private property. A crucial site of ideological struggle is accordingly
the nation state as the location of formal political subjectivity constituted in
indifference to economic or class distinctions. The critical effort for radical
democracy is to supplant a discourse of rights, founded in and maintaining
property rights, by a discourse of exploitation so that the interpellative force
of abstract national identifications can be countered by a material analysis of
class positions. The class struggle is guided then not, as has too often
been suggested, by a notion of class as essence but by a recognition of its
differential construction within social relations governed by exploitation
(cf. Spivak 1988, pp. 276–9). The class struggle, which is devoted to the

dissolution of class and, crucially, of the division of labour, takes the economic sphere as its principal site not because of the materialist's secret metaphysical yearning for an essential ground but precisely because capitalism itself has transformed all social relations into economic differentials. Though the effects of class permeate every aspect of social life, the specific terrain of class struggle is defined not by culture or ethos, but by the projects which are aimed ultimately at the dissolution of the class formation itself. Minimal or fragmentary as those individual projects at times appear, whether strikes, go-slows, product boycotts, occupations, the concept of class at once regulates them and establishes the terms of its own dissolution.[18]

Something similar can be argued of minority discourse as a political formation, especially when we recognise that it is in the first place precisely a political as opposed to an economic formation. That is to say, just as the concept of class emerges in the sphere of the economic, so that of the minority emerges at the point where civil society requires the state and its correlative, the formal political individual. Only within the context of representative government and the ethical state formation can the concept of the minority emerge as the differential antithesis of the majority.[19] The processes of representation, however, which constitute the minority, introduce a different and contradictory logic. Political representation is from the outset a contradictory concept, since the narrative movement it involves demands the negation at one level, that of the ethical state, of the particular or local interests which are to be represented to the state. This contradiction is rendered as precisely an ethical movement from locality to universality. The effect of this topological argument is to convert a minority status based on an intersection between cultural difference and geographic dispersal into a condensed figure for local attachment and, correlatively, underdevelopment, given the narrative which, as we earlier saw, simultaneously leads by way of development from partiality to universality. It becomes accordingly impossible for minorities ever to escape this logic which constitutes them as generic: precisely that which constitutes minorities as 'interest groups' susceptible of representation deprives them of the capacity to enter fully into the larger narrative of representation. For whereas the general logic of representation assumes its ground to be the formal individual whose contingent interests are none the less sublated in ethical development, the minority is constituted as an impossibility of sublation, as a generic individual whose particularity represents a difference inassimilable to the universal ends of the representative state.

Hence the distinction which it is necessary to make between a minority and a class position (which is not to say that there are not constant and crucial overlaps between the two). Within liberal discourse, working-class subjects become the objects of a figural localisation. The insistence on the narrow horizons, the local interests, the lack of far-sightedness or large vision which is the staple of anti-working-class rhetoric indicates sufficiently for now the metaphorical basis of this figuration. In principle, however, there is no obstacle to the working-class subject overcoming this 'localism' in the sphere of politics. That is, indeed, the very assumption of the formal politics of the democratic state and the rationale of the division of spheres, just as, one might say, the transformation involved in becoming a unit of abstract labour is the ground of participation in a formal politics. For the minority, as such, this option is categorically impossible. Assimilation demands the mere negation rather than the sublation of the ethnic individual as minority, producing that contradiction which Norma Alarcón has succinctly formulated as 'I am a citizen / I am not a citizen' (Alarcón forthcoming).

This is not simply a contingent consequence of a choice to assimilate or not to assimilate. The discourse of choice is irrelevant to the logic of assimilation, in so far as that logic demands the production of the minority individual as generic, as constructed around cultural elements and formations inassimilable to dominant culture. Here the construction of minorities ceases to be a question of interests and becomes one of cultural identities. Accordingly, minority politics exhibits the tendency to commence in a politics of rights but points always towards the terms in which that politics of rights begins to manifest its aporetic structure once the unilaterality of its cultural formations begins to be recognised. As I have argued elsewhere, the unilateral nature of the western cultural formation is fundamental to the constitution of its public sphere around the formal abstract subject and is inseparable from the racist structure of its political formations.[20] Within such a construction, the claim of minorities to 'equal rights' is inseparable from the demand that minorities constitute themselves as individuals, a demand that is in contradiction with their constitution, *as minorities*, as generic rather than individual subjects. It is at this point, though through a different sphere of antagonisms, that a minority politics in completing its logic rejoins a class struggle, without the specificity of either struggle being dissolved: the logic of both demands the critique of what Benjamin designated the 'property system' which the discourse of rights subserves.

This is not the space to explore the relation between the construction of the racial formation of the state and its function in containing and defusing class formations. More important in the present context is to note that the constitution of minorities occurs when a racial formation based on pure exclusion, on a 'crude' racism which simply disenfranchises those it constitutes as others, gives way to a formation based on the need to assimilate and whose racism is, as Fanon put it, a cultural racism directed against ways of living rather than individuals (Fanon 1967, p. 15). This racism remains a mode of exclusion around which the contradictory processes of assimilation become apparent in the constitution of minorities as a mode of 'residue' and from which derives the impetus consciously to retrieve or construct alternative subjectivities in the face of negation from the perspective of the subject. But it is crucial to recognise, in terms which go beyond Williams's famous formulation, that this residue is not to be seen as belonging to the superseded prehistory of the inevitable advent of the modern. The political stakes lodged in the dialectic of ethnic culture and minority discourse are those which hold that not only is the 'residual' itself a moment of the modern, but precisely that in the forms of the residual are to be traced the terms of an emergent transformation of the dominant social order. If ethnic culture is determined by the dominant narrative as a pre-political space of the private sphere, those terms are challenged wherever the ethnic community conceives itself as in fact an alternative kind of public sphere. By the same token, minority discourse, forged in the political sphere, dissolves the concept of the political precisely in its resistance to the narrative of ethical sublation into representation.

That resistance is articulated in the name of the specific ethnic culture from which the individual as minority is to be separated. By the same token, the modes of resistance will vary between different ethnic cultures even if it is the indiscriminate racism of white cultural structures that more often that not is the first stimulus to resistance. For this reason, the articulation of various ethnic struggles with one another takes place not by the positing of analogies between disparate cultures and their histories but in a constant interchange between cultural specificities and the space we have designated that of 'minority discourse'. The force of these struggles is to derive the terms of a critique of the assimilative state formation from the very space in which minorities are interpellated into identity. An analogical manoeuvre, posing equivalences between profoundly different cultures, runs the risk of per-forming the same homogenising gesture as state culture itself, raising cultures to a point of identity where the specificities that it is finally a question of maintaining tend to evaporate.[21] Accordingly, minority politics moves beyond the affirmation of civil rights within the present state formation towards a fundamental questioning of the reason of state itself as a critical stage in the pursuit of the conditions by which the radical self-determination of various social formations could become possible. It is not for us, at this critical juncture, to spell out the terms of that self-determination, terms in any case probably impossible to discern in the fluctuations of what Gramsci terms 'subaltern' histories; we can, however, assist in the dismantling of those dominant structures which continue to legitimate a single mode of historical verisimilitude for humanity and to stem the force of those other histories even as they emerge.

Notes

1 In thinking through the concept of the residual as a counter-formation produced by assimila-tion, I am indebted to the work of Zita Nunes on Brazil: see Nunes (1990) and the essay in

this volume. One of the valuable effects of her turn on the term is to suggest that formations produced by assimilation as residual in the sense that Raymond Williams gives the word in *Marxism and literature* can become the grounds for emergent resistance precisely by refusing the temporal structure imposed by assimilation. See Williams (1977), pp. 121–7.

2 On the concept of *Herkunft*, see 'Niezsche, genealogy, history' in Foucault (1980), pp. 139–64. I prefer this term to 'origins' for the sense of displacement it suggests.

3 For valuable critical and historical summary of the usage of the concept, see Omi and Winant (1986), pp. 14–24.

4 For a fuller elaboration of 'aesthetic culture', see Lloyd (1990b).

5 Williams (1980), pp. 31–7, is an excellent summary of concepts of determination and base and superstructure in the Marxist tradition of cultural studies.

6 In this respect, even Althusser's 'Letter on art' (Althusser 1971, pp. 221–7) reproduces Marx's own idealism on the permanent charm of aesthetic emotions in his 'Introduction' to the *Grundrisse* (Marx 1973, pp. 110–11). Sprinker (1987) maintains a transhistorical view of the aesthetic throughout. For a critique of this tendency in Marxist aesthetics, see Lloyd (1990b).

7 I have been influenced here by Lowe (1992 and forthcoming), essays in which she elaborates the relevance of Althusser's work to minority discourses and the necessary transformation of his concepts which is required in this redeployment. Guha (1988, p. 83) has also been in mind, as he speaks in related terms of the idealism of Marxist historiography and its constitutive blindness to subaltern history's contradictory formations.

8 In Lloyd and Thomas (1991) we have elaborated a similar argument concerning working-class culture and its radical resistance to emergent conceptions of culture in the first half of the nineteenth century. There also, resistance to culture involves an alternative conception of the very divisions of the social that are taken for granted.

9 Tomás Rivera's *Y no se lo tragó la tierra* (1987) similarly constructs in its form as in its representations of the 'internal dialogues' of the Chicano community a portrait of the community in continual self-constitution and without representatives. In general, minority writers have been as profoundly critical of their own communities as of the dominant communities – I think, among others here, of Sandra Cisneros, Richard Wright, Ralph Ellison, Toni Morrison, Maxine Hong Kingston, Toni Cade Bambara, as well as cultural critics like bell hooks. A similar phenomenon often causes consternation in American classes on Third World literature, in reading, for example, O'Flaherty, Beckett, Achebe, Ngugi or Emecheta: their negativity with regard to their own people's conflicts and divisions, often along class and gender lines, is often at first shocking to the good will of American students but has to be understood as a returning of history and agency to peoples whom colonialism has attempted to 'scotomise', to use Fanon's term (cf. Fanon 1968, p. 41). The understanding of contradictions within one's own society, historically and actually, is crucial to the recognition of one's own historicity. It is also a process which is deeply antagonistic to the celebratory nationalism of 'Celtic Twilight' or 'Negritude' formations which reverse the stereotype but thereby preserve predominant social relations as the given. For a very persuasive argument for the necessity of criticism within an ethnic culture, in this case the Asian American, see Lowe (1991a). See also hooks (1990).

10 The tension between topographical and developmental schemas here requires a rethinking both of Lacan's famous essay 'On the mirror stage' and of the use made of it by Louis Althusser in 'Ideology and ideological state apparatuses' (in Althusser 1971). In some ways, the present chapter is a contribution to a fuller rethinking of those works, and follows the line suggested by Frantz Fanon in his all too brief discussion of 'On the mirror stage' in *Black skin, white masks* (Fanon 1986, pp. 161–4n.). I have discussed both Fanon's work and the constitution of the citizen-subject in Lloyd (1991).

11 For a fuller account of this condition of minority status, see Lloyd (1990a).

12 Fanon (1986, pp. 141–2) speaks suggestively of the difference between the even passage from family to state for the colonisers and the contradictory relation between family and civil society for the colonised. A similar dynamic operates in the relation between the minority subject and the ethnic community.

13 For a rather more extended discussion of this assumption and its relations to the cultural formation of the subject, see Lloyd (1990a).

14 See Marx (1978), where he makes the fundamental distinction between political and human emancipation. For a more extensive account of 'On the Jewish question' in relation to Marxist theories of the state and politics, see Thomas (1984).

15 The classic text on this process of dissolving traditional bonds is of course Marx and Engels (1967). On this fundamental element of modernity, see Berman (1982, pp. 87–130), though it is a little uncritical of modernity itself. For a more nuanced and critical take on the processes of rational critique and rationalisation in modernity, see Horkheimer (1978), a still invaluable essay. Deleuze and Guattari (1977) describe capitalism as a perpetual process of decodings and recodings, and provide a very valuable means of understanding the contradictory production of resistance and difference within the overarching processes of rationalisation that capitalism entails. This analysis of capitalism is useful for the understanding of the complex relation of ethnic and minority cultures to the capitalist social formation, of the constant refunctioning of commodity culture in the extension and transformation of cultural traditions.

16 For instances of these processes, see for example Lipsitz (1990b), Hebdige (1979), or hooks (1990). As Lipsitz (1990b) has argued, the work of artists is of paramount importance here as theoretical as well as aesthetic understanding. In an essay which I have found of enormous value to my thinking throughout this chapter, Martin Carnoy (1989) has argued that capitalist hegemony depends on an uneven process of negotiation with and domination of subordinate groups, a process which may involve both concessions to the subordinate groups and the necessary adoption of hegemonic language for the expression of counter-hegemonic projects by those groups.

17 See not only the well known work of Laclau and Mouffe (1985) but also Radhakrishnan (1988), McKinnon (1992), West (1988), Hall (1988). As Radhakrishnan's work indicates, one of the most fruitful encounters in this area has been that between Gramsci and Foucault, though, as Gayatri Chakravorty Spivak has pointed out (1988), there is a crucial analytical distinction to be made between a Marxist analysis of *exploitation* (which I would concur in viewing as indispensable) and a Foucaulian analysis of domination or subjectification. For one excellent conjunction of Gramsci and Foucault which does not make that confusion, but which emphasises rather the heterogeneity and 'heterotopicality' of interlocking discursive formations, see Lowe (1991b, chapter 1).

18 Benjamin, in his essay 'Critique of violence', argues that the strike has the crucial effect of using the discourse of legality in the service of its fundamental overthrow, an understated but brilliant insight on the nature of class politics (1978, pp. 291–3).

19 On the 'ethical state', see Gramsci (1971, p. 263), where the institutions of civil society are seen to be crucial to the formation of citizens for the state.

20 See Lloyd (1991). A vexed question currently in legal studies is that of the place for *group* as opposed to individual rights within bourgeois legal systems. I have neither the brief nor the expertise to discuss this issue as fully as it merits here, but the tendency of my argument is to suggest that resolution of the question is probably impossible within the current legal and political constitution. For some of the issues involved, see Omi amd Winant (1986).

21 There has not been space here to address fully the relation between gender or sexual and minority politics as I have attempted to do with class and minority politics. To do so properly would have demanded a further essay, and I have preferred to suspend the question rather than address it inadequately. The terms of the kind of articulation that I would want

to make between the infamous triad 'race, class, gender' are perhaps discernible here, since I would want to insist on taking into account in gender and sexual politics the crucial way in which the capitalist state divides its spheres, not in order to affirm them but in order to understand specific domains and determinants of constantly overlapping but never identical struggles. For this reason, I would say that recent attempts in feminist studies to displace the Marxist model of class or relations of production with models of gender subordination or the critique of the production/reproduction dichotomy are unhelpful precisely because they fall into a kind of negative analogical mode and try to establish equivalences between a mode of analysis specific to the economic sphere and those needed to critique the construction of sexuality, reproduction, the family and so forth, as belonging to the 'private' sphere (see for example, McKinnon (1992) and Nicholson (1987)). As I argue in the body of the chapter, concepts like class are by no means essential but are precisely differential constructions which can be grasped only in relation to their specific spheres of formation. More useful in defining the relation of feminism to the public sphere has been Carol Pateman's recent work, especially *The sexual contract* (1985), which demonstrates how the public sphere itself is necessarily constructed through the exclusion of women into a private sphere outside the social contract. In this fashion, as with minority discourse, though through a different set of terms, feminism approaches the critique of the state and reconnects with class politics also. Donna Haraway's essay 'The cyborg manifesto' is instructive here, in so far as, in its systematic laying out of the domains of gender oppression, it is possible to discern how the specificity of *gender* oppression diminishes the closer the subject comes to the state. That is to say, where oppression is virtually entirely gender-specific within the 'private' sphere of the family, it is not nearly so much so in labour relations and yet less so in relation to citizenship (Haraway 1991, p. 171). Needless to say, these remarks have an application limited to the western democratic state, and have no necessary relevance beyond that formation. I am indebted to Ronke Oweyumi for her reflections on the problems of importing western private/public dichotomies as analytical tools for examining gender relations in non-western social formations.

Social justice and the crisis
of national communities

RENATO ROSALDO

Modern nation states, such as the United States, operate with coercive ideologies designed to forge all their citizens into a single homogeneous national community. The possibility of formal equality before the law, according to official state ideology, requires uniformity of language and culture among all members of the national community. The national community thus derives from shared identity, common values and uniform consensus, rather than from the solidarity born of diverse identities, a social division of labour and a sense of shared fate. In making immigrants into citizens the state 'naturalises' and polices them. It also embarks on a systematic process of assimilation that the educational system (as part of what Althusser would call the ideological state apparatus) reinforces by preparing each successive generation of children for the nation's version of adult citizenship. In what ways has the equation of conformity and equality always been in question? And in what ways are present-day efforts to renegotiate the national contract at odds with the coercive ideological conflation of sameness and equity?

Although the homogenising force of assimilationist state policies and schooling in civics as preparation for citizenship has long been recognised, social analysts have been less quick to notice that state-induced forms of subordination have created the conditions for movements of resistance. The inequities of class, race and gender were encoded in the North American constitution's provisions for and simultaneous, if less celebrated, exclusions from suffrage. Constitutionally based forms of exclusion have proven consequential over the long run in creating conditions that fostered, firstly, movements for women's suffrage and the abolition of slavery and, in more recent periods, an array of civil rights movements to combat white supremacy, misogyny and homophobia. The context for such movements has been the contradictions between official state ideals of equal citizenship for all and enforced sameness of identity in the national community as well as state-sanctioned forms of subordination based on class, race, gender and sexual orientation. State-sponsored notions that all citizens were created equal have proved to be at odds with both coercive uniformity and the subordinating exigencies of capital.

The critical project of this chapter attempts to clarify present-day efforts to reforge the national community in ways that allow for the mutual recognition of socially significant differences of gender, sexual orientation and race without losing sight of equity and social justice. Difference need not entail inequality; sameness need not be the condition of equality. Difference can promote solidarity; sameness can promote division and exclusion. My project calls for a revision of ethical and political visions so that they better accord with processes of progressive social change now widely under way. The analysis proposed calls for a remaking of the historically received models of national communities in order to accommodate emergent social formations potentially deriving from current renegotiations of national contracts. This chapter contributes an ethical vision that calls for greater inclusion and democratisation in national communities whose solidarity emerges more from diversity than from homogeneity.

The modern nation state has historically imposed a common culture and rallied around shared values and common life-ways (such as The American Way of Life (see Perin 1988), Englishness (see Gilroy 1987), and so on) that attend to citizens who are included and not to those who are excluded. From the perspective of unity based on the cultural homogeneity of the citizenry, diversity appears to be a threat (see Williams 1989). Yet in states like California one cannot help but be overwhelmed by rapidly increasing demographic diversity, the enduring power of the colour line, and persisting divisions of class, gender and sexual orientation. In the elementary and high schools of California, non-white so-called minorities have become the numerical majority. Thus the question of how to (and not whether or not to) enfranchise the emerging majority population has become an urgent issue. Otherwise the United States condemns itself to being more like South Africa of 1980 than it already is.

The analysis in this chapter was conditioned by two recent events, one quite general and the other rather particular. The more general event is the Gulf War. For me, this was strangely like dreamtime. When the war ended I had difficulty discerning whether it was late January or late March. Time seemed to have come to a standstill. Yet the war's conclusion involved a rude awakening. The war had been neither another Vietnam (as then President Bush had warned it would not be – 'no more Vietnam syndrome') nor the Second World War (as the then president had tried to convince us it would be – 'a moral crusade against the new Hitler'). Nor was it the War of 1898 (as I had been saying it would be – 'a big bully nation fighting a small-fry country'). Instead it more nearly resembled the late-nineteenth-century battle of Wounded Knee against the Sioux nation. It was a massacre.

During the dreamtime of war yellow ribbons sprouted everywhere. They were multi-vocal symbols. Some people used them to say that they supported the troops but opposed the war; others meant to say that they supported both the war and the troops. Who could resist the yellow ribbons? In the meantime, public opinion polls supporting then President Bush shot up as if they were thermometers whose bulbs were in the grip of a hot thumb. Many who opposed the war began to feel uncomfortable going to the movies out of fear of being surrounded by flag-waving Americans with yellow ribbons in their teeth. Yet the public opinion polls seemed unbelievable, as if they had been manufactured for the nightmare moment. Had the nation been hood-winked? Or was this the welling-up of spontaneous national sentiment? Was the mobilisation for war the paradigmatic instance of a national community?

A second event conditioning this chapter was more particular. In January 1991 I attended a conference on national culture in Tijuana, Mexico (Valenzuela Arce 1992). There, two Mexican social scientists engaged in intense debate on the topic. The late Mexico City anthropologist Guillermo Bonfil Batalla argued that national culture was imagined in the sense of being false. Mexican national culture, a vision of the homogeneous *mestizo* community, had been manufactured by bourgeois metropolitan intellectuals who ignored and probably knew nothing of the highly variegated and pervasive presence of indigenous cultures among working-class and hinterland populations. There was, he said, no such thing as a singular homogeneous Mexican national culture outside the minds of a few Mexico City intellectuals. Speaking as one living on the USA–Mexico border, Tijuana sociologist Jorge Bustamante argued that Mexican national culture was well defined and that it was a culture of resistance to domination from the United States. He spoke from the border where international relations of inequality were a paramount reality. Bustamante also said that indigenous groups who had migrated to Tijuana, such as the Mixtecans, participated so little in Mexican national culture that their presence could be overlooked. Each analyst's social position clearly influenced their analysis.

From a Chicano perspective, to add a third social position to the debate, both speakers ignored what happens to Mexicans who cross the border and move from being the majority population to becoming a national minority. Structurally speaking, Chicanos in the United States occupy a niche comparable to that of Mixtecans in Tijuana. For us, national culture in the United States signifies marginalisation and exclusion, not pride, belonging and empowerment. Through schooling, the media and the practices of everyday life, the national community renders Chicanos invisible.

Elementary and high school history classes in the United States teach a master narrative about the founding of Jamestown, the original thirteen colonies, immigration from Europe and westward expansion. The fact that the ancestors of certain Chicanos lived within the present boundaries of the United States in settled colonies founded before Jamestown does not enter the narrative. Nor do the history books explain that the ancestors of many Chicanos did not immigrate westward. Instead they stood still and the border

moved southward in the aftermath of the Mexican War of 1848, transforming them overnight from Mexican citizens to citizens of the United
States. Similarly, Native Americans can only wonder about whether or not
they have any place at all in schoolbook histories of a nation of immigrants;
African Americans may well ask who booked their passage before they set
sail across the Atlantic; Asian Americans say theirs is a story of eastward, not
westward movement. The national community, as represented in conventional
elementary and high school history textbooks, overlooks more Californians
than it includes.

How can Chicanos and other minority groups have a place in national
communities? Can we be who we are and still belong as full members in a
participatory democracy? How can the renegotiation of belonging in the
United States be a democratising process? Although the following speaks
primarily about the Philippines, I shall be concerned to view issues from the
viewpoint of both the dominant national community and the historically
subordinated groups within it, including Mixtecans in Mexico, Chicanos in
the United States and Ilongots in the Philippines. What difference does it
make, in forging national communities, if the analyst's primary point of
attachment is that of a subordinated minority group?

Cultural citizenship

In northern Luzon, Philippines, members of one of the cultural minority
groups, the Ilongots (M. Rosaldo 1980; R. Rosaldo 1980), speak of themselves as *bugkalut* and lowlanders as 'those Filipinos'. In other words, Ilongots
do not regard themselves as belonging to the nation state; they do not see
themselves as citizens. Yet, over the period I have known them, from 1967
to the present, they have started joining the nation, albeit in small ways.
Ilongots have had little choice in the matter because the nation has imposed
itself on them through landgrabbing, mining, hydroelectric projects, resettlement projects, elementary schools and missionisation.

In response, Ilongots have prepared their children to face a changing
world by sending them to secular schools, encouraging them to convert to
evangelical Christianity and urging them to learn wet rather than dry rice
agriculture. The changes thus brought have created a chasm between parents
and their children. In a short span of years, they have moved from a purely
oral to a partially literate world. Their children's conversion to evangelical
Christianity involves the end of oratory, magical spells, songs and a host of
other cultural practices. Parents say that by giving up shifting cultivation and
taking up the plough their children will no longer be Ilongots. The ongoing
change in identity has been drastic.

There is no law that says that in order to be Filipino one has to go to
school, belong to a major world religion or do wet rice agriculture. Yet to be

utterly unschooled is to be incompetent in the lowlands. Ilongots have also found that in practice the phrase 'pagan Filipino' is virtually an oxymoron: one can be either a pagan or a Filipino, but not both. Finally, they have encountered tremendous prejudice against people who practise dry rice cultivation, and they recognise that as settlers move in their midst they must limit themselves to a single plot of land for which they can gain legal title. The legal code and the practicalities of vernacular citizenship fail to coincide in a number of important domains.

The Ilongot case raises more general questions about what I have chosen to call cultural citizenship. Cultural citizenship refers to the right to be different and to belong, in a democratic, participatory sense. In this context, the term 'citizenship' broadly encompasses a sense of belonging, as in full citizenship versus second-class citizenship, and more narrowly includes legal definitions, where one either is or is not a citizen. It emphasises participation and influence in the national and local polity; it stresses local, informal notions of membership, entitlement and influence. The word 'cultural' underscores vernacular definitions of community, identity, and human dignity, particularly those of subordinated minority groups.

In the case at hand, rapid changes brought by incorporation into the nation state and capitalist penetration have made it difficult to fix identities and culture. Both the Ilongot ethnic community and the Filipino national community continue to be under negotiation rather than being settled once and for all. Under such circumstances, affirmations of Ilongot identity often appear problematic and at odds with informal notions of citizenship in the nation. At the same time notions of national citizenship that do not fit significant numbers of people legally entitled to them are thrown into jeopardy. (Indeed, a number of observers would follow William Henry Scott, a noted historian of the Philippines, in asserting that current lowland prejudices against their upland neighbours reflect a colonised mentality that persists in a postcolonial nation state. He argues that the Ilongots, among others, should be first-class citizens of the Philippines because their cultures have been comparatively undeformed by the 350 years of Spanish and then American colonial regimes.)

Questions of national identity thus appear not only as collective fictions (where the line between something made and a falsehood can be difficult to draw) but also as arenas of negotiation, dispute and conflict. How do racialised ethnic minority groups navigate between local identities and participation in the state? Such matters are often negotiated around issues of religion, education, land rights, modes of subsistence, wage labour, health care delivery, taxes and the right to vote. From the vantage point of state officials, such matters quickly become practical administrative matters that must be reduced to fiscal and other solutions. From the position of historically subordinated groups, such matters often involve questions of human well-being and dignity as well as distinctive senses of value and community. Social analysts should aspire to tack between the perspective of state officials and that of historically subordinated groups. Under conditions of rapid change, the interplay between state citizenship, the national community, and ethnic nationality involves conflict and complex processes of negotiation more than stable conceptions of identity and community. Such situations test, at once reflecting and redefining, the often tacit boundaries where official national communities draw lines of inclusion, marginalisation and exclusion.

Cultural analysis, subject position, contestation

In terms of methodology, studies of national communities and their inclusions, marginalisations and exclusions require cultural analysis, the recognition of divergent subject positions and studies of contestation. The national community must be understood as a cultural artefact, a coercive ideology and not as a fact of nature. Not unlike other social phenomena, ranging from the self to childhood, nationhood has been historically and socially constructed by human beings. Rather than being given in nature, as ideology often would have it, states have invented national communities over a long period of time. Notions of national communities have histories – rising, falling, meandering, coming into focus, blurring – and they cannot be reduced to such seeming brute facts as human nature or the conduct of 'men in groups'. Such cultural analysis must avoid the pitfall of seeing only cerebral construction and failing to ask about the strength and nature of attachments. If national communities are mere inventions, why are people so often willing to die for them? Why, when and for whom is nationalism compelling? Social analysis requires a double vision that can apprehend both the coercive force of cultural artefacts *and* their socially invented character.

Social analysts must also consider how cultural artefacts look and feel from different positions (see R. Rosaldo 1989). Such positions can be purely structural, based on class, age, gender, sexual orientation, ethnicity, race and so on, taken singly or together in various combinations. Rather than being positioned in a single unified manner, individuals live at the intersection of multiple subject positions (white, upper middle class, male, political prisoner, for example). These positions can be relatively consistent, contradictory or both. Structural positions can be described along such axes as top versus bottom (as in history from below) or centre versus margins (as in women's history). Such positions can also derive from distinctive experiences, such as those of combat soldiers, recent immigrants, political prisoners or parents of children killed in war. They can also range from patriotic zeal and national fervour to exclusion and degradation.

Cultural artefacts are contested or negotiated rather than being fixed; they often encompass both sites of struggle and zones of consensus. When a consensus arises, one can ask, 'Who was not in the room when the consensus was formed?' This approach suggests that social analysts should study the intersections of relations of inequality, such as gender, age, caste, class, race and ethnicity. Although certain dimensions of inequality may be considered universal (age and gender), their content is always local. It is socially and historically formed, politically and economically conditioned and culturally specific. In this approach, one attempts to discern historical processes of conflict and change rather than to discover timeless essences of universal human nature.

The cultural analysis of imagined national communities

What follows involves the detailed assessment of Benedict Anderson's book, *Imagined communities* (1983), a provocative and deservedly influential cultural analysis of nationalism. Anderson's analysis gains its critical edge by transforming a social formation from the naturalised realm of common sense to that of the culturally constructed. This critical passage from the natural to the cultural allows one to call official state national communities into question. Yet I find that Anderson's analysis attends with such care to who is included in his imagined communities that he fails to gain a deeper critique of ideology by considering the position of those who are marginalised and excluded.

Anderson begins with the observation that nationalism has proven a more recalcitrant and enduring fact of life than theorists of either the left or the right predicted. Nationalism, he says, must be understood as a cultural artefact (requiring historical and cultural analysis) rather than as a natural object (transparent to common-sense understandings). The imagined communities of nationalism are fictions in the sense of something made or constructed, but not in that of a falsehood. Not unlike other human inventions, nationalism acts back on its inventors; it shapes, even as it is shaped by, human lives. Indeed one's nationality has come to be treated not as an invention but as if it were a human fatality given at birth and subject to change only by the individual's undergoing the ordeal of so-called naturalisation.

From the outset Anderson combines invention (imagined national communities) with attachment (nationality as human fatality). Culturally speaking, one's nationality belongs with a family of fatalities, such as one's skin colour, genetic endowment, gender, parentage, life-era, and so on. In accord with the ideology of nationhood, human beings cannot do much about the nationalities they are born into, except live with them as best they can.

Too numerous to know each other, members of the nation none the less imagine their national communities as if they were small-scale and face-to-face entities. Their national community is regarded as sovereign and finite. Its limited boundaries never extend to the whole of humankind. Yet, as Anderson notes with biting critical irony, people willingly give their lives for their limited national imaginings. 'What', he asks, 'makes the imaginings of recent history (scarcely more than two centuries) generate such colossal sacrifices?' (p. 16).

Perhaps using the term with more precision than he intends, Anderson describes the horizontal egalitarian ties that bind the members of a nation as fraternal. Readers can probably anticipate that I shall in due time reconsider the question of fraternal relations from the perspective of gender studies.

Anderson goes on to develop an analytically revealing ideal typic contrast between the imagined national community and that of its historical predecessor, the dynastic realm. He suggests that the key historical shift involves the change from the dynastic realm's notion of its subjects to the national community's notion of its citizens. He then argues that the transition between social orders fundamentally redefined cultural notions of space and time.

In spatial terms, the dynastic realm defines human relations vertically by their connection with divinity which is, in turn, linked in a hierarchical series to such earthly representatives as the monarch, the lords and the vassals. In this vertical social order altitude is the key dimension; it emphasises centres, not borders. In contrast, the nation state exercises sovereign control over a flat, homogeneous territory defined by its boundaries rather than by its middles.

In temporal terms, the dynastic realm finds meaning through linkages with divine providence rather than through human causality. Thus an earlier human event can be said to announce or promise a later event which, in turn, fulfills it. In contrast, the national community exists in homogeneous empty time where significant linkages occur through a single moment of secular rather than through widely separated moments of divinely ordained time. Anderson suggests, for example, that the sense of national community grows in part from the socially shared experience of reading about the disparate events that, on any single day, comprise the front page news.

Anderson also speaks of the nineteenth-century novel and its ability to link characters in ways that create an imagined national community. A knows B and B knows C, thus A and C (who do not know one another) become linked in what the reader perceives as a single network. In particular, Anderson uses the opening of Philippine national hero José Rizal's novel *Noli me tangere* (1968; originally published 1887). In this scene, Don Santiago de los Santos is giving a dinner party. Throughout Manila, numerous unnamed people, who do not know each other, are simultaneously discussing the up-coming dinner party in a manner that conjures up a sense of the imagined national community where everybody will be together in the same room at the same time. Later I shall reconsider this example.

Anderson argues more generally that print capitalism transforms human linguistic diversity (and the fact that any finite individual can learn only a tiny portion of all spoken languages) by making a specific language the official medium of communication (for commerce, politics and education) over a bounded territorial expanse. (Richard Handler (1985) has suggested that the classic anthropological concept of culture reflects the coercive ideals of the state in forging a bounded territory that is homogeneous in terms of language and culture.)

After thus defining the key parameters of the nation as a cultural artefact (the imagined community), Anderson proceeds with a historical sketch which falls into three periods. Firstly, he demarcates the period between 1776 and 1838 when the initial generation of nation states emerged in a relatively rapid succession ranging from the thirteen colonies through the French Revolution to the series of nations founded in the Americas.

Secondly, the years between 1820 and 1920 were marked by the consolidation of nationalism as ideology in Europe. If the first phase of nationalism was relatively improvised, the later two phases were distinguished by a tension between spontaneous national movements and an official version of nationalism. Based more on the exigencies of the state than on the aspirations of the populace, the latter developed in large measure to contain the former.

Thirdly, the period following the Second World War was marked by a series of new nations formed out of prior colonial territories. In the new nations the tension between ardent populism and official nationalism became especially acute. The latter was inculcated through the mass media, popular education and administrative regulations. The former grew out of anticolonial popular movements of national liberation.

Subject position and the remaking of national communities

Anderson's cultural analysis of the nation as an imagined community attends more carefully to questions of inclusion than of exclusion. His analysis of imagined national communities situates itself from the vantage point of the state rather than from that of its more marginalised citizens. In failing to consider divergent subject positions, Anderson misses the opportunity for a critical analysis that would carry him beyond the important step he does take of studying the socially constructed character of national communities.

Consider, for example, Anderson's analysis of the opening scene of José Rizal's *Noli me tangere*. Anderson underscores the universality of the verbal net Rizal casts as he creates the imagined national community. Marked by Rizal's macabre humour and his Gothic sense of the grotesque, passages such as the following lend credence to Anderson's view: 'So the news of his dinner party ran like an electric shock through the community of spongers, hangers-on, and gate-crashers whom God, in His infinite wisdom, had created and so fondly multiplied in Manila' (1968, p. 1). The image of riff-raff spreading the news suggests that everybody in Manila was planning to attend the dinner party being given by Don Santiago de los Santos. Yet lines of marginalisation were evident by the time the great event began. The narrator says that the few women present congregated in a room separate from the men. Only one person, a 'kindly-faced' cousin of the host, bothered to welcome the women. The mean-spirited narrator notes that: 'Her hospitality and good manners did not extend beyond offering the Spanish ladies cigars and betel-nut chew on a tray, and giving her hand to be kissed by her compatriots, exactly like a friar' (p. 4). In a double ethnic cross-over, the welcomer demeaned the Spanish by offering them 'lowly' Filipino fare, cigars and quids of betel-nut at the same time that she insulted her Filipino compatriots by offering her hand to be kissed in the manner of a haughty Spanish friar.

The party centres on men who often pretend to be of eminence and their occasional wives rather than on distinguished women and their husbands. Indeed the male guests described at the party are clergy, officials, military officers, businessmen and men of affairs generally rather than vagabonds, rogues or members of the working class. If gender differentially shapes the treatment of the guests who do arrive, social class determines whose names are placed on the guest list in the first place.

Aside from the segregation of men from women in the novel's opening scene, women find multiple ways to absent themselves throughout the novel. (I am indebted to anthropologist Anna Tsing for suggesting the lines of analysis in this and the following paragraphs.) Women's absences often enable men to become heroic patriots that measure up to international stan- dards. The perceived need to protect indigenous women, especially mothers and virgin daughters, from predatory Spaniards brings a number of Filipino male characters into consciousness as nationalists. Women thus become the enabling condition and the source of inspiration for the mobilisation of a patriotic male defence of the nation.

Women also find more literal ways to remove themselves so that men can create the revolutionary fraternal ties that bind. In the *Noli*, Maria Clara, the only daughter of Don Santiago de los Santos who hosted the opening scene's dinner party, was betrothed from an early age to the novel's hero, Crisostomo Ibarra. After a number of Spaniards repeatedly use foul play to foil the young couple's amorous intentions, the hero flees because he has been charged with rebellion and Maria Clara literally takes herself out of the incipiently bonding men's way by entering a convent and going mad. In the novel's concluding scene, she becomes little more than a frightful apparition, 'a white figure standing almost on the ridge of the roof, its arms stretched out to the sky and its face turned pleadingly upward while the heavens replied with thunder and lightning' (p. 406). Rizal's novel establishes a hydraulic relation between horizontal egalitarian relations among men and the exclusion of women. The marginalisation of women allows men to forge the fraternal bonds that unite the imagined national community in egalitarian solidarity. The linked dynamics of fraternal egalitarianism and sororal exclusion constitute the process of forging the national community.

Gender relations in Rizal's novel have a notable precedent in the French Revolution which, for a series of successors, has become an exemplary model of both revolution and the modern nation state. Indeed Anderson's phrase concerning the imagined community's fraternal bonds appears tacitly to draw on the French Revolutionary slogan of liberty, equality and fraternity. Yet it is only recently that scholars such as Joan Landes (1988) have called attention to the relations of gender and the nation. Landes argues that under dynastic realms the absolutist public sphere did not exclude women. Instead it put them at something of a disadvantage because of their supposed weaker character and baser nature. Under the republic, however, women's gender became the basis of twin differences. On the one hand, women enjoyed a certain moral superiority, especially as manifest in motherhood and domesticity. On the other hand, they were virtually excluded from the public realm of politics and civil society, as seen in the following:

> The subordination of women to men and a rigid sexual differentiation were encapsulated in the uniform body of laws codified by Napoleon during the first decade of the [nineteenth] century. The Civil Code excluded women from the definition of citizenship even as it recognized the equal rights of all citizens. (p. 170)

Feminism as we know it today, Landes says, emerged in part from the contradiction between equal rights for all citizens and the explicit exclusion of women from citizenship. In the long run, such lines of exclusion produce new social movements that demand changes on behalf of newly recognised citizen subjects.

Contestation

Once one recognises the import of different and unequal subject positions, questions of conflict, contestation and negotiation become central. Social analysis must become fundamentally historical because contestation always is in process and its outcomes are uncertain. Although structural factors may constrain events, they do not determine them. In this respect, Anderson's work has set in motion a series of new studies that begin where his left off.

In addition to the marginalisation of women and the working class, the *Noli* fails even to acknowledge the existence of racialised cultural minorities. My companions of some three years, the Ilongots in the hills to the north, neither were invited to nor heard about the party given by Don Santiago de los Santos. In the present, the Philippine imagined national community often fails to include such cultural minorities. As one can probably anticipate, the feeling is by and large mutual. Or at any rate, as I said, Ilongots do not regard themselves as Filipinos.

Recent works suggest a need to supplement Anderson's historical schema. Begin with the conception of the nation as a bounded homogeneous territory. Within this delimited territory, as Max Weber said, the state exercises a monopoly on the legitimate use of violence. The term 'legitimate' refers, of course, to the state's vantage point and not to the people against whom the violence is directed. Ilongots, Kurds, Basques and Mohawks probably do not find state violence legitimate.

Increasingly over Anderson's second phase (1820–1920) the idea of nationality took on the appearance of a fact of nature. Indeed the term 'naturalisation' became current in this period and one's nationality, as Anderson says, increasingly had the character of a fatality given at birth. From the viewpoint of the state, its individual citizens were equal and the same; they were uniform in language and culture. From this perspective, however, national (linguistic and ethnic) diversity within the state became a threat because it challenged the normative order that posited uniformity among the citizenry in the name of a coercive congruence between state and nation (see Williams 1989).

During this period, certain citizens came to fulfil the norms of the national community and thus became culturally invisible to themselves (Rosaldo 1989). Upwardly mobile citizens who succeeded in entering the bourgeois bureaucratic chambers (corporate, military, legal, medical, educational) were called upon to abandon local attachments and 'parochial' cultural attributes. No matter how parochial they may have been, ancient Athenian and western European educational classics were regarded by many in positions of privilege as if they embodied universal thought, reason and cultivation. From another angle of vision, so-called universal thought could be described, despite the protestations of its adherents, as the distinctive cultural systems of the bourgeoisie in each nation founded in Europe and the Americas between 1776 and 1838.

If the state fully enfranchised certain individuals (e.g., white male property holders), it simultaneously disenfranchised others (e.g., women, people of colour, white men without property). In this context, the privileged full citizens of nations founded between 1776 and 1838 saw themselves as universal, rational and cultivated, whereas states regarded their subordinated second class citizens as cultural in the sense of being local, ethnic and different from the dominant norms of the national community. From a top-down perspective, the more empowered a group the less cultural it was and the more cultural the group the less powerful it was, at least in terms of the entitlements of full citizenship. One can then ask whether this ratio of culture and power applies as aptly to the nations formed after the Second World War as it does to those created between 1776 and 1838. This question requires comparative exploration.

Benedict Anderson's path-breaking work has made questions of citizenship in the national community a productive area for further enquiry. Membership in national communities appears to be a contract that requires constant renegotiation. Using the metaphor of Rizal's opening scene, one can fruitfully ask who was and who was not invited to the party. How do such inequalities as age, gender, class, race, caste and ethnicity intersect in conflicts and negotiations? Which groups have been excluded or marginalised by national imaginings? How do marginalised groups imagine themselves and the nations they inhabit?

Arguably, the study of nations under imperialism now works from a present in which the useful fiction of the nation state as a territorially bounded homogeneous territory is at once strongly present and breaking down owing to such global transformations as the new international division of labour, immigration of unprecedented magnitude and the implosion of the Third World into the first. The idea of the melting pot can no longer be sustained. Even newer images, such as the salad bowl and the stewing pot, meant to highlight diversity within an encompassing entity, fail to recognise that the container itself is leaking. Think of New York in the mid-1980s when over one-third of its seven million inhabitants were from the Caribbean. Consider the demographic changes in California where, in 1945, 91 per cent of the population was Anglo and 5 per cent Latino; now the population is 25 per cent Latino and by 2030 it is projected to be 50 per cent Latino. The container does not contain.

National communities and processes of incorporation into and resistance against the nation state require historical and comparative study from a present that renders the entities under study increasingly problematic. In studying relations of dominant and subordinant populations within nation states a number of analysts have found it useful to distinguish between states and nations (e.g., Guidieri *et al.* 1988). States often contain more than one nation (in this context, nation and ethnic group are nearly synonymous) and a single nation often inhabits more than one state (in extreme cases, one speaks of diasporas). Current processes of globalisation should enable social analysts to reconsider cases that once seemed closed. The central question raised by the concept of cultural citizenship is whether one can be different and be a full citizen too. Need more different mean less equal? Do mechanisms of assimilation cross the colour line? What are other comparable lines of insolubility? By what coercive means have states tried to enforce sameness and conformity within their bounded national territories?

Let me conclude by returning to my opening reflections. The Gulf War raised the question of whether it produced a spontaneous outpouring of national sentiment, a manufactured mobilisation of consensus or both. One should note well that the national consensus took the form of like-mindedness. It evoked images of men in groups and men on teams. Much as Benedict Anderson's work would anticipate, the emerging New World Order appears quite literally fraternal. Yet the war moved me beyond the spontaneous versus manufactured issues to the rather chilling realisation that national mobilisation for war appears to be the best example of nationalism in Anderson's sense. Hopefully, such realisations can open those with democratic aspirations to the remaking of national communities.

The remaking of national communities requires a blend of the known world and the hoped-for future. Such ethical and political efforts require comparative assessment in a manner that tacks between dominant and subordinate perspectives. What makes the subordinated members of internally diverse national communities thrive and feel violated? How do marginal or excluded groups imagine themselves and their nations? Can one move from notions of homogeneity as the basis of consensus to something more like a weave whose strength and solidarity resides in a combination of overlap and difference? Can polyglot citizens become the national norm? For historically subordinated groups, questions of social justice and full citizenship in national communities are not academic but matters of sheer survival.

The angel of progress: pitfalls
of the term 'postcolonialism'

ANNE McCLINTOCK

His face is turned towards the past ... The angel would like to stay, awaken the dead, and make whole that which has been smashed. But a storm is blowing from Paradise; it has got caught in his wings with such violence that the angel can no longer close them. This storm irrestistibly propels him into the future to which his back is turned, while the pile of debris before him grows skyward. This storm is what we call progress. (Walter Benjamin)

To enter the Hybrid State exhibition on Broadway, you enter The Passage. Instead of a gallery, you find a dark antechamber, where one white word invites you forward: COLONIALISM. To enter colonial space, you stoop through a low door, only to be closeted in another black space – a curatorial reminder, however fleeting, of Fanon: 'The native is a being hemmed in' (Fanon 1968, p. 29). But the way out of colonialism, it seems, is forward. A second white word, POSTCOLONIALISM, invites you through a slightly larger door into the next stage of history, after which you emerge, fully erect, into the brightly lit and noisy HYBRID STATE.

I am fascinated less by the exhibition itself than by the paradox between the idea of history that shapes 'The Passage', and the quite different idea of history that shapes the 'Hybrid State' exhibition itself. The exhibition celebrates 'parallel history':

Parallel history points to the reality that there is no longer a mainstream view of American art culture, with several 'other,' lesser important cultures surrounding it. Rather there exists a parallel history which is now changing our understanding of our transcultural understanding. (Hybrid State Exhibition Brochure 1991)

Yet the exhibition's commitment to 'hybrid history' (multiple time) is contradicted by the linear logic of The Passage ('A brief route to freedom'), which, as it turns out, rehearses one of the most tenacious tropes of colonialism. In colonial discourse, as in The Passage, space is time, and history is shaped around two, necessary movements: the 'progress' forward of humanity from slouching deprivation to erect, enlightened reason. The other movement presents the reverse: regression backwards from (white, male) adulthood to a primordial, black 'degeneracy' usually incarnated in women. The Passage rehearses this temporal logic: progress through the ascending doors, from primitive prehistory, bereft of language and light, though the epic stages of colonialism, post-colonialism and enlightened hybridity. Leaving the exhibit, history is traversed backwards. As in colonial discourse, the movement forward in space is backwards in time: from erect, verbal consciousness and hybrid freedom – signified by the (not very free) white rabbit called 'Free' which roams the exhibition – down through the historic stages of decreasing stature to the shambling, tongueless zone of the pre-colonial, from speech to silence, light to dark.

The paradox structuring the exhibition intrigues me, as it is a paradox, I suggest, that shapes the term 'post-colonialism'. I am doubly interested in the term, since the almost ritualistic ubiquity of 'post-' words in current culture (post-colonialism, postmodernism, post-structuralism, post-Cold-War, post-Marxism, post-apartheid, post-Soviet, post-Ford, post-feminism, post-national, post-historic, even post-contemporary) signals, I believe, a widespread, epochal crisis in the idea of linear, historical 'progress'.

In 1855, the year of the first imperial Paris Exposition, Victor Hugo announced: 'Progress is the footsteps of God himself.' 'Post-colonial Studies' has set itself against this imperial idea of linear time – the 'grand idea of Progress and Perfectability', as Baudelaire called it. Yet the term 'post-colonial', like the exhibition itself, is haunted by the very figure of linear 'development' that it sets out to dismantle. Metaphorically, the term 'post-colonialism' marks history as a series of stages along an epochal road from 'the precolonial' to 'the colonial' to 'the post-colonial' – an unbidden, if disavowed, commitment to linear time and the idea of 'development'. If a theoretical tendency to envisage 'Third World' literature as progressing from 'protest literature' to 'resistance literature' to 'national literature' has been criticised as rehearsing the Enlightenment trope of sequential, 'linear' progress, the term 'post-colonialism' is questionable for the same reason. Metaphorically poised on the border between old and new, end and beginning, the term heralds the end of a world era, but within the same trope of linear progress that animated that era.

If 'post-colonial' *theory* has sought to challenge the grand march of western historicism with its entourage of binaries (self–other, metropolis–colony, centre–periphery, etc.), the *term* 'post-colonialism' none the less re-orients the globe once more around a single, binary opposition: colonial/post-colonial. Moreover, theory is thereby shifted from the binary axis of *power* (coloniser/colonised – itself inadequately nuanced, as in the case of women) to the binary axis of *time*, an axis even less productive of political nuance since it does not distinguish between the beneficiaries of colonialism (the ex-colonisers) and the casualties of colonialism (the ex-colonised). The 'post-colonial scene' occurs in an entranced suspension of history, as if the definitive historical events have preceded us, and are not now in the making. If the theory promises a decentring of history in hybridity, syncreticism, multi-dimensional time and so forth, the singularity of the term effects a re-centring of global history around the single rubric of European time. Colonialism returns at the moment of its disappearance.

The word 'post', moreover, reduces the cultures of peoples beyond colonialism to *prepositional time*. The term confers on colonialism the prestige of history proper; colonialism is the determining marker of history. Other cultures share only a chronological, prepositional relation to a Eurocentred epoch that is over (post-), or not yet begun (pre-). In other words, the world's multitudinous cultures are marked not positively by what distinguishes them but by a subordinate, retrospective relation to linear, European time.

The term also signals a reluctance to surrender the privilege of seeing the world in terms of a singular and ahistorical abstraction. Rifling through the recent flurry of articles and books on 'post-colonialism', I am struck by how seldom the term is used to denote *multiplicity*. The following proliferate: '*the* post-colonial condition', '*the* post-colonial scene', '*the* post-colonial intellectual', '*the* emerging disciplinary space of post-colonialism', 'post-coloniality', '*the* post-colonial situation', 'post-colonial space', '*the* practice of post-coloniality', 'post-colonial discourse', and that most tedious, generic hold-all: '*the* post-colonial Other'.

I am not convinced that one of the most important emerging areas of intellectual and political enquiry is best served by inscribing history as a single issue. Just as the singular category 'Woman' has been discredited as a bogus universal for feminism, incapable of distinguishing between the varied histories and imbalances in power among women, so the singular category 'post-colonial' may license too readily a panoptic tendency to view the globe within generic abstractions voided of political nuance. Much post-structural theory, with its insistence on infinite textuality, has disavowed the idea of 'history', while none the less charting its own theory in very broad historical sweeps: the Enlightenment, modernity, postmodernity, postcolonialism and so forth. The arcing panorama of the horizon, however, becomes thereby so expansive that international imbalances in power remain effectively blurred. Historically voided categories such as 'the other', 'the signifier', 'the signified', 'the subject', 'the phallus', 'the postcolonial', while having academic clout and professional marketability, run the risk of telescoping crucial geopolitical distinctions into invisibility.

The authors of the recent book *The empire writes back*, for example, defend the term 'post-colonial literature' on three grounds: it 'focuses on that relationship which has provided the most important creative and psychological impetus in the writing'; it expresses the 'rationale of the grouping in a common past', and it 'hints at the vision of a more liberated and positive future' (Ashcroft, Griffiths and Tiffin 1989, p. 24). Yet the inscription of history around a single 'continuity of preoccupations' and 'a common past' runs the risk of a fetishistic disavowal of crucial international distinctions that are barely understood and inadequately theorised. Moreover, the authors decided, idiosyncratically to say the least, that the term 'post-colonialism' should not be understood as everything that has happened since European colonialism but rather 'all the culture affected by the imperial process from the moment of colonization to the present day' (p. 2). Which means turning back the clocks and unrolling the maps of 'post-colonialism' to 1492, and earlier. Whereupon, at a stroke, Henry James and Charles Brockden Brown, to name only two on their list, are awakened from their *tête-à-tête* with time, and ushered into 'the postcolonial scene' alongside more regular members like Ngugi Wa Thiong'o and Salman Rushdie.

Most problematically, the historical rupture suggested by the preposition 'post-' belies both the continuities and discontinuities of power that have shaped the legacies of the formal European and British colonial empires (not to mention the Islamic, Japanese, Chinese and other imperial powers). Political differences *between* cultures are thereby subordinated to their temporal distance *from* European colonialism. But 'post-colonialism' (like postmodernism) is unevenly developed globally. Argentina, formally independent of imperial Spain for over a century and a half, is not 'post-colonial' in the same way as Hong Kong (destined to be independent of Britain only in 1997). Nor is Brazil 'post-colonial' in the same way as Zimbabwe. Can most of the world's countries be said, in any meaningful or theoretically rigorous sense, to share a single 'common past', or a single common 'condition', called 'the post-colonial condition', or 'post-coloniality'? The histories of African colonisation are certainly, in part, the histories of the collisions between European and Arab empires, and the myriad African lineage states and cultures. Can these countries now best be understood as shaped exclusively around the 'common' experience of European colonisation? Indeed, many contemporary African, Latin American, Caribbean and Asian cultures, while profoundly affected by colonisation, are not necessarily primarily preoccupied with their erstwhile contact with European colonialism.

On the other hand, the term 'post-colonialism' is, in many cases, prematurely celebratory. Ireland may, at a pinch, be 'post-colonial', but for the inhabitants of British-occupied Northern Ireland, not to mention the Palestinian inhabitants of the Israeli Occupied Territories and the West Bank, there may be nothing 'post' about colonialism at all. Is South Africa 'post-colonial'? East Timor? Australia? By what fiat of historical amnesia can the United States of America, in particular, qualify as 'post-colonial' – a term which can only be a monumental affront to the Native American peoples who opposed the confetti triumphalism of 1992. One can also ask whether the emergence of Fortress Europe in 1992 may not also signal the emergence of a new empire, as yet uncertain about the frontiers of its boundaries and global reach.

My misgivings, therefore, are not about the theoretical substance of 'post-colonial theory', much of which I greatly admire. Rather, I wish to question the orientation of the emerging discipline and its concomitant theories and curricula changes, around a singular, monolithic term, used ahistorically, and haunted by the very image of linear 'progress' that much of that same work challenges theoretically. Nor do I want to banish the term to some chilly, verbal Gulag; there seems no reason why it should not be used judiciously in appropriate circumstances, in the context of other terms, if in a less grandiose and global role.

One might distinguish theoretically between a variety of forms of global domination. Colonisation involves direct territorial appropriation of another geopolitical entity, combined with forthright exploitation of its resources and labour, and systematic interference in the capacity of the appropriated culture (itself not necessarily a homogenous entity) to organise its dispensations of power. Internal colonisation occurs where the dominant part of a country treats a group or region as it might a foreign colony. Imperial colonization, by extension, involves large-scale, territorial domination of the kind that gave Britain and the European 'lords of humankind' control over 85 per cent of the earth in the nineteenth century, and the USSR totalitarian rule over Hungary, Poland and Czechoslovakia in the twentieth century.

Colonisation, however, may involve only one country. Currently, China keeps its colonial grip on Tibet's throat, as does Indonesia on East Timor, Israel on the Occupied Territories and the West Bank, and Britain on Northern Ireland. Since 1966 South Africa, in defiance of a UN General Assembly Resolution and a 1971 World Court Order, kept its colonial boot on Namibia's soil. Only in 1990, having stripped Namibia of its last diamond resources, was South Africa content to hand back the economically empty shell to the Namibians. Israel remains in partial occupation of Lebanon and Syria, as does Turkey in Cyprus. None of these countries can, with justice, be called 'post-colonial'.

Different forms of colonisation have, moreover, given rise to different forms of decolonisation. Where *deep settler colonisation* prevailed, as in Algeria, Kenya, Zimbabwe and Vietnam, colonial powers clung on with particular brutality.[1] Decolonisation itself, moreover, has been unevenly won. In Zimbabwe, after a seven-year civil war of such ferocity that at the height of the war five hundred people were killed every month, and 40 per cent of the country's budget was spent on the military, the Lancaster House Agreement choreographed by Britain in 1979 ensured that one-third of Zimbabwe's arable land (12 million hectares) was to remain in white hands, a minute fraction of the population (Meldrum 1991, p. 13). In other words, while Zimbabwe gained formal political independence in 1980 (holding the chair of the 103-nation Non-Aligned Movement from 1986 to 1989) it has, economically, undergone only *partial decolonisation*.

Breakaway settler colonies can, moreover, be distinguished by their formal independence from the founding metropolitan country, along with continued control over the appropriated colony (thus displacing colonial control from the metropolis to the colony itself). The United States, South Africa, Australia and New Zealand, remain, in my view, breakaway settler colonies that have not undergone decolonisation, nor, with the exception of South Africa, are they likely to in the near future.

Most importantly, orienting theory around the temporal axis colonial/ postcolonial makes it easier not to see, and therefore harder to theorise, the continuities in international imbalances in imperial power. Since the 1940s, the United States' imperialism-without-colonies has taken a number of distinct forms (military, political, economic and cultural), some concealed, some half-concealed. The power of US finance capital and huge multinationals to direct the flows of capital, commodities, armaments and media information around the world can have an impact as massive as any colonial regime. It is precisely the greater subtlety, innovation and variety of these forms of imperialism that makes the historical rupture implied by the term 'post-colonial' especially unwarranted.

'Post-colonial' Latin America has been invaded by the United States over a hundred times in the twentieth century alone. Each time, the USA has acted to install a dictatorship, prop up a puppet regime or wreck a democracy. In the 1940s, when the climate for gunboat diplomacy chilled, United States' relations with Latin America were warmed by an economic imperialist policy euphemistically dubbed 'good Neighbourliness', primarily designed to make Latin America a safer backyard for the United States' virile agribusiness. The giant cold-storage ships of the United Fruit Company circled the world, taking bananas from poor agrarian countries dominated by monocultures and the marines to the tables of affluent US housewives (Enloe 1989, pp. 124–50). And while Latin America hand-picked bananas for the United States, the United States hand-picked dictators for Latin America. In Chile, Allende's elected socialist government was overthrown by a US-sponsored military coup. In Africa, more covert operations such as the CIA assassination of Patrice Lumumba in Zaire had consequences as far-reaching.

In the Cold War climate of the 1980s, the USA, still hampered by the Vietnam syndrome, fostered the more covert military policy of 'low intensity' conflicts (in El Salvador and the Philippines), spawning death squads and proxy armies (Unita in Angola, and the Contras in Nicaragua) and training and aiding totalitarian military regimes in anti-democratic, 'counter-insurgency' tactics (El Salvador, Honduras, South Africa, Israel and so forth). In Nicaragua in February 1990 the 'vote of fear' of continuing, covert war with the USA brought down the Sandinistas.

The United States' recent fits of thuggery in Libya, Grenada and Panama, and most calamitously in Iraq, have every characteristic of a renewed military imperialism, and a renewed determination to revamp military hegemony in a world in which it is rapidly losing economic hegemony. The attacks on Libya, Grenada and Panama (where victory was assured) were practice runs for the new imperialism, testing both the USSR's will to protest and the US public's willingness to throw off the Vietnam syndrome, permitting thereby a more blatant era of intervening in Third World affairs. At the same time, having helped stoke the first Gulf War, the USA had no intention of letting a new boy on the block assert colonial dominance in the region.

For three years before the Gulf War, the US arms trade had been suffering a slump. After what one military industrialist gloatingly called the Gulf War's 'giant commercial-in-the-sky', US arms sales have soared. None the less, if the USA had the political muscle to resuscitate a nearly defunct Security Council and strong-arm a consensus through the UN, and the military capacity to make short shrift of 150,000 Iraqi soldiers and an estimated 200,000 civilians in one month, it did not have the economic means to pay for the war. Saddled with its own vast debts, the USA has been massively paid off in reimbursements (an estimated $50 billion) by Saudi Arabia, Kuwait, Japan and Germany, so that it now appears in fact to have profited from the war to the tune of $4–5 billion. At the same time, most of the estimated $20 billion necessary to restore Kuwait will go to western, largely US, companies. The war has thus made ever more likely a global security system based on military muscle, not political co-operation, policed by the United States' mercenary army (and perhaps NATO), moving rapidly and lightly around the world, paid for by Germany and Japan, and designed to prevent regional, Third World consensuses from emerging. Far from heralding the end of imperial intervention, the second Gulf War simply marks a new kind of interventionism. Not only is the term 'postcolonial' inadequate to theorise these dynamics, it actively obscures the continuities and discontinuities of US power around the globe.

While some countries may be 'post-colonial' with respect to their erstwhile European masters, they may not be 'post-colonial' with respect to their new colonising neighbours. Both Mozambique and East Timor, for example, became 'post-colonial' at much the same time, when the Portuguese Empire decamped in the mid-1970s, and both remain cautionary tales against the utopian promise and global sweep of the preposition 'post'. In East Timor, the beds of the Portuguese were scarcely cold before the Indonesians invaded, in an especially violent colonial occupation that has lasted nearly two decades. The colonial travail of the East Timoreans has gone largely unprotested by the UN – the familiar plight of countries whose pockets aren't deep, and whose voices don't carry.

In Mozambique, on the other hand, after three centuries of colonial drubbing, the Portuguese were ousted in 1975 by Frelimo, Mozambique's socialist independence movement. But across the border, white Rhodesians, resentful of Mozambique's independence and socialist promise, spawned the Mozambique National Resistance (MNR), a bandit army bent only on sowing ruin. After Zimbabwe itself became politically independent of Britain in 1980, the MNR has continued to be sponsored by South Africa. A decade of the MNR's killing-raids and South Africa's predations has subjected the country to a fatal blood-letting and displaced nearly two million people, in a war so catastrophic that Frelimo has been forced to renounce Marxism and consider shaking hands with the bandits. Now Mozambique is in every sense a country on its knees. What might have been a 'post-colonial' showpiece has instead become the killing fields of Southern Africa.

Yet neither the term 'post-colonial' nor 'neocolonial' is truly adequate to account for the MNR. Neocolonialism is not simply a repeat performance of colonialism, nor is it a slightly more complicated, Hegelian merging of 'tradition' and 'colonialism' into some new, historic hybrid. In recent years, the MNR has become inextricably shaped around local inter-ethnic rivalries, distinct religious beliefs and notions of time and causality (especially ancestral intervention) which cannot be reduced to a western schema of linear time. More complex terms and analyses, of alternative times, histories and causalities, are required to deal with complexities that cannot be served under the single rubric 'post-colonialism'.

Singular universals such as 'the postcolonial intellectual' obscure international disparities in cultural power, electronic technology and media information. The role of 'Africa' in 'post-colonial theory' is different from the role of 'post-colonial theory' in Africa. In 1975 the entire continent had only 180 daily newspapers, compared with 1,900 for the USA, out of a world total of 7,970. By 1984, the number of African dailies dropped to 150, then staggered back to 180 in 1987 (the same figure as in 1955). In 1980, the annual production of films in the continent was seventy. In contrast, the production of long films in Asia was 2,300 in 1965, and 2,100 in 1987 (Kinfe 1990, pp. 47–9). The film industry in India remains the largest in the world, while Africa's share of television receivers, radio transmittors and electronic hardware is minuscule.

The term 'post-colonialism' is prematurely celebratory and obfuscatory in more ways than one. The term becomes especially unstable with respect to women. In a world where women do two-thirds of the world's work, earn 10 per cent of the world's income and own less than 1 per cent of the world's property, the promise of 'post-colonialism' has been a history of hopes postponed. It has generally gone unremarked that the national bourgeoisies and kleptocracies that stepped into the shoes of 'post-colonial' 'progress' and industrial 'modernisation' have been overwhelmingly and violently male. No 'post-colonial' state anywhere has granted women and men equal access to the rights and resources of the nation state. Not only have the needs of 'post-colonial nations' been largely identified with male conflicts, male aspirations and male interests, but the very representation of 'national' power rests on prior constructions of gender power. Thus even for Fanon, who at other moments knew better, both 'coloniser' and 'colonised' are unthinkingly male: 'The look that the native turns on the settler is a look of lust... to sit at the settlers' table, to sleep in the settler's bed, with his wife, if possible. The colonized man is an envious man' (Fanon 1968, p. 30). Despite most anti-colonial nationalisms' investment in the rhetoric of popular unity, most have served more properly to institutionalise gender power. Marital laws, in particular have served to ensure that for women citizenship in the nation state is mediated by the marriage relation, so that a woman's political relation to the nation is submerged in, and subordinated to, her social relation to a man through marriage.

The global militarisation of masculinity, and the feminisation of poverty have thus ensured that women and men do not live 'post-coloniality' in the same way, or share the same singular 'post-colonial condition'. In most countries, IMF and World Bank policy favoured cash-cropping and capital surplus in the systematic interests of men, and formed a predictable pattern where men were given the training, the international aid, the machinery, the loans and cash. In Africa, women farmers produce 65–80 per cent of all agricultural produce, yet do not own the land they work, and are consistently bypassed by aid programmes and 'development' projects.

The blame for women's continuing plight cannot be laid only at the door of colonialism, or footnoted and forgotten as a passing 'neocolonial' dilemma. The continuing weight of male economic self-interest and the varied under-tows of patriarchal Christianity, Confucianism and Islamic fundamentalism continue to legitimise women's barred access to the corridors of political and economic power, their persistent educational disadvantage, the bad infinity of the domestic double day, unequal childcare, gendered malnutrition, sexual violence, genital mutilation and domestic battery. The histories of these male policies, while deeply implicated in colonialism, are not reducible to colonialism, and cannot be understood without distinct theories of gender power.

Finally, bogus universals such as 'the post-colonial woman', or 'the post-colonial other' obscure relations not only between men and women but among women. Relations between a French tourist and the Haitian woman who washes her bed linen are not the same as the relations between their husbands. Films like *Out of Africa*, clothing chains like Banana Republic and perfumes like 'Safari' all peddle neocolonial nostalgia for an era when European women in brisk white shirts and safari green supposedly found freedom in empire: running coffee plantations, killing lions and zipping about the colonial skies in aeroplanes – an entirely misbegotten commercialisation of white women's 'liberation' that has not made it any easier for women of colour to form alliances with white women anywhere, let alone parry criticisms by male nationalists already hostile to feminism.

How, then, does one account for the curious ubiquity of the preposition 'post' in contemporary intellectual life, not only in the universities but in newspaper columns and on the lips of media moguls? In the case of 'post-colonialism', at least, part of the reason is its academic marketability. While admittedly another PC word, 'post-colonialism' is arguably more palatable and less foreign-sounding to sceptical deans than 'Third World Studies'. It also has a less accusatory ring than 'Studies In Neocolonialism', say, or 'Fighting Two Colonialisms'. It is more global, and less fuddy-duddy, than 'Commonwealth Studies'. The term borrows, moreover, on the dazzling marketing success of the term 'postmodernism'. As the organising rubric of an emerging field of disciplinary studies and an archive of knowledge, the term 'post-colonialism' makes possible the marketing of a whole new generation of panels, articles, books and courses.

The enthusiasm for 'post-' words, however, ramifies beyond the corridors of the university. The recurrent, almost ritualistic incantation of the pre-position 'post-' is a symptom, I believe, of a global crisis in ideologies of the future, particularly the ideology of 'progress'.

The first seismic shift in the idea of 'progress' came with the abrupt shift in US Third World policy in the 1980s. Emboldened in the 1950s by its econ-omic 'great leap forward' (space, again, is time), the USA was empowered to insist globally that other countries could 'progress' only if they followed the US road to mass-consumption prosperity. W. W. Rostow's 'Non-communist manifesto' envisaged the so-called 'developing' nations as passing through similar stages of development, out of tradition-bound poverty, through an industrialised modernisation overseen by the USA, the World Bank and the IMF, to mass-consumer prosperity. None the less, except for the Japanese 'miracle' and the Four Tigers (Taiwan, Singapore, Hong Kong and South Korea), the vast majority of the world's populations have, since the 1940s, come to lag even further behind the consumer standards set by the west (Arrighi 1991, p. 40).

Then, between 1979 (the second oil shock) and 1982 (the Mexican default), the world economy began to creak. Increasingly, it became clear that the USA was no longer destined to be the only economic power of the future. Hobbled by its phenomenal debts, and increasingly diminished by the twin shadows of Japan and Germany, the USA summarily abandoned the doctrine of global 'progress' and 'development'. During the Reagan era, the USA instituted instead a bullying debt-servicing policy towards poorer countries, bolstered by aggressive competition with them on the market, and defended by sporadic fits of military gangsterism, as in Grenada and Panama. The cataclysmic war in the Gulf served only to underscore the point.

For many poorer countries, the shift in US policy meant abandoning overnight the *fata Morgana* of capitalist 'progress', and settling for chronically stricken positions in the global hierarchy. Henceforth, they could aspire only to tighten their belts, service their debts and maintain some credit. In 1974, Africa's debt-service ratio was a manageable 4.6 per cent. Thirteen years later it had rocketed to 25 per cent. But the collapse of the US model of 'progress' has also meant the collapse, for many regimes, of the legitimacy of their national policies, in the panicky context of worldwide economic crisis, ecological calamity and spiralling popular desperation. Indeed, perhaps one reason, at least, for the burgeoning populist appeal of Islamic fundamentalism is the failure of other models of capitalist or communist 'progress'. As a senior Libyan aide, Major Abdel-Salam Jalloud, has said of the destiny of the FIS in Algeria: 'It's impossible to turn back. The FIS has an appointment with history; it will not miss it'.

A monotonously simple pattern has emerged. Despite the hauling down of colonial flags in the 1950s, revamped economic imperialism has ensured that America and the former European colonial powers have become richer, while, with a tiny scattering of exceptions, their ex-colonies have become poorer (Payer 1974, 1982).[2] In Africa before decolonisation, World Bank projects were consistently supportive of the colonial economies. Since formal decolonisation, contrary to the World Bank's vaunted technical 'neutrality' and myth of expertise, projects have aggressively favoured the refinement and streamlining of surplus extraction, cash crop exports, and large-scale projects going to the highest bidders, fostering thereby cartels and foreign operators, and ensuring that profits tumble into the coffers of the multinationals. During 1986, Africa lost $19 billion through collapsed export prices alone. In 1988 and 1989, debt service payments from the Third World to the USA were $100 billion. At the same time, as Fanon predicted, Third World kleptocracies, military oligarchies and warlords have scrambled over each other to plunder the system. To protect these interests, the tiny, male elites of 'developing' countries have spent almost $2.4 trillion on the military between 1960 and 1987, almost twice the size of the entire Third World debt (Broad, Cavanagh and Bello 1992, p. 100).[3] Now, after the 1980s 'desperate decade' of debt, drought and destabilisation, the majority of Third World countries are poorer than they were a decade ago. The World Bank has concluded that 'fifteen African countries were worse off in a number of economic categories after structural adjustment programs' (Broad, Cavanagh, and Bello, p. 96). In Africa 28 millions face famine, and in countries like Mozambique, Ethiopia, Zaire and the Sudan the economies have simply collapsed.

The United States' 'development' myth has had a catastrophic impact on global ecologies. By 1989, the World Bank had $225 billion in commitments to poorer countries, on condition that they, in turn, endure the purgatory of 'structural adjustment', export their way to 'progress', cut government spending on education and social services (with the axe falling most cruelly on women), devalue their currencies, remove trade barriers and raze their forests to pay their debts (George 1988, 1990). Under the financial spell of

the USA (and now Japan), and in the name of the fairy-tale of unlimited tech-
nological and capital 'growth', the World Bank engineered one ecological disaster after another: the Indonesian Transmigrasi programme, the Amazonian
Grande Carajas iron-ore and strip-mining project, and Tucurui Dam de-
forestation project, and so on. The Polonoroeste scheme in Brazil carved a
paved highway through Amazonia, luring timber, mining and cattle ranching
interests into the region with such calamitous impact that in May 1987 even
the President of the World Bank, Mr. Barber Conable, confessed he found the
devastation 'sobering' (Hancock 1989, p. 131).

The Four 'miracle' Tigers have paid for progress with landscapes pitted
with poisoned water, toxic soil, denuded mountains and dead coral seas. In
'miracle' Taiwan, an estimated 20 per cent of the country's farmland is
polluted by industrial waste, and 30 per cent of the rice crops contain unsafe
levels of heavy metals, mercury and cadmium (Broad, Cavanagh, and Bello
1992, p. 91). A World Bank report in 1989 concluded gloomily that 'adjustment programs' carry the by-product that 'people below the poverty line will
probably suffer irreparable damage in health, nutrition and education' (Broad,
Cavanagh, and Bello 1992, p. 95). Now Japan, insatiably hungry for timber
and raw resources, is the major foreign aid donor, to the tune of $10 billion.
In short, the World Bank and IMF 'road to progress' has proved a short road
to what Susan George has called 'a fate worse than debt'.

To compound matters, the collapse of the US myth of 'progress' was
swiftly followed by the collapse of the Soviet Union, which dragged down with
it an entire master narrative of communist 'progress'. The zigzag of Hegelian–
Marxist 'progress', managed by a bureaucratic, command economy, had been
destined to arrive inevitably at its own utopian destination. The toppling of
the Soviet Empire has meant, for many, the loss of a certain privileged
relation to history as the epic unfolding of linear, if spasmodic progress, and
with it the promise that the bureaucratic, communist economy could one
day outstrip the USA in providing consumer abundance for all. As a result,
there has also been some loss of political certitude in the inevitable role of the
male (and, as it turns out, white) industrial working class as the privileged
agent of history. If the bureaucracy of the Soviet Union fell, it was not under
the weight of popular, industrial mobilisation, but rather under the double
weight of its economic corruption and manic military spending. The irony is
not lost that the ascendant economies of Japan and Germany were historically
denied the unsupportable burden of the arms race. Thus, despite the fact that
men are slaughtering each other around the globe with increased dedication,
there has been a certain loss of faith in masculined militarism as the inevitable
guarantee of historical 'progress'. For the first time in history, moreover, the
idea of industrial 'progress' impelled by technocratic 'development' is meeting
the limits of the world's natural resources.

Ironically, the last zone on earth to embrace the Enlightenment ideology of capitalist 'development' may be the one now controlled by Mr. Yeltsin and his allies. The world has watched awestruck as Yeltsin and his fellow travellers swerved dizzyingly off the iron road of the centralised, communist, command economy and lurched bumpily on to the capitalist road of decentralisation, powered no longer by the dialectic as the motor and guarantee of 'progress' but by tearaway competition and mad marketeering. Never mind that this swerve is likely to unleash a disaster on a scale comparable to the famines that followed the original Bolshevik revolution, nor that the rough beast that slouches out of the chaos may, indeed, not be western capitalism at all but a particularly grisly form of fascism.

For both communism and capitalism, 'progress' was both a journey forward and the beginning of a return; for, as in all narratives of 'progress', to travel the 'road of progress' was to cover, once again, a road already travelled. The metaphor of the 'road' or 'railway' guaranteed that 'progress' was a *fait accompli*. The journey was possible because the road had already been made (by God, the Dialectic, the *Weltgeist*, the Cunning of History, the Law of the Market, Scientific Materialism). As Hegel decreed, 'progress' in the realm of history was possible because it has already been accomplished in the realm of 'truth'. But now, if the owl of Minerva has taken flight, there is widespread uncertainty whether it will return.

The collapse of both capitalist and communist teleologies of 'progress' has resulted in a doubled and overdetermined crisis in images of future time.[4] The uncertain global situation has spawned a widespread sense of historic abandonment, of which the apocalytic, time-stopped prevalence of 'post-' words is only one symptom. The storm of 'progress' had blown for both communism and capitalism alike. Now the wind is stilled, and the angel with hunched wings broods over the wreckage at its feet. In this calm at 'the end of history', the millenium has come too soon, and the air seems thick with omen.

Francis Fukuyama has declared history dead. Capitalism, he claims, has won the grand Hegelian agon with communism, and is now 'post-historic'. Third World countries lag behind in the zone of the 'historic', where matters are decided by force (Fukuyama 1990, p. 3). Far from the 'end of history' and the triumph of US consumer capitalism, however, the new order of the day is most likely to be multi-polar competition between the four currently decisive regions of the world: Japan, the United States, Fortress Europe and the Middle East, with new power centres emerging in India, Brazil, Nigeria and the Pacific rim. The arms trade will continue, as the military industrial wizards of Armageddon turn their attention from Cold War scenarios to multiple, dispersed wars of attrition, fought by the US mercenary army and other proxies, and paid for by Japan and Germany. Within the USA, with the vanishing of international communism as a rationale for militarism, new enemies will be found: the drug war, international 'terrorism', lesbians and gays, feminists, the PC hordes and 'tenured radicals', and any number of international 'ethnic' targets.

For this reason, there is some urgency in the need for innovative theories of history and popular memory. Asking what single term might adequately replace 'post-colonialism', for example, begs the question of rethinking the global situation as a multiplicity of powers and histories, which cannot be marshalled obediently under the flag of a single theoretical term, be that feminism, Marxism or post-colonialism. Nor does intervening in history mean lifting, again, the mantle of 'progress' or the quill-pen of empiricism. 'For the native,' as Fanon said, 'objectivity is always directed against him'. Rather, a *proliferation* of historically nuanced theories and strategies is called for, which may enable us to engage more effectively in the politics of affiliation, and the currently catastrophic dispensations of power. Without a renewed will to intervene in the unacceptable, we face being becalmed in an historically empty space in which our sole direction is found by gazing back, spellbound, at the epoch behind us, in a perpetual present marked only as 'post'.

Notes

This article expands on comments I made during the Symposium at Essex in 1991. The article first appeared in *Social text*, 31/32 (1992), pp. 84–98.

1 During the Algerian war of resistance, over a million Algerians died out of about nine million.
2 The international monetary system set up at the Bretton Woods Conference in 1944 excluded Africa (still colonised) and most of what is now called the Third World, and was designed to achieve two explicit objectives: the reconstruction of Europe after the Second World War and the expansion and maintenance (especially after decolonisation) of international trade in the interests of the colonial powers and America. The President of the World Bank and the deputy managing director are always American, while by tradition the managing director is European.
3 A few African socialist states, like Angola and Mozambique, tried to dodge the IMF and World Bank's blandishments, until national economic mismanagement and South Africa's regional maulings forced them to bend the knee.
4 Ironically, following the swift jettisoning of the doctrine of 'progress' by the captains of capital in the 1980s, the 'hybridity' and 'syncreticism' celebrated by much postcolonial theory has become increasingly celebrated by the mass-consumption media-market.

References

Abdel-Malek, Anouar (1981) *Nation and revolution*, trans. Mike Gonzalez, Albany.

Abrams, M. H. (1971) *The mirror and the lamp: Romantic theory and the critical tradition*, New York.

Adam, Ian and Helen Tiffin, eds (1991) *Past the last post: theorizing post-colonialism and post-modernism*, London.

Adas, Michael (1989) *Machines as the measure of men: science, technology, and the ideologies of western dominance*, Ithaca.

Adorno, Rolena (1986) *Guaman Poma de Ayala: writing and resistance in colonial Peru*, Austin.

—— ed. (1982) *From oral to written expression: native Andean chronicles of the early colonial period*, Syracuse.

Adorno, Theodor (1985) *Minima moralia: reflections from damaged life*, trans. E. F. N. Jephcott, London.

Ahmad, Aijaz (1989) 'Jameson's rhetoric of otherness and the "national allegory"', *Social text*, 17, pp. 3–25.

—— (1992) *In theory: classes, nations, literatures*, London.

Alarcón, Norma (forthcoming) *T(r)opics of hunger: subjectivity in Chicano literature*.

Allen, Sheila and Carol Wolkowitz (1987) *Homeworking: myths and realities*, London.

Althusser, Louis (1971) *Lenin and philosophy and other essays*, trans. Ben Brewster, New York.

Anderson, Benedict (1983) *Imagined communities: reflections on the origin and spread of nationalism*, London.

Angier, Carole (1990) *Jean Rhys*, London.

Appiah, K. A. (1988) 'Out of Africa: topologies of nativism', *Yale journal of criticism*, 1, 2, pp. 153–78.

—— (1990) 'Is the post- in postmodernism the post- in postcolonial?', *Critical inquiry*, 17, 2, pp. 336–57.

—— (1991) 'Tolerable falsehoods: agency and the interests of theory', in Jonathan Arac and Barbara Johnson, eds *Some consequences of theory*, Baltimore, pp. 63–90.

Apte, Hari Narayan, ed. (1897) *Sangītaratnākara*, Gwalior.

Aravamudam, Srinivas (1989) 'Being God's postman is no fun, yaar: Salman Rushdie's *The satanic verses*', *Diacritics*, 9, 2 (summer), pp. 3–20.

Armah, Ayi Kwei (1967) 'African socialism: utopian or scientific?' *Presence Africaine*, 64 (4th quarterly), pp. 6–30.

Arnold, A. James (1981) *Modernism and negritude: the poetry and poetics of Aimé Césaire*, Cambridge, Mass.

Arnold, Matthew (1984) *Culture and anarchy*, ed. J. Dover Wilson, Cambridge.

Aronowitz, Stanley (1981) *The crisis in historical materialism*, New York.

—— (1989) 'Postmodernism and politics', in Ross, ed. (1989), pp. 46–62.

Arrighi, Giovanni (1991) 'World income inequalities and the future of socialism', *New left review*, 189, pp. 39–65.

Ashcroft Bill, Gareth Griffiths and Helen Tiffin (1989) *The empire writes back: theory and practice in post-colonial literatures*, London.

Attwell, David (1990) 'The problem of history in the fiction of J. M. Coetzee', in Trump, ed. (1990), pp. 94–133.

Atwood, Roger (1988) 'Brazil marks 100 years of abolition but blacks are still bitter', *Reuters*, 11 May.

Auchterlonie, T. B. (1898) 'The city of Benin', *Transactions of the Liverpool Geographical Society*, 6, pp. 5–11.

Bacon, Commander R. H. (1897) *Benin, the city of blood*, London.

Bakhtin, Mikhail (1968) *Rabelais and his world*, trans. Helen Iswolsky, Cambridge, Mass.

—— (1987) *Speech genres and other late essays*, trans. Vern W. McGee, Austin.

Baldwin, James (1961) 'Princes and powers', in his *Nobody knows my name*, New York, pp. 24–54.

Balfour, H. (1893) *The evolution of decorative art*, London.

Bandyopadhyay, P. (1971) 'One sociology or many – some issues in radical sociology', *Sociological review*, 19, pp. 5–29.

Barker, F. *et al.*, eds (1983) *The politics of theory*, Colchester.

—— (1985) *Europe and its others*, 2 vols, Colchester.

—— (1992) *Postmodernism and the re-reading of modernity*, Manchester.

Barman, Roderick J. (1988) *Brazil: the forging of a nation*, Stanford.

Barthes, Roland (1972) *Mythologies*, trans. Annette Lavers, London.

Baudrillard, Jean (1983a) *In the shadow of the silent majorities*, trans. Paul Foss, Paul Patton and John Johnston, New York.

Baudrillard, Jean (1983b) *Simulations*, trans. Paul Foss *et al.*, New York.

Bayliss-Smith, T. P. *et al.* (1989) *Islands, islanders and the world: colonial and post-colonial experience of Eastern Fiji*, Cambridge.

Benjamin, Walter (1970) *Illuminations*, trans. Harry Zohn, London.

—— (1978) *Reflections: essays, aphorisms and autobiographical writings*, ed. Peter Demetz, New York.

Berman, Marshall (1982) *All that is solid melts into air: the experience of modernity*, London.

Berman, Russell (1988) 'Rights and writing in South Africa', *Telos*, 75, pp. 161–72.

Bernal, Martin (1987) *Black Athena: the Afroasiatic roots of classical civilization*, London.

Besant, Annie (1913) *Wake up, India*, Adyar.

Bhabha, Homi K. (1984) 'Of mimicry and men: the ambivalence of colonial discourse', *October*, 28, pp. 125–33.

—— (1985) 'Signs taken for wonders: questions of ambivalence and authority under a tree outside Delhi, May 1817', in Barker *et al.*, eds (1985), I, pp. 80–106.

—— (1988) 'The commitment to theory', *New formations*, 5, pp. 5–23.

—— (1990) 'DissemiNation: time, narrative, and the margins of the modern nation', in Bhabha, ed. (1990), pp. 291–322.

—— (1993) *The location of culture*, London.

—— ed. (1990) *Nation and narration*, New York.

Bhatnagar, Rashmi (1986) 'Uses and limits of Foucault: a study of the theme of origins in Edward Said's *Orientalism*', *Social scientist* (Trivandrum), 158, pp. 3–22.

Bideau, Alain and Jean-Pierre Bardet (1988) *De la Renaissance à 1789: histoire de la population française*, vol. 2, Paris.

Biko, Steve (1988) *I write what I like*, Harmondsworth.

Birdwood, G. (1903) 'Conventionalism in primitive art', *Journal of the Society of Arts*, 51, pp. 881–9.

Birkett, Dea (1992) *Mary Kingsley: imperial adventuress*, London.

Bjornson, Richard (1991) *The African quest for freedom and identify: Cameroonian writing and the national experience*, Indiana.

Bloch, Ernst (1970) *Philosophy of the future*, trans. John Cumming, New York.

—— (1977) 'Non-synchronism and the obligation to its dialectics', *New German critique*, 11, pp. 22–38.

—— (1988) 'Something's missing: a discussion between Ernst Bloch and Theodor W. Adorno on the contradictions of Utopian longing', *The utopian function of art and literature: selected essays*, trans. Jack Zipes and Frank Mecklenburg, Boston, pp. 1–17.

—— (1991) *Heritage of our times*, trans. Neville and Stephen Plaice, Cambridge.

Boddam-Whetham, J. W. (1879) *Roraima and British Guiana*, London.

Boehmer, Elleke (1991) 'Transfiguring body into narrative in post-colonial writing', unpublished paper.

Bolt, Christine (1971) *Victorian attitudes to race*, London.

Bongie, Chris (1991) *Exotic memories: literature, colonialism and the fin de siècle*, Stanford.

Booth, C. (1892–1903) *Life and labour of the people of London*, London.

Bose, Mandakranta (1990) '*Lāsya*: dance or drama?', in Bimal Krishna Matilal and Purushottam Bilimoria, eds *Sanskrit and related studies*, Delhi.

Boswell, James (1953) *Boswell on the grand tour: Germany and Switzerland 1764*, ed. Frederick A. Pottle, London.

Boswell, John (1988) *The kindness of strangers: the abandonment of children in western Europe from late antiquity to the Renaissance*, New York.

Boumelha, Penny (1988) ' "And what do the women do?" *Jane Eyre*, Jamaica and the gentleman's house', *Southern review*, 21, pp. 111–22.

Brah, Avtar (1992) 'Difference, diversity, differentiation', in Donald and Rattansi, eds (1992), pp. 126–45.

Brathwaite, Edward (1971) *The development of creole society in Jamaica, 1770–1820*, Oxford.

—— (1974) *Contradictory omens: cultural diversity and integration in the Caribbean*, Mona.

Brett, Guy (1987) *Through our own eyes: popular art and modern history*, Philadelphia.

Brewer, John (1990) *The sinews of power: war, money and the English state 1688–1783*, Cambridge, Mass.

Brink, Andre (1983) *Mapmakers: writing in a state of siege*, London.

Broad, Robin, John Cavanagh and Walden Bello (1992) 'Sustainable development in the 1990's', in C. Hartman *et al.*, eds *Paradigms lost: the post cold war era*, London, pp. 89–111.

Brontë, Charlotte (1934) *Jane Eyre* [1847], London.

—— (1969) *Jane Eyre, an autobiography* [1847], ed. Jane, Jack and Margaret Smith, Oxford.

—— (1987) *An edition of the early writings of Charlotte Brontë*: volume I, *The Glass Town saga, 1826–1832*, ed. Christine Alexander, Oxford.

Brown, R. and A. Gilman (1972) 'Pronouns of power and solidarity' [1958], in Pier Paolo Giglioli, ed. *Language and social context*, Harmondsworth, pp. 252–82.

Buchloch, B. (1989) 'The whole earth show', *Art in America*, May, pp. 150–8, 211–13.

Bunn, David and Jane Taylor, eds (1987) *From South Africa: new writing, photographs, and art*, Chicago.

Burrow, J. W. (1966) *Evolution and society: a study in Victorian social theory*, Cambridge.

Burton, Antoinette M. (1990) 'The white woman's burden: British feminists and the Indian woman, 1865–1915', *Women's studies international forum*, 13, 4.

Butler, Guy (1986) 'English in the new South Africa', *English academy review*, 3, pp. 163–76.

Cabral, Amilcar (1973) *Return to the source: selected speeches by Amilcar Cabral*, ed. Africa Information Service, New York.

—— (1974) 'National liberation and culture', *Transition*, 45, pp. 12–17.

—— (1980) *Unity and struggle: speeches and writings*, trans. Michael Wolfers, London.

Callinicos, Alex (1989) *Against postmodernism: a marxist critique*, Oxford.

Camargo, Suzana (1977) *Macunaíma: ruptura e tradiçao*, São Paolo.

Carnoy, Martin (1989) 'Education, state and culture in American society', in Henry A. Giroux and Peter McLaren, eds *Critical pedagogy, the state and cultural struggle*, Albany, New York, pp. 3–23.

Carter, Hannah (1968) 'Fated to be sad' [interview with Jean Rhys], *The guardian*, 8 August.

Carusi, Annamaria (1989) 'Post, post and post; or, where is South African literature in all this?', *Ariel*, 20, 4, pp. 79–95.

Centre for Cultural Studies, eds (1982) *The empire strikes back: race and racism in seventies Britain*, London.

Césaire, Aimé (1972) *Discourse on colonialism*, trans. Joan Pinkham, New York.

—— (1983) *Collected poetry*, trans. with an introduction by Clayton Eshleman and Annette Smith, Berkeley.

Chabram, Angie (1990) 'Chicana/o studies as oppositional ethnography', *Cultural studies*, 4, 3, pp. 228–47.

Chace, Russell E. (1989) 'Protest in post-emancipation Dominica: the "guerre nègre" of 1844', *The journal of Caribbean history*, 23, 2, pp. 118–41.

Chakrabarty, Dipesh (1992) 'Open space / public place: garbage, modernity and India', *Economic and political weekly*, 27, 10–11 (7–14 March), pp. 541–7.

Chartier, Roger (1991) *The cultural origins of the French revolution*, trans. Lydia G. Cochrane, Durham, NC.

Chatterjee, Partha (1986) *Nationalist thought and the colonial world: a derivative discourse?* Delhi.

Chattopadhyay, Aparna (1967) 'The institution of the "devadāsis" according to the Kathāsarit-sāgara', *Journal of the Oriental Institute*, 16, 3 (March), pp. 216–22.

Chrisman, Laura (1990) 'The imperial unconscious? representations of imperial discourse', *Critical quarterly*, 32, 3, pp. 38–58.

Cisneros, Sandra (1989) *The house on Mango Street*, New York.

Clastres, Pierre (1987) *Society against the state: essays in political anthropology*, trans. Robert Hurley with Abe Stein, New York.

Clegg, Ian (1979) 'Workers and managers in Algeria', in Robin Cohen, Peter C. W. Gutkind and Phyllis Brazier, eds *Peasants and proletarians: the struggles of third world workers*, New York.

Clifford, James (1988) *The predicament of culture: twentieth-century ethnography, literature, and art*, Cambridge, Mass. and London.

—— (1991) 'Four Northwest Coast museums: travel reflections', in Karp and Levine, eds (1991), pp. 212–54.

—— and George E. Marcus, eds (1986) *Writing culture: the poetics and politics of ethnography*, Berkeley.

Clingman, Stephen (1986) *The novels of Nadine Gordimer: history from the inside*, London.

CO = Colonial Office Papers, Public Record Office, Kew, London.

Coetzee, J. M. (1977) *In the heart of the country*, Johannesburg.

—— (1988) *White writing*, New Haven and London.

Collier, George, Renato Rosaldo and John D. Wirth, eds (1982) *Inca and Aztec states*, New York.

Coombes, Annie E. (1985) '"For God and for England", contributions to an image of Africa in the first decade of the twentieth century', *Art history*, 8, 4 (December), pp. 453–66.

—— (1988) 'Museums and the formation of national and cultural identities', *Oxford art journal*, 11, 2, pp. 57–68.

—— (forthcoming) *Anthropology and popular imagination in the invention of Africa*, New Haven.

—— and Jill Lloyd (1986) '"Lost and found" at the Museum of Mankind', *Art history*, 9, 4 (December), pp. 540–5.

Cornejo Polar, Antonio (n.d.) *La novela indigenista*, Lima.

Cornell, Margaret (1981) ed. *Europe and Africa: issues in post-colonial relations*, London.

Corner, John and Sylvia Harvey, eds (1991) *Enterprise and heritage: crosscurrents of national culture*, London.

Coutts-Smith, Kenneth (1991) 'Some general observation on the problem of a cultural colonialism', in Susan Hiller, ed., *The myth of primitivism: perspectives on art*, London, pp. 14–31.

Crapanzano, Vincent (1986) *Waiting: the whites of South Africa*, London.

Cronin, Jeremy and Raymond Suttner, eds (1986) *Thirty years of the freedom charter*, Johannesburg.

Crow, Thomas E. (1985) *Painters and public life in eighteenth-century Paris*, New Haven.

Cultural Affairs Committee of the Parti Socialist Unifié (1978) 'Beaubourg: the containing of culture in France', *Studio international*, 1, pp. 27–36.

Curtin, Philip (1969) *The Atlantic slave trade: a census*, Madison.

da Costa, Emilia Viotti (1989) *Da senzala a colónia*, São Paulo.

da Cunha, Euclides (1966) *Os sertões*, in his *Obra completa*, vol. II, Rio de Janeiro.

da Silva Brito, Mário (1970) 'A revoluçao modernista', *A literatura no Brasil*, vol. III, ed. Afrânio Coutinho, Rio de Janeiro.

Dalton, O. M. (1898a) 'Booty from Benin', *English illustrated magazine*, 18, pp. 419–29.

Dalton, O. M. (1898b) *Report on ethnographic museums in Germany*, London.

Dash, Michael (1973) 'Marvellous realism: the way out of negritude', *Caribbean studies*, 13, 4, pp. 57–70.

——, Joe Slovo and Anthony Wilkinson (1976) *Southern Africa: the new politics of revolution*, Harmondsworth.

Davin, Anna (1978) 'Imperialism and motherhood', *History Workshop Journal*, 5, pp. 9–63.

de Andrade, Mario (1984) *Macunaíma*, trans. E. A. Goodland, New York.

—— (1986) *Macunaíma: o herói sem nenhum caráter*, Belo Horizonte.

—— (1988) *Macunaíma: o herói sem nenhum caráter*. Coleçao arquivos, ed. Telê Porto Ancona Lopez, Brasilia.

de Certeau, Michel (1988) *The writing of history*, trans. Tom Conley, New York.

de Hollanda, Heloisa Buarque (1978) *Macunaíma: da literatura ao cinema*, Rio de Janeiro.

de Kok, Ingrid and Karen Press, eds (1991) *Spring is rebellious*, Cape Town.

de Sade, Marquis (1966) *Philosophy in the bedroom in three complete novels: Justine, Philosophy in the bedroom, Eugenie de Franvel and other writings*, trans. Richard Seaver and Austryn Wainhouse, intro. Jean Poulhan and Maurice Blanchot, New York.

Dean, Seamus (1988) *Celtic revivals: essays in modern Irish literature: 1880–1980*, London.

Degler, Carl (1971) *Neither black nor white: slavery and race relations in Brazil and the United States*, New York.

Deleuze, Gilles and Félix Guattari (1977) *Anti-Oedipus: capitalism and schizophrenia*, trans. Robert Hurley, Mark Seem and Helen R. Lane, New York.

Dening, Greg (1980) *Islands and beaches. Discourse on a silent land: Marquesas 1774–1880*, Honolulu.

Depestre, René (1976) 'Problems of identity for the black man in the Caribbean', in John Hearne, ed. *Carifesta Forum*, Jamaica, pp. 61–7.

Derrida, Jacques (1984) 'My chances / *mes chances*: a rendezvous with some Epicurean stereophonies', in Joseph Smith and William Kerrigan, eds *Taking chances: Derrida, psychoanalysis and literature*, Baltimore, pp. 1–32.

—— (1985) 'Racism's last word', *Critical inquiry*, 12, 1, pp. 290–9.

—— (1986) *Glas*, trans. John P. Leavey, Jr, and Richard Rand, Lincoln.

—— (1989) *Of spirit: Heidegger and the question*, trans. Geoffrey Bennington and Rachel Bowlby, Chicago.

Desani, G. V. (1986) *All about H. Hatterr*, New Paltz.

Diawara, Manthia (1990–91) 'The nature of mother in *Dreaming rivers*', *Third text*, 13, pp. 73–84.

—— (1991) 'Englishness and blackness: cricket as discourse on colonialism', *Callaloo*, 13, 4, pp. 830–44.

Diderot, Denis (1875) *Oeuvres complètes*, 20 vols, ed. J. Assézat et M. Tourneaux, Paris.

—— (1955) *Essais sur la peinture*, textes établis et commentés par Robert Desné, vol. 5 of *Les Classiques du peuple*, Paris.

—— (1964) 'The encyclopedia', in *Rameau's nephew and other works*, trans. Jacques Barzun and Ralph H. Bowen, Indianapolis.

—— (1971) 'Apologie pour Raynal', in *Textes politiques*, preface et notes par Yves Benot, Paris.

—— (1990) *Oeuvres complètes de Diderot*, ed. Jacques Chouillet and Anne-Marie Chouillet, 26 vols to date, Paris.

Dollimore, Jonathan (1991) *Sexual dissidence: literatures, histories, theories*, Oxford.

—— and Alan Sinfield (1990) 'Culture and textuality: debating cultural materialism', *Textual practice*, 4, 1, pp. 91–100.

Dominica (1844) *Minutes of the House of Assembly*, Roseau.

—— (1883–1952) *Register of Baptisms*, St George's Parish, Morne Rouge.

Donald, James and Ali Rattansi, eds (1992) *Race, culture and identity*, London.

Duchet, Michèle (1971) *Anthropologie et histoire au siècle des lumières*, Paris.

Duncan, C. and A. Wallach (1980) 'The universal survey museum', *Art history*, 3, 4 (December), pp. 448–69.

During, Simon (1989) 'Waiting for the post: some relations between modernity, colonization, and writing', *Ariel*, 20, 4, pp. 31–61.

Eagleton, Terry (1990a) *The ideology of the aesthetic*, Oxford.

—— (1990b) 'Nationalism: irony and commitment', in Terry Eagleton, Fredric Jameson, and Edward Said, *Nationalism, colonialism, and literature*, Minneapolis, pp. 23–39.

Ellison, Ralph (1967) 'Some questions and some answers' [1958], in his *Shadow and act*, London, pp. 261–72.

Emery, Mary Lou (1990) *Jean Rhys at 'World's End': novels of colonial and sexual exile*, Austin.

Enloe, Cynthia (1989) *Bananas, beaches and bases: making feminist sense of international politics*, Berkeley.

Errol, Lawrence (1982) 'Just plain common sense: the roots of racism', in Centre for Contemporary Cultural Studies, eds (1982), pp. 87–94.

Ethnic Minority Rights Group (1985) *Education for all: the report of the committee of inquiry into the education of children from ethnic minority groups*, London.

Fanon, Frantz (1967) *Toward the African revolution*, trans. Haakon Chevalier, New York.

—— (1968) *The wretched of the earth*, trans. Constance Farrington, New York.

—— (1986) *Black skin, white masks*, trans. Charles Lam Markman, intro. Homi Bhabha, London.

Ferguson, R. Brian and Neil L. Whitehead, eds (1992) *War in the tribal zone: expanding states and indigenous warfare*, Santa Fe.

Ferguson, Russell et al., eds (1991) *Out there: marginalization and contemporary cultures*, New York.

Filho, Joao Etienne (1986) Introduction to de Andrade (1986).

Fisher, J. (1987) 'The health of the people is the highest law', *Third text*, * (winter), pp. 63–75.

Forster, E. M. (1952) *A passage to India*, New York.

Foster, Hal (1985) 'The "primitive" unconscious of modern art, or white skin black masks', in his *Recodings: art, spectacle, cultural politics*, Washington, pp. 181–208.

Foucault, Michel (1980) *Language, counter-memory, practice: selected essays and interviews*, ed. Donald F. Bouchard, Ithaca.

—— and Arlette Farge, eds (1982) *Le Desordre des familles: lettres de cachet des Archives de la Bastille*, Paris.

Fox, Richard G., ed. (1990) *National ideologies and the production of national cultures*, American Ethnological Society Monograph Series, no. 2, Washington.

Francis, Paulo (1990) 'Lamurias da galeria e glasnost', *Folha de São Paulo*, 3 Feb., p. E-10.

Franco, Jean (forthcoming) *Border patrol*, Cambridge.

Freud, Sigmund (1961), 'The uncanny', in *The standard edition of the complete psychological works*, trans. James Strachey *et al.*, New York, vol. 17, pp. 218–56.

—— (1977) *Case Histories I: 'Dora' and Little Hans*, ed. Angela Richards [Penguin Freud Library, vol. 8], Harmondsworth.

—— (1985) 'Group psychology and the analysis of the ego' in *Civilization, society and religion*, trans. James Strachey, ed. Albert Dickson, Harmondsworth, pp. 91–178.

Freyre, Gilberto (1946) *The masters and the slaves*, trans. Samuel Putnam, New York.

—— (1987) 'A estetica da miscigenaçao', in his *Vida, forma e cor*, Rio de Janeiro.

Friel, Brian (1981) *Translations*, London.

Fukuyama, Francis (1990) 'Forget Iraq – history is dead', *The guardian*, 12 August, p. 3.

Fuss, Diana (1989) *Essentially speaking: feminism, nature and difference*, London.

García Canclini, Néstor (1982) *Las culturas populares en el capitalismo*, Mexico City.

—— (1988) 'Culture and power: the state of research', *Media, culture and society*, 10, pp. 467–97.

—— (1989) *Culturas híbridas: estrategias para entrar y salir de la modernidad*, Mexico City.

Gates, Jr, Henry Louis (1990) 'Afterword: critical remarks', in Goldberg, ed. (1990), pp. 319–32.

—— (1991) 'Critical Fanonism', *Critical inquiry*, 17, 3, pp. 457–70.

George, Susan (1988) *A fate worse than debt*, London.

—— (1990) 'Managing the global house: redefining economics', in J. Legget, ed. *Global warming: the Greenpeace report*, Oxford.

Gilroy, Paul (1987) *There ain't no black in the union jack: the cultural politics of race and nation*, London.

—— (1990) 'One nation under a groove: the cultural politics of "race" and racism in Britain', in Goldberg, ed. (1990), pp. 263–82.

—— (1993) ' "Cheer the weary traveller": W. E. Dubois and the politics of displacement', in his *The Black Atlantic: modernity and double consciousness*, Cambridge, Mass.

Glissant, Edouard (1981) *Le Discours antillais*, Paris.

—— (1989) *Caribbean discourse: selected essays*, trans. Michael Dash, Virginia.

Goldberg, David Theo (1990) 'The social formation of racist discourse', in Goldberg, ed. (1990), pp. 295–318.

——, ed. (1990) *Anatomy of racism*, Minneapolis.

Gordimer, Nadine (1989) *The essential gesture*, Harmondsworth.

Goubert, Pierre and Michel Denis (1964) *1789: les français ont la parole: Cahiers de doleances des Etats généraux*, Paris.

'Gough, Kathleen (1968) 'New proposals for anthropologists', *Current anthropology*, 9, pp. 403–7.

Graham-Brown, Sarah (1988) *Images of women: the portrayal of women in photography of the Middle East, 1860–1950*, London.

Gramsci, Antonio (1971) *Selections from the prison notebooks*, ed. Quintin Hoare and Geoffrey Nowell Smith, New York.

Green, David (1982) 'Veins of resemblance: Francis Galton, photography and eugenics', *Oxford art journal*, 2, pp. 3–16.

Greenfield, Jeanette (1989) *The return of cultural treasures*, Cambridge.

Grosz, Elizabeth (1990) 'Judaism and exile: the ethics of otherness', *New formations*, 12, pp. 77–88.

Guéhenno, Jean (1966) *Jean-Jacques Rousseau*, trans. John and Doreen Weightman, 2 vols, New York.

Guaman Poma de Ayala, Felipe (1980) *Nueva coronica y buen gobierno y justicia* [1613], ed. Franklin Pease, Caracas.

Guha, Ranajit (1983) *Elementary aspects of peasant insurgency in colonial India*, Delhi.

—— (1986a) 'On some aspects of the historiography of colonial India', in Ranajit Guha, ed. *Subaltern studies I: Writings on South Asian history and society*, Delhi, pp. 1–8.

—— (1986b) 'The prose of counter-insurgency', in Ranajit Guha, ed. *Subaltern studies II: Writings on South Asian history and society*, Delhi, pp. 1–42.

—— (1988) 'The prose of counter-insurgency', in Ranajit Guha and Gayatri Chakravorty Spivak, eds *Selected subaltern studies*, foreword by Edward Said, Oxford, pp. 45–86.

—— (1989) 'Dominance without hegemony and its historiography', in Ranajit Guha, ed. *Subaltern studies VI: Writings on South Asian history and society*, Delhi, pp. 210–309.

Guidieri, Remo, Francesco Pellizzi and Stanley J. Tambiah, eds (1988) *Ethnicities and nations: processes of interethnic relations in Latin America, Southeast Asia, and the Pacific*, Austin.

Gunew, Sneja (1985) 'Australia 1984: a moment in the archaeology of multiculturalism', in Barker *et al.*, eds (1985), I, pp. 178–93.

Habermas, Jürgen (1979) 'Consciousness-raising or redemptive criticism: the contemporaneity of Walter Benjamin', *New German critique*, 17, pp. 30–59.

—— (1987) *The philosophical discourse of modernity: twelve lectures*, trans. Frederick Lawrence, Cambridge, Mass.

Haddon, A. C. (1894) *The decorative art of Papua New Guinea: a study in Papuan Ethnography*, Dublin.

—— (1895) *Evolution in art*, London.

Hainard, Jacques and Roland Kaehr, eds (1985) *Temps perdu, temps retrouvé: voir des choses du passé au present*, Neuchâtel.

Hall, Stuart (1980a) 'Cultural studies: two paradigms', in *Media, culture and society*, 2, pp. 57–72.

—— (1980b) *Culture, media, language: working papers in cultural studies*, London.

—— (1987) 'Minimal selves', in *The real me: postmodernism and the question of identity*, ICA documents, 6, London, pp. 44–6.

—— (1988a) 'The toad in the garden: Thatcher amongst the theorists', in Nelson and Grossberg, eds (1988), pp. 35–73.

—— (1988b) *The hard road to renewal: Thatcherism and the crisis of the left*, London.

—— (1988c) 'New ethnicities', in *Black film British cinema*, ICA documents, 7, London, pp. 27–31.

—— (1990) 'Cultural identity and diaspora', in J. Rutherford, ed. *Identity, community, culture, difference*, London, pp. 222–37.

Hancock, Graham (1989) *The lords of poverty*, London.

Handler, Richard (1985) 'On having a culture: nationalism and the preservation of Quebec's *patrimoine*', in George W. Stocking, Jr, *Objects and others: essays on museums and material culture*, Madison, pp. 191–217.

Haraway, Donna (1991) *Simians, cyborgs and women: the reinvention of nature*, New York.

Harris, Wilson (1970) 'History, fable and myth in the Caribbean and Guianas', *Caribbean quarterly*, 16, pp. 1–32.

—— (1974) *History, fable and myth in the Caribbean and Guianas*, Georgetown, Guyana.

—— (1980) 'Carnival of psyche: Jean Rhys's *Wide sargasso sea*', *Kunapipi*, 2, 2, pp. 142–50.

—— (1985) 'Jean Rhys's "tree of life"', *Review of contemporary fiction*, 5, 2, pp. 114–17.

Harrison, J. D. (1988) '"The Spirit Sings" and the future of anthropology', *Anthropology today*, 4, 6 (December), pp. 6–9.

Harth, Erica (1988) 'The virtue of love: Lord Hardwicke's marriage act', *Cultural critique*, 9, pp. 123–54.

Hartman, Chester and Pedro Vilanova (1992) *Paradigms lost: the post cold war era*, London.

Hearne, John (1974) 'The *Wide sargasso sea*: a West Indian reflection', *The Cornhill magazine*, 1080, pp. 323–33.

Hebdige, Dick (1979) *Subculture: the meaning of style*, London.

Hewison, Robert (1987) *The heritage industry: Britain in a climate of decline*, London.

Heywood, Christopher (1987) 'Yorkshire slavery in *Wuthering Heights*', *Review of English studies*, n.s. 38, 150, pp. 184–98.

Hiller, Susan, ed. (1991) *The myth of primitivism: perspectives on art*, London.

Hodgkin, Thomas (1956) *Nationalism in colonial Africa*, London.

Hofmeyr, Isabel (1987) 'Building a nation from words: Afrikaans language, literature and ethnic identity, 1902–1914', in Marks and Trapido, eds (1987), pp. 95–123.

Hoggart, Richard (1970) *The uses of literacy: aspects of working-class life* [1959], New York.

Holston, James (1989) *The modernist city: an anthropological critique of Brasilia*, Chicago.

Honychurch, Lennox (1984) *The Dominica story*, Roseau.

hooks, bell (1990) 'Representations: feminism and black masculinity', in her *Yearning: race, gender and cultural politics*, Boston, pp. 65–78.

Horkheimer, Max (1978) 'The end of reason,' in Andrew Arato and Eike Gebhardt, eds *The Frankfurt school reader*, New York, pp. 26–48.

—— and Theodor W. Adorno (1987) *Dialectic of Enlightenment*, trans. John Cumming, New York.

House of Commons (1844) 'Copies or extracts of correspondence relative to the late disturbances among the negroes in the island of Dominica', in *Accounts and paper* (3), 34, pp. 235–49.

—— (1845) 'Copies or extracts of correspondence relative to the late disturbances among the negroes in the island of Dominica', in *Accounts and papers* (4), 31, pp. 81–187.

Howells, Coral Ann (1991) *Jean Rhys*, London.

Hulme, Peter (1986) *Colonial encounters: Europe and the native Caribbean, 1492–1797*, London.

—— (1990) 'Dancing with Mr. Hesketh: Jean Rhys, Dominica, and the last of Caribs', *Sargasso*, 7, pp. 18–26.

—— and Ludmilla Jordanova, eds (1990) *The Enlightenment and its shadows*, London.

—— and Neil L. Whitehead, eds (1992) *Wild majesty: encounters with Caribs from Columbus to the present day*, Oxford.

Hurston, Zora Neale (1979) 'What it feels like to be colored me', in her *I love myself when I'm laughing*, ed. Alice Walker New York.

Husband, Charles, ed. (1982) *'Race' in Britain: continuity and change*, London.

Hyams, Jacques Louis (1971) *Leopold Sedar Senghor: an intellectual biography*, Edinburgh.

'Hybrid state exhibit brochure' (1991) Exit Art, New York.

Igbafe, P. A. (1979) *Benin under British administration: the impact of colonial rule on an African kingdom 1897–1938*, London.

Irele, Abiola (1970) 'The theory of negritude', in *Proceedings of the seminar on political theory and ideology in African society*, Edinburgh, pp. 162–90.

—— (1986) 'Contemporary thought in French speaking Africa', in Isaac James Mowoe and Richard Bjornson, eds *The legacies of empire*, New York, pp. 121–58.

Isbell, Billie Jean (1976) 'La otra mitad esencial: un estudio de complementaridad sexual en los Andes', *Estudios andinos*, 5, 1, pp. 37–56.

—— (1978) *To defend ourselves: ecology and ritual in an Andean village*, Austin.

James, Louis (1978) *Jean Rhys*, London.

Jameson, Fredric (1984) 'Postmodernism, or the cultural logic of late capitalism', *New left review*, 146, pp. 53–92.

—— (1986) 'Third-world literature in the era of multinational capital', *Social text*, 15, pp. 65–88.

JanMohamed, Abdul (1983) *Manichean aesthetics: the politics of literature in colonial Africa*, Amherst.

—— (1986) 'The economy of Manichean allegory', in Henry Louis Gates, Jr, ed. *'Race', writing and difference*, Chicago, pp. 78–106.

—— and David Lloyd, eds (1990) *The nature and context of minority discourse*, Oxford. (This volume is a slightly revised form of *Cultural critique*, nos 6 and 7, 1987.)

Jordan, Winthrop D. (1982) 'First impressions: initial English confrontations with Africans', in Husband, ed. (1982), pp. 42–58.

Jules-Rosette, B. (1984) *The messages of tourist art*, New York.

Kant, Immanuel (1867) 'Beantwortung der Frage: was ist Aufklärung?', *Immanuel Kants Sämmtliche Werke in chronologischer Reihenfolge*, ed. G. Hartenstein, Leipzig.

Karp, Ivan and Stephen Levine, eds (1991) *Exhibiting cultures: the poetics and politics of museum display*, Washington.

Kavi, Manavalli Ramakrishna, ed. (1926) *Nāyaśāstra*, with the commentary of Abhinavagupta, Baroda.

Kinfe, Abraham (1990) 'The media crisis: Africa's exclusion zone', *SAPEM* (September), pp. 47–9.

Kitaj, R. B. (1989) *First diaspora manifesto*, London.

Koch-Grunberg, Teodor (1981) *Del Roraima al Orinoco*, tomo II, trans. Frederica de Ritter, Caracas.

Kruger, Barbara and Phil Mariani, eds (1989) *Remaking history*, Seattle.

Kumar, Kamala (1987) 'Improving quality of life and status of women through enhancing effectiveness of organizations working for women's development', Asian centre for organisation, research and development, New Delhi.

Kumar, Raj (1981) *Annie Besant's rise to power in Indian politics 1914–1917*, New Delhi.

Laclau, Ernesto (1990) *New reflections on the revolution of our time*, London and New York.

—— and Chantal Mouffe (1985), *Hegemony and socialist strategy: towards a radical democratic politics*, London.

Landes, Joan (1988) *Women and the public sphere in the age of the French Revolution*, Ithaca.

Lazarus, Neil (1987) 'Modernism and modernity: T. W. Adorno and contemporary white South African Literature', *Cultural critique*, 5, pp. 131–55.

—— (1990a) *Resistance in postcolonial African fiction*, New Haven.

—— (1990b) 'Imperialism, cultural theory, and radical intellectualism today: a critical assessment', *Rethinking Marxism*, 3, 3–4, pp. 156–64.

—— (1991) 'Doubting the new world order: marxism, realism, and the claims of postmodernist social theory', *differences*, 3, 3, pp. 94–138.

Le Ridant, Pierre (1770) *Code matrimonial au recueil complet de toutes les loiz canoniques et civiles de France*, Paris.

Legget, Jeremy, ed. (1990) *Global warming: the Greenpeace report*, Oxford.

Lenin, V. I. (1969) *What is to be done? Burning questions of our movement*, New York.

Lipsitz, David (1990a) *Time passages: collective memory and American popular culture*, Minneapolis.

—— (1990b) 'Listening to learn and learning to listen: popular culture, cultural theory, and American studies', *American quarterly*, 42 (December), pp. 615–36.

Lloyd, David (1990a) 'Genet's genealogies: European minorities and the ends of the canon', in JanMohamed and Lloyd, eds (1990), pp. 369–93.

—— (1990b) 'Analogies of the aesthetic: the politics of culture and the limits of materialist aesthetics', *New formations*, 10 (spring), pp. 109–26.

—— (1991) 'Race under representation', *Oxford literary review*, 13, pp. 62–94.

—— and Paul Thomas (1991) 'Culture and society or "Culture and the state"?', *Social text*, 30, pp. 27–56.

Look Lai, Wally (1968), 'The road to Thornfield Hall', *New beacon reviews*, ed. John La Rose, London.

López-Baralt, Mercedes (1979) 'La persistencia de las estructuras simbólicas andinas en los dibujos de Guaman Poma', *Journal of Latin American lore*, 1, pp. 83–116.

Lowe, Lisa (1991a) 'Heterogeneity, hybridity, multiplicity: marking Asian American differences', *Diaspora*, 1, pp. 24–44.

—— (1991b) *Critical terrains: British and French orientalism*, Ithaca.

—— (1992) 'Imagining Los Angeles in the production of multiculturalism', *Emergences*, 5/6 (spring).

—— (forthcoming) 'Canons, institutions, identities: contradictions for Asian American studies', in David Palumbo-Liu, ed. *Revisions of the ethnic canon*, Minneapolis.

Lumley, Robert, ed. (1988) *The museum time machine*, London.

Macherey, Pierre and Etienne Balibar (1978) 'Literature as an ideological form', *Oxford literary review*, 3, 1, pp. 4–12.

McKendrick, Neil, J. H. Plumb and John Brewer, eds (1982) *The birth of a consumer society: the commercialization of eighteenth-century England*, Bloomington.

McKinnon, Catherine (1992) 'Feminism, Marxism, method and the state: an agenda for theory', *Signs*, 7, 3 (spring), pp. 515–44.

McNab, Robert, ed. (1908) *Historical records of New Zealand*, 2 vols, Wellington.

Malan, Rian (1990) *My traitor's heart*, London.

Mandela, Nelson (1965) *No easy walk to freedom*, London.

Marglin, Frédérique Apffel (1985) *Wives of the god-king: the rituals of the devadāsis of Puri*, Delhi.

Marks, Shula and Stanley Trapido, eds (1987) *The politics of race, class and nationalism in twentieth-century South Africa*, London.

Martins, Wilson (1970) *The modernist idea: a critical survey of Brazilian writing in the twentieth century*, New York.

Marx, Karl (1973) *Grundrisse*, trans. Martin Nicolaus, Harmondsworth.

—— (1978) 'On the Jewish question', *Early writings*, intro. Lucio Colletti, trans. Rodney Livingstone and Gregor Benton, New York, pp. 211–42.

—— and Friedrich Engels (1967) *The communist manifesto*, ed. A. J. P. Taylor, Harmondsworth.

Mayall, James and Anthony Payne, eds (1991) *Fallacies of hope; post-colonial record of the Commonwealth Third World*, Manchester.

Mayhew, Henry (1968) *London labour and the London poor*, intro. John D. Rosenberg, 4 vols, New York.

Meldrum, Andrew (1991) 'Zimbabwe', *The Guardian*, Thursday 25 April.

Memmi, Albert (1969) *Dominated man: notes toward a portrait*, New York.

—— (1990) *The colonizer and the colonized*, trans. Howard Greenfeld, London.

Mercer, Kobena (1990) 'Black art and the burden of representation', *Third text*, 10, pp. 61–78.

Messenger, P. Mauch (1989) *The ethics of collecting cultural property*, Albuquerque.

Meyer, Susan (1991) 'Colonialism and the figurative strategy of *Jane Eyre*', in Jonathan Arac and Harriet Ritvo, eds *Macropolitics of nineteenth-century literature: nationalism, exoticism, imperialism*, Pittsburgh, pp. 159–83.

Mezei, Kathy (1987) '"And it kept its secret": narration, memory, and madness in Jean Rhys's *Wide sargasso sea*', *Critique*, 28, pp. 195–209.

Miceli, Sérgio (1979) *Intelectuais e classe dirigente no Brasil (1920–1945)*, São Paolo.

—— et al. (1984) *Estado e cultura no Brasil*, São Paolo.

Miller, Christopher L. (1990) *Theories of Africans: francophone literature and anthropology in Africa*, Chicago.

Millones, Luis and Mary Louise Pratt (1989) *Amor brujo: imagen y cultura del amor en los Andes*, Lima. (Translated as *Amor brujo: image and culture of love in the Andes*, Syracuse, 1990.)

Miquelon, Dale (1987) *New France, 1701–?: 'A supplement to Europe'*, Toronto.

Mishra, Vijay and Bob Hodge (1991) 'What is post(-)colonialism?' *Textual practice*, 5, pp. 399–414.

Mitra, Subrata K. (1990) *Post-colonial state of Asia: dialectics of politics and government*, London.

Moraga, Cherrie (1983) *Loving in the war years: lo que nunca pasa por sus labios*, Boston.

Moreira Leite, Dante (1983) *O caráter nacional brasileiro*, São Paolo.

Mort, Frank (1987) *Dangerous sexualities: medico-moral politics in England since 1830*, London.

Mphahlele, Ezekiel (1971) 'Remarks on negritude', in Hyams (1971), appendix VI.

Mudimbe, V. Y. (1988) *The invention of Africa: gnosis, philosophy and the order of knowledge*, London.

Murra, John (1980) 'Introduction' to Felipe Guaman Poma de Ayala, *Nueva coronica y buen gobierno y justicia*, Mexico City.

Narayan, R. K. (1980) *The guide*, New York.

—— (1989a) *My days: a memoir*, London.

—— (1989b) *A story-teller's world*, New Delhi.

Ndebele, Njabulo (1986) 'Rediscovering the ordinary: some new writings in South Africa', *Journal of Southern African studies*, 12, 2, pp. 143–57.

—— (1987) 'The English language and social change in South Africa', in Bunn and Taylor, eds (1987), pp. 217–35.

Ngugi Wa Thiong'o (1986) *Decolonizing the mind*, London.

Nelson, Cary and Lawrence Grossberg, eds (1988) *Marxism and the interpretation of culture*, Urbana/Chicago.

Neuberger, B. (1986) *National self-determination in post-colonial Africa*, Boulder.

Nicholls, Henry Alford Alfred (1893) 'Notes on the negro outbreak of 1844, written by Dr Alford Nicholls, on the 15th December, 1893, for the information Sir Robert G. C. Hamilton K. G. B., Her Majesty's Commissioner, to enquire into the present condition of the Island of Dominica', MS.

Nicholson, Linda (1987) 'Feminism and Marx: integrating kinship with the economic,' in Seyla Benhabib and Drucilla Cornell, eds *Feminism as critique: on the politics of gender*, Minneapolis.

Nochlin, Linda (1991) 'The imaginary Orient', in her *The politics of vision*, London, pp. 33–59.

Norris, Christopher (1990) *What's wrong with postmodernism: critical theory and the ends of philosophy*, Baltimore.

Nunes, Zita (1990) ' "Os males do Brasil": antropofagia ea questo da raca', *Papeis Avulsos do CIEC*, 22, Rio de Janeiro.

O'Connor, Teresa F. (1986) *Jean Rhys: the West Indian novels*, New York.

O'Hanlon, Rosalind (1988) 'Recovering the subject: *Subaltern studies* and histories of resistance in colonial South Asia', *Modern Asian studies*, 22, 1, pp. 184–224.

—— (1989) 'Cultures of rule, communities of resistance: gender, discourse and tradition in recent South Asian historiographies', *Social analysis*, 25, pp. 95–114.

Olinder, Britta, ed. (1984) *A sense of place: essays in post-colonial literatures*, Göteborg.

Oliver, Vere Langford (1927) *The monumental inscriptions of the British West Indies*, Dorchester.

Omi, Michael and Howard Winant (1986) *Racial formation in the United States*, New York.

Omvedt, Gail (1983) 'Devadasi custom and the fight against it', *Manushi*, 19.

Ong, Walter (1982) *Orality and literacy: the technologizing of the word*, London and New York.

Ortiz, Fernando (1978) *Contrapunto cubano* [1947], Caracas.

Ourliac, Paul and J. de Malafosse (1968) *Le Droit familial*, vol. 3 of *Histoire du droit privé*, Paris.

Palomino Flores, Salvador (1984) *El sistema de oposiciones en la comunidad de Sarhua: la complementaridad de los opuestos en la cultura andina*, Lima.

Parry, Benita (1987) 'Problems in current theories of colonial discourse', *Oxford literary review*, 9, 1–2, pp. 27–58.

Pateman, Carol (1988) *The sexual contract*, Stanford.

Payer, Cheryl (1974) *The debt trap: the International Monetary Fund and the Third World*, New York.

—— (1982) *The World Bank: a critical analysis*, New York.

Pécault, Daniel (1990) *Os intellectuais e a política no Brasil*, São Paulo.

Pêcheux, Michel (1982) *Language, semantics and ideology*, trans. Harbans Nagpal, London.

Pechey, Graham (1983) 'The story of an African farm: colonial history and the discontinuous text', *Critical arts*, 3, 1, pp. 65–78.

—— (1990) 'Voices of struggle', *Southern African review of books*, December–January, pp. 3–5.

Perin, Constance (1988) *Belonging in America: reading between the lines*, Madison.

Pillorget, René (1979) *La Tige et le Rameau: familles anglaise et français XVIe–XVIIIe siècle*, Paris.

Pinney, C. (1989) 'Appearing worlds', *Anthropology today*, 5 (June), pp. 26–8.

Prado, Paulo (1931) *Retrato do Brasil*, Rio de Janeiro.

Prakash, Gyan (1990) *Bonded histories: genealogies of labor servitude in colonial India*, New York.

Pratt, Mary Louise (1991) 'Arts of the contact zone', *Profession*, New York, pp. 33–40.

—— (1992) *Imperial eyes: travel writing and transculturation*, London.

Proença, Cavalcanti (1987) *Roteiro de Macunaíma*, São Paulo.

Quick, Richard (1900) 'On bells', *The reliquary*, 6, pp. 226–41.

Radhakrishnan, R. (1988) 'Toward an effective intellectual: Foucault or Gramsci?', in Bruce Robbins, ed. *Aesthetics, politics, academics*, Minneapolis, pp. 57–99.

Rama, Angel (1982) *Transculturación narrativa en América Latina*, Mexico.

Ramchand, Kenneth (1983) *The West Indian novel and its background*, 2nd ed., London.

Raynal, Guillaume-Thomas (1783) *Histoire philosophique et politique des établissements et du commerce des Européens dans des Deux Indes*, 4 vols, Genève.

Read, Charles H. (1899) *Antiques from the city of Benin and other parts of West Africa in the British Museum*, London.

Reis, Fidelis (1931) *Pais a organizar*, Rio de Janeiro.

Rhys, Jean (1968) *Wide sargasso sea* [1966], Harmondsworth.

—— (1981) *Smile please: an unfinished autobiography*, Harmondsworth.

—— (1985) *Letters 1931–66*, ed. Francis Wyndham and Diana Melly, Harmondsworth.

—— (MS a) 'Black exercise book', University of Tulsa Special Collections.

—— (MS b) 'Smile please folders', in the David Plante papers, University of Tulsa Special Collections.

Ribeiro, A. (1979) 'Turquerie: Turkish dress and English fashion in the eighteenth century', *Connoisseur*, 201, pp. 16–23.

Rivera, Tomas (1987) *Y no se lo tragó la tierra*, trans. Evangelina Vigil-Piñon, Houston.

Rizal, José (1968) *Noli me tangere* [1887], trans. León Ma. Guerrero, New York.

Robbins, Bruce (1992) 'Comparative cosmopolitanism', *Social text*, 31/32, pp. 169–86.

Roche, Daniel (1989) *La Culture des apparences: une histoire du vêtement XVIIe–XVIIIe siècle*, Paris.

Rooney, Caroline (1991) 'Are we in the company of feminists?; a preface for Bessie Head and Ama Ata Aidoo', in Harriet Devine Jump, ed. *Diverse voices*, Hemel Hempstead, pp. 214–46.

Rosaldo, Michelle Z. (1980) *Knowledge and passion: Ilongot notions of self and social life*, Cambridge.

Rosaldo, Renato (1980) *Ilongot headhunting, 1883–1974: a study in society and history*, Stanford.

—— (1989) *Culture and truth: the remaking of social analysis*, London.

Ross, Andrew, ed. (1989) *Universal abandon? The politics of postmodernism*, Edinburgh.

Rousseau, Jean-Jacques (1960) *Julie ou la Nouvelle Héloïse*, ed. R. Pomeau, Paris.

—— (1968) *The social contract*, trans. and intro. Maurice Cranston, Harmondsworth.

—— (1984) *A discourse on the origin of inequality*, trans. and intro. Maurice Cranston, Harmondsworth.

Rowntree, B. S. (1901) *Poverty: a study of town life*, London.

Rustin, Michael (1989) 'The politics of post-Fordism: or, the trouble with "New Times"', *New left review*, 175 (May–June), pp. 54–77.

Ryder, Alan (1977) *Benin and the Europeans, 1485–1897*, London.

Sachs, Albie (1991) 'Preparing ourselves for freedom', *Red letters*, 29, pp. 8–10; also in de Kok and Press, eds (1991), pp. 19–29.

Said, Edward (1978) *Orientalism*, London.

—— (1988) *Yeats and decolonization*, Derry.

—— (1989) 'Representing the colonised: anthropology's interlocutors', *Critical inquiry*, 15, pp. 205–25.

—— (1990a) 'Figures, configurations, transfigurations', *Race & Class*, 32, 1, pp. 1–16.

—— (1990b) 'Yeats and decolonization', in Terry Eagleton, Fredric Jameson and Edward W. Said, *Nationalism, colonialism, and literature*, Minneapolis, pp. 69–95.

—— (1993) *Culture and imperialism*, London.

San Juan, Epifanio Jr (1988) *Ruptures, schisms, interventions: cultural revolution in the Third World*, Manila.

Sanchez, Rosaura (1990) 'Ethnicity, ideology and academia', *Cultural studies*, 4, 3, pp. 294–302.

Sangari, Kumkum (1987) 'The politics of the possible', *Cultural critique*, 7, pp. 157–86.

Sartre, Jean Paul (1976) *Black Orpheus* [1948], trans. S. W. Allen, Paris.

Schiller, Friedrich (1967) *On the aesthetic education of man, in a series of letters*, ed. Elizabeth Wilkinson and L. M. Willoughby, Oxford.

Scott, Walter (1851) *Tales of a grandfather*, Edinburgh.

Searle, G. R. (1976) *Race and representation: eugenics and politics in Britain 1900–1914*, Leyden.

Sheehy, J. (1980) *The rediscovery of Ireland's past: the Celtic revival 1830–1930*, London.

Shohat, Ella (1991) 'Imagining terra incognita: the disciplinary gaze of empire', *Public culture*, 3, 2, pp. 41–70.

—— (1992) 'Notes on the "post-colonial"', *Social text*, 31/32, pp. 99–113.

Shramshakti (1988) National Commission on Self-employed Women & women in the informal sector, New Delhi.

Sivanandan, A. (1983) 'Challenging racism: strategies for the 80's', *Race and class*, 25, pp. 1–11.

Skidmore, Thomas E. (1974) *Black into white: race and nationality in Brazilian thought*, New York.

Slovo, Joe (1976) 'South Africa – no middle road', in Davidson, Slovo and Wilkinson (1976), pp. 106–210.

Smith, Adam (1937) *An enquiry into the nature and causes of the wealth of nations*, ed. Edwin Cannon, New York.

Smith, Paul (1988) *Discerning the subject*, Minneapolis.

Snead, James (1988) 'Black independent film', in *Black film British cinema*, ICA documents, 7, London, pp. 47–50.

Sole, Kelwyn (1988) 'The days of power: depictions of politics and community in four recent South African novels', *Research in African literatures*, 19, 1, pp. 65–87.

South African Communist Party (1962) *The road to South African freedom*, London.

—— (1989) *The path to power*, London.

Soyinka, Wole (1976) *Myth, literature and the African world*, Cambridge.

Spengler, Joseph J. (1938) *France faces depopulation*, Durham, NC.

Spivak, Gayatri Chakravorty (1985) 'Three women's texts and a critique of imperialism', *Critical inquiry*, 12, 1, pp. 243–61.

—— (1987) 'Feminism and critical theory', in her *In other worlds: essays in cultural politics*, New York, pp. 77–92.

—— (1988) 'Can the subaltern speak?', in Nelson and Grossberg, eds (1988), pp. 271–313.

—— (1990a) 'Practical politics of the open end' (interview with Sarah Harasym), in *The postcolonial critic: interviews, strategies, dialogues*, ed. Sara Harasym, New York and London, pp. 95–112.

—— (1990b) 'Woman in difference: Mahasweta Devi's "Douloti the Bountiful"', *Cultural critique*, 14 (winter), pp. 105–28.

—— (1991) 'Marxist feminism', *Frontier*, 23–4 (26 January).

—— (1993) 'The burden of English', in Carol A. Breckenridge and Peter van der Veer, eds *Orientalism and the postcolonial predicament*, Philadelphia, pp. 134–57.

Sprinker, Michael (1987) *Imaginary relations: aethetics and ideology in the theory of historical materialism*, London.

Srinath, C. N. (1986) *The literary landscape: essays on Indian fiction and poetry in English*, Delhi.

Srinivasan, Amrita (1988) 'Reform or conformity? Temple "prostitution" and the community in the Madras presidency', in Bina Agarwal, ed. *Structures of patriarchy: state, community and household in modernizing Asia*, Delhi.

Stern, Steve J., ed. (1987) *Resistance, rebellion and consciousness in the Andean peasant world, 18th to 20th centuries*, Madison.

Stone, Lawrence (1977) *The family, sex and marriage in England, 1500–1800*, New York.

Swanton, John R. (1929) *Myths and tales of the southeastern Indians*, Washington, DC.

Szombati-Fabian, Ilona and Johannes Fabian (1976) 'Art, history, and society: popular painting in Shaba, Zaire', *Studies in the anthropology of visual communication*, 3, 1.

Taussig, Michael J. (1988) *Shamanism, colonialism and the wild man: studies in terror and healing*, Chicago.

Taylor, Anne (1992) *Annie Besant: a biography*, New York.

Taylor, Patrick (1989) *The narrative of liberation: perspectives on Afro-Caribbean literature, popular culture, and politics*, Ithaca.

Terdiman, Richard (1985) *Discourse / counter discourse: the theory and practice of symbolic resistance in nineteenth-century France*, Ithaca.

Tharoor, Shashi (1989) *The great Indian novel*, New York.

Thomas, Paul (1984) 'Alien politics', in Terence Ball and James Farr, eds *After Marx*, Oxford, pp. 124–40.

Thorner, Daniel and Alice Thorner (1962) *Land and labour in India*, Bombay.

Tiffin, Helen (1987) 'Post-colonial literatures and counter-discourse', *Kunapipi*, 9, 3, pp. 17–34.

—— (1991) 'Introduction', in Adam and Tiffin, eds (1991), pp. vii–xvi.

Traer, James F. (1980) *Marriage and the family in eighteenth-century France*, Ithaca and London.

Trinh, T. Minh-ha (1989) *Woman, native, other: writing postcoloniality and feminism*, Bloomington.

Trump, Martin (1990) 'Part of the struggle: Black writing and the South African liberation movement', in Trump, ed. (1990), pp. 161–85.

—— ed. (1990) *Rendering things visible: essays in South African literary culture* Johannesburg.

Tylor, E. B. (1871) *Primitive culture: researches into the development of mythology, philosophy, religion, language, art and customs*, London.

UNESCO (1970) *Race and class in post-colonial society*, Paris.

Valenzuela Arce, José Manuel, ed. (1992) *Decadencia u auge de las identidades: cultura nacional, identidad cultural y modernización*, Tijuana.

Vaughan, Michael (1990) 'Storytelling and politics in fiction', in Trump, ed. (1990), pp. 186–204.

Vaughan, W. (1990) 'The Englishness of British art', *The Oxford art journal*, 13, 2, pp. 11–23.

Villareal, José Antonio (1970), *Pocho*, intro. Pamon E. Ruiz, New York.

Volosinov, Valentin (1973) *Marxism and the philosophy of language*, trans. Ladislaw Matejka and I. R. Titunik, New York.

Walvin, James (1982) 'Black caricature: the roots of racialism', in Husband, ed. (1982), pp. 59–72.

Webster, Charles, ed. (1981) *Biology, medicine and society, 1840–1940*, Cambridge.

Weeks, Jeffrey (1981) *Sex, politics and society: the regulation of sexuality since 1800*, London.

West, Cornel (1985) 'The dilemma of the black intellectual', in *Cultural critique*, 1, pp. 109–24.

—— (1988) 'Marxist theory and the specificity of Afro-American oppression', in Nelson and Grossberg, eds (1988), pp. 17–33.

—— (1989) 'Black culture and postmodernism', in Kruger and Mariani, eds (1989), pp. 87–96.

Williams, Brackette (1989) 'A class act: anthropology and the race to nation across ethnic terrain', in *Annual review of anthropology*, ed. Bernard J. Siegel, Alan R. Beals and Stephen A. Tyler, Palo Alto, 18, pp. 401–44.

Williams, Raymond (1977) *Marxism and literature*, Oxford.

—— (1980) 'Base and superstructure in marxist critical theory', in his *Problems in materialism and culture*, London, pp. 31–49.

—— (1983) *Culture and society, 1780–1950* [1958], New York.

Willis, A. and T. Fry (1988–9) 'Art as ethnocide: the case of Australia', *Third text*, 5 (winter), pp. 3–21.

Wilson, Arthur M. (1972) *Diderot*, New York.

Withey, Lynne (1987) *Voyages of Discovery: Captain Cook and the exploration of the Pacific*, Berkeley.

Wolf, Eric R. (1982) *Europe and the people without history*, Berkeley.

Wollen, Peter (1990) 'Tourism, language and art', *New formations*, 12, pp. 43–59.

Wollstonecraft, Mary (1975) *Maria or the wrongs of woman*, intro. Moira Ferguson, New York.

Wood, Charles H. and José Alberto Magno de Carvalho (1988) *The demography of inequality in Brazil*, New York.

Woodhead, Leslie (1987) *A box full of spirits: adventures of a film-maker in Africa*, London.

Worringer, Wilhelm (1907) *Abstraktion und Einfuehlung*, Munich.

Worsley, Peter (1972) 'Frantz Fanon and the "lumpenproletariat"', in J. Savile and R. Miliband, eds *The Socialist Register*, London, pp. 193–230.

Wright, Patrick (1985) *On living in an old country*, London.

Wright, Richard (1966) *Black boy: a record of childhood and youth*, New York.

Young, Robert (1990) *White mythologies: writing, history and the west*, London.

Notes on contributors and editors

Francis Barker teaches Literature at the University of Essex. He is the author of *The tremulous private body* (1984), and of *The culture of violence* (1993). He is writing a book on artificiality, with the working title *Breathing simulacra*.

Annie Coombes teaches History of Art and Cultural Studies at Birkbeck College, University of London. She has published on anthropology and museology in the nineteenth and twentieth centuries. Her book *Anthropology and popular imagination in the invention of Africa* will be published later this year.

Simon During teaches English at the University of Melbourne. His *Foucault and literature* appeared in 1992, and he is the author of several articles about the notions of the postcolonial and the postcultural.

Peter Hulme teaches Literature at the University of Essex. He is the author of *Colonial encounters: Europe and native Caribbean, 1492–1797* (1986) and joint editor (with Neil Whitehead) of *Wild majesty: encounters with Caribs from Columbus to the present day* (1992).

Margaret Iversen is a lecturer in the department of Art History and Theory at the University of Essex. Her *Alois Riegl: art history and theory* appeared recently. She is currently working on a book entitled *Poststructuralist theory and modern art*, and planning another on psychoanalytic aesthetics.

Neil Lazarus teaches in the department of English and the Center for Modern Culture and Media at Brown University. He is the author of *Resistance in postcolonial African fiction* (1990) and of the forthcoming *Hating tradition properly*.

David Lloyd teaches English at the University of California, Berkeley. He is the author of *Nationalism and minor literature* (1987) and *Anomalous states: Irish writing and the post-colonial moment* (1993), and joint editor with Abdul JanMohamed of *The nature and context of minority discourse*.

Anne McClintock teaches gender and cultural studies at Columbia University. Her book *Maids, maps and mines: gender and imperialism* was published in 1993, and she is currently working on a book on women and the sex industry.

Zita Nunes teaches Comparative Literature at Columbia University, and has written on Brazilian nationalism and *modernismo*.

Benita Parry is the author of *Conrad and imperialism* (1983) and of several articles on post-colonial theory. She is currently working on a study entitled *The discourses of imperialism*.

Graham Pechey teaches English at the University of Hertfordshire. He has published several articles about Bakhtin (a book entitled *Postmodern Bakhtin* is forthcoming) and on South Africa. He is currently working on the introduction to a selection of essays by Njabulo Ndebele.

Mary Louise Pratt teaches in the Departments of Spanish and Comparative Literature at Stanford University. She is the author of several books, most recently *Imperial eyes: transculturation and travel writing* (1992).

Renato Rosaldo teaches in the Department of Anthropology at Stanford University. He is the author of several books, including *Culture and truth* (1989).

Gayatri Chakravorty Spivak teaches English and Comparative Literature at Columbia University. She has published widely on postcolonial theory, including her book *In other worlds: essays in cultural politics* (1987). *Outside in the teaching-machine* and *Imaginary maps* will be published during 1993.

Index